WITHDRAWN BY THE
UNIVERSITY OF MICHIGAN

The *Logos* Reader

The *Logos* Reader
RATIONAL RADICALISM AND THE FUTURE OF POLITICS

Edited by
Stephen Eric Bronner and
Michael J. Thompson

THE UNIVERSITY PRESS OF KENTUCKY

Copyright © 2006 by The University Press of Kentucky

Scholarly publisher for the Commonwealth, serving Bellarmine University, Berea College, Centre College of Kentucky, Eastern Kentucky University, The Filson Historical Society, Georgetown College, Kentucky Historical Society, Kentucky State University, Morehead State University, Murray State University, Northern Kentucky University, Transylvania University, University of Kentucky, University of Louisville, and Western Kentucky University.

All rights reserved.

Editorial and Sales Offices: The University Press of Kentucky
663 South Limestone Street, Lexington, Kentucky 40508-4008
www.kentuckypress.com

10 09 08 07 06   5 4 3 2 1

Library of Congress Cataloging-in-Publication Data

The logos reader : rational radicalism and the future of politics / edited by Stephen Eric Bronner and Michael J. Thompson.
    p. cm.
  Includes index.
  ISBN 0-8131-2368-2 (hardcover : alk. paper)—ISBN 0-8131-9148-3 (pbk : alk. paper)   1. Liberalism.   2. Socialism.   3. Political science.
  I. Bronner, Stephen Eric, 1949–   II. Thompson, Michael, 1973–
  JC574.L65 2005
  320.51—dc22   2005025882

Cloth ISBN 978-0-8131-2368-4
Paper ISBN 978-0-8131-9148-5

This book is printed on acid-free recycled paper meeting the requirements of the American National Standard for Permanence in Paper for Printed Library Materials.

Manufactured in the United States of America.

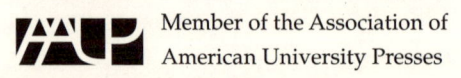

Member of the Association of American University Presses

CONTENTS

Acknowledgments   vii
Introduction   1

Part I. Whither America?

Stephen Eric Bronner, American Landscape: Lies, Fears, and the Distortion of Democracy   9

Jeffrey Goldfarb, How to Be an Intelligent Anti-American   17

R. Claire Snyder, The Federal Marriage Amendment and the Attack on American Democracy   27

Kurt Jacobsen, Fahrenheit 9/11: The Real Lowdown   39

Charles Noble, The Never-ending War on the Welfare State   45

Part II. Theoretical Encounters

Nicholas Xenos, Leo Strauss and the Rhetoric of the War on Terror   59

Jürgen Habermas, Dual-Layered Time: Reflections on T. W. Adorno in the 1950s   75

Geoffrey Kurtz, Anthony Giddens's Third Way: A Critique   81

Christine Kelly, How Dinesh Gets Over: The Unmeritorious Scholarship of Dinesh D'Souza   99

Stanley Aronowitz, A Mills Revival?   117

Part III. Political Recollections

Michael J. Thompson, The Price of Heavenly Peace: Tiananmen Square Fifteen Years Later   141

Fred Dallmayr, But on a Quiet Day . . . A Tribute to Arundhati Roy   149

Patricia Cholakian, Flight from Van: Memories of an Armenian Genocide Survivor   165

Meera Nanda, Dharma and the Bomb: Postmodern Critiques of Science and the Rise of Reactionary Modernism in India   179

Irene Gendzier, The Political Legacy of Edward Said   195

Alexis de Tocqueville, Second Letter on Algeria (August 22, 1837)   201

Part IV. Israel and Palestine

Henry Pachter, Who Are the Palestinians?   217

Ernest Goldberger, The Power of Myths in Israeli Society: Historical Realities and Political Dogmatism   227

Menachem Klein, The Logic behind the Geneva Accord   233

Marwan Bishara, West Bank Settlements Obstruct Peace: Israel's Empire State Building   247

Lawrence Davidson, Orwell and Kafka in Israel–Palestine   253

Part V. Iraq: Imperialism and Invasion

Keith D. Watenpaugh, The *Guiding Principles* and the U.S. "Mandate" for Iraq: Twentieth-Century Colonialism and America's New Empire   269

Eric Rouleau, The Iraqi Conflict and Its Impact on the Israeli–Palestinian Conflict   279

James Jennings, Iraqnophobia versus Reality   283

Wadood Hamad, Whither Independence? Iraq in Perspective: From Despotism to Occupation   293

Part VI. Transnational Realities

Douglas Kellner, September 11 and the Terror War: The Bush Legacy and the Risks of Unilateralism   303

Dick Howard, Europe as a Political Project   323

Drucilla Cornell and Philip Green, Multilateralism: For a New Political Enlightenment   331

Manfred B. Steger, Globalism: The New Market Ideology   341

Ulrich Beck, The Silence of Words and Political Dynamics in the World Risk Society   353

List of Contributors   369

Index   373

ACKNOWLEDGMENTS

This book is the culmination of the combined efforts of many people whose only motivation was their commitment to *Logos*. Without each of them it would have been impossible to keep the journal afloat. Gregory Zucker has been a tireless and precocious managing editor. Eli Merenzon and Debbie Wolf made important contributions setting up our Web site; Brian Graff, Kai Artur Diers, Elena Mancini, Jeffrey Craig Miller, and Valery de Lame provided us with translations; Michal Shmulovich and Pauline Zalkin helped with editing and transcriptions; and Brett Stoudt, Drew Martin, Sam Aboelela, Hedda Smulewicz, and Eliot Katz helped us in innumerable ways. We'd also like to thank Moataz Hamza for compiling the index. In addition to the contributors to this volume there are other writers and artists who have made *Logos* what it is. We can't thank any of you enough.

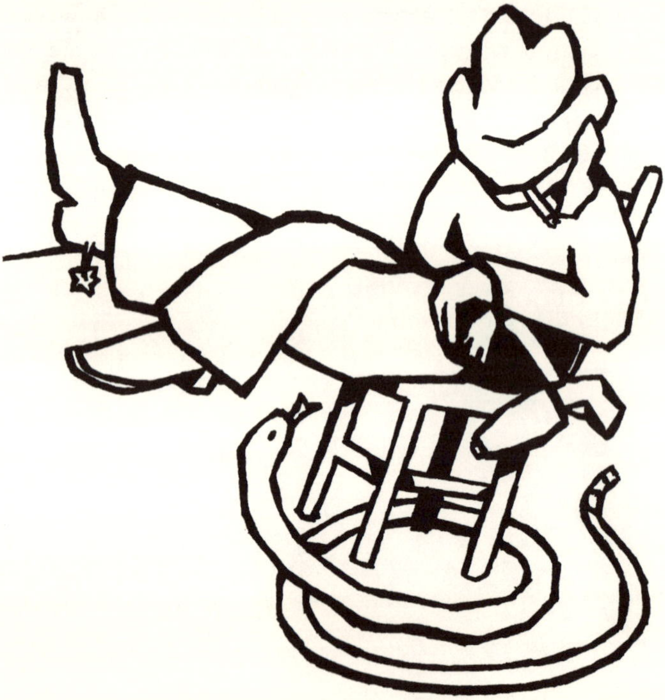

INTRODUCTION

Logos was founded in the shadow of September 11, 2001, when the new millennium had barely begun. It was conceived as a journal, but also as part of a larger political and cultural project. A palpable chill had already pervaded the cultural climate. Neoconservatism was becoming the intellectual fashion, and a new preoccupation with world hegemony was defining American politics. That situation has only grown worse. The aftermath of 9/11 has witnessed the rise of religious traditionalism, exaggerated nationalism, and America's withdrawal from the global discourse even as the world is becoming increasingly interdependent. The mass media as well as the classic organs of public debate made little room for a critical perspective in the wake of 9/11 and the subsequent global war on terror. Radical voices, even now, can barely be heard.

Logos was launched to intervene in this state of affairs. Its express purpose is to resurrect eroding democratic principles, concerns with social justice, and the broad-minded cosmopolitanism originally associated with the Enlightenment and then with the great progressive movements of modernity. Weary of hyperintellectualized professional journals, suspicious of the anti-intellectual bias of many publications seeking to engage a "broader public," *Logos* seeks to create a new public, one oriented toward critical reflection and political and social praxis. Our intent was to chart a new course in a responsible, intellectual manner. Both new and established writers from around the world would engage in a collective project of critique and political reconstruction on a global scale, bringing fresh ideas to pertinent issues.

Logos fosters what we like to call a *rational radicalism,* an interdisciplinary perspective, and a commitment to critique with a positive political purpose. No less than the language of the vernacular or the attempt to move outside narrow disciplinary boundaries, such an enterprise has always been associated with the ethical imperative of confronting asymmetrical relations of power. Our journal is therefore engaged in a distinctly public enterprise. It is intent on dealing with trends deriving from the end of the cold war that have only now begun to yield their fruit, a new freedom for the market that is redistributing income upward in so many nations, and the way in which what was once called the "end of history" has given way to new forms of regional and global conflict. No less than democracy or cosmopolitanism, therefore, an unfashionable socialist impulse also informs our enterprise.

And so, if *Logos* is primarily the offspring of a reaction against narrow intellectualism and rank populism, it is also grounded in a radical engagement with the contemporary public sphere, domestically and globally. That should become apparent in our choice of the best political articles published by *Logos* during the first three years of its existence. It should also be evident from these articles that the editorial ethos of *Logos,* though obviously a journal of the Left, is free of any narrow ideological agenda and demands no particular form of analysis.

Too many liberal and left-wing journals and magazines have allowed ideology to trump the critical faculty and pervert political and ethical judgment. Such a strategy, we believe, has alienated more readers than it has enlightened or engaged. Again, however, *Logos* is not simply a response to a crisis of theory. It is, above all, a project to intervene in a historical conjuncture that has left everyday people of good faith disorientated. The turn toward religion and a new provincialism, possessive individualism, and an anachronistic notion of capitalism, imperialism, and nationalism, is real. *Logos* is explicit in its support for secularism and science, solidarity with the dispossessed, and mitigating the whip of the market, no less than realizing an ethics of human dignity and the moral precepts of universalism.

America and its brand of culture, politics, and economics are continuing to drive this kind of Enlightenment project—both domestically and globally—into the ground: its culture industry is privileging the lowest common denominator; its economic values are degrading any meaningful notions of citizenship; its new obsession with "security" is constricting civil liberties; and its foreign policy is driving whole regions toward chaos. The articles collected in this volume not only intervene in the crucial political issues and debates of our time but also probe deeper, more enduring themes. The six parts represent the various concerns that have occupied *Logos* for the past three years.

Part I, "Whither America?" examines the current state of American politics and society. Stephen Eric Bronner examines the "distortion of democracy" that has resulted from the excesses of the neoconservative project both at home and abroad. Jeffrey Goldfarb confronts the discourse of anti-Americanism, arguing that America's critics have as much to learn from American democratic traditions as modern Americans do. R. Claire Snyder provides an insightful polemic on the issue of gay marriage and its relation to American liberal political principles. Kurt Jacobsen's essay on Michael Moore's controversial film *Fahrenheit 9/11* is no period piece—it interprets Moore's documentary, highlighting the salient issues of the Bush administration's neoconservative agenda. Finally, Charles Noble provides a detailed critique of the recent push against the welfare state by America's newest conservative elite.

Part II, "Theoretical Encounters," brings together essays on various intellectual figures and the impact they have had on modern politics and society, as well as their continued relevance for the present. Nicholas Xenos analyzes the antidemocratic elements of the political philosophy of Leo Strauss and its connection with the neoconservative ideas that have come to dominate contemporary American political thought. Jürgen Habermas provides an intellectual portrait of T. W. Adorno on the one-hundredth anniversary of his birth, then examines his teacher's continued relevance for modern thought and society. Anthony Giddens and his idea of a more compromising and moderate "third way" for social democracy is criticized by Geoffrey Kurtz, and Christine Kelly provides an intellectual portrait that skewers conservative ideologue Dinesh D'Souza. Stanley Aronowitz's intellectual sketch of C. Wright Mills upholds his salience for the current American cultural and intellectual context, placing emphasis on the decline of the critical public intellectual.

Part III, "Political Recollections," consists of essays with a more personal bent toward political events and figures from around the world. Michael J. Thompson looks back on the political demonstrations in Tiananmen Square in 1989, seizing on that event as a chance to discuss the problems of global capitalism and development and the way that democracy often takes a backseat to economic interests. Fred Dallmayr paints an elegant and incisive political portrait of the Indian writer and activist Arundhati Roy, and Patricia Cholakian weaves a startling account of the Armenian genocide of 1915 into a broader interrogation of the horrors of genocide. Meera Nanda looks at the rise of Hindu nationalism in India and its affinities with postmodern critiques of Western science, and Irene Gendzier sketches the "political legacy" of Edward Said. The last essay in this part is Alexis de Tocqueville's 1837 "Second Letter on Algeria," which discusses his views on imperialism and the relationship between Islam and the West.

The Middle East has been an area of special concern for *Logos,* particularly the Israeli–Palestinian conflict, which is the subject of Part IV. The essay on the Palestinians by the late Henry Pachter, which caused a bit of a sensation when it was first published, sets the historical and political stage for a discussion of the conflict. Ernest Goldberger confronts various myths essential to the Israeli national identity, and Menachem Klein makes a firm argument for the Geneva Accord as a viable and just settlement to the Israeli–Palestinian conflict. Marwan Bishara's piece on the Israeli settlements outlines the empirical realities that serve as obstacles to peace in the region. Lawrence Davidson's essay invokes the imagery of George Orwell and Franz Kafka to bring home the harsh realities of the politics and history behind the conflict between Israel and Palestine.

Part V concerns the Iraqi war. Keith Watenpaugh's historicopolitical essay frames the context for imperial designs on Iraq, going back to the 1916 Sykes-Picot agreement, and connects it to the United States' new mandate for the region. Eric Rouleau draws important parallels between the conflict in Iraq and the problems in Palestine, and James Jennings examines how ignorance of the Middle East has led to a violent posturing toward Iraq and the region as a whole. Wadood Hamad's essay discusses the negative impact of Iraq's transition from despotic rule to its present state of occupation, stressing the political implications for a democratic future.

To a certain extent, all these parts build on and interconnect with one another to provide a sense of the cosmopolitan world that marks our present and future. Part VI, "Transnational Realities," brings the collection to a close. Globalization and its effects are the focus of Douglas Kellner and his polemic on the implications of September 11 and the "terror war." Dick Howard probes the problems faced by Europe as it moves toward political integration, while Drucilla Cornell and Philip Green look at the antidemocratic implications of American unilateralism. Manfred Steger dissects the various approaches to globalization, stressing the inegalitarian effects of the global market and the ways it undercuts attempts at political modernization and democratization. Ulrich Beck sets out to cast the emerging global order as a "world risk society" premised on technological and institutional complexity.

Each of these articles in its own way seeks to change the way we think about politics and society. They question the usual assumptions about democracy, globalization, fundamentalism, terror, anti-Americanism, war and peace, the important thinkers of our age, and the conflicts that are currently redefining it. Each signals a concern with the problem of political conformity and the commonplace understandings of current affairs. They offer a critical sensibility and a desire to reinvigorate the impulse for democratic change. All of them, whatever the differences among their authors, reflect the insight offered by Immanuel Kant when he wrote in 1784: "revolutions may be able to abolish despotism, profit seeking. But they are unable, by themselves, to transform ways of thinking."

It is worth saying a bit more about the rational radicalism that lies at the heart of *Logos:* the standpoint that privileges cosmopolitanism over provincialism, equality over hierarchy, and human freedom over servitude, oppression, and the constraints of ideology. Rational radicalism is a practical enterprise that insists on resurrecting the link between ideas and reality, principles and interests, theory and practice. Just as the abstruse political notions embraced by postmodernism and poststructuralism surrender the practical element, which proved so crucial for labor movements and others struggling for liberty, the neoconservatives attempt to mix a crude and bellicose form of hyperrealism with what Ernst Cassirer liked to call "mytho-poetic thinking." Above all, however, rational radicalism is concerned with constraining the arbitrary exercise of institutional power whether on the level of economics, politics, or culture. This is what unites democrats and socialists, *philosophes* and muckrakers, genuine idealists and materialists intent on bettering the world. Rational radicalism is what unites the authors who have contributed to this volume. It is also what will continue to define the intellectual undertaking of *Logos* in the years ahead.

Part I
Whither America?

American Landscape
Lies, Fears, and the Distortion of Democracy

Stephen Eric Bronner

Lying has always been part of politics. Traditionally, however, the lie was seen as a necessary evil that those in power should keep from their subjects. Even totalitarians tried to hide the brutal truths on which their regimes rested. This disparity gave critics and reformers their sense of purpose: to illuminate for citizens the difference between the way the world appeared and the way it actually functioned. Following the proclamation of victory in the Iraqi war, however, that sense of purpose became imperiled, along with the trust necessary for maintaining a democratic discourse. The Bush administration boldly proclaimed the legitimacy of the lie, the irrelevance of trust, and the mainstream media essentially looked the other way.

Not since the days of Senator Joseph McCarthy has such purposeful misrepresentation, such blatant lying, so dramatically tainted the American landscape. It has now become clear to all except the most stubborn that justification for the war against Iraq was based not on "mistaken" interpretations or "false data" but on sheer mendacity. Current discussions among politicians and investigators focus almost exclusively on the false assertion contained in sixteen words of a presidential speech to the effect that Saddam Hussein sought to buy uranium in Africa for his weapons of mass destruction. The forest has already been lost for the trees. We are told that the problem derived from faulty intelligence by subordinates rather than purposeful lying by those in authority. CIA officials, however, have openly stated that they were pressured to make their research results support governmental policy. Secretary of State Colin Powell has still not substantiated claims concerning the existence of weapons of mass destruction that he made in his famous speech to the United Nations. Doing so would be difficult. The chief American inspector for Iraq, Charles A. Duelfer, has offered a report and testified before Congress that, under pressure from the United Nations, Iraq ended its nuclear program in 1991 and closed down its last biochemical weapons plant in 1996; he also found no evidence of an attempt to restart those programs (*New York Times,* October 7, 2004).

But then various members of the Bush inner circle cheerfully admitted that the threat posed by Iraq had been grossly exaggerated. No matter: hyping the threat was useful in building a consensus for war. The Bush administration itself nonchalantly verified what critics always knew: that American policy was propelled by greedy thoughts of an oil-rich Iraqi nation, the desire to control water in an arid region, the opportunity to throw the fear of the Western God into Tehran and Damascus, and the chance to establish an alternative to the military presence that once existed in Saudi Arabia. Wrong on every count in Iraq—the existence of weapons of mass destruction, the threat posed by the decrepit dictatorship, the degree of popular support for American intervention, and the degree of possible resistance—the CIA was either incompetent beyond all reason or, more likely, served to protect the president from domestic criticism by acting as what Thomas Powers called a "foreign ministry of spin." Former director of the CIA George Tenet ultimately took the fall. But the Bush administration has chastised none of the principal advisers who championed its catastrophic policy in Iraq, even as attacks by the Democratic Party with respect to the war and its conduct were qualified to the point of insignificance.

"Leaders" of the so-called opposition party cowered in their offices. They obviously feared being branded disloyal. As they quaked in their boots and wrung their hands, they had little time for issues pertinent to the national interest. It was not their fault that debate over the broader justification of the war had been steadily disappearing from the widely read right-wing tabloids such as the *New York Post* and, at best, retreating to the middle pages of more credible newspapers. Elected politicians in both parties, scurrying for cover, routinely made sure to note that their support for the war did not rest on the existence of weapons of mass destruction in Iraq. Few considered it necessary to mention that the lack of such weapons, combined with the inability to find any proof of a link between Saddam Hussein and al Qaeda, invalidated the claim that Iraq posed a national security threat to the United States. Everyone in the political establishment now points to humanitarian motives. For the most part, however, such concerns were not uppermost in the minds of those occupying the "war room" of the White House *then*, and there is little reason to believe that they consider them decisive now. Human rights became important for self-styled "realists" such as Paul Wolfowitz and Richard Perle only when claims concerning the imperiled national interests of the United States were revealed to be vacuous.

President Bush and members of his cabinet no longer bother to insist that the weapons will ultimately be found or that links to al Qaeda will soon be unveiled. This acknowledges that the evidence did not exist when the propaganda machine initially began to roll out its arguments for war. The administration had untold intellectual resources from which to learn that the United States would not be welcomed as the liberator of Iraq and that serious problems would plague the postwar reconstruction. But it wasn't interested. Decision makers within the administration remained content to forward a position and then find information to back it up. This begs two obvious questions: Would the American public have supported a war against Iraq had they known the truth? And perhaps more importantly, did this self-induced ignorance about conditions in Iraq help produce the current morass in which billions of dollars have been wasted and every day more American soldiers are injured or killed?

Millions of dollars were spent by a special prosecutor investigating false allegations of financial impropriety by Bill and Hillary Clinton. Impeachment proceedings were begun following the revelation of an affair between President Clinton and an intern. The media were up in arms. Many still pat themselves on the back for their role in bringing about the Watergate hearings. But when it comes to the chorus of untruth perpetrated over the invasion of Iraq, which has already cost more than 1,500 American lives and (according to the *Lancet* Web site) 100,000 Iraqi lives and billions of dollars, the public interest is apparently best served by "bipartisan" committees and a press corps that is scared of its own shadow. Just as the Republican Party was flagrant in its refusal to rationally justify its war of "liberation," the Democratic Party seemed less concerned with self-criticism and its inability to offer a principled alternative stance on foreign policy than with defending against the possibility of the Far Left—led by the erstwhile supporters of Governor Howard Dean (D-Vt.)—taking over its apparatus.

Important members of the Democratic Leadership Council poignantly asked during the 2004 primaries whether the party wished "to vent or govern," and when questioned whether its current disarray was more a product of Republican success or Democratic blunders, Senator Evan Bayh of Indiana, chairman of the organization, was quick to blame the antiwar critics by responding that it was a matter of "assisted suicide." He and the rest of his comrades talk big about the failings of the Left. But their tone changes when it comes to their feeble efforts to define their message and their willingness to swallow whatever the Bush administration puts on their plates. Democrats were quick to use leaks from the intelligence community, many of whose members were aghast at the misuse of their research, to condemn the Bush administration. But they were never able to explain how they or their staffers ignored the flood of disbelief on the Internet concerning supposed links between Saddam and al Qaeda, the existence of a nuclear program, and the idea that Iraq posed a threat to the United States. Their credulity in the face of the propaganda blitz, or their cynical cowardice in refusing to stand against it, makes these Democrats almost as culpable as the Republicans for what transpired.

The mainstream "opposition" still has not acknowledged that it was bamboozled or that the war was a disaster from the beginning. Unable to admit their complicity in bringing the war about and their lack of either nerve or a critical sensibility, the "responsible," moderate, and—above all—"patriotic" leaders of the Democratic Party always speak the language of pragmatism and moderation. Unfortunately, however, their pragmatism is anything but pragmatic. They conveniently forget the congressional elections of November 2002. By all serious accounts, it was their inability to offer any meaningful alternative to the policies of President Bush that led to the worst nonpresidential-year losses in American history. It also apparently doesn't matter to them that the American public has never embraced "bipartisan" candidates like Joseph Lieberman. Unwilling to take a stand on principle, since it *might* cost them some votes, they don't seem to mind that being a little less right wing than the Republicans on tax cuts, social welfare, and the war is undermining any genuine loyalty to a party that once identified with FDR, Bobby Kennedy, and Paul Wellstone. Senator Bayh and his friends haven't a clue: the Democratic Party can neither vent *nor* govern. Democrats should worry about their image—especially since they don't have one.

The United States appears less like a functioning democracy in which ideologically distinct parties and groups debate the issues of the day and more like a one-party state ruled by shifting administrative factions. Free speech exists, but having a formal right and making substantive use of it are very different matters. Consensus and bipartisanship are becoming increasingly paranoid preoccupations of the media and party professionals, whose range of debate extends from Humpty to Dumpty. Noam Chomsky may not be to everyone's taste, but his little collection of interviews *9/11* (Seven Stories Press) was *the* best-selling work on that terrible event. When was the last time you saw him interviewed by the mainstream media?

It is the same with Frances Fox Piven and any number of other radical or progressive public figures. Every now and then, of course, Cornel West may pop up for an interview on MSNBC. Robert Scheer continues to write for the *Los Angeles Times* and Paul Krugman for the *New York Times.* Sean Penn can still pay for a full-page advertisement to express his critical views on the war. A few genuinely progressive politicians such as Barbara Lee (D-Calif.), Sherrod Brown (D-Ohio), and Lynn Woolsey (D-Calif.) will occasionally speak their minds. In fact—though only after the emergence of a groundswell from below—even former vice president Al Gore challenged the veracity of the Bush administration.

But their voices certainly don't dominate what conservatives and right-wing pundits—always ready to view themselves as victims of the system they control—castigate as the "liberal" media. Career talking heads usually just nod and counsel prudence. Most of them are taught to be careful. They know how the game is played, and they hedge their bets. So long as some element of a statement made by the president is technically true, the boss will be let off the hook. Others are in the pocket of the administration, a few are bribed, and eyes are closed all around when it comes to the use of staged photographs and faked interviews. The false justifications for what can only be considered one of the major blunders of American foreign policy in the past century were ultimately treated—or, better, "interpreted"—with the same degree of esoteric obscurantism as a complex business contract or a convoluted literary text.

This revolting display by the mainstream media brings to mind the vision of a society dominated by what Herbert Marcuse termed "repressive tolerance"— a world in which establishmentarians can point to the rare moment of radical criticism to better enjoy the reign of an overwhelming conformity. The evidence is everywhere. CNN is only a minor player when compared with the combined power of television news shows with huge audiences hosted by mega-celebrities such as Rush Limbaugh, Bill O'Reilly, and Pat Robertson. Belief in the reactionary character of the American public has generated a self-fulfilling prophecy: the public gets the shows it wants, which in turn only strengthen the original prejudices. Edward R. Murrow, so courageous in his resistance to the hysteria of the 1950s, is often invoked by the fourth estate, but that invocation is merely symbolic.

Hardly a word is said about the skepticism of the millions who participated in the mass demonstrations or how criticism by the mainstream affected Tony Blair and the English political landscape. Neither the intensity of the criticism nor the bravery of the critics was matched in the United States during the early days of the conflict. More than fifty former officials of the English foreign affairs ministry castigated Blair's decision to support the United States in its invasion of Iraq. Indeed, according to the *Independent* of June 18, 2003, the former secretary of state for international development, Clare Short, and the former foreign secretary, Robin Cook, publicly insisted that "half truths, exaggerations, and reassurances that were not the case" were employed, along with "selective intelligence," to produce the "honorable deception" required to lead England into a shameful war.

One criterion for judging democracy is the plurality of views presented to the public; the number of views expressed usually reflects the number of political options from which the public can choose. A chill is passing over America. It is striking to reflect on the range of debate during the Progressive Era, the New Deal, and the 1960s. Even so, governmental attempts to constrict civil liberties in moments of crisis have been a fundamental trend of American history. But this trend is currently being celebrated in a new way and with new force. It is sobering to consider how debate over the legitimacy of a terrible war has been narrowed—with the acquiescence of most establishmentarian critics—to sixteen words in a presidential speech and an increasingly corrupt evaluation of policy options.

It is no wonder that the American public has proved itself increasingly incapable of grasping how much distrust its government inspires elsewhere. A current Pew poll of more than forty-four countries, directed by former secretary of state Madeleine Albright, shows that distrust of the United States has grown in an exceptionally dramatic fashion in each of them. This includes sensitive nations such as Pakistan, Saudi Arabia, Turkey, and Indonesia, where unfavorable ratings of the United States have gone from 36 percent in the summer of 2002 to 83 percent in May 2003. And this only makes sense: the paternalism with which the will of the world was treated by this administration, coupled with its mixture of bluster and mendacity, is unprecedented.

The "streets" of Europe and, more importantly, the Arab world have been lost. Perhaps they will be regained at a future time. But the numbers in this poll express anger at a basic reality. Trust and loyalty cannot be commanded by military power. With its new strategy of the "preemptive strike" buttressed by a $420 billion defense budget, bigger than that of eighteen of the most "well-defended" nations put together, the United States has rendered illusory the idea of a "multipolar world." It has become the hegemon amid a world of subaltern states, and it has no need to listen or debate. The difference between truth and falsehood no longer matters. There remains only the fact of victory, the fall of Saddam Hussein, and the bloated self-justifications attendant on what Senator J. William Fulbright, the great critic of the Vietnam War, termed "the arrogance of power."

Americans have traditionally tended to rally around the president in times of war. Fulbright himself accepted President Johnson's claim that an American military vessel had been attacked in the Gulf of Tonkin and, in 1964, voted in the Senate for a decision that would ultimately be used to bolster the U.S. role in Vietnam. When asked about his decision later, Fulbright supposedly replied, "Was I supposed to call the President of the United States a liar?" That would have been almost unprecedented at the time, and it would have been hard to expect from a senator. But then is not now. The "liberals" in the Democratic Party really should have learned something from the conduct of presidents during the Vietnam War, Watergate, and Iran-contra. It would be sad if they didn't, since this war against terror is not like other wars. President Bush has admitted that it has no end in sight. The question is: how much rope will "responsible" liberals give before he hangs them?

A new department of "homeland security" has been created, and the civil liberties of citizens are imperiled. Justification is supplied by manipulative and self-serving "national security alerts" in which the designation of danger shifts from yellow to orange to red and then back again without the disclosure of any evidence regarding why a certain color was chosen and why it was changed. The "bully pulpit" of the president, as Theodore Roosevelt called it, can go a long way in defining the style of national discourse and a sense of what is acceptable to its citizenry. This is where leadership asserts itself; the Democrats can go home now. Nevertheless, it is precisely on this question of leadership, for which President Bush has received such lavish praise, where he is weakest.

Beyond all social policy concerns or disagreements over issues of foreign policy, this president is presiding over a newly emerging culture in which truth is subordinate to power, reason is the preserve of academics, paranoia is hyped, and know-nothing nationalism is celebrated. No longer is the constructive criticism of genuine democratic allies taken seriously; better to rely on a corrupt "coalition of the willing" whose regimes have been bribed, whose economies have been threatened, and whose soldiers have been exempt from fighting this unending war on terror. The opportunity for self-reflection has been missed, no dialogue over the decline of American standing in the world has taken place, and there has been no hint of an apology by the Bush administration for its conduct in the weeks before the war broke out. In 2001, Donald Rumsfeld closed down the short-lived Office of Strategic Influence, lodged in the Pentagon, which covertly fed propaganda and misinformation to the media to shape opinion in enemy and neutral nations; now, apparently, its approach is being resurrected to meet American needs in the Middle East. That such false information will find its way back home is only logical. The question, then, for the American public, and for the citizens of other nations, is this: how can one trust a liar whose arrogance is such that he finds it unnecessary to conceal the lie?

Democracy remains elusive in Iraq, Afghanistan is languishing in misery, and new threats to the national security of the United States are already waiting to be determined. Iran trembles; Syria, too. And, if all else fails, there is always Cuba or North Korea. The enemy can change in the wink of an eye. The point about arbitrary power is, indeed, that it is arbitrary. What happens once the next lie is told and the next gamble is made? It is perhaps useful to think back to other powerful nations whose leaders liked to lie and loved to gamble—and who won and won and won again until finally they believed their own lies and gambled once too often.

NOTE

This chapter is written in memory of my student Rute Moleiro.

How to Be an Intelligent Anti-American

Jeffrey Goldfarb

The original idea for this paper dates back to 1996. At that time, I was teaching in Cracow, Poland, in a summer institute on democracy and diversity. Since 1992, I had been teaching a course on democratic culture, utilizing the political theory of both major Western thinkers, particularly Hannah Arendt, and major thinkers and political actors from around the old bloc, particularly Adam Michnik and Vaclav Havel. Since the early 1970s, I had studied and worked with the developing democratic movement in central Europe, particularly Poland. The course was a continuation of these activities. But something new and different presented itself in 1996. In a region where (outside official circles) Ronald Reagan could do no wrong, students started presenting fairly standard—but, from this part of the world, very exciting—critical judgments of America.

The students came from eastern, central, and western Europe, North and South America. In the first years of the institute, the young Westerners' automatic critical approach to liberal capitalism and their insufficient appreciation of the force of totalitarianism led to strong disagreements across the old political divide. Suddenly, in 1996, there was an informed and not so well informed anti-American consensus articulated around our seminar table, with some forceful dissenters. I found myself caught in between the consensus and the dissent, between automatic condemnation and automatic celebration. With that in mind, rather than proceeding with the seminar discussion and ending the last class of the term on an informal note, as is my custom, I presented a formal lecture. It was my first anti-American advisory.

My second advisory was presented just a few months ago. One of the students in the original class, Jacek Kucharczyk, is now the vice-director of Poland's major social science think tank. He had had an idea for a conference on European integration, and there were sessions on political, economic, and cultural integration. My paper framed a discussion about the cultural relationships among Poland, western Europe, and the United States. The paper was well received, meaning that it stimulated a spirited discussion. Particularly pleasing to me was my friendly public debate with the Polish film director Krzystof Zannusi over the films of Steven Spielberg. I was appreciative. He was dismissive.

The two advisories were presented to democratic and intellectual friends and colleagues. We were sympathetic critics of contemporary democratic practices talking among ourselves. I was trying to use irony to provoke a principled distinction between criticism of American practices and unthinking dismissal of the principles and promises of democracy. I present here the second of the two advisories. I believe that the advisory to my European colleagues is worth sharing more broadly, but I must add a post-9/11 note. There are anti-Americans who need to be reminded of American democratic practice and promise in order to temper, refine, and inform their criticism. They can become intelligent anti-Americans, which we Americans sorely need. But there are also those who are anti-American because they are against democratic practice and promise in principle. In the twentieth century, totalitarians of the Left and Right held this position. In our young century, such figures again revealed themselves in New York, Washington, and Pennsylvania. They are much more than unintelligent anti-Americans. They are democracy's enemies. Anti-Americanism in the twenty-first century first appeared as comedy, then as tragedy. I present this advisory from New York with a sense of profound personal loss and with the hope that I can combat the new postmodern totalitarians by informing democratic criticism. With this in mind, here is my part of the dialogue I had with Polish and other European colleagues.

THE POLISH FASCINATION with things American has long been coupled with a sense that there is something underdeveloped and naive about the American way of life. Fascination is centered on American economic, military, and geopolitical power. Dismissal is centered on the cultural, even the political-cultural. The "American model" has been viewed with profound ambivalence. On the one hand, learning from the bitter lessons of communism, America's steadfast anticommunism has been viewed with admiration, and its antistatist approach to the economy has been judged as the height of wisdom. On the other hand, at least among the intellectual elite, the American happy ending and the Hollywood mentality more generally have been viewed with disdain. Especially on the latter point, Polish intellectuals have been good Europeans. And like all good Europeans, they recognize the vitality of American popular culture, but this is combined with strongly critical appraisals.

Things are even more complicated than this, of course. Whereas a certain segment of the intellectual elite has been persuaded by the American political economic model, others, those on the short end of shock therapy who do not understand the workings of the global economy, have been very critical. And as the Polish intellectual elite shares its critical judgment of American mass culture with its western European colleagues, their compatriots (both eastern and western Europeans) vote with their feet, so to speak, selecting Hollywood productions and African American hip-hop culture over indigenous cultural fare. Elite sensibilities run up against popular, dare I say democratic, choice.

Each group—eastern and western Europeans, the cultural elites, and broader cross sections of the population—has its own reasons for being anti-American: the elite because of their disdain for popular culture; the disadvantaged, and those concerned with the disadvantaged, because of the perceived cruelties of the American economic model. This suggests a need to pause and reflect. If everything seems to be the responsibility of the new hegemonic power—the banalities of popular culture, the cruelties of the market, the heartlessness of globalism—is there not a danger that a new unthinking ideology is replacing the old verities of the cold war?

It used to be that anti-Americanism was the easy ideology of the communist authorities. It would be a terrible shame if the mirror image of such foolishness came to be understood as the entrance fee for full European status. It is a mark of political maturity that all things American are no longer automatically viewed in a positive light. It is also a mark of maturity not to unthinkingly move in the opposite direction. Intelligent pro- and anti-Americanism are two sides of the same coin. This means looking at American actions concretely, not as a unified model but as a set of experiences to be observed and judged from one's own distinctive point of view.

As far as the distinctiveness of the central European point of view, first I must say that I realize that the people of Poland (and of eastern and central Europe more generally) have experienced remarkable changes in the past decade, including major transformations of their systems of governance and the economy. The dictatorship of the proletariat and party vanguards is gone; instead, you have groping efforts to establish liberal democracy. Five-year plans are things of the past; instead, you have attempts to raise foreign and domestic capital to fuel the economic growth of a free-market system. The way the population gets through its days, weeks, months, and years has been reorganized. No longer do people pretend to work and the authorities pretend to pay them. Now is the time to carefully plan careers and get on with the projects of personal and societal development, working to avoid a crushing unemployment rate and to address the economic conditions that foster it.

The changed circumstances not only mean a redirection of personal lives and economic prospects. They also present fundamental challenges to the cultural and political life of society, with fundamental changes in the political culture of the region. Many of these are well known and often commented on: the relative success of the countries of central Europe in establishing a normal economy; the precarious nature of democratization in Russia and its meaning for the region's stability; the rise of xenophobic nationalism, which in the Balkans has meant a brutal war; and the reemergence of anti-Semitism, without Jews, which was present in the communist period but has reached new heights in recent years.

But the biggest surprise for an old eastern European hand such as myself is the rise of anti-Americanism in the region, although, upon reflection, it seems quite natural. There was a time, not too long ago, when it seemed that America could do no wrong in the eyes of eastern and central Europeans. There was no place in the world where Americans were so openly welcomed. It seems like only yesterday that I had to explain to my bewildered friends why I did not think that Ronald Reagan was a perfect president, an ideal leader of the free world, and why the appearance of a McDonald's in Warsaw did not strike me as a sign of great cultural and economic progress. But today, dissatisfaction with American power and culture can be observed everywhere—resentment over the domination of the American mass media, concern with the military strength of the American armed forces, discontent with the presumption of American scholars and intellectuals who propose to apply their models of economic, political, and cultural life, with happy results, to the countries of the former Soviet bloc. American triumphalism is being rejected, and, as usual, we Americans are hard-pressed to understand why this is.

I hope, though, that you would concede, at least for a little while, that good intentions are at the root of America's active participation in the internal affairs of the postcommunist world. To be sure, these good intentions include the identification of U.S. corporate and geopolitical interests with the principles of democracy and freedom. This is clearly something to be critically examined, but as good European realists, you should not expect otherwise. You know that principles rarely wander far from interests. Yet, as an interested observer seeking to be objective, I would remind you that the specificities of these principles and interests, and their relations, differ greatly, forcing us to examine and judge them on their own terms. Although democracy cannot simply be identified with the American way of life, the history and potential of modern democracy are intimately involved in the history and promise of this way of life. "Democracy in America" is not the only way to realize democracy, but its accomplishments and problems are instructive for those who take their democratic commitments seriously. They can be considered with benefit for Americans and non-Americans alike. To criticize American practices is a necessity; to overlook the meanings of the American experience is folly.

It is a sign of cultural strength that you, the citizens of eastern and central Europe, can now turn your critical eyes in the direction of America, but there is a danger that you will be blinded by your visions. In Latin America, the United States often played the role of an imperial power. It made and broke dictators and often undermined the development of indigenous democratic political forces. Yet it is now clear to those with critical stakes in the region, from both the left and right sides of the political spectrum, that the obstacles to a democratic life and a free society in Latin America had as much to do with the political culture and institutions of the countries themselves as they did with interference from big brother to the north. The loud shouts of "Yankee go home!" distracted those who were democratically disposed from considering their own problems closer to home. Some were alarmed by the communist threat that often seemed to be looming behind the slogan; others thought that the realization of the slogan's intent would solve all problems.

Such distraction and preoccupation with the foreign other, I believe, may now exist on the eastern European horizon, and it may be promoted from points more immediately west on the European continent. Yet there is a need to develop a critical approach to the American role in the new world order that takes into account both the problematic influence of American power and culture and the importance of the democratic experiment that America is. There is a need to be an intelligent anti-American.

There is much to be critical about when it comes to the American way of life. It is racist. It is unusually violent. The works produced by the American culture industry—music, films, television programs, and software products—often seek the lowest common denominator, a level of mediocrity that should not be acceptable to Americans or foreigners. We Americans are preoccupied with our own internal affairs and are remarkably ignorant of the rest of the world. There is only a dim recognition that some people beyond America's boundaries live in fundamentally different ways than Americans do, and there is little awareness that what we do and do not do as a nation have direct effects on their lives, and not always for the better. Ours is a society that has confused the pursuit of consumer goods with the common good, and we propagate this confusion to the rest of the world. Overly individualistic, we have lost a sense of community; overly materialistic, all sorts of spiritual fundamentalisms have invaded our public life. From certain points of view—from the critical point of view of radical socialists, to the point of view of Burkean conservatives, to the point of view of traditional Catholics—America seems to be at the vanguard of the decline and fall of the West.

But the problem with this opinion is that it is based on half-truths, ill-considered appraisals, and a rush to judgment. America is judged as a caricature of itself, not as the complex society that it is.

Consider American racism. The fact that the exclusion of African Americans is at the core of American political culture is undeniable. The very definition of freedom, as it is understood by Americans, emanates from the opposite of the condition of black servitude in the United States. The long and harsh history of slavery; the unofficial reign of terror of the Ku Klux Klan in the South during post–Civil War Reconstruction; the Jim Crow laws from the turn of the twentieth century to the 1960s, which yielded a state-enforced apartheid in the South and a socially enforced system of segregation and subordination in the great cities of the North, all point to the unfreedom that makes freedom so dear. On one side, there is the slave; on the other, the freeman, in the language of the antebellum era. On the side of servitude is the unfreedom of a separate and decidedly unequal economic and political life, and on the side of freedom is America as the land of opportunity.

And the problem of race is far from being exclusively historical; it overshadows much of our public life. The injustices of our educational, social welfare, and judicial systems, as they process blacks and whites, yield incredibly depressing statistics. There are more young black men in their teens and twenties caught in the prison system as prisoners, defendants, or parolees than there are in the educational system as students. The income disparity between blacks and whites is still systemic—at all levels of education and for both men and women. African Americans still face daily indignities in their everyday lives in a white-dominated society. There is a systematic assumption that blacks are not capable of doing both menial and challenging intellectual tasks.

For those who have been to America, remember and take as significant the fact that you saw more immigrants doing attractive service jobs, such as driving airport limousines, and holding sales positions in lucrative enterprises than African Americans, and this is indicative of hiring policies in small factories as well. Surveys of employers reveal a marked preference for immigrant labor over African Americans, even among African American entrepreneurs. This bias, in effect, systematically relegates a large portion of the African American population to the rural and urban underclass, beyond the system of steady jobs and salaries, beyond the hope of upward social mobility. On the other side of the stratification spectrum, affirmative action serves as an excuse for racists to minimize the accomplishments of blacks who hold positions of power, prestige, and privilege. To racists, it seems that all these jobs came off the backs of qualified whites. Black accomplishment defines a new white servitude.

But when you, in this part of the world, think about the problems of American society as they relate to you, I suspect that you are not much concerned with American racism. You all too readily understand the nature of our problems. The high level of heterogeneity that exists in the United States is practically beyond eastern and central European imagination. You may be sympathetic with our race problem. You may understand that the problem of American violence is somehow related to it. Your understanding may or may not have racist qualities. But given the different problems of race, ethnicity, and nationality here, you can hardly afford to feel self-satisfied and depict yourselves in a completely positive fashion. You know that we confront problems in the course of our domestic relations that have led to modern barbarism here, and while you may cast a critical glance on the racial situation in America, you would be well advised to consider how Americans struggle to deal with the problems of difference, with successes and failures, as the ugly face of xenophobia again raises its head in the lands of the European killing fields.

But do not think that I am suggesting that the way to be an intelligent anti-American is to be pro-American. I concede that your critical approaches to the American way of life are important to the viability of your cultural identity and, in my judgment, may help us in our democratic life as well.

Probably the most unfortunate and problematic aspects of American life observable abroad are the products of our culture industry. There is much to dismiss here, much to be against, and it seems to me that resistance to the idiocies of our mass culture wherever it comes from is welcome—the more forceful the better. But be forewarned. The critique of American mass culture can easily slide into the rejection of democracy and the rejection of democratic cultural forms. The most famous case of this is the completely wrongheaded rejection of jazz by Theodor Adorno.

An extraordinary American comic strip, *Pogo*, comes to mind. One of its characters famously announced during an apparently nonsensical interaction: "we have met the enemy and it is us." During the Vietnam War, when this strip was created, the referent hardly needed explanation. But remember that the key to the success of American mass culture is its popularity, both in the United States and abroad. We, as intellectuals—indeed, as intellectuals who attempt to be intelligent anti-Americans—should be cautious in our condemnation of American mass culture unless we are comfortable with the role of philosopher king. Do we really want to hold an intellectual position that boldly declares, paraphrasing a great line from *Pogo*, that we have met the enemy and it is the people? Can we commit ourselves to a politics or even a cultural position that claims to know better what is in the people's interest after the close of a bloody century of ideological wars?

Perhaps not, I hope you would reply, but surely we should take some care to distinguish the banal from the fine, the enriching from the stupefying. I agree. But an intelligent anti-American will proceed with caution. Some things are easy. The mindless violence of American television and films that increasingly dominates the European and American markets should be condemned, boycotted; perhaps some form of national cultural policy, short of official censorship, should attempt to ensure the creation of alternative local, regional, and national markets to compete with Hollywood productions. The economies of scale allow Hollywood to dominate the world market for slick entertainment, disseminating a worldview that is clearly objectionable not only here in Europe but also in the United States, not only in South Africa but also in Latin America and central Asia. Our politicians attempt to make political points out of this, and surely so will yours. The stuff Hollywood produces creates the greatest audiences; establishing the conditions for the profitability of smaller audiences is clearly desirable, both here and there.

But I am referring so far to relatively easy matters. What about a situation where the line between trash and excellence is not so easily drawn? What about the exportation of works that intelligently address a mass audience in effective aesthetic fashion but, with the power of wealth and know-how, overwhelm smaller, more difficult alternatives? To refer to a specific and telling case in point, what about films such as *Schindler's List?*

It is one of the oddities of life in Cracow that one can go to the former Jewish section of Kazimierz and take a guided tour of the sites of mass killings, the liquidation of the ghetto, and the Holocaust as they were depicted for a mass audience in Steven Spielberg's film. Given the facts of what actually happened on (at least very close to) those grounds, this is grotesque to the extreme, an awful Americanization of the perception of modern evil. It seems that for those who sponsor the tour and for those who go on it, the grounds of great suffering attain a higher reality for having been represented in a film than for simply being the reality that they are. The film, with its popularity and power, has made the destruction of the Jews a reality for a mass audience. It facilitates memory where horror and forgetting interacted in the service of ignorance. But I wonder, as I am sure some of you do, whether the melodramatic qualities of its story line, the focus on the good German and its happy ending, create a kind of memory that is worse than ignorance. If this should become the Holocaust on film, there is a danger that there will be little room to remember anything and anyone other than its memorable characters and their fate: the sadistic prison commandant, the loyal Jewish accountant, the German rogue who helps it all work out in the end, the hero of the story. From the perspective of what we know about the makers and victims of the Holocaust, the simplification is overwhelming.

Yet simplification is not all it offers; there is more to this brilliant film than its melodrama. In its incredible portrayal of the liquidation of the Jewish ghetto, the absolute horror of the experience of the Nazi terror becomes accessible to those who were not there. Using all the tricks and wealth of the American film industry, Spielberg helps the world remember things easily forgotten, consider things that are beyond the imagination of most of us. And most important, despite all the problems of its presentation—exhibiting the limitations of American movies as opposed to the refinements of European films—the film has reached a large and broad audience, many of whom hardly ever thought about the Holocaust before. The democratic art form that film is attains its distinction. Yes, the limitations of an American happy ending are evident. Yes, more sophisticated treatments of the horrors of our century are available in all sorts of forms, often presented with far greater insight. But the great majority of the

Schindler's List audience would never have turned to these forms. Intelligent anti-Americans, refine your criticisms, even when they generally apply.

Serious criticisms of American activities in foreign lands are especially concerned with the anomaly of Americans being both remarkably ignorant of the world about them and remarkably willing to interject themselves into that world about which they are so ignorant. Perhaps even this presentation is vulnerable to this objection. Who am I to tell you what an intelligent form of anti-Americanism should be? Why do Americans think that they can best advise people what form their democracies should take? Is American advice on democracy too similar to the advice given by the big brother to the east? Is democracy *à la Americain* just another dominant ideology?

These are difficult questions. But I think they can be answered simply. It requires a perception of the texture—not just the formal structure—of democracy, America, and anti-Americanism. When we consider the problems of democracy in a nonutopian way, in a way that is practical and not simply idealistic, we think of specific modern institutions: constitutions and elections, competing political parties, modes of representation and association, liberal rights of free speech and property, the rule of law. But we must remember that these institutions require, if they are successful within a supportive cultural context, a democratic culture. Such a culture, in contrast to an authoritarian one, is far from being univocal. It is filled with paradoxes and anomalies, tensions and dilemmas, which in principle cannot be resolved definitively. It is unclear whether democracy requires a common set of cultural commitments, as the advocates of Americanism believed at the turn of the twentieth century, or whether differences can work to hold the democratic polity together, as advocates of multiculturalism (and the pluralists before them) have maintained. Democracy is about the robust and open contestation between these positions. With such openness, it cannot easily function as an instrumental ideology in the fashion of Soviet Marxism.

Criticism of the American way of life is a basic part of the American way of life. In a sense, anti-Americanism is a great American tradition. When I propose to you an intelligent anti-Americanism as opposed to one that is not so intelligent, I suggest that it be based on knowledge of the problems of democracy in America. I suggest that it be critical, but not cynical; informed about the accomplishments and promise of the American experiment in democracy; and judged against existing practices.

Americans, especially when they travel abroad, may confuse the promise with the ongoing reality. This may be especially convenient for those who work in and for official governmental institutions. But it would be a pity if this tendency overshadowed attempts to overcome them. It would be a shame if independent voices of criticism were not heard, along with the voices of appreciation. When advice comes from America, you should judge the quality of its understanding of American society and its practices, and its understanding of the situation of the countries being advised. Likewise, when I hear anti-Americanism from abroad, I will judge it for its self-understanding and its appreciation of the complexities of American life. If it has such qualities, it will substantiate the prospects of the democratic project. We in America, like you in this part of the world, need intelligent anti-Americanism, that is, a critical democratic culture.

The Federal Marriage Amendment and the Attack on American Democracy

R. Claire Snyder

For centuries there have been powerful voices to condemn homosexual conduct as immoral, but this Court's obligation is to define the liberty of all, not to mandate its own moral code.
—U.S. Supreme Court, *Lawrence v. Texas* (2003)

Marriage in the United States shall consist only of the union of a man and a woman. Neither this Constitution, nor the constitution of any State, shall be construed to require that marriage or the legal incidents thereof be conferred upon any union other than the union of a man and a woman.
—Proposed Federal Marriage Amendment (2004)

The American Constitution created a secular government that acts to protect the civil rights and liberties of individuals rather than imposing a particular vision of the "good life" on its citizens. Freedom of conscience and the separation of church and state are central to the political philosophy of liberal democracy. These principles, enshrined in our founding documents, have become almost universally accepted norms in U.S. society today. Nevertheless, conservative religious organizations are currently mobilizing their supporters across the country to undermine these basic principles, appealing to popular prejudice against an unpopular minority. Claiming to speak for the People, they seek to deny lesbians and gay men legal equality and the right to *civil marriage* through the passage of the Federal Marriage Amendment, which would impose a religiously rooted definition of marriage as the law of the land. While conservative Americans are free to practice their religious beliefs and live their personal lives however they choose, neither federal nor state government in the United States can legitimately generate public policy imposing a particular religious worldview on all Americans. Nor can it let the beliefs of some—even a majority—violate the civil rights of other individuals in society or deny equality before the law to certain groups of citizens.

LIBERAL DEMOCRACY OR CHRISTIAN NATION?

Liberal political theory constitutes the most important founding tradition of American democracy. Both liberal Democrats and neoliberal Republicans endorse its basic principles—individual freedom, religious liberty, equal rights, constitutional government, and impartial laws—although they interpret these concepts in different ways. According to the liberal founding myth of "social contract," self-interested individuals left the state of nature in order to better secure their natural rights and liberties. Consequently, they established a constitutional government of impartial laws that would protect all citizens equally. The Declaration of Independence stated the basic values of liberal political theory—"all men are created equal and . . . are endowed by their creator with certain unalienable rights, among them life, liberty, and the pursuit of happiness"—while the U.S. Constitution created a secular government that would not discriminate against those who do not practice the dominant religion or who espouse unpopular beliefs.

Despite the First Amendment's prohibition against the establishment of religion by government, Christian conservatives often insist that America is really a "Christian nation." They argue that the American founders believed that democratic political institutions would work only if grounded on religious mores within civil society, emphasizing a comment made by John Adams: "Our Constitution was made only for a moral and religious people. It is wholly inadequate to the government of any other." William Bennett has contributed greatly to this right-wing project of revisionist historiography with *Our Sacred Honor: Words of Advice from the Founders,* a volume that catalogs stories, letters, poems, and speeches that emphasize the religious beliefs that animated many in the founding generation (among other things). The Christian Right hopes that once the religious beliefs of the American founders are established, a theory of constitutional interpretation that privileges "original intent" will authorize the imposition of Christian moral precepts on American society at large.

Although the relationship between religion and democracy in the American context is a complicated one, the fact remains that the founding generation *intentionally* took the extremely radical step of constructing a secular government that was constitutionally required to remain neutral toward religion. As Isaac Kramnick and R. Laurence Moore rightly stress in *The Godless Constitution,* "God is nowhere to be found in the Constitution, which also has nothing to say about the social value of Christian belief or about the importance of religion for a moral public life." Indeed, the fact that the American Constitution institutionalized a secular state was both revolutionary and controversial. While conservatives are certainly correct that the Bill of Rights protected states' rights, not individual rights, leaving the states free to establish religion, in fact, only five states actually permitted the establishment of religion. Thus, the conservative attempt to redefine America as a Christian nation completely ignores the fact that this country was remarkable for its intentionally secular Constitution.

THE LOGIC OF LIBERALISM

In principle, the Bill of Rights has protected individual rights from the tyranny of federal and state governments and majoritarianism ever since ratification of the Fourteenth Amendment after the Civil War. This important amendment extended the liberal principle of legal equality by mandating "equal protection" of the law for all U.S. citizens. Though never fully actualized in practice, the principle of legal equality has been used successfully to justify progressive change. African Americans utilized this principle during the civil rights movement in their struggle to end segregation. While the Right violently opposed legal equality at the time, contemporary conservatives have largely accepted the principle of color-blind law. At the same time, however, color blindness in the law is completely compatible with the New Right's "new racism," wherein de jure legal equality is used to challenge affirmative action and other remedial measures that seek to address institutional racism.

The struggle for gender-blind law has also been largely successful. Although feminists lost the battle for the Equal Rights Amendment (ERA) during the 1970s, since that time, the principle of legal equality for women has been largely implemented through the courts, which are charged with following the logic of liberalism as they apply the principles of the Constitution to new areas. Although historical custom and reactionary political agendas have resulted in some unfortunate constitutional rulings, overall, the level of legal equality within American society has increased over time.

A consistent application of the philosophical principles of liberalism also justifies same-sex marriage. A secular state committed to legal equality cannot legitimately deny *civil marriage*, with all its benefits, to particular citizens on the basis of gender or sexual orientation. To do so would be to violate the basic principles of the United States as a liberal democracy. Though I would argue that the Christian Right is losing its battle to prevent the extension of civil rights to lesbians and gay men, there is no guarantee that politically appointed judges will rule in a principled way. The courts are, however, slowly beginning to recognize this logic. The Massachusetts Supreme Court has actually legalized same-sex marriage. Societal attitudes are also changing. Fifty-eight percent of first-year college students now think that "gay and lesbian couples should have the right to 'equal marital status,' i.e., civil marriage"—including half who identify themselves as "middle-of-the-road" or "conservative."[1]

ILLIBERAL REACTION

Despite the compelling logic of philosophical liberalism, traditionalists on the Right have always actively opposed increasing levels of legal equality—first for African Americans, then for women, and now for lesbian, gay, bisexual, transgender, and queer (LGBTQ) people. The Old Right explicitly supported white supremacy at a time when it was socially acceptable to publicly denigrate African Americans and claimed that racial equality would destroy the American way of life. It vehemently opposed the Supreme Court's principled ruling in *Brown v. Board of Education,* accused the justices of legislating from the bench, and mobilized one of the largest grassroots campaigns in U.S. history to attack all attempts to enact racial equality.

Opposition to racial equality included a ban on interracial marriage—and an attempt in 1912 to amend the U.S. Constitution to that effect. State bans on interracial marriage continued until 1967, when the Supreme Court ruled antimiscegenation laws unconstitutional in *Loving v. Virginia,* stating, "the freedom to marry has long been recognized as one of the vital personal rights essential to the orderly pursuit of happiness . . . one of the 'basic civil rights of man' . . . and cannot be infringed by the State."

The Republican Party was able to become competitive in the historically Democratic South by capturing the racist vote, attracting southerners who came to reject the Democratic Party when it started backing civil rights legislation under the Kennedy and Johnson administrations. In 1964 the Republican Party supported Barry Goldwater for president, who opposed the Civil Rights Act; he wanted the states to decide for themselves how to deal with racial issues.

With the landslide defeat of Goldwater and the acceptability of explicit racism on the decline among the general public, right-wing leaders began repackaging their message to make it more appealing to mainstream Americans. The conservative mobilization against feminism—in particular the ERA and abortion rights—helped solidify this New Right during the 1970s and played an important role in its success, the election of Ronald Reagan in 1980, and the rightward shift in U.S. politics. Antifeminism provided a link with evangelical Christian churches, mobilized traditional homemakers who felt that their position was being threatened by changing laws and mores, and focused the reaction against cultural and political change. Remarkably, Reagan inaugurated his 1980 election campaign by promoting "states' rights"—a southern code word for segregation—in Philadelphia, Mississippi, scene of the murder of three civil rights workers sixteen years before.

Feminism and the LGBTQ civil rights movement are linked theoretically through the political philosophy of liberalism and politically through common struggle. Although unprincipled liberals sometimes try to deny this connection out of political expediency, those on the Right quickly recognized that the logic of liberalism provided the potential for unity between women and LGBTQ individuals and used it to their advantage. In its rise to power, the New Right successfully manipulated homophobia to increase opposition to gender equality as well as explicitly condemning all attempts to accord nonheterosexuals the equal protection of the law.

CHRISTIAN RIGHT THEOLOGY AND THE ATTACK ON RELIGIOUS FREEDOM

Current right-wing opposition to gay marriage not only constitutes another example of the Right's fundamentally antidemocratic, antiliberal politics but also forms a central part of the Christian Right's larger agenda that seeks to reverse the progress of feminism, reinforce male dominance, and restore the patriarchal family with its traditional gender roles as the hegemonic family form in America. Because many Americans balk at the prospect of disconnecting marriage from its traditional heterosexual moorings, members of the Christian Right hope that the gay marriage issue will help galvanize support for their larger agenda, just as opposition to the ERA helped them consolidate their base during the 1970s.

While Christian Right organizations claim to speak for the American people when they oppose civil marriage for lesbians and gays, they are actually trying to impose their own particular religious worldview on U.S. society, in direct violation of the separation of church and state. They define marriage as a sacred religious institution and homosexuality as a sin. According to the Family Research Council, marriage is "the *work of heaven and every major religion* and culture throughout world history." Concerned Women for America proclaims that marriage is *"a covenant established by God* wherein one man and one woman, united for life, are licensed by the state for the purpose of founding and maintaining a family." For Focus on the Family, "marriage is *a sacred union, ordained by God* to be a life-long, sexually exclusive relationship between one man and one woman." Indeed, because of this religious worldview, all three groups have made opposition to same-sex civil marriage a centerpiece of their political agenda.

The Christian Right's vision of heterosexual marriage directly relates to its understanding of gender difference, which it bases on its particular interpretation of the Bible. To justify male dominance, the Christian Right privileges the second version of the creation story in Genesis, in which God created Eve out of Adam's rib to be his "helper" and declared that the man and his wife would become "one flesh" (Gen. 2:18–24), rather than the first story, in which

"God created man in his own image, in the image of God he created him; *male and female he created them*" (Gen. 1:26–27, emphasis added). Additionally, instead of reading the latter version as establishing gender equality at the origin, as some religious scholars do, the Christian Right interprets it to mean that "God's purpose for man was that there should be two sexes, male and female. Every person is either a 'he' or a 'she.' God did not divide mankind into three or four or five sexes."[2] Right-wing Christians bolster their selective reading of the Old Testament with a few New Testament verses, such as woman is the "weaker vessel" (1 Pet. 3:7), "man was not made from woman, but woman from man" (1 Cor. 11:8), "the head of a woman is her husband" (1 Cor. 11:3), "wives be subject to your husbands, as to the Lord," and "the husband is the head of the wife as Christ is the head of the church" (Eph. 5:22–23).

The Christian Right's selectively literalist interpretation of the Bible not only emphasizes the natural authority of husbands over their wives but also condemns homosexuality as a particularly grave sin. This condemnation relies on just a few passages in the entire Bible. For example, they interpret God's destruction of Sodom and Gomorrah (Gen. 18:16–19:29) as punishment for homosexuality. Yet religious scholars vigorously disagree about the meaning of that story. The dominant contemporary interpretation is that the city was destroyed for the sin of inhospitality—considered a "sacred obligation" in ancient times—not for homosexuality.

In addition, the Christian Right stresses the two sentences in Leviticus that proclaim, "you shall not lie with a male as with a woman; it is an abomination" (Lev. 18:22) and "if a man lies with a male as with a woman, both of them have committed an abomination; they shall be put to death" (Lev. 20:13), completely ignoring the fact that the Ten Commandments does not prohibit homosexuality. At the same time, the Christian Right disregards the wide array of other practices prohibited in Leviticus, such as eating pork or touching a football made of pigskin (Lev. 11:7–8), wearing cotton-polyester blends (Lev. 19:19), and trimming the hair on the side of the face (Lev. 19:27). "Ex-gay" Stephen Bennett stresses that Leviticus refers to male homosexuality as an "abomination" but fails to mention that it also refers to eating shellfish as an "abomination" (Lev. 11:10).

While the Right makes much of the English term *abomination*, the original Hebrew word *to'evah* comes from *'to'eh ata ba*, which means "you go astray because of it." Rebecca Alpert argues that the original meaning of the word implies that engaging in homosexual acts is not intrinsically evil but simply has negative consequences, which in ancient or medieval times might have meant not reproducing or abandoning your wife.

My point here is not to establish any one reading of the Bible as definitive, but rather to complicate the Christian Right's claim that the meaning of Scripture is self-evident. Not all religious people agree that homosexuality is a sin or that same-sex couples should be denied the right to civil marriage. In fact, some religious denominations not only support civil marriage but also perform *religious* marriage or some comparable form of union for lesbian and gay couples—Reform and Reconstructionist Judaism, some Episcopal congregations, the Metropolitan Community Church, and the Unitarian Universalists, for example. Moreover, no consensus exists among religious folks even when it comes to the definition and meaning of heterosexual marriage. For example, Christianity restricts marriage to one man and one woman, but Islam allows polygamy. Catholics consider marriage a sacrament, whereas Protestants do not.

Nevertheless, despite the diversity of beliefs and interpretations within a religiously pluralistic society such as the United States, the Federal Marriage Amendment, if passed, would impose one particular, religiously rooted definition of marriage on all the citizens of the United States, Christian or not. The amendment directly violates the separation of church and state, and so it undermines the principles of liberal democracy on which the United States was founded. In a liberal society, conservative Christian churches certainly have the religious liberty to define marriage for their parishioners in any way they see fit; however, the liberal democratic state cannot legitimately make one particular interpretation of revealed religion the law of the land.

PHONY POPULISM ON THE RIGHT

Right-wing opponents of gay marriage claim that they stand for the interests of ordinary people when they oppose legal equality for all. This rhetorical strategy worked well during the 1970s, when opponents of the ERA portrayed feminism as advancing the interests of elite career women at the expense of housewives and working-class women. In reality, however, according to a 1994 study by Sara Diamond, it was middle-class women who performed the daily activist tasks essential to the anti-ERA movement.

In fact, Lisa McGirr's recent study of the origins of the New Right reveals its mass base to be composed of not the farmers and blue-collar working folks of George Wallace's segregationist South, or even the lower-middle-class white ethnics who became "Reagan Democrats," but rather the educated, affluent, upwardly mobile white suburbanites, who reap material benefits from tax cuts and reduced government spending, from real estate development and the military-industrial complex, and from the traditional entitlements of white Christian America.

In its attack on same-sex marriage, the Right continues its pseudopopulist pose, claiming to speak for the interests of ordinary people who are supposedly being attacked by an elite "homosexual lobby." As Chip Berlet and Matthew

Lyons have argued, Christian Right propaganda frequently portrays gay men, like feminists, as a wealthy, privileged elite that wants to impose its immoral, self-serving agenda on American society. For example, a Family Research Council fund-raiser says, "the Human Rights Campaign [HRC] and the other groups in the homosexual lobby have very deep pockets. Big corporations, elite foundations, and Hollywood celebrities underwrite the homosexual lobby with tens of millions of dollars every year." Similarly, the executive director of the Traditional Values Coalition calls the HRC "the wealthiest extremists of the left." In reality, however, antigay groups outspend LGBTQ groups "by at least a four-to-one ratio." Moreover, contrary to myth, gay men actually earn 20 to 25 percent less than do heterosexual men. "Lesbians appear to earn about the same as heterosexual women, but lesbian couples earn less than straight couples because women, on average, earn less than men." Finally, many state and local anti-gay marriage groups that promote themselves as "grassroots" are actually funded by wealthy national organizations.[3]

DOES SAME-SEX MARRIAGE REALLY HARM MEN, WOMEN, AND CHILDREN?

Although the Christian Right claims to speak for the good of society, it actually seeks to reconsolidate male dominance and reestablish the patriarchal family as the dominant family form in the United States, despite "extensive feminist analysis and empirical evidence" documenting that "gender role differentiation in families is connected to stratification in economic, political and social life" in a way that harms women.[4] Because no evidence exists that same-sex couples are less functional than heterosexual ones or that their children are more likely to suffer negative effects, allowing same-sex couples to marry and have children would clearly undermine the myth that the patriarchal heterosexual family is the superior family form.

The conservative "fatherhood movement" blames feminism and single mothers for the social problems caused by men and teenaged boys. Though the packaging of their arguments varies slightly, advocates make a similar claim: By refusing to respect natural gender differences, feminists have pathologized masculinity and futilely attempted to change the behavior of men and boys. They have undermined the rightful authority of men as the head of the household, attempted to change the natural division of labor between mothers and fathers, and propagated the idea that a woman can fulfill the role traditionally played by a man, thus rendering fathers superfluous to family life. Consequently, men have lost interest in fulfilling their traditional family responsibilities, and boys have no one to teach them how to become responsible men.

Detached from the civilizing influence of the traditional patriarchal family, males increasingly cause a wide array of social problems, and everybody suffers.

Focus on the Family president James Dobson makes this argument from a Christian Right perspective. In *Bringing Up Boys*, he argues that traditional gender roles are natural and cannot be changed. He points to the continued power of men in society as evidence of their natural "biochemical and anatomical" dominance. Dobson strongly opposes attempts to change the gender socialization of children and explicitly links this "unisex" idea to "the powerful gay and lesbian agenda," whose propagandists are teaching a revolutionary view of sexuality called "gender feminism," which insists that sex assignment is irrelevant. Although Dobson sees this as dangerous for both sexes, it is particularly harmful for boys: "Protect the masculinity of your boys, who will be under increasing political pressure in years to come."

Dobson believes that a breakdown of traditional gender roles within the family fosters homosexuality in children. The prevention of homosexuality among boys requires the involvement of a properly masculine heterosexual father, especially during the early years. Dobson relies on the work of Dr. Joseph Nicolosi, a leading proponent of the Christian Right's "ex-gay" movement, who urges parents to monitor their children for signs of "prehomosexuality" so that professionals can step in before it is too late. While "feminine behavior in boyhood" is clearly a sign, so is "nonmasculinity," defined as not fitting in with male peers. "The father," Nicolosi asserts, "plays an essential role in a boy's normal development as a man. The truth is, Dad is more important than Mom." In order to ensure heterosexuality, the father "needs to mirror and affirm his son's maleness. He can play rough-and-tumble games with his son, in ways that are decidedly different from the games he would play with a little girl. He can help his son learn to throw and catch a ball. . . . He can even take his son with him into the shower, where the boy cannot help but notice that Dad has a penis, just like his, only bigger."

Based solely on the work of Nicolosi, Dobson concludes, "if you as a parent have an effeminate boy or a masculinized girl, I urge you to get a copy [of Nicolosi's book] and then seek immediate professional help." He warns parents, however, to beware of "secular" mental health professionals, who will most certainly "take the wrong approach—telling your child that he is homosexual and needs to accept that fact." Instead, Dobson recommends a referral from either Exodus International, the leading organization of the ex-gay ministries, or the National Association for Research and Therapy of Homosexuality, founded to oppose the 1973 decision by the American Psychological Association to stop classifying homosexuality as an emotional or mental disorder.

While Dobson and the burgeoning fatherhood movement stress the harm that the feminist and the LGBTQ movements have supposedly done to men and boys, the Right insists that these movements for gender equality harm women as well. Concerned Women for America, which claims to be the largest women's group in the country, blames feminism—in particular, its support for legal equality, reproductive freedom, female sexual pleasure, and no-fault divorce—for eroding the "protections" supposedly provided women by traditional marriage and family law, making it easier for men to renounce their familial responsibilities and causing the feminization of poverty. In its view, the LGBTQ movement continues these allegedly destructive trends by further undermining traditional gender roles, advocating diverse family forms, and reinforcing the disconnection between sexual pleasure and reproduction.

Some on the Right insist that women's role in the traditional family has already been undermined by feminism, and the specter of same-sex marriage threatens to render women completely useless. For example, William Mattox, a *USA Today* columnist and Alliance for Marriage supporter, argues that "in the same way that polygamy teaches that women are inferior to men, 'gay marriage' implicitly teaches that women are superfluous to men, that women make no unique and irreplaceable contribution to family life. Indeed, 'gay marriage' teaches that the most basic unit of human society—marriage—does not need a woman to be complete."

Despite this interesting rhetorical strategy, however, same-sex marriage does not actually undermine the position of women. In fact, the majority of same-sex couples seeking marriage are women—57 percent of same-sex couples who wed in San Francisco between February 12 and March 11, 2004, 71 percent of those who wed in Portland between March 3 and April 20, 2004, and 66 percent of first-day applicants in Massachusetts were women, as are two-thirds of those seeking Vermont civil unions. Since access to the civil benefits of marriage will help these women take care of each other and any dependent children they may have, gay marriage clearly helps rather than hurts the position of women by making it easier for them to survive outside the bounds of patriarchal marriage—which is exactly what the Right opposes.

The Christian Right wants to continue to portray lesbians and gay men as inordinately driven by sexual desire and thus unable to form long-term relationships. The visibility of committed same-sex couples illustrates the ordinariness of most lesbian and gay people's lives and demonstrates an alternative to the Christian Right's rigid view of proper gender roles and its narrow definition of what constitutes a family. Because of their particular theological beliefs, right-wing Christians insist that men and women are fundamentally different beings who come together to reproduce and must remain coupled in order to rear their children. Because homosexuality disconnects sex from reproduction, they reason, homosexual relationships must be fleeting, driven by sexual gratification alone. As Concerned Women for America founder Beverly LaHaye put it, "it is the compulsive desire for sexual gratification without lasting commitment, the high rate of promiscuity, and the self-defined morality among homosexuals that sap the vitality of the family structure, making it something less than it was, is, and should be." Consequently, "homosexual relationships are not only the antithesis to family, but also threaten its very core."

Clearly the desire of many same-sex couples to marry and to raise children demonstrates that lesbians and gay men are not primarily seeking hedonistic gratification. In fact, the first same-sex couple to receive a marriage license in San Francisco had been together for fifty years, whereas half of all heterosexual marriages end in divorce. Most lesbians and gay men want the same types of relationships that straight people do. In fact, an estimated "64 to 80 percent of lesbians and 46 to 60 percent of gay men report that they are in committed partner relationships," and "studies show that gay and lesbian relationships are comparable to opposite-sex relationships in terms of quality of the relationship and satisfaction in the relationship." Furthermore, according to 2000 census data, "lesbian couples . . . parent at about three quarters of the rate of married straight couples, and gay male couples parent at about half the rate as married straight couples"—and this includes only couples with at least one child living with them.[5] Nevertheless, despite empirical evidence, Christian Right groups purposely disseminate misinformation in an attempt to bolster their political agenda of marginalizing lesbians and gay men and reconsolidating the tradition of male dominance.

CONCLUSION

In their fight against legal equality for lesbians and gay men, the Christian Right appeals to the religious assumptions, historical customs, social anxieties, and unexamined prejudices of many Americans, yet their overarching agenda actually undermines American democracy's most precious political principles, including the separation of church and state, legal equality, and personal liberty. Although liberal democracy has its limitations, its virtue is that it maximizes the freedom of all by allowing individuals to organize their personal lives as they see fit. The government may respond to the will of its citizens by providing a default set of legal entanglements that makes it easier for individuals to establish families (i.e., civil marriage), but it may not legitimately deny equal protection of the law to unpopular minorities or enshrine a particular religious definition of marriage as the law of the land. Consequently, the state should ensure equal access to civil marriage and leave religious marriage where it belongs—in the synagogues, churches, and mosques.

NOTES

1. Paul Varnell, "College Freshmen Support Gay Marriage," *Chicago Free Press*, January 30, 2002. http://www.indegayforum.org/articles/varnell85.html.
2. Stephen Bennett, "Homosexuality and the Bible: What Does God Say?" (Huntington, Conn.: Stephen Bennett Ministries, n.d.), 3. For an alternative view, see Anne Fausto-Sterling, *Sexing the Body: Gender Politics and the Construction of Sexuality* (New York: Basic Books, 2000).
3. Quotes and statistics cited in Sean Cahill, *Same-Sex Marriage in the United States: Focus on the Facts* (Lanham, Md.: Lexington Books, 2004).
4. Jyl J. Josephson and Cynthia Burack, "The Political Ideology of the Neo-Traditional Family," *Journal of Political Ideologies* 3, no. 2 (1998): 213–31.
5. Cahill, *Same-Sex Marriage*, 55, 57.

Fahrenheit 9/11
The Real Lowdown

Kurt Jacobsen

Agitprop, by any other name, is still agitprop. Even our heartiest approval of a refreshingly candid viewpoint within this dubious medium doesn't change that fact. But so what? In the trumped-up second Persian Gulf war, didn't the mainstream U.S. media operate, as if by a tap of a wicked witch's wand, as an enormous fawning agitprop apparatus for the Bush White House (as anchorman Dan Rather admitted, with the saving grace of traces of shame)? Agitprop is what every government assiduously churns out every day in calculated streams of tactical news bites, although the purveyors usually give it a suitably anodyne label, such as "public information." The disingenuous official briefings that reporters in Vietnam dubbed the "Five o'Clock Follies" have since been resurrected and refined into holy writ, especially by the watch-the-bomb-scoot-down-the-chimney cable news networks, among which Fox is only the worst offender. Can we have some whopping correctives, please?

Agitprop is customarily dismissed as politically skewed messages wrapped in the guise of art or news reporting. Yet the redoubtable Michael Moore, after a mercifully brief dalliance with presidential candidate and former NATO commander Wesley Clarke, owes no special party allegiances and loudly tells anyone who wants to know that his cunningly corrosive and $100 million–grossing *Fahrenheit 9/11* is damned well intended to capsize (if not abet the impeachment of) the floundering Bush administration. Most agitprop, these ultra-hip days, is heavily cloaked as dispassionate analysis, not as ringing calls to man the barricades or, more to the point, flock to local polling places to throw out the bums. With that infinitely affable tenacity that is his gift and trademark, Moore has become the insistent, inquisitive voice of everyday Americans who wear their baseball caps unfashionably peak forward and want to know what the hell is really going on.

In *Fahrenheit 9/11* Moore deftly strings a chain of seamy episodes into a big picture of the media manipulation of that huge chunk of working America that is informed, if that is the word, mostly by glossy TV and radio networks or by a remarkably servile local press. You needn't peruse David Brock's *The Republican Noise Machine* or Joe Conason's *Big Lies* or anything by Robert McChesney to notice the monotonous right-wing tone of U.S. airwaves—just hit "scan" on your car radio or flip through eighty-seven TV channels and find nothing (else) on news stations. An incandescent right-wing rage has erupted because Moore miraculously managed to break—maybe just sprain—the Right's grip on misreporting the news. If he accomplishes nothing else, Moore is finally getting the word out that al Qaeda and Saddam Hussein had nothing to do with each other. The circulation of that piquant fact alone is a public service for which we should smooch the ground Moore walks on. In a mass media vehicle, Bush at last wears a tall dunce's cap, and not the avenging angel's wings that his righteous supporters imagine.

The big guns were rolled out. Christopher Hitchens, in a typical and deviously reasoned essay, assails *Fahrenheit 9/11* as "a sinister exercise in moral frivolity, crudely disguised as an exercise in seriousness." For Hitchens, a born-again Bush apologist, the horde of contradictions that, as Moore vividly points out, infests Bush's antiterrorism policy is grist to be twisted sophistically into Moore's own contradictions. Moore, for example, archly asks why so few U.S. troops were dispatched so tardily to catch Osama bin Laden if Bush's urgent concern were really terrorism. Moore also asks what influence the Saudis, as well as other major moneybags both domestic and foreign, have exerted over U.S. policy. Hitchens, therefore, asserts that either the Saudis run U.S. policy or they do not. If not, then nothing the Saudis do matters. Now there's a fine analytical mind for you. (By the way, according to Hitchens, everything is going swimmingly in arid Afghanistan, where nary a burka mars the scenic landscape anymore.)

Coming into play is the twitty Brit view that only they savor the exquisiteness of irony, while those perky Yanks cannot evolve beyond commonplace sarcasm. Because the pallid 9/11 Commission and Richard P. Clarke see nothing wrong with the peculiar nature of the Saudis' exit, it's okay then. Bush and Blair together are doing profound work. Iraq was indeed in noncompliance with United Nations resolutions, as were the United States and Israel, but never mind about them. There admittedly was a "bad period" when Washington preferred Saddam in the 1980s (and maybe a bit before), but, hey, that's history. Hitchens credits the rumor that Saddam dispatched agents to snuff the elder Bush. For eleven years, those sanctified no-fly zones were imposed by Britain and the United States, not the UN. Hitchens studiously misses any uncongenial point. Moore ridicules counterterrorism stinginess not because he craves massive spending but because the war on terror is plainly a pretext. The "matches and lighters" episode in the documentary underlines the hefty business influence on an obliging government, at the minor cost of common sense. Blacks are happy to be in the army, Hitchens says, because, you know, that's what the civil rights movement was all about, although Martin Luther King might like to have had a word with Hitchens about this little misapprehension.

He even equates Moore's aversion to Bush with a hatred of "Western democracy and an admiration of totalitarianism." I'm not kidding. A jowly literal-mindedness smothers Hitchens, who is by far still the smartest among the multitude of critics.

WHY ALL THE FUSS? Could a mere documentary decide the next U.S. presidential election? Moore, so far as the jittery Bush administration was concerned, was one of the most dangerous critters at large in America. They rightly reckoned that in a close race, Moore could cost Bush many vital votes. No documentary has ever exerted the seditious public impact that Moore's *Fahrenheit 9/11* made at the box office. If the numbers in the first few weeks were anything to go by, Moore was not just wittily preaching to the converted but also reaching the shopping mall cineplex masses, a majority of whom still believed the carefully cultivated fib that Saddam Hussein instigated the 9/11 attacks. If not, then even more people might venture to ask just what was the point of the Iraq invasion and its soaring costs anyway?

Films rarely matter a whit in the real world, except as money-spinning reaffirmations of conventional wisdom and shopworn fantasies. In times of war, even undeclared war, films reverently wave Old Glory and duly demonize the appointed foe. Commercial flicks are especially reluctant to upset popular prejudices and illusions, preferring to play along in order to attract ticket-buying crowds. Yet Moore, creator of the black-humored probes *Roger & Me* and *Bowling for Columbine,* slipped past the wary gatekeepers of the corporate entertainment industry to score a sizzling success. Far scarier than routine images of slavering foreign fanatics in faraway climes lusting to cut our throats is the sneaking suspicion that our own "wartime" government is the worst enemy that ordinary Americans have: picking our pockets, grabbing our kids for service, spying on our toilet habits, raising prices, lying prolifically, gutting the Constitution, and violating civil liberties. If "by their deeds ye shall know them," then no one hates our freedom more than the devious denizens of the Bush administration do.

Moore's magical knack is capturing raw truths on screen that his audience may suspect but are too timid or unsure to say aloud. In the opening weeks of *Fahrenheit 9/11,* people dashed to see his heartachingly funny exposé of Bush's long trail of truculent twaddle, despite the fact that original distributor Disney stupidly balked at releasing it. *Fahrenheit 9/11* publicizes blistering facts that ought to have been in plain sight all along. Behold footage of the 2001 inauguration, where Bush's presidential stretch limo is pelted with eggs by crowds incensed at his theft of the election through canny Florida vote-rigging, a staged "riot" of middle-class Republican bullies to stop a county-level recount, and the inexcusable 5–4 decision by conservative Supreme Court appointees (two of whom should have recused themselves for having sons working for the Republican campaign) to select Bush, who managed to mistake it for a coronation.

Is Moore just a simpering Democratic Party flack? Well, Moore does not shy away from displaying the spineless acquiescence of Democratic Party leaders to the 2000 electoral travesty. Not one senator of either party had the nerve to sign a demand by black congresspersons for a formal debate of the certification of the 2000 election to address the deliberate, illegitimate disenfranchisement of tens of thousands of black Florida voters, which helped hand the presidency to Bush—an outrage that has yet to be remedied. Al Gore, who chaired the proceedings, looks like a perfectly obliging fool. One can bet that if the positions were reversed, Republicans would have battled as fiercely and dirtily as possible. What is most shocking, though, is that many Americans were never informed because such scenes were withheld or underplayed by national news networks.

Still, the starkly clear news slowly dawns on bewildered Americans that there is no level to which Bush's band of corporate bullies, neoconservative firebrands, and faux Christian fundamentalists would not stoop for the sake of grabbing more power. Moore insinuates that it is the authoritarian urges of George W. Bush, not Osama bin Laden, that have done the most to make the United States an increasingly scary and strange land for its inhabitants. With bemused distaste, *Fahrenheit 9/11* charts how wealthy cronies repeatedly bailed the young, feckless Bush out of business flops in order to gain precious access to his former secret policeman daddy in the White House. Bush was virtually lifted into multimillionaire status through the indulgent auspices of these influence-seeking big businessmen, and with lavish Saudi backing, too. All these touchingly devoted pals deeply appreciate that there is no higher or quicker return on investment than that which can be gained through medleys of tax breaks, government contracts, and other special favors.

The supremely idealized America that John Wayne valiantly defended in myriad 1950s movies is long gone. Bush, the self-styled "war president," is actually the carefree and careless National Guard pilot during Vietnam, whose closest chum in that safe branch of the service became a Saudi representative. Moore cites the mammoth cash flow over three decades from the Saudis to Bush's family and friends. Moore isn't peddling a conspiracy theory, just painting a picture of coziness. Quid pro quo reigns way up there in the economic stratosphere, which is why, just a day or two after 9/11, more than a hundred members of bin Laden's billionaire clan were spirited out of the United States while police were tossing less well-connected foreigners into prisons, throwing away the keys, and thumbing through recycled Gestapo manuals. Why, Moore even has the gall to remind viewers (most of whom never had an inkling) that bin Laden was once tenderly nurtured by U.S. agencies. In the

1980s in Afghanistan, the United States ponied up plenty of arms and cash for bin Laden and other feudal fundamentalists because a Soviet-backed modernizing regime obviously "hated the freedom" of those sweet Afghan warlords. Bush's backers have quite a soft spot for feudal allies.

Moore's patented in-your-face bonhomie is downright enchanting as he collars glib U.S. politicians who squirm or sprint away as he tries to enlist their children in the Iraqi war that they approved. For once, their smooth glad-handedness or Olympic disdain counts against them. Far better, Moore goes after the Patriot Act, which was nothing but a shameless compilation of devoutly desired things that closet reactionaries yearned to impose the first chance they got. Moore circles Capitol Hill in a rickety ice cream van, reading passages of this draconian law that our legislators signed without going through the patriotic chore of reading first.

Moore, the savvy blue-collar boy, senses what tropes will get through to his audience. His mockery of the motley crew making up the "coalition of the willing" has drawn PC squeals in some pursed-lipped quarters. (Do the Dutch really need defending against a languid, hash-smoking stereotype?) The archetypal shot is Bush sitting, eerily clueless, in a primary school classroom for what seems like eons after being told of the 9/11 attacks—the very antonym of the cool, "take-charge" guy his handlers project. Then there's Georgie boy in his nifty flight suit smirking on the carrier deck with that "Mission accomplished" banner unfurled like a tombstone inscription above. Bush's macho threat vis-à-vis the Iraqi resistance to "smoke 'em out" intersects with a sublime cheap shot from a musty old cowboy flick—the sort where he no doubt picked up this B-movie expression.

Moore shows how U.S. troops, mostly trawled by sharp-eyed recruiters from neighborhoods laid waste by neglect, were dispatched to serve the interests not of the nation but of Halliburton, Unocal, and Bechtel. An Iraqi family, raided at night by a snatch squad of GIs, weeps and trembles before their new masked masters. In wavering flashlight beams, tiny children cower as another "suspect" is swept up, mostly because he fits that key criminal category: young man. Moore provides Abu Ghraib–like glimpses of routine racist mistreatment of liberated Iraqis. As Moore sadly says, "Immoral actions lead to more immoral actions." Sordid systematic abuses are what happen when cynical elites send ignorant youngsters off to fight for trumped-up reasons. The troops righteously imagine that they are exacting revenge for 9/11—a stupefying lie. But what next?

A close relative of mine is an army combat veteran. Once, long ago, he wandered by mistake into the "closed ward" of a veterans' hospital, where the unsightly cases are delicately tucked away. What he glimpsed inside left him shaken. You should have seen his darting eyes as he told the tale. In *Fahrenheit*

9/11 Moore unfurls the taboo images of ghastly wounds, charred corpses of U.S. mercenaries dangling on a bridge, and rows of flag-draped metal coffins. All so hush-hush. Yet even these hideous costs might be marginally bearable if they had really been necessary to ensure safety. No way. Moore's interview with parents of a dead American soldier peels away the reflex-like obedience that passes for patriotism in many quarters of America.

The real strife, Moore rousingly sums up, is a covert class war waged on Americans by their own callous leadership. This Orwellian "endless war" stirs fear and reduces citizens to suckers for the genuine agenda, which is upholding the social hierarchy and looting rights. Why else would the police plant spies inside innocuous do-gooder groups while Bush gives bin Laden a two-month head start to get away, hmm? Why does this mendacious administration, which tried to cut counterterrorism funds before 9/11, try so hard to slash money for military veterans? Oil, of course, is far too vulgar a motive for our most sophisticated minds to accept as a key reason, if not *the* reason, for intruding into Iraq. The scene of American firms holding a dreary jamboree at which to divvy up the taxpayer-funded spoils of war is a clincher.

If there is a glaring omission in *Fahrenheit 9/11*, it is, as leftist critics complain, the intimate link between Bush neoconservatives and the truculent Israeli right wing. Is Moore really more afraid of the Israeli lobby than of the Bush administration? An interesting, even instructive, question.

Moore flatly, scandalously, openly says *j'accuse,* that the reasons Americans have been given for the war are hopelessly phony ones. The venerable repertoire of gimmicks that power elites rely on is not working terribly well nowadays. A CBS News/*New York Times* poll in mid-July 2004 found that a majority (51 percent) believe that the United States should have left well enough alone and stayed out of Iraq. Almost two-thirds (62 percent) said that the war has not been worth the cost. Apart from tens of thousands of dead and mutilated Iraqis, the war has exacted, based on lowball official estimates, some 1,600 American lives, 12,000 wounded, and $300 billion. Word leaked out that the Bush people were scrambling to contrive possible pretexts to suspend the November elections. One suspects, too, that there are fretful aides on their knees in the White House praying for another fundamentalist attack on the United States—and that a stray intergalactic meteor, dispatched by their cruel backwoods god named Mammon, strikes down Michael Moore.

The Never-ending War on the Welfare State

Charles Noble

Commenting on the administration's decision to create a new drug benefit for seniors, one highly respected liberal columnist recently observed that "political considerations seemed to be pushing George W. Bush further and further into the New Deal way of life."[1] But Bush's obvious ploy to pick up senior votes should be cold comfort to anyone who cares about public provision. The Right still intends to undo the welfare state. And there is a good chance that it might succeed.

For one thing, at least in social policy, the Right's strategy is carefully crafted and brilliantly conceived. Moreover, American conservatives enjoy enormous political advantages that are not likely to go away soon. Finally, the Left has not yet worked out a practical political response to retrenchment.

STRATEGY

The Right's strategy consists of three interrelated and hard to defend against elements. First, conservatives are working overtime to impose a fiscal straitjacket on social policy. The welfare state depends on government's ability to raise revenues that can be spent on public purposes. The Keynesian welfare state that spread widely in the West after World War II assumed a virtuous cycle in which public spending would stimulate the economy, leading to higher tax revenues, leading in turn to even more generous social spending. In this way, governments could commit themselves simultaneously to promoting economic growth and maintaining a variety of safety-net programs.

But using the economic troubles of the 1970s as political cover, conservatives set out in the 1980s to undo this accord. Although the Right claimed that it only wanted to put the government's fiscal house in order, the Reagan administration's indifference to the deficits caused by its simultaneous embrace of tax cuts and military spending made it clear that fiscal probity was not high on its agenda. To the contrary, some conservatives saw in the huge shortfall an opportunity to tighten the noose around federal spending. David Stockman, Reagan's first budget director, admitted as much at the time.[2] More recently, Irving Kristol, a founding neoconservative, unashamedly confessed that the Right cared little for the niceties of economic theory or "the accounting deficiencies of government." Rather, "political effectiveness . . . was the priority."[3]

As soon as the federal budget came back into balance in the late 1990s, another Republican administration adopted the same strategy. Immediately on taking office, the Bush White House simultaneously proposed record tax cuts and a massive buildup of the military. Worse, even as economic forecasters warned of looming deficits in Medicare and Social Security, the administration sought to lock in these regressive changes in the tax code, making it impossible to even imagine that the federal government might one day find the revenues needed to save these two safety-net programs from draconian cuts. Just as the enormous federal budget deficits run up in the Reagan years handicapped liberal Democrats in the 1990s, Bush's record-setting deficits will tie the hands of future, even decidedly more liberal, presidents.

This conservative about-face on deficit spending poses an enormous challenge to the welfare state. By starving the federal government of resources, the Right is able to argue for cuts in social spending in order to "save" the same programs it hopes to eviscerate. Liberals are boxed into a corner. If they focus on the deficits, the Right responds by demanding even greater tax cuts, arguing that the promised economic growth, which they recklessly assume will be forthcoming, will balance the budget. If liberals ignore the deficits and push for increased social spending, they are blamed for the fiscal mess. All the while, those on the Right who remain true to old-style fiscal conservatism maintain a steady chorus condemning government spending in principle. And because the tax cuts are skewed so mightily to upper-income groups, they increase inequality, making life that much harder for people who depend on the benefit programs that the Right wants to cut.

Explained this way, of course, it is easy to see through the Right's rhetoric. But the complexity of the strategy makes it hard for voters to grasp what's going on, particularly as the Right denies all responsibility for the problem. And as usual, the media fail to connect the dots, leaving the public entirely in the dark about the long-term implications of this ground shift in welfare state politics.

The Right's retrenchment strategy also targets the way social programs are designed and implemented. Conservatives want to both change the legal status of benefits from "rights" or "entitlements" to "privileges" and, wherever possible, privatize welfare state functions.

The attack on entitlements is well under way. The historic 1996 welfare reform act, which replaced Aid to Families with Dependent Children with Temporary Assistance for Needy Families, did far more than impose work obligations and push millions of people off the rolls. Even more ominously, it replaced the 1935 Social Security Act's open-ended entitlement to public assistance with a block grant: the federal and state governments are no longer required to help everyone who qualifies; people can be denied benefits simply because Congress or the state legislatures fail to appropriate enough money to meet their needs. This is a direct and, to this point, successful challenge to the hard-won idea that income security is a social "right" rather than charity to be doled out at the discretion of willing benefactors.

Privatizers intend an equally radical reversal of direction. In some cases, privatization means that government contracts with for-profit corporations and nonprofit agencies to run programs previously administered by public agencies. After the 1996 welfare reform, a wide variety of for-profit firms jumped into this suddenly lucrative market, competing for state contracts to provide social services to welfare state clients. In other cases, such as public housing, clients are given vouchers to purchase services on their own. In still other instances, tax credits are used to encourage people to save money on their own, whether for "medical savings accounts" or individual retirement plans.

There are very good reasons to be skeptical of efforts to turn social programs, particularly those that serve the most vulnerable, over to the private sector. For one, far from lowering costs, private provision often increases them, if only because of the administrative inefficiencies that follow when implementation is farmed out to hundreds if not thousands of competing private providers. This notion flies in the face of the received wisdom that competition and privatization always save money. But the fact that the United States, which relies so heavily on private insurers, spends twice as much on administrative costs (as a percentage of total health care costs) as Canada spends, with its government-run, single-payer system, should put that notion to rest.[4] Private providers expect a fair rate of return on their investment and pay their executives salaries that far outstrip those of even the best-paid public bureaucrats. Wall Street investment firms have poured millions of dollars into the campaign to privatize Social Security because they expect to make billions off the fees they will charge individuals to manage their accounts—fees that will far exceed the administrative costs of the current public system.

Private corporations are just as likely, if not more so, to misspend money as public agencies are. For example, after Maximus, a for-profit Wisconsin corporation responsible for serving welfare clients in Milwaukee, was charged with misusing public funds, an independent state audit determined that the company could not account for nearly three-fourths of the expenditures it had claimed.[5]

But these complaints mean little to the Right, as shown by ongoing efforts to "reform" Medicare by offering public subsidies to for-profit HMOs that take in more seniors, as well as the decision to create a Medicare drug benefit that does nothing to cap the costs of pharmaceuticals. In fact, as Bush's entirely duplicitous campaign to pass the drug benefit bill indicates, the Right is willing to spend even more—at least in the short run—if that will ensure that control over the welfare state is transferred to the private sector.

Some suggest that privatization can be managed fairly and efficiently. Certainly it would be possible in principle for the government to insist that private providers watch what they spend and how they treat clients. But it has proved quite hard to hold private corporations and agencies accountable to these sorts of standards. Private contractors almost always try to exercise as much discretion as possible in meeting government mandates; it's one way they cut costs and increase profits. Given what we know about how large corporations treat their consumers and workers, it's hard to believe that they will treat welfare clients and the elderly any better. It's difficult for anyone who has tried to get Blue Cross or Aetna to correct a billing error to imagine that these companies will be more responsive once they've been given large chunks of the welfare state to administer.

Moreover, as the Right pushes to means-test more benefits and to more tightly supervise the behavior of people who use public benefits, the problem will get worse. Imagine a future in which private corporations impose personal standards on people in need, denying benefits to those who don't meet some arbitrary ideological or behavioral test in order to enhance their bottom lines. Handing over welfare state administration to "faith-based" charities will not improve the situation. Besides being likely to discriminate among beneficiaries, these institutions are also likely to demand a great deal of behavioral and even ideological conformity in return for help. Given the Right's eagerness to impose a conservative Christian view of the world on people's behavior, this could get ugly.

In the end, of course, that, and not money, may be the point. The Right wants privatization because it challenges the notion that recipients are citizens with rights and, as such, should be treated with equal respect—regardless of whether they have jobs or read the Bible.

As the third element in its retrenchment strategy, the Right has mounted a carefully conceived ideological offensive against the very idea of public provision. Here too, conservatives typically hide their true intent. Rather than directly challenge the notion that, as members of a political community, people have a valid claim on that community's resources in times of need, the Right has sought to portray public provision as a violation of core American values, including personal responsibility, property rights, and limited government.

Two themes are regularly repeated as if they were intuitively obvious and unassailable. First, any effort to redistribute income or wealth is an inherently "unfair" taking of property; people have a right only to what they've earned or saved (or, apparently, inherited). Never mind that private property depends on public institutions for its very existence or that the poor often pay a greater, not lesser, percentage of their income in taxes or that government always redistributes property in some fashion—it is impossible to imagine spending and benefit programs, whatever their objective, that reward people in precise proportion to their "contributions"—or that those contributions could be measured in a variety of ways, including service to the community, family, or nation. The Right insists that any public claim on private property is inherently suspect.

Second, the Right insists that government almost never does a better job than the private sector. Though examples of private-sector inefficiency and waste are legion, the Right argues that these are exceptions to the rule, whereas examples of public-sector malfeasance illustrate the norm. Sophisticated theoretical reasons are offered for this claim, but these models always idealize the free market and demonize bureaucrats and legislators. They never admit the myriad market failures that everyone but the most ideological laissez-faire economists recognize or the long list of things that the government has done well, from public health to the creation of the Internet. Big government simply cannot get it right.

To support these theoretical arguments, the Right resorts to a series of false claims and mythical ideas for which there is little if any empirical evidence. Social spending, we are told, is always at odds with job creation, while the tax system punishes work and investment and rewards sloth. Public assistance is so generous that it allows those who don't want to work to live a life of leisure, all the while encouraging childbearing by women who wouldn't (or shouldn't) have had kids otherwise. These programs, in turn, are the root source of the government's budgetary problems. Finally, the welfare state has largely benefited racial minorities at the expense of the majority white population.

POWER

Conservatives are also winning their war against welfare because the balance of political power has turned so sharply against the Left. Though obvious, this point bears repeating, if only because the media still seem to take seriously the idea that America is run by "liberal elites."

Capital's power in Washington and the state capitals has grown significantly since the 1960s because corporations have poured billions of dollars into political campaigns and lobbying, fighting for and winning a broad pro-business agenda. Cuts in public assistance are not at the top of this list, but tax cuts are, as are cutbacks in any public benefits that might shelter workers from the discipline of labor markets. Wherever we find "independent" organizations such as the Concord Coalition and "nonpartisan" studies arguing for "fiscal responsibility," we are likely to find corporate funding and corporate-friendly scholars on the payroll. And even though a mountain of research contradicts every one of the Right's myths, these fantasies remain alive and well, spread by this network of well-funded conservative propagandists comfortably housed in think tanks and showcased by friendly media mega-corporations.

Cutting the welfare state also dovetails nicely with the New Right's political agenda. Even though other issues matter more to this jerry-rigged coalition of neoconservatives, free-market ideologues, and religious fundamentalists, each of these groups has found it useful to bash the welfare state in its campaign against the horrors of liberal government.

For their own reasons, both political parties have gone along for the ride. Republicans have appealed to the middle class with images of "slackers" and "welfare queens" while promising to give back the money saved through retrenchment. Whether or not the promised tax cuts ever get to the middle class—few do—this campaign has convinced just enough middle-class voters to defect from liberalism to create real problems for the Democrats. For their part, Democrats have chosen to defend specific programs, notably Social Security and Medicare, but not the underlying principles that animate the welfare state. This appeal to the self-interest of seniors has worked on occasion, but it comes at a great political cost because the Democrats have all but ceded the ideological ground to the Right.

The decline of organized labor has enormously complicated progressive efforts to defend public provision. In fact, labor's own political and bargaining strategies, which have privileged the negotiation of private, job-based benefits from employers rather then universal benefits for workers as a class, have undermined efforts to put together a broad coalition in defense of social welfare. Until quite recently, organized labor's reluctance to join with advocates for the poor and for immigrants in their efforts to defend programs targeted toward unorganized workers has made matters worse.

The way that American liberals went about building the welfare state has also made social provision vulnerable. Put simply, there is far too little universalism (too many benefits are targeted toward specific populations), the benefits are incomplete (there is next to no publicly funded job training, for example), and there are far too few cost controls (the pharmaceutical companies will make a killing off the new drug benefit, as doctors and hospitals once did off Medicare). This costly but incomplete and inefficient version of the welfare state has led to a vicious circle of overselling, underfunding, policy failure, and political alienation, leading to calls for further cuts.

Finally, the Right's willingness, even eagerness, to exploit the troubled relationship between welfare and race in the United States has further undermined public support for public provision. Welfare states are most easily defended when they are perceived as a shared reward for shared sacrifice, as another way to assert a national, communal identity. It is not accidental that the modern welfare state expanded dramatically in the aftermath of the two world wars, when the citizens of the Western democracies saw themselves as having pulled together to resist foreign aggression. But the assertion of a shared national identity is easiest in homogeneous societies, or at least in societies where racial, ethnic, and language differences have been incorporated into the political system in settled and legitimate ways. The United States is neither. Initially, blacks were simply denied benefits. Even the landmark Social Security Act excluded the two principal sectors—agriculture and domestic work—where blacks were concentrated. When the civil rights movement finally made racial exclusion politically nonviable, the Right worked overtime to make it seem as if blacks had blackmailed politicians into granting them these benefits rather than earning them, as whites had done.

HOW TO RESPOND

The Right is also winning because none of the Left's responses are gaining any political traction. Moving out from the center, the least ambitious response is to try to hold on to the New Deal and Great Society vision of social justice while building a welfare state that appeals to the mainstream because it emphasizes work, market competition, and personal responsibility. These progressives believe that they can cut costs by introducing market incentives and encouraging individuals to save for their own retirement and health care while selectively introducing some new benefits for the working poor, including health insurance coverage and even a modified "living" wage. This is essentially the New Democrats' strategy and was, at bottom, Bill Clinton's approach.

Unlike the Right's war against the welfare state, and contrary to what some on the Left fear, this strategy is not intended as a Trojan horse to gut social protection. Contrary to the Republican Right, Democratic Party centrists actually believe in the basic idea of public provision; they just don't like the idea that government must always take the lead. That is true, of course, but it doesn't address the larger political problem: although this strategy is supposed to appeal to the mainstream, it actually captures no one's imagination, apart from the policy analysts and business-friendly Democrats who designed it. That was clear in the struggle over welfare reform in 1996, when the Republicans were able to replace Clinton's initial proposal, which supported work and expanded social services, with a far more punitive work requirement that did little to actually help the poor.

Moreover, because it does not clearly address the fiscal straitjacket the Republicans have imposed on welfare state spending, it is unclear how the centrist strategy might be financed. These two problems are related: without a political movement in support of such a program, it is hard to imagine mobilizing enough political support to restructure the tax system to pay for it. However long and hard Matt Miller may call for devoting 2 percent of the gross domestic product to a renewed social compact, it is hard to believe that this or any Congress that might be elected in the near future is going to allocate the requisite $220 billion a year.[6] In fact, as Al Gore's promise in 2000 to create a Social Security "lock box" illustrates, even Democrats have a hard time endorsing an expansion of the welfare state beyond core New Deal programs.

Putting off a new round of welfare state spending until the budget is once again in surplus is not going to solve the problem, because Democratic Party efforts to balance the budget are likely to be exploited by Republicans, who are eager to squander any and all surpluses on the military and on tax cuts.

The interest-group politics of this centrist solution are not obvious either. If recent history is any indication, middle-class voters don't care much about the working poor, let alone the truly dispossessed. And the rich are likely to resist any effort to means-test programs like Social Security and Medicare. Nor is there any fiscally sound way to increase medical benefits without doing one or more of the following: forcing private providers to take less, forcing recipients into managed care, forcing drug companies to charge less, and cutting insurance companies out. All are politically explosive.

But while it's easy to criticize the New Democrats' strategy, it's harder to figure out what to do differently. For one thing, there are deep differences on the Left about whether existing programs are even worth defending. Work-based welfare reinforces capitalist norms. Is that our goal? Should progressives lobby to expand social services so that mothers can go to work, or should they push, instead, for expanded cash grants so that these poor women can stay home and care for their children? There is also little consensus on what to do next—in particular, on how to move from fighting against retrenchment to a more offensive strategy—or whether that is even possible in the current political climate.

Consider the social democratic agenda. Clearly it's more radical and more humane than the New Democratic one. But at the end of the day, it is also organized around the idea that people should work and that social policy should reward and support that effort. But increases in labor productivity and capital flight threaten job creation throughout the West, while global competition makes it even harder for nation-states to adopt Keynesian-style economic policies.

It's also doubtful that social democracy can be sustained politically. Events in Europe suggest just how dire the situation is. Recently, mass demonstrations and major strikes in Italy failed to stop a new decree restricting pension rights. Though unpopular, the Raffarin government in France continues to press pension reform—despite the Right's electoral losses. In Germany, IG Metall ended a strike to extend the thirty-five-hour work week eastward without winning any concessions—the union's most dramatic defeat in fifty years. And while European social democrats have recently shown some interest in returning to Keynesian demand management techniques, it's not at all clear that the European Union's budgetary rules, however flexible, will actually allow that.

Recognizing that reformist social democracy may be played out, those on the "postindustrial" Left have argued for an entirely different approach based on the idea that social policy should be used not to prepare workers for routine jobs in industry and the service sector but to teach new ways of working, thinking, and being. Rather than "train" people, government should provide individuals with the resources to educate, enrich, and enlighten themselves. The goal is not only to create more productive workers but also to encourage a more sophisticated and enlightened society. Certainly, enlightenment would have economic benefits: presumably, better-educated workers would be more productive and more flexible and find it easier to adapt to a changing workplace. But the real payoff would be social: these enlightened workers would make better citizens too.

But as attractive as this vision sounds, it's hard to figure out how to get there from here. If it's not easy to imagine cobbling together a political coalition to reenergize social democracy, which would at least appeal to organized labor and advocates for the poor, it is doubly difficult to figure out how to build a political coalition in support of postindustrial social policy. The middle class stands to benefit, but it would likely see only the increased tax burden. To firms, the economic benefits are both long term and hard to capture. Because they are "public goods," no one is likely to lobby for them or be willing to pay the bill. Moreover, if the government provides universal cash grants to people to invest in themselves, as advocates of this sort of social policy innovation want, this program would be extraordinarily expensive. Conversely, if it is targeted toward those in greatest need, it would likely devolve into a small-scale, means-tested, showcase project with little impact. It is important to remember that both social democratic and postindustrial social policies have been on the table in Europe for decades, and even those welfare states have run out of steam. It's hard to imagine that the United States would finish this course when it is, in fact, running full speed in the opposite direction.

Some on the Left suggest that whatever we do about the welfare state should be part of a more radical and populist assault on American capitalism. They think that the Left should harness the anger and discontent now directed at a host of targets, from big government to corporate pirates, to take on corporate capitalism itself, demanding more from the state, reasserting the logic of community against the market and the disenfranchised against the rich. Rather than tinker with social policy or worry about labor productivity, the Left should demand that government take care of basic human needs at whatever cost. As long as we begin from capitalist premises, people will be forced to depend on the kindness of markets and enlightened capitalists. That logic should be rejected in its entirety. Radically redistributive taxes, basic income grants, community control of local economic development—this vision combines the best of progressive social policy with community activism and the goals of the anticorporate globalization movement.

Forging alliances between college students protesting the International Monetary Fund and poor mothers forced off welfare, building coalitions of unionists, environmentalists, small businesses, and feminists, this strategy certainly represents the Left at its best. But it also seems entirely unrealistic at the moment. These radical movements are only trace elements in American society. And organized labor is in decline. Moreover, although there is really very little in the short run for the blue-collar working class or even the white-collar middle class in this strategy, it will go nowhere without them. As the New Democrats understand, reformers still have to win elections.

Nonetheless, there are some reasons to be optimistic, some developments that bear watching, and some openings that can be exploited.

For one, Western democracies are likely to see a steady erosion of social protection in the coming years, if only because capitalism is getting harder on everyday life and government has fewer resources to cushion the blows. This may move significant numbers of people to the Left, if only for help. A real crisis in the provision of health care or a major reduction in pensions could spark a serious movement for reform. Ironically, the steady decline of organized labor in the United States means that private, union-negotiated security arrangements that have sheltered so many workers and made them less dependent on public benefits are not likely to survive, forcing those once-privileged employees into the same boat as other, less fortunate workers. Additionally, some of the racial and ethnic rivalries that undermine efforts to defend public provision may moderate as millions of recent immigrants are assimilated and African Americans are more fully incorporated into the American economy and society. All these things could change the political calculus suddenly, making new alliances and coalitions possible.

Obviously, we're not there yet. Particularly in the United States, it may be a long time before the Left can bring the Right to bay. But progressives need to be very clear about just how much is at stake whenever the Right turns its attention to the welfare state.

NOTES

1. Russell Baker, "In Bush's Washington," *New York Review of Books*, May 13, 2004, 25.
2. William Greider, "The Education of David Stockman," *Atlantic Monthly*, December 1981. http://www.theatlantic.com/politics/budget/stockman.htm.
3. Paul Krugman, "The Tax-Cut Con," *New York Times*, September 14, 2003.
4. S. Woolhander and D. U. Himmelstein, "The Deteriorating Administrative Efficiency of the U.S. Health Care System," *New England Journal of Medicine* 324 (1991): 1253–58.
5. Karyn Rotker, "Corporate Welfare for Welfare Corporations—Welfare Reform in Wisconsin," *Dollars and Sense*, January 2001. http://articles.findarticles.com/p/articles/mi_m2548/is_2001_Jan/ai_70396233.
6. Matthew Miller, *The 2% Solution: Fixing America's Problems in Ways Conservatives and Liberals Can Love* (New York: Public Affairs, 2003).

Part II
Theoretical Encounters

Leo Strauss and the Rhetoric of the War on Terror

Nicholas Xenos

A very curious piece appeared on the op-ed page of the *New York Times* on June 7, 2003. Its author was Jenny Strauss Clay, a professor of classics at the University of Virginia, and the title was "The Real Leo Strauss." Highlighted in a box midway down the page were the words, "My father was a teacher, not a right-wing guru." Clay wrote:

> Recent news articles have portrayed my father, Leo Strauss, as the mastermind behind the neoconservative ideologues who control United States foreign policy. He reaches out from his 30-year-old grave, we are told, to direct a "cabal" (a word with distinct anti-Semitic overtones) of Bush administration figures hoping to subject the American people to rule by a ruthless elite. I do not recognize the Leo Strauss presented in these articles.

The "recent news articles" had appeared in an array of magazines and newspapers, including the *New York Times*, the *Boston Globe*, the *International Herald Tribune*, and the *New Yorker*. In only one of these does the term *cabal* appear. That one was Seymour Hersh's *New Yorker* article, the opening line of which is, "They call themselves, self-mockingly, 'The Cabal,' a small cluster of policy advisers and analysts now based in the Pentagon's Office of Special Plans." Abram Schulsky, "a scholarly expert in the works of the political philosopher Leo Strauss," directs this self-identified cabal, according to Hersh.

In Clay's apologia on behalf of her father, she wrote, "My father was not a politician. He taught political theory, primarily at the University of Chicago." It is not incidental that Leo Strauss rarely, if ever, referred to what he taught as political theory, but I will come back to that. "He was a conservative insofar as he did not think that change is necessarily for the better," which is a rather bland description of a conservative. "Leo Strauss believed," she wrote,

> in the intrinsic dignity of the political. He believed in and defended liberal democracy, although he was not blind to its flaws. He felt it was the best form of government that could be realized, "the last best hope." He was an enemy of any regime that aspired to global domination. He despised utopianism, in our time Nazism and communism, which is predicated on a

59

denial of a fundamental and even noble feature of human nature, love of one's own. His heroes were Churchill and Lincoln.

Keep in mind a few of the things that come up in this paragraph. Among these is the notion of the "dignity of the political." We still need to know exactly what Leo Strauss thought the political was, as well as what he thought liberal democracy was and in what sense he was a defender of it. The use of the word *regime* on the part of his daughter is not entirely innocent, as I show later on, and the notion that Churchill and Lincoln were his heroes and Nazism and communism were the things he abhorred I address in due course.

Professor Clay went on to say, "The fact is that Leo Strauss"—and this is very important and is the reason why the issue is ultimately of much more than academic interest—

> also recognized a multiplicity of readers, but he had enough faith in his authors to assume that they, too, recognized that they would have a diverse readership. Some of their readers, the ancients realized, would want only to find their own views and prejudices confirmed. Others might be willing to open themselves to new, perhaps unconventional or unpopular, ideas. I personally think my father's rediscovery of the art of writing for different kinds of readers will be his most lasting legacy.

Strauss's students are aware of the impression their admiration for him makes on outsiders. Allan Bloom was the best known of those students, thanks to his best-selling 1987 antiegalitarian diatribe *The Closing of the American Mind* and, more recently, to his having been "outed" by his old friend Saul Bellow in Bellow's novel *Ravelstein*. In a tribute to his former teacher, published after Strauss's death, Bloom observed that "those of us who know him saw in him such a power of mind, such a unity and purpose of life, such a rare mixture of the human elements resulting in a harmonious expression of the virtues, moral and intellectual, that our account of him is likely to evoke disbelief or ridicule from those who have never experienced a man of this quality."[1] Bloom's rhetorical strategy here of appropriating a projected criticism—the fawning admiration Straussians have for their teacher-founder and turning it around—also has the effect of demarcating an out-group that does not understand from an in-group that has experienced the truth, which is another characteristic feature of the style and substance that constitute a Straussian.

It is partly the aura that emanates from Strauss that gives credence to the claims of conspiracy when Straussians are involved in something, if that is in fact the claim that people make. More particularly, the prominence given to the notion of a charismatic founder within the Straussian fold means that it quickly begins to look like a cult.

WHO WAS LEO STRAUSS? He was born in Germany in 1899 and died in the United States in 1973. As was the case for many German Jewish intellectuals of his generation, he was active in Jewish youth groups in the 1920s. The ones that he was involved with were mostly inspired by the German nationalist youth movement. In Strauss's case, he admired the sense of spiritual unity that was promulgated in these German youth groups, and it was that sort of nationalist or spiritual element that was appealing to him. He wrote a book on Spinoza published in 1930 and left Germany in 1932 on a Rockefeller Foundation grant for research on Thomas Hobbes in Paris and London. He was thus in Paris when the Nazis took power. However, Strauss should not be confused with the anti-Nazi refugees who soon arrived in the French capital, because at the time he was a committed antiliberal, in the German sense of the term, which is to say, among other things, an antiparliamentarian. Also in 1932, he wrote an extended review of a book by the German legal and political theorist Carl Schmitt entitled *The Concept of the Political,* in which Schmitt articulated his notion that the core of the political problem is the distinction between friends and enemies. Schmitt later became a member of the Nazi Party and a leading figure in the main legal organization of the Third Reich. In Strauss's review, he criticized Schmitt from the political right. He argued that "the critique introduced by Schmitt against liberalism can . . . be completed only if one succeeds in gaining a horizon beyond liberalism. In such a horizon Hobbes completed the foundation of liberalism. A radical critique of liberalism is thus possible only on the basis of an adequate understanding of Hobbes."[2] His point was that Schmitt was, in his criticisms of liberalism, working within the bounds of liberal society because liberalism had become so dominant that it was difficult to see beyond it anymore, so it was necessary to go back to Hobbes to see what had been there before. And what had been there before was a very strong sense of the absolute dichotomy of good and evil. For Strauss, Hobbes represented the foundation of liberalism and modernism in the claim that these notions of good and evil are nominalist; they simply do not exist in anything other than our judgment about them. So Strauss was suggesting that you had to go back before liberalism to reconnect with the sort of absolutist distinctions on which Schmitt was attempting to ground the political.

While Strauss's review of Schmitt's book is fairly well known among scholars, the most striking document from Strauss's early period is a letter he wrote in May 1933 to the German scholar Karl Löwith. Five months after Hitler's appointment as chancellor and a month after implementation of the first anti-Jewish legislation, Strauss wrote to Löwith, "just because Germany has turned to the right and has expelled us [Jews], it simply does not follow that the principles of the right are therefore to be rejected. To the contrary, only on the basis of principles of the right—fascist, authoritarian, *imperial* [emphasis in original]—is it possible in a dignified manner, without the ridiculous and pitiful appeal to 'the inalienable rights of man' to protest against the mean nonentity [the Nazi Party]." In other words, he is attacking the Nazis from the right in this letter. He wrote that he had been reading Caesar's *Commentaries* and valued Virgil's judgment that "under imperial rule the subjected are spared and the proud are subdued." And he concluded, "There is no reason to crawl to the cross, even to the cross of liberalism, as long as anywhere in the world the spark glimmers of Roman thinking. And moreover, better than any cross is the ghetto."

Two months later, in July 1933, he wrote to Schmitt—he did not realize that Schmitt had joined the Nazi Party and seemed not to fully understand what the regime was about in terms of anti-Semitism—asking for help in getting entrée to Charles Maurras, the French right-wing Catholic leader of the Action Française. What all this suggests is that in the 1930s Strauss was not an *antiliberal* in today's sense of the term but an *antidemocrat* in a fundamental sense, a true reactionary. Strauss was somebody who wanted to go back to a previous preliberal, prebourgeois era of blood and guts, of imperial domination, of authoritarian rule, of pure fascism. Like Schmitt, what Strauss hated about liberalism, among other things, was its inability to make absolute judgments, its inability to take action. And, like Schmitt, he sought a way out in a kind of preliberal decisiveness. I suggest that this description of fascist, authoritarian, imperial principles accurately describes the current imperial project of the United States. Because of this, examining the foundational elements of Strauss's political theory helps us see something important about our current situation, independent of any kind of Straussian direct influence, although there is certainly some of that.

IN 1935 STRAUSS PUBLISHED A BOOK ON HOBBES as well as a book entitled *Philosophy and Law*. The latter, on Maimonides and other Jewish themes, is the book in which he announced the discovery of what he called "the forgotten kind of writing," to which his daughter referred. This entailed writing for different kinds of audiences simultaneously. Strauss had been studying Maimonides, and he came to the conclusion that in order to understand Maimonides, he had to understand the writers to whom Maimonides was relating. This led Strauss to Alfarabi, the medieval Islamic philosopher. In these authors, and in Machiavelli and Spinoza and ultimately in Plato, Strauss thought that he had discovered something about the way they wrote. In an oral presentation entitled "A Giving of Accounts," recorded near the end of his life, he said, "I arrived at a conclusion that I can state in the form of a syllogism: philosophy is the attempt to replace opinion by knowledge, that opinion is the element of the city, hence philosophy is subversive, hence the philosopher must write in such a way that he will improve rather than subvert the city." That is, the philosopher has to conceal what he is actually doing.

> In other words, the virtue of a philosopher's thought is a certain kind of *mania* [inspired frenzy], while the virtue of the philosopher's public speech is *sophrosyne* [discretion or moderation]. Philosophy is as such transpolitical, transreligious, and transmoral, but the city is and ought to be moral and religious. . . . To illustrate this point, moral man, merely moral man, the *kalosgathos* in the common meaning of the term [that is, the good man], is not simply closer to the philosopher than a man of the dubious morality of Alcibiades.[3]

The suggestion here is that philosophy always has to go underground, to conceal itself in some way, because philosophy deals with truth while society is based on opinion, and truth subverts opinion. This is the basis of what Strauss calls a "philosophic politics." In his book *On Tyranny*, which I discuss in more detail later, he explains:

> In what then does philosophic politics consist? In satisfying the city that the philosophers are not atheists, that they do not desecrate everything sacred to the city, that they reverence what the city reverences, that they are not subversives, in short that they are not irresponsible adventurers but good citizens and even the best of citizens. This is the defense of philosophy that was required always and everywhere, whatever the regime might have been.[4]

Philosophers have to convince the city that they are not subversive. What is entailed here is that philosophers such as Maimonides and the others he described wrote for at least two different audiences. To one audience was addressed the so-called *exoteric* meaning of their texts, which was the edifying, superficial level, while to another audience was addressed an *esoteric* meaning, embedded in the text, that only some people were capable of drawing out. This "discovery" is what his daughter says is going to be his lasting contribution. Now there is something right about the claim that some writers conceal to some degree their real intentions, but Strauss raised this observation to an art form, or he thought that it was raised to an art form by the authors with whom he was dealing.

What is particularly interesting about this to me is that while he described this quite clearly in the early 1930s, in his study of Alfarabi and Maimonides, he did not start to write in this mode himself until after he came to the United States in 1936. This is an issue concerning Strauss that people gloss over too easily. The question, starkly posed, is: why did Strauss start to write in this esoteric-exoteric manner only after he came to an "open" society, to the United States? It is often said that Strauss's discovery was somehow situated in terms of the Nazi regime and its repression, but that does not explain why he would revert to this kind of writing only when he came here. I suggest that Strauss's political position, which he articulated in the letter to Löwith and in his critique of Schmitt, never fundamentally changed, but when he came to the United States, it had to take on a more prudent presentation. Strauss's criticisms of liberal-democratic societies did not stop at liberalism but went all the way through to the core—he was, in other words, far more reactionary than many contemporary critics suggest.

The notion of esoteric and exoteric writing means that one has to read writers, as Strauss put it, "between the lines," and he developed an elaborate system of reading that included silences, things that are not included in the text, and obvious errors or thematic points that appear to pop up out of nowhere. I do not want to get into this conception of writing too deeply, but to characterize it a little bit, Strauss held that the great books were written by authors who had complete and total control of their texts. Thus there were no errors, no false starts; everything was very tightly, beautifully constructed so that the initiated could pick up on little mistakes, little openings in the text and find their way in. Strauss himself adopted a system of using many interrelated footnotes and references and of quoting people whose position he did not overtly take while pointing to the fact that that was indeed his position by other clues in the text, among other techniques. It is almost impossible to avoid the term *Talmudic* to describe the way he read and later wrote books. Two of his books are particularly instructive.

STRAUSS'S *ON TYRANNY* WAS PUBLISHED IN 1948. This complex book consists of his translation of Xenophon's dialogue *Hiero,* also known as *Tyrannicus*—a work and an author that Strauss considered unjustly ignored by modern scholars—along with an interpretive essay that partly decodes it and partly adds another layer or layers of convoluted meanings. In beginning his commentary, Strauss says that contemporary social science cannot identify the very tyranny that it faces. He writes of what he calls the modern form of tyranny:

> Not much observation and reflection is needed to realize that there is an essential difference between the tyranny analyzed by the classics and that of our age. In contradistinction to classical tyranny, present-day tyranny has at its disposal "technology" as well as "ideologies"; more generally expressed, it presupposes the existence of "science," i.e., of a particular interpretation, or kind, of science. Conversely, classical tyranny, unlike modern tyranny, was confronted, actually or potentially, by a science that was not meant to be applied to "the conquest of nature" or to be popularized and

diffused. But in noting this one implicitly grants that one cannot understand modern tyranny in its specific character before one has understood the elementary and in a sense natural form of tyranny which is premodern tyranny. The basic stratum of modern tyranny remains, for all practical purposes, unintelligible to us if we do not have recourse to the political science of the classics.[5]

In reference to the structure of such a political science, which he sees as a subdivision of philosophy, he goes on to say that "socratic rhetoric is meant to be an indispensable instrument of philosophy, its purpose is to lead potential philosophers to philosophy, both by training them and by liberating them from the charms which obstruct the philosophic effort, as well as to prevent the access to philosophy of those who are not fit for it." Strauss then claims:

> The experience of the present generation has taught us to read the great political literature of the past with different eyes and with different expectations. The lessons may not be without value for our political orientation. We are now brought face to face with a tyranny which holds out the threat of becoming, thanks to "the conquest of nature" and in particular of human nature, what no other tyranny ever became: perpetual and universal. Confronted by the appalling alternative that man, or human thought, must be collectivized either by one stroke and without mercy or else by slow and gentle processes, we are forced to wonder how we could escape from this dilemma. We consider therefore the elementary and unobtrusive conditions of human freedom.[6]

Strauss's warning that modern society is heading toward a kind of tyranny is not directed only toward Hitler and Stalin, toward fascism and communism; he is talking about the development of Western civilization generally: the diffusion of modern science and technology, the spreading of education throughout the entire population, the foundation of democratic claims in the notion of popular sovereignty. This is the beginning of the end of a certain notion of the political, of a certain relation to the world that Strauss wants to reinvigorate. The tyranny that he is writing about in 1948 is the tyranny that he experiences, or thinks he experiences, in the West. It is under the threat of that tyranny that he adopts this dual form of writing, and this book is a great example of that form.

The other text, or collection of texts, from the period that is relevant here is entitled *Persecution and the Art of Writing*. It was published in 1952, but most of the essays in it were written in the 1940s. He writes there of the literature of multiple meanings: "The fact which makes this literature possible can be expressed in the axiom that thoughtless men are careless readers, and only thoughtful men are careful readers."[7] Obviously, Strauss is writing for careful readers, and careless readers are going to give up on his texts after a certain point. In that same book, he writes: "What attitude people adopt toward freedom of public discussion depends decisively on what they think about popular education and its limits. Generally speaking, premodern philosophers were more timid in this respect than modern philosophers."[8] Here again, Strauss identifies with the premodern philosophers, which is to say that his attitude toward popular education is completely negative. Strauss's entire orientation here is a criticism of Western modernity. This becomes especially clear at the end of the passage, when he writes:

> Those to whom such books [i.e., esoteric books] are truly addressed are, however, neither the unphilosophic majority nor the perfect philosopher, as such, but the young men who might become philosophers: the potential philosophers are to be led step by step from the popular views which are indispensable for all practical and political purposes to the truth which is merely and purely theoretical, guided by certain obtrusively enigmatic figures in the presentation of the popular [i.e., exoteric] teaching—obscurity of the plan, contradiction, pseudonyms, inexact repetitions of earlier statements, strange expressions, etc. Such features do not disturb the slumber of those who cannot see the woods for the trees, but act as awakening stumbling blocks to those who can. All books of that kind owe their existence to the love of the mature philosopher for the puppies of his race, by whom he wants to be loved in turn. All esoteric books are "written speeches caused by love."[9]

This last comment is one of the meanings of the "love of one's own" to which Jenny Strauss Clay referred.

RETURNING TO THE BIOGRAPHY, we see that Strauss comes to the United States, gets a teaching position at the New School—his daughter said that he was first and foremost a teacher, but he did not start teaching until he was thirty-eight years old and here in the United States—and then goes to Chicago in 1949 as professor of political philosophy. Now, his daughter said that he taught political theory, but Strauss never said that he taught political theory; he taught political philosophy. As Strauss understood it, political philosophy is the face that philosophy turns to the public. It is the way that philosophers address the public to convince them that they are not subversive at the same time that they are embedding another kind of message to those who will understand. Strauss taught in Chicago for twenty years, and it was there that he established his reputation.

This signals the establishment of Strauss as an academic influence in the United States. Up until this period, I have been discussing his books alone. In Chicago he begins to have students, schooling them in the techniques of his own writing, including, perhaps most centrally, irony. However, for Strauss, what philosophers say to one another, to their friends, in conversation someplace out of the public realm is one thing; what they say in writing to any group beyond that is another. The exoteric-esoteric distinction applies only to writing, and so we find Strauss's students emphasizing the conversations they had with Strauss in class, which means that those who were students of Strauss have a privileged knowledge that those who were not his students are lacking. Thus one begins to see a kind of network building outward from his charismatic center, where the truth is spoken in small groups and seminar rooms and then conveyed in secondary ways to a larger group.

Besides his teaching activities, Strauss rather skillfully turned his attention, after he got to the University of Chicago, to struggles within academe rather than struggles in the popular, political arena. Positioned in a social science department, he started attacking social science for its value neutrality. He and his associates began attacking elements of contemporary society through their supposed representation in social science and other academic disciplines rather than out in the open as a direct political attack, and doing it in a way that made it seem that he and his students and friends were defending the principles of liberal-democratic society at the same time. This collective struggle was another element in the building of a Straussian network, one that continued after his death primarily through attacks on so-called multiculturalism and postmodernism.

The Straussian network is really an amazing thing. Any political theorist or anyone who has been around political science departments has seen it at work. Long before attaining public attention, the Straussians were often ridiculed for their cultlike qualities: they speak and write the same way, they write the same books on the same themes over and over again, they dress alike, they are almost all men, they went to the same schools—those sorts of things. It thus comes as a shock to discover that Leo Strauss may turn out to be the most influential political theorist of the last fifty years in the United States with respect to the exercise of political power.

If the Straussians were only one academic school among others, that would be one thing. But in the mid-1980s some commentators suddenly realized that they had begun to follow the lead of their liberal academic neighbors in heading for Washington, D.C. At that time, it was noticed that something strange was going on in the Reagan administration. The first sign of this was in an article by Stephen Toulmin, a historian of science, in the *New York Review of Books* in 1984. In the middle of a review of a book on Margaret Mead, Toulmin used Mead as an example to which he compared the State Department policy planning staff, which, he said, consisted of people who were better acquainted with the writings of Leo Strauss than with the cultures they had to deal with.[10]

Probably few people knew what he was talking about until Nathan Tarcov, a University of Chicago professor and a former student of Strauss, wrote a letter to the *Review* because he recognized himself in Toulmin's description and attempted to defend himself and the staff on which he served. One year later, the classicist F. M. Burnyeat, in another article in the *New York Review*, took up the theme again and did a very thorough critique of Strauss's writings and the whole basis of the Straussian school (it may be the best single piece anyone has written on the Straussians).[11] Burnyeat tackled the subject not just because it was an academic issue but because he knew that there were influential Straussians in Washington. In the Reagan administration there were Tarcov, Carnes Lord, who was a member of the national security staff, and Paul Wolfowitz. Later on, William Kristol and Carnes Lord were part of Vice President Dan Quayle's staff. The Straussians clearly were aligning themselves with certain elements of the right wing of the Republican Party.

STRAUSSIANS HAVE BEEN AROUND WASHINGTON for twenty years. In a sense, they invite the criticism of being a cult or a conspiracy by the networking they do, by their purposive replication, and by the use of a certain kind of coded language. (For example, whenever Strauss talked about someone's theory, he referred to his "teaching," and this is a term similarly deployed by all Straussians.) Strauss and his descendants use all kinds of stilted, often archaic language, and some of that language has found its way into the rhetoric of the so-called war on terror.

The most obvious example is the administration's use of the term *regime*. Some people were surprised by what "regime change" turned out to mean, but they would not have been surprised if they had been familiar with Leo Strauss's writings or those of the Straussians. *Regime* is the term that Strauss used to translate the Greek *politeia*, an Aristotelian category, and Strauss understood it to mean—what it more or less meant to Aristotle—the form of a city; that is, its essence as opposed to the unformed humans, the matter, that the city forms. Aristotle, in Book Three of the *Politics*, makes the case that there are different kinds of polities—democracies, aristocracies, and so on—and that in each case, if one kind changes into another kind, it changes essentially; it changes its form into something else. The citizens too are different, are changed—a citizen of a democracy is not a citizen of an aristocracy—so it is a total transformation of the city's essence, a formal transformation. Thus Strauss wrote that "a change of regime transforms a given city into another city," into something totally different. So a "regime change," which was a relatively new term in the discourse of international relations, meant a total transformation of the model of the society in question rather than a simple change of government in the narrow sense. This has had immediate effects in terms of the policy in Iraq.

But in Strauss's mind, what was important about using this term was that it leads necessarily to the question of the "best" city. Strauss thought that if one starts talking about fundamentally different forms, it necessarily leads to a comparison of those forms, and the comparison leads to a judgment about the best or worst sort of city. This is apparent, too, in the current discourse. On the one hand, the Bush administration always says that it is not making judgments; on the other hand, it is clear that there is a preferred form for the transformation it seeks to effect, which it calls liberal democracy—a combination of market economics and the appearance of representative political institutions. So regime is one clear example of Straussian influence on the administration's rhetoric and the thinking behind it. And indeed, William Kristol and a coauthor, in an article entitled "What Was Leo Strauss Up To?" point to the notion of regime as an instance of Strauss's influence.[12]

Another important element is the "good versus evil" trope. Here William Kristol and Robert Kagan can show us the way toward an understanding. They coauthored an article in *Foreign Affairs* in 1996 entitled "Towards a Neo-Reaganite Foreign Policy."[13] They urged conservatives to put moral judgments back at the center of American foreign policy, as Reagan had with the notion of the "evil empire." Carnes Lord, who now teaches at the U.S. Naval College and was a member of the Reagan administration and the Quayle staff, as well as a translator of Aristotle, wrote an article in 1999 in which he argued that the crisis of liberalism was a crisis of the political class, of the leadership in this country. He blamed the agenda of "multiculturalism" in both domestic and foreign affairs for the fact that, as he saw it, we had lost our way in this country.[14]

Straussians are dogged critics of what they call multiculturalism in academia in general and in society as a whole, and the supposed spread of multiculturalism in American society was castigated by Lord on both the domestic and foreign levels. Thus there was the need for an effort, he wrote, aimed at "arresting the decline of American education, reviving a sense of citizenship and civic responsibility, and repairing vital national institutions such as the armed forces." He was concerned that the next time there was a crisis and the president called us to sacrifice, would we be ready to do that? So the Straussians were talking about the need to infuse foreign policy with a moral language during both the George H. W. Bush and the Clinton administrations, and of course it came to fruition after September 11, 2001.[15]

In this context, an op-ed piece written by William Bennett in the *Wall Street Journal* in September 2002, entitled "Teaching September Eleventh," is worthy of note. Bennett wrote, "An appropriate response to September eleventh begins with a kind of moral clarity, a clarity that calls evil by its true name, terms like evil, wrong, and bad were rightly put back into the lexicon. September eleventh also requires that we point to what is good and right and true. The dark day was pierced with rays of courage, honor, and sacrifice and they should be upheld for all to see, they too are enduring lessons." That kind of reliance on courage and honor is prebourgeois and aristocratic, and it falls into Strauss's whole framework of the way "gentlemen" behave. Strauss saw the world as divided up into three layers: there are the *vulgar,* there are *gentlemen,* and there are the *wise.* Honor and courage are the virtues of the gentleman; the virtue of the wise is wisdom. The wise need the gentlemen to govern. And the gentlemen, these elite, do not operate with wisdom but with the "simple virtues" that they are able to grasp and assert.

Another element of the administration's rhetoric, of course, is the division of the world into friends and enemies. Strauss said that the way of the philosopher is the way of Socrates, of the pursuit of wisdom, of the good in itself. But the way of the world is the way of Thrasymachus. And the argument for justice that Thrasymachus makes in Plato's *Republic* is that justice is helping friends and hurting enemies. And this is, in fact, the moral compass that Straussians adopt in the world. It accounts, partly, for the network they have constructed. And when the friends are philosophers, that is a really good thing, but if they are not philosophers, well, that is the way the world works anyway—you help friends, you hurt enemies. It is a form of realism, but it is realism in the hidden interests of wisdom. Now, this attitude and this kind of language do not derive only from Strauss, but it is notable the degree to which this administration, in particular, has articulated the world in terms of friends and enemies from September 11 on. That is the way the world has been divided by this administration, and it does what it can for its friends, regardless of what regime they may have, and it does what it can to its enemies, or what the administration perceives as its enemies, domestic and foreign.

The trickiest element in the current rhetorical structure of things is "tyranny." As in the case of *regime,* one perks up one's ears with the sudden ubiquity of the term *tyranny.* The term had not been used in contemporary political discourse until recently. Academic political science and public political discourse had used terms such as *authoritarian* or *dictatorship* or *despotism* to describe varieties of political domination throughout the last century. For the last half of it, the category of *totalitarian* was added. Despite Strauss's effort in 1948, it is only now that *tyranny* has entered the speechwriters' lexicon, and it seems clear that it is the work of Strauss's descendants.

This is the most complicated part of Strauss's thinking and the most important in terms of understanding the current political situation. In the passage quoted earlier, Strauss referred to an ancient teaching on tyranny with which he contrasted a problematic modern tyranny. In the ancient teaching, which is the teaching he wishes to identify himself with, it is possible for the wise man to move a tyranny toward its best possible form. That is, there are tyrannies and there are tyrannies; there are really bad ones and relatively good ones. In the good ones, the tyrant rules beneficially for his subjects, but does so beyond the law. And Strauss says in his book, through the words of Xenophon, the author of the *Hiero*, that the rule of a good tyrant is better than misrule under law, so that tyrannical rule can be superior to constitutional rule or to the rule of misguided political elites. It is simply not the case that Strauss is entirely hostile to the notion of tyranny; he is hostile to the modern notion of tyranny, which is articulated in the passages already cited and then further articulated by Strauss in his response to Alexandre Kojève's review of his book.

In Strauss's post-Nietzschean view, the modern form of tyranny leads necessarily to a flattening out of experience, to the so-called last man. Society eventually becomes uninteresting when it is permeated by technology and science and a generalized level of education, the flattening out of experience that Tocqueville partly anticipated for democratic societies and that Nietzsche railed against. Strauss held out the hope, under those circumstances, for some rebellion, for acts of courage or honor to reverse this trend, this so-called tyranny. For Strauss, tyranny is a problem in the modern sense, not in the ancient sense, and I suggest that his admiration for Churchill and Lincoln was based on the fact that they mirrored, to some degree, the ancient notion of the tyrant, especially Lincoln, who sidestepped the Constitution during the Civil War.

Straussians love Lincoln, and they love him for a couple of reasons, one of which is that he was not reluctant to set the law aside when he felt it was necessary. But they also venerate Lincoln because he quite consciously set about the business of constructing a mythology about American identity, a patriotic mythology. Lincoln made the claim, in his Lyceum speech in 1838, that those who had had the experience of fighting for the establishment of the country in the Revolution were dying out as a generation and that future generations would have to revive this experience through myths and stories that they told about this founding generation. And that is what Straussians do in terms of American culture, primarily through the myth of the founding fathers, the notion of this aristocratic elite that established America and the way that it was established. So Lincoln is a very important figure for them because he resorted to tyrannical measures when he had to and because he sought to mythically restore heroic virtues.

As for Churchill, who was also something of a tyrant, the issue is somewhat different. Churchill stood up to Hitler, and Hitler is a representative of the bad kind of tyrant. It is embedded in the Straussian notion of the vulgar that they are thoughtless readers, but they can see things. One can construct images—Strauss develops this out of Plato's notion of the noble lie—that it is easier for people to see through than to glimpse the principles that lie behind them. What was important about Churchill was his image as a figure representing this opposition; that one could raise the question of good and evil by having this figure confront Hitler. Then, once Hitler is labeled as evil and Churchill as good, one is into that dialectic of good and evil, which is so important to Strauss and such a fundamental element of what he understood the political to be about— that is, about struggle, about this sort of confrontation. So when Jenny Strauss Clay says that her father was opposed to all kinds of utopianisms, and she cites the Nazi and communist ones, there is more to it than that. For some, there is the utopia of a peaceful world, a Kantian sort of utopia, an end to conflict, a resolution of grievances through peaceful means. For Strauss, that eliminates the struggle that is at the core of the political and is necessary in the political realm while philosophers are busy doing whatever it is that philosophers do.

One modern philosopher who is important in a complicated sort of way for Strauss is Martin Heidegger. Strauss says that he encountered Heidegger for the first time in the early 1920s when Strauss "attended his lecture course from time to time without understanding a word, but sensed that [Heidegger] dealt with something of the utmost importance to man as man." But despite his disclaimer of limited understanding, Strauss broke with what he called Heidegger's moral teaching, which he describes in this way: "The key term" in Heidegger's vocabulary "is 'resoluteness,' without any indication as to what are the proper objects of resoluteness. There is a straight line that leads from Heidegger's resoluteness to his siding with the so-called Nazis in 1933. After that I ceased to take any interest in him for about two decades."[16] In this post-Nietzschean world, where nothing really matters anymore, one possible moral position to take is to say: well, you choose something and you adhere to it with resoluteness; you affirm it, even though there is really no foundation for it other than your affirmation of it. Where Strauss differs with Heidegger is that Strauss wants to put truth in that place; the thing that you adhere to with resoluteness is truth. If you are going to hold society together, and keep it from becoming completely chaotic, you must affirm the notion of an absolute truth. And that is where he makes the break with Heidegger, though actually they are on the same ground. He is also on very similar ground with all the political and philosophical movements that descend from Heidegger, including a voluntarist existentialism and deconstruction.

I do not want to leave the impression that I think that Straussians are the root cause of all contemporary political problems. They have clearly contributed on the rhetorical level. They have helped codify certain notions, and they have helped push a war of images, but I do not for a second think that there are no material interests at stake in American foreign policy. Perhaps what is most worrisome about the Straussian influence is the way some of this language has permeated public discourse generally, and not just what is coming from this administration. Paul Berman, for example, in *Terror and Liberalism*, wants to characterize everything that is opposed to liberalism, as he understands it—a liberal sentiment—as "terror." This is falling into the kind of dichotomous and problematic constructions that Strauss articulated.

Liberalism is itself fearful, in most instances, of popular power, of—for want of a better term—the power of the people. The big event in Allan Bloom's life, aside from meeting Strauss and writing a best seller and becoming rich, happened at Cornell University while he was teaching there, when armed black students took over the student center. In many respects, Straussian cultural criticism is a reaction against the countercultural and political movements of the 1960s, including the student movement. But there has been a liberal reaction to that, too. And a liberal discourse that talks about the need for civic education, that talks about the need for a patriotic discourse, is really moving in the same area as the Straussian discourse. There are some crossover types, as well. Mark Lilla, a professor in the Straussian redoubt of the Committee on Social Thought at the University of Chicago and an associate director of the Olin Center there, published an article in the "liberal" *New York Review of Books* on the importance of the concept of tyranny. What is troubling in a lot of ways, more than anything else, is that the Straussians have begun to dominate the terms of public discourse. A fearful liberalism and a political elite and punditry have been fertile ground for Straussian seeding. It was shocking in some ways when the *New York Times* hired David Brooks as a regular columnist, but it was not a shock when he wrote a column on the persecution of conservatives in American universities and interviewed Straussian professors to drive the point home. There is no conspiracy at work here, but rather a conflation of a Straussian and a liberal discourse that is very, very troubling. And both of them are fundamentally antidemocratic.

NOTES

1. Allan Bloom, "Leo Strauss," *Political Theory* 2, no. 4 (1974): 372.
2. Leo Strauss, "Notes on Carl Schmitt, *The Concept of the Political*," in Heinrich Meier, *Carl Schmitt and Leo Strauss: The Hidden Dialogue*, trans. J. Harvey Lomax (Chicago: University of Chicago Press, 1995), 119.
3. Jacob Klein and Leo Strauss, "A Giving of Accounts," in Leo Strauss, *Jewish Philosophy and the Crisis of Modernity*, ed. Kenneth Hart Green (Albany: State University of New York Press, 1997), 463.
4. Leo Strauss, *On Tyranny*, ed. Victor Gourevitch and Michael S. Roth (New York: Free Press, 1991), 205–6.
5. Ibid., 23.
6. Ibid., 27.
7. Leo Strauss, *Persecution and the Art of Writing* (Chicago: University of Chicago Press, 1952), 25.

8. Ibid., 33.
9. Ibid., 36.
10. Stephen Toulmin, "The Evolution of Margaret Mead," *New York Review of Books* 31, no. 19 (December 1984).
11. F. M. Burnyeat, "Sphinx without a Secret," *New York Review of Books* 32, no. 9 (May 1985).
12. Steven Lenzner and William Kristol, "What Was Leo Strauss Up To?" *Public Interest* (Fall 2003).
13. William Kristol and Robert Kagan, "Towards a Neo-Reaganite Foreign Policy," *Foreign Affairs* (July–August 1996).
14. Carnes Lord, "Thoughts on Strauss and Our Present Discontents," in *Leo Strauss, the Straussians, and the American Regime,* ed. Kenneth L. Deutsch and John A. Murley (Lanham, Md.: Rowman and Littlefield, 1999), 413–17.
15. Ibid.
16. Klein and Strauss, "A Giving of Accounts," 461.

Dual-Layered Time
Reflections on T. W. Adorno in the 1950s

Jürgen Habermas

What seems to be trivial in retrospect could not be taken for granted by the time I joined the Institut für Sozialforschung (Institute for Social Research): that its reputation would be more dependent on Theodor Adorno's incessant productivity, which was only then heading for its climax, rather than on the success of the empirical research with which the institute was supposed to legitimize itself in the first place. Although he was the nerve center of the institute, Adorno could not handle administrative power. Rather, he constituted the passive center of a complex area of tension. When I arrived in 1956 there were symmetrical differences among Max Horkheimer, Gretel Adorno, and Ludwig von Friedeburg that were defined by the fact that their respective expectations toward Adorno were thwarted.

Friedeburg had a legitimate interest in a content-based cooperation with Adorno, which would lead to a more theoretical orientation of the empirical research. Separate from this, Gretel wanted the personal success of the philosopher both as a scientist and as a writer, which Adorno actually gained only posthumously. For Horkheimer, it was Adorno's task to establish a public prestige for the institute through politically pleasant and academically impressive studies, but without denying their common philosophical intentions and without harming its nonconformist character—an important image in terms of attracting students.

To me, Adorno had a different significance: time had a dual-layered quality in the institute. During the 1950s, there was probably no other place in the whole Federal Republic in which the intellectual 1920s were so explicitly present. Certainly, the old staff members of the institute such as Herbert Marcuse, Leo Löwenthal, and Erich Fromm, as well as Franz Neumann and Otto Kirchheimer, had remained in America. However, names such as Walter Benjamin and Gershon Scholem, Siegfried Kracauer and Ernst Bloch, Bertolt Brecht and Georg Lukács, Alfred Sohn-Rethel and Norbert Elias, Thomas and Erika Mann, Alban Berg and Arnold Schönberg, Kurt Eisler, Lotte Lenya, and Fritz Lang circulated in a completely natural fashion among Adorno, Gretel, and Horkheimer.

This was no name-dropping. In an astonishingly natural way, these names were used to refer to people they had known for decades. The names belonged to people they were either friends with or, more importantly, fought against. Bloch, for example, was still persona non grata by the time Adorno wrote *Die große Blochmusik*. The irritatingly casual presence of these minds caused a discrepancy in my sense of time. For "us," the Weimar Republic was lying beyond an abyss-like caesura, whereas for "them," the continuation of the 1920s had only recently ended in emigration. Hardly three decades had passed since Adorno used to visit his future wife in Berlin, where she was a trained chemist and carried on her father's leather goods factory. On one of these occasions he had also met Benjamin. Benjamin's *Angelus Novus*, which George Bataille, who by that time was librarian at the Bibliothèque Nationale, had taken into safekeeping, was hanging on the wall right next to the entrance in Gretel's room. Then the picture became Scholem's property and now hangs in the room of the Hebrew University where the unique library of this obsessive collector is housed. When I came to Frankfurt, Benjamin was for me, as he was to almost all the younger ones, a stranger. But I was soon to learn about the significance of this picture.

Gretel and Teddy Adorno had just published Benjamin's first essays with Suhrkamp Publishers. Since the public response had been weak, Gretel asked me to write a review. Therefore, I got a hold of those light-brown leather-bound volumes that retrieved Benjamin from oblivion. My wife Ute and I immersed ourselves in the dark shimmering essays, and in a peculiar way, we were moved by the opaque connection of lucid sentences and apocryphal allusions, which did not seem to fit in any genre.

I was not completely unprepared for the aspects of the dual-layered temporality of everyday life at the institute. However, they made me aware of the academic milieu of German-Jewish tradition and of the extent of the moral corruption of a German university that had not directly engaged in, but had at least tacitly accepted, the expulsion and annihilation of this spirit. In those days I began to imagine the state of mind of those colleagues who must have been staring at empty chairs at the first faculty meeting of the summer term 1933. The young university owed the fame it had found during the Weimar Republic to its nondiscrimination policy and its hiring procedures that were unbiased toward Jews, but in Frankfurt, the faculty was reduced by almost a third.

Intellectually I entered a new universe in 1956. In spite of familiar issues and sets of questions, it was different and fascinating at the same time. Compared with the environment of Bonn University, here the lava of thought was moving. Never before had I encountered such subtly differentiated intellectual complexity at its embarkation, in the mode of movement before finding its literary manifestation. What Schelling had developed in the summer term, 1802, in his Jena lectures to serve as a method of academic studies and as an idea of the German university—namely, to "construct the whole of one's science out of oneself and to present it with inner and lively visualization"—this is what Adorno practiced in this summer term in Frankfurt.

Effortless as it seemed, he presented the dialectic production of speculative thoughts without notes but in a polished style. Gretel had asked me to accompany her to the lecture that still took place in those days in the small lecture hall. In the following years, when I was already busy with other things, I noticed that she hardly ever missed one of Teddy's lectures. The first time I struggled to follow the talk; blinded by the brilliance of expression and by the way he presented it, I was lagging behind the diction of the thought. Only later did I notice that this dialectics often fossilized into mere manner or affectation. The main impression was the sparkling pretense of enlightenment that was still in the darkness of the not understood, the promise to make concealed connections transparent.

HOW A WHOLE NEW WORLD OPENS UP

Those unknown authors and thoughts, Freud and Durkheim, psychoanalysis and sociology of religion, did not enter as from outside, as a reduction into the holy realm of German idealism. With help from Freud's superego and Durkheim's collective consciousness, Adorno did not examine the miserable other side of the categorical imperative, its inappropriate usage, in order to denounce Kant's free will, but he did so to denounce the repressive circumstances that made this potential fade away. What Paul Riceour later called the "hermeneutics of suspicion" was not Adorno's thing. This was due to the protective impulse, which was just as strong as the critical one that served anyone, at least that is how it appeared to me. We had studied at the morally deteriorated universities of the Adenauer era that were marked with self-pity, suppression, and insensitiveness. In the mind-fetishizing shallow and murky environment of the "loss of the center," our vague need for an act of a comprehending catharsis could not be satisfied. Only the intellectual fervency and the intense analytical work of a solitary working and defiant Adorno saved the substance of our own great traditions for us in those days. He did this in the only possible way: by relentlessly criticizing their views.

The imperative consciousness of needing to be absolutely modern was combined with Proust's gaze of remembrance to the wildly leveling off of progress in a modernization devoid of any remembering. Hardly anywhere was modernization as overpowering as in the hastily and roughly performed corrections in the wounded streets of a town as hard hit as the Frankfurt Berliner Strasse. Whoever was listening to Adorno could not fail to tell the avant-garde spirit of modernity from the fake, aesthetically self-destructing progress of the "reconstruction." This haste had lost touch with the insight into this forward-looking dialectics of the nonconformist, which had been dismissed as obsolete. To me, new and outrageous—in a philosophical context—aesthetic arguments gained immediate political affirmation.

If I remember correctly the ambivalence of my first impressions in this new environment, to me, with all my intellectual excitement, it was a mixture of disconcertment and admiration. I felt like a character in a novel by Balzac, the clumsily uneducated boy from the province whose eyes were opened by the big city. I became aware of the conventionality of my way of thinking and feeling. I had grown up in the dominant traditions, which had persisted during the Nazi era, and now I found myself in a milieu where everything was alive that had been eliminated by the Nazis. It is easy to remember those unknown issues that had to be learned about then. However, it is hard to describe how a universe of concepts and mentalities changes through the opening of a whole new world. This is what happened shortly after my arrival while attending this memorable series of lectures held by Alexander Mitscherlich and Horkheimer on the occasion of Sigmund Freud's one-hundreth birthday anniversary. All these new thoughts were eye-opening, overwhelming.

At least I was prepared for Adorno and the reconciliation of philosophy and sociology and of Hegel and Marx, even though I was not used to the systematic style that promised to live up to the radical expectations of a social theory. Adorno gave new life to the systematically used and amalgamated concepts of Marx, Freud, and Durkheim. By means of a contemporary sociological thinking, he removed the simple historical from everything that I already knew from the Marx discourse of the 1920s and made it very current. It was only in the melting pot of this enlightened culture informed by social theory critique that the vague concepts of my Bonn University days dissolved. But the fog would not have lifted as fast had I not convinced myself of the scientific character of the new perspective on the facts.

THE POWER OF NEGATING THOUGHT

The now-legendary Freud lectures were very helpful in this. At that time in the United States, England, Holland, and Switzerland, psychoanalysis was at the peak of its reputation. The groundbreaking works of Erik Erikson, René Spitz, Ludwig Binswanger, Franz Alexander, Michael Balint, Gustav Bally, and many more (among which was Anna Spitz, of course) enjoyed worldwide respect. Hardly more than one decade after the end of the war this elite circle of scientists addressed a German audience to report on the progress of this discipline that had been ousted shamefully in 1933. I do not know what fascinated me more, after having encountered Freud only in derogatory contexts: the impressive individuals or the brilliant talks. In this respectable environment, Adorno's and Marcuse's contributions to the Horkheimer Festschrift received an enhanced scientific character.

At that time, I did not know the research agenda of the old institute and was not aware of the fact that it was these two authors alone who continued the tradition without even considering a discontinuity. Leo Löwenthal's most productive days lay behind him; Otto Kirchheimer and Franz Neumann had always gone their own ways; Erich Fromm was now considered a "revisionist" from the perspective of the core of the institute circle; Friedrich Pollock had practiced theoretical abstinence since the discussion on state capitalism in the early 1940s.

Not everything was different in a liberating sense. Someone who had graduated from a traditional philosophy department noticed irritating gaps in the Frankfurt canon. Those I considered the philosophical "contemporaries," the great authors of the 1920s and 1930s such as Scheler, Heidegger, Jaspers, and Gehlen, but also Cassirer, even Plessner, and Carnap and Reichenbach, did not appear in seminar or lecture. If at all, they were mentioned only in a bon mot like the one from Horkheimer: "If it has to be Jaspers then preferably Heidegger." The hermeneutic tradition from Humboldt to Dilthey was branded as idealist. The Phenomenological School did not have a better position either: Husserl's development seemed to stop before his transcendental change. Of the neo-Kantians, only Cohen and Cornelius, Horkheimer's teacher, were mentioned with a certain respect.

The relevant history of philosophy seemed to end with Bergson, Georg Simmel, and the Göttingener Husserl, hence before World War I. Only while reading the posthumously published inaugural lecture on the "Actuality of Philosophy" did I discover with a certain astonishment that Adorno must have taken a good look at Heidegger's *Being and Time* as an outside lecturer; *The Jargon of Authenticity*, which had been published shortly after that, had not been able to convince me of this fact. Nevertheless, I have to add that this first Adorno lecture was not the only one I visited over the course of one whole semester. I often attended the Hegel seminars. The absence of the philosophy of the 1920s created a somewhat old-fashioned air of the Frankfurt discourse. Even stronger was the contrast to the spirit of the aesthetic and Freudian avantgarde that was expressed by Adorno in a radical way, from head to toe.

If I want to try to describe the change in consciousness and the impact of the mental influence that the daily contact with Adorno brought about in me, it is best captured by the distancing from the familiar vocabulary and the outlook of the very German historical humanities that are rooted in Herder's romanticism. The sobering sociological perspective on the complexity of the tied-up whole of a mutilated life framework yet to be understood was connected with the trust in the analytical power of a negating thinking that would unravel the knot.

NOTE

This essay was translated from the German by Kai Artur Diers.

Anthony Giddens's Third Way
A Critique

Geoffrey Kurtz

The story goes that Michael Harrington and Paul Jacobs, the socialists in an early War on Poverty task force, liked to end their policy memos by noting: "Of course, there is no real solution to the problem of poverty until we abolish the capitalist system."[1] Harrington and Jacobs's complaint, tongue in cheek as it was, suggests something vital about left politics at its best: a relentless vigilance toward the limits and trade-offs implicit in available political options, matched by a willingness to slog it out in the trenches of pragmatic reformism.

Anthony Giddens's recent trio of slim manifestos shows plenty of eagerness for practical politics. As an adviser to Tony Blair and Bill Clinton, Giddens is the central intellectual exponent of one side—the winning side, so far—in an ongoing debate within parties of the Left around the world. Giddens champions a "renewal of social democracy" through a new appreciation of market economics and a revised understanding of core left values such as equality. Convinced that globalization and other aspects of modernization bring a new complexity to the political spectrum and a heightened salience for the politics of individual life choices, Giddens calls for a redefinition of social democrats' political aspirations.

However, Giddens exhibits a stark lack of concern for what might get lost in the transition to a "modernized" Left. With Giddens, there are no grumbles about the limitations of feasible reforms. Giddens has been accused by people to his left of surrendering to the neoliberalism of Margaret Thatcher and Ronald Reagan. But this estimation misses the point: Giddens does not believe that he is calling for a compromise, much less a surrender. Business-friendly reforms, in Giddens's eyes, deserve enthusiasm from social democrats.

There is no room for regrets, no counting of costs and benefits. Giddens's Third Way is a celebration.

GLOBALIZATION, RISK, AND THE THIRD WAY

Published in 1998, the year after the Labour Party's first electoral victory in nearly two decades, *The Third Way: The Renewal of Social Democracy* offers intellectual underpinnings for the political project championed by leaders such as Blair and Clinton. *The Third Way* introduces themes that include the political and cultural impact of globalization, the notion of risk, the rise of a "life politics" of individual self-definition, the new irrelevance of a strict Left–Right political divide, the need to relegitimate political institutions, and the potential for a new version of social democracy that can meet all these challenges. *The Third Way and Its Critics* (2000) summarizes his opponents' key arguments and elaborates his ideas, the principle of equality in social democratic thought, and global governance—although never responding systematically to the criticisms he cites. In *Runaway World: How Globalization Is Reshaping Our Lives* (2001), originally a set of lectures for the BBC, Giddens offers a series of conversational riffs on how globalization and the rise of new forms of risk are reshaping traditions and the family, and how politics can and must respond to these changes. These three books provide complementary, overlapping accounts of a unified argument—an argument with adherents, or at least friendly listeners, now governing countries from Europe to South America.

Third Way policy positions are well known by now. Politicians influenced by Third Way ideas have shown enthusiasm for lowering labor costs and decreasing workers' job security, suspicion toward unions and traditional social welfare programs, support for "supply-side" tax and economic policies, and caution in public spending, apart from a willingness to "invest" in education and worker training. Giddens's purpose in these three books is not to offer detailed policy arguments or to review the accomplishments of Third Way governments but to put "theoretical flesh . . . on the skeleton of their policy-making."[2]

At the heart of Giddens's call for a Third Way is the notion that economic globalization has brought with it a displacement of nation-state politics in favor of both more local and more global arenas, as well as deep changes in everyday life. This "new individualism" means the "retreat of tradition and custom" and a "moral transition" that allows individuals to "live in an open and reflexive manner." Giddens concedes that globalization—or, more precisely, liberalized international trade—can bring with it increased inequalities. But this is a mere side effect. What matters, Giddens maintains, is the "global cosmopolitan society" that is on the horizon, heralding a process of detraditionalization and an "active, open approach to life" for individuals.[3]

The sea change of globalization is, for Giddens, closely bound up with the rise of new kinds of risk. For Giddens, the notion of risk helps make sense of an array of relatively new problems, and of new ways that old problems confront us. Environmental problems are the paradigmatic example of these new risks. The personal strain resulting from the erosion of traditional marriage and family customs is another.[4] Giddens's extensive discussions of criminal justice policy also point to the risks that accompany social dislocation.

Modern, future-oriented societies have sought ways to calculate and control risk, Giddens writes. However, the more we intervene in the world to shape the future, the more we face "manufactured risks" that "rebound upon us." With the increasing rapidity of social and technological change wrought by globalization, there is "a new riskiness to risk," since we cannot reliably estimate the new risk we create. Claims about what is and is not risky become intensely political. New risks affect the whole world and demand global responses.[5]

While Giddens gives the nod to the potential usefulness of the "precautionary principle"—according to which changes with uncertain results should be avoided—and to social democracy's historic commitment to providing security, his tone in discussing questions of risk is resoundingly upbeat. Yes, risks mean real problems. Still, risk is "the energizing principle of a society that has broken away from tradition," and "active risk-taking is a core element of a dynamic economy and an innovative society." Boldness and daring, not caution, are called for.[6]

Risk, like other Third Way themes, has been a prominent category in Giddens's work for some time. His discussions of risk elsewhere strike similar notes, but with more conceptual resonance. In *Beyond Left and Right* (1994), Giddens emphasizes the ways that manufactured risk—that is, risk arising from human actions—troubles the Enlightenment's presumed link between knowledge and control. Enlightenment thinkers believed that knowledge about the world allows human beings to better control their fates. Giddens suggests that with modern risk situations, knowledge reveals the limits of human control or provides the basis for actions, the results of which end up outside human control. Risk, then, marks the limits of modernity. Much of the socialist project in particular has been predicated on the assumption that knowledge of social forces and relations allows for human control of society. The rise of manufactured risk means that the Left can no longer see its work as simply an attempt to solve the problems that humanity has set for itself. New conceptions of politics, of welfare, and of what it means to be radical are thus necessary.

THE POLITICS OF LIFE CHOICES

Because globalization and risk have brought new freedoms and uncertainties to individuals' lives, Giddens argues that a new "life politics" is disrupting the old political spectrum. Issues of life politics, Giddens insists, "nearly all raise value or ethical questions, but not only to do with social justice. Ageing is a good case in point. We have to consider problems such as what the proper role of older people should be in a society where ageing is changing its meaning." Life politics, in Giddens's *Beyond Left and Right* formulation, is about *"lifestyle*

... about how (as individuals and as collective humanity) we should live in a world where what used to be fixed either by nature or tradition is now subject to human distinctions."[7]

A commitment to a radical life politics means welcoming the breakdown of traditional limits on individual life choices. Here Giddens is enthusiastic in following through the logic of his analysis. It is worth noting that this is the area in which Giddens's policy recommendations diverge most sharply from those of some of his best-known advisees. Tony Blair, for instance, has stressed an ethic of "social moralism," emphasizing traditional family forms, and has willingly cut public assistance benefits for single mothers.[8] Giddens, in contrast, declares that "the persistence of the traditional family," at least in its inegalitarian and coercive aspects, "is more worrisome than its decline." The decline of traditional family forms, for Giddens, has made possible a "democracy of the emotions" that is "on the front line in the struggle between cosmopolitanism and fundamentalism."[9]

Giddens links his embrace of cosmopolitan values, gender equality, and individual freedom to the notion of "detraditionalization" most clearly articulated in *Runaway World*. Under globalization, Giddens writes, traditions in both public institutions and everyday life remain. However, their hold on people is broken, and they can no longer be defended through their own internal claims to truth but must be justified externally. Although traditions of some sort might be useful, in the way that disciplinary traditions structure academic research, detraditionalization is fundamentally a positive change. By introducing "a large dollop of rationality" into all remaining traditions, the process of detraditionalization makes possible a "cosmopolitan morality" in which various traditions can coexist. Giddens is also enthusiastic about the new individual freedoms that accompany detraditionalization. "Self identity," he writes, is now "created and recreated on a more active basis than before," opening up new worlds of life-choice possibilities.[10]

REVISING LEFT VALUES

For Giddens, the politics of life choices is distinct from the Left's traditional concern with "emancipation." Giddens admits that emancipatory politics—the politics of equality and "life chances"—has not become obsolete. What is crucial is the way Giddens relates life politics and emancipatory politics. The relationship is described most clearly in *Beyond Left and Right* and can be found only between the lines of his more recent books. Giddens stipulates that we should "regard life-political questions as central to emancipatory politics, rather than simply working the other way around. . . . To speak of 'lifestyle' with regard to the poor and hungry of the world initially sounds odd; but a response to poverty today can no longer be regarded as purely economic."[11]

Life politics, thus, is not simply an additional category. Rather, life-political issues redefine the older issues of emancipatory politics. Life politics, for Giddens, sets the framework in which other issues are understood. This is a profound shift from the Left's traditional stance, in which questions of emancipation are primary and define other concerns. Giddens plays out the implications of this shift by offering a new understanding of the Left's core principle of equality and calling for an end to the Left's "obsession with inequality."[12]

The goal of equal outcomes leaves too little room for "pluralism and lifestyle diversity," Giddens writes. Equality of opportunity is a better model for the modern Left, even though it may be untenable in its extreme meritocratic forms. Giddens's preferred reformulation of the principle of equality is "equality as *inclusion* and inequality as *exclusion*." Equality as inclusion is, fundamentally, Giddens's response to the fading of class as an experienced reality and the corresponding rise of life politics and concern for "self-realization."[13] Inclusion, for Giddens, "refers in its broadest sense to citizenship, to the civil and political rights and obligations that all members of a society should have . . . as a reality of their lives. It also refers to opportunities and to involvement in public space. In a society where work remains central to self-esteem and standard of living, access to work is one main context of opportunity. Education is another."[14]

Exclusion, then, can mean either the involuntary exclusion of those at the bottom—the unemployed and uneducated, most notably—or the voluntary self-exclusion of elites. Giddens's policy proposals follow this logic relentlessly: if inclusion in the labor market is the kind of equality that matters, then the existence of pensions and fixed retirement ages must be questioned, since they exclude the elderly from the labor market.[15] Income inequality is a secondary concern at best, and social welfare programs must be conceived as investments in human capital—in other words, as aids to life choices rather than to life chances.[16] The enthusiasm of Third Way politicians for education and worker training programs clearly fits with this line of thinking.[17]

If the old Left–Right political spectrum can no longer make sense of key political issues, Giddens argues, the political center need not mean a position that offers only compromise between Left and Right. Rather, the notions of an "active middle" or "radical center" can indicate resolute efforts to "take [new issues] by the roots."[18] The term *center-left*, for Giddens, thus does not mean a moderate Left: it means a genuinely new response to unprecedented political conditions:

> A renewed social democracy has to be left of centre, because social justice and emancipatory politics remain at its core. But the "centre" shouldn't be

regarded as empty of substance. Rather, we are talking of the alliances that social democrats can weave from the threads of lifestyle diversity. Traditional as well as novel political problems need to be thought about in this way.... The equation between being on the left and being radical no longer stands up, if in fact it ever did.[19]

DEMOCRACY WITHOUT ACTIVISM

The rise of life politics, Giddens contends, is behind the widespread discontent with existing forms of democratic government that many social observers have noted in recent decades. New demands for "individual autonomy and the emergence of a more reflexive citizenry" require a corresponding "democratization of democracy." Giddens proposes an eclectic set of reforms that, he insists, will "reassert" the legitimacy and power of government. New levels of transparency and business-inspired efficiency, along with experiments such as electronic referenda, will inspire confidence in government. Both devolution and the development of transnational forms of governance—Giddens offers the European Union as a model—will allow government to respond to new needs more effectively than nation-state institutions can. Likewise, a new conceptualization of government as a "risk manager" must lead to reform of welfare and other state functions, bringing them into line with people's new needs and new self-understandings. Giddens also places great value on a renewal of civil society. Here, Giddens means primarily new relationships between government and nonprofit organizations. Local initiatives, volunteerism, and face-to-face groupings of all kinds, he suggests, can also help foster a "civic culture" that, while outside the state, will help relegitimate public life as a whole.[20]

Social movements, strikingly, play a negligible role in Giddens's conception of democratic renewal. Unions, for instance, are explicitly discussed only once in the three books, in a passage advocating closer labor–management cooperation—although a brief oblique reference to "special-interest groups" in *The Third Way* seems to be a jab at the labor movement.[21] Likewise, decades of feminist activism seem to have played no part in the equalization of gender relations that Giddens lauds, and lesbian and gay movements have nothing to do with increased freedoms regarding gender and sexual identity; such changes, in Giddens's description, seem to result purely from impersonal social forces.

At best, Giddens suggests, social movements can raise new issues and pose symbolic challenges to hidebound practices. In general, however, Giddens sees social movements more as symptoms of the crisis of depoliticization than as helpful responses to that crisis. Movements distract from the mainstream parties and state institutions that, in the final analysis, matter most of all. Giddens dismisses the ideas of theorists such as German sociologist Ulrich Beck, who sees a "subpolitics" of social movement activism as a vital but limited new form of democratic politics.[22]

ULRICH BECK ON INEQUALITY, DANGER, AND RISK

Giddens's criticism of Beck is important in part because the two thinkers share many points of agreement. Arriving independently at themes of risk, detraditionalization, and what Giddens calls "the politics of life choices," the two thinkers have collaborated increasingly in recent years.[23] In many respects, their ideas run parallel, but the place of social movements in modern politics is only one of several significant areas where the two diverge. The contrasts between Giddens and Beck highlight an underlying, deeply problematic, pattern in Giddens's work.

Like Giddens, Beck is concerned with the way modern societies experience and produce risk. Beck relates the emergence of "risk society" to processes of "individualization," a close parallel to Giddens's notions of detraditionalization and life politics. However, Beck's understanding of risk, unlike that of Giddens, emphasizes the continuity of old inequalities, the creation of new inequalities, and the dangers inherent in risk. Beck describes risk as a "systematic way of dealing with hazards and insecurities induced and introduced by modernization itself," in particular by the modern process of wealth creation. Modern risks, for Beck, are defined by the immense threat of destruction they pose, and by the fact that they are invisible or latent until described and defined—unlike older forms of risk that tended to be personal, limited in scope, and obvious. For Giddens, in contrast, what makes modern risks new is primarily that their causes are new: we don't have enough experience dealing with them to reliably calculate the likelihood of particular effects.[24]

Unlike Giddens, Beck stresses that existing societies have only partly completed a transition from a society focused on wealth distribution to one focused on risk distribution. This means, first of all, that conflicts over wealth are far from over. All the conflicts and inequalities of capitalist societies remain. Old inequalities even shape new conflicts, Beck argues. Movement toward gender equality, for instance, is constrained by inegalitarian economic institutions, and new ecological risks hit hardest among the poor. Accordingly, Beck advocates policies that reduce material inequalities—not just inequalities of opportunity—and that aim at "limiting and cushioning market relationships."[25] The contrast with Giddens's vision of equality as inclusion in market relationships could hardly be more striking.

For Beck, the fact that inequality has "lost significance as an issue" in public life does not mean that material inequalities affect people's lives any less. Rather, the change in the social prominence of issues of inequality heralds "a new chapter in the history of classes," one apparently fraught by "illusory and ideological . . . claims" that individual fates now transcend class categories.[26] Where Giddens sees the reduced salience of class politics as a change to be taken at face value, Beck sees it as a complex problem to be understood and, perhaps, addressed.

Beck also traces the development of new inequalities based on "risk position," an analogue to the class positions of groups in societies existing up to this point. Although he agrees with Giddens that the inclusive and global nature of modern risks is part of what makes them distinctive, Beck also argues that "some people are more affected than others by the distribution and growth of risks," and he underlines the inequalities between "those afflicted by risks and those who profit from them," as well as inequalities in how well prepared people of different groups are to deal with the risks and changes they face.[27]

Where Giddens calls for boldness in the face of risk, Beck's understanding of risk emphasizes danger. Modern risk is not, for Beck, a matter of uncertainty per se; it is fundamentally about "the threat of self-destruction of all life on Earth." Safety and risk prevention are, for Beck, paramount issues.[28]

These differences are revealed in the two authors' discussions not only of policy issues but also of the ways people respond to distinctly modern changes in their individual lives. In particular, Giddens and Beck offer tellingly different interpretations of the widespread appeal of psychotherapy in modern societies. For Giddens, Freudian psychoanalysis is "in effect . . . a method for the renewal of self-identity" that makes it easier for individuals to create and re-create their own identities "on a more active basis than before." Beck, in contrast, argues that the move toward a risk society is accompanied by incredible "fear and anxiety." The process of individualization means that "social crises appear as individual crises," despite their social nature, leading to an intense "pressure to work out insecurity by oneself." This pattern, in turn, leads to "new demands on social institutions [including] therapy" and a "revival of interest in psychology."[29]

These positions may not be strictly incompatible, but their radically different emphases matter. Giddens's understanding of risk and related social changes points him away from recognizing and addressing dangers and conflicts. Whenever possible, he describes changes in contemporary societies in positive terms. Although Beck does not have easy solutions to offer, he does not succumb to Giddens's blithe optimism. Instead, Beck focuses on the ways that dangers are inextricably tied to modernization.

Beck's interest in what he calls the subpolitics of social movement activism parallels his other key differences from Giddens. For Beck, the nation-state's capacity to effect change has been severely reduced. In part, this is a result of the success of liberal democracy and the welfare state in creating a reflexive citizenry. These changes, however, have happened along with others: the economy has become the engine of change, and state-centered politics has reached a "stand-off." The real site of democratic political action, for Beck, is now the new social movements.[30]

Contrasting his own position with Beck's, Giddens argues that "the idea that [social movement] groups can take over where government is failing, or can stand in place of political parties, is fantasy. . . . Movements . . . cannot govern."[31] But this is not what Beck has said. Beck claims, more modestly, that subpolitics is a kind of politics that is on the rise for a variety of reasons. Beck does suggest that the participatory and immediate qualities of social movement politics make subpolitics a crucial part of the relegitimation of political life in modern societies. However, he does not argue that subpolitics can fill the gap left by the stagnation of state-centered politics with regard to the basic functions of governance and policy making. For Beck, the fading capacity and legitimacy of state-centered politics are unavoidable effects of modernization. Giddens insists that a solution to the state's problems must exist, but Beck avoids making such claims, and the possibilities he sees in subpolitics are, he suggests, not a replacement for conventional politics. When Giddens argues that a renewed social democracy can relegitimate conventional politics, Beck might accuse him of wearing blinders and of missing the stark limitations on state-centered politics under current conditions.

GIDDENS AND THE POLITICS OF ROSE-COLORED GLASSES

Giddens consistently refuses to acknowledge downsides to the policies he advocates. It would be a mistake to see the Third Way argument—at least Giddens's version—as a compromise between social democracy and neoliberalism. "Compromise" suggests regret, a conscious falling short of goals or aspirations. Giddens, however, sees his policy framework as normatively defensible on its own terms, not as a mere expedient.

This is most evident in Giddens's attitude toward markets. Responding to critics, Giddens admits that markets can "breed a commercialism that threatens other life values" and that "ethical standards . . . have to be brought from the outside" into market interactions.[32] However, this sense of caution toward markets is never integrated into his analysis and seems quickly forgotten. In redefining equality as inclusion, for instance, Giddens writes primarily about inclusion in labor markets. Here, he breaks sharply with the insights of the social democratic tradition in ways that he does not adequately acknowledge.

Karl Marx, notably, argued that the sale of one's labor power, that is, participation in the labor market, is a matter of exploitation, not of freedom. For Marx, freedom exists only outside the labor market:

> And the worker, who for twelve hours weaves, spins, drills, turns, builds, shovels, breaks stones, carries loads, etc.—does he consider this twelve hours' weaving, spinning, drilling, turning, building, shoveling, stone breaking as a manifestation of his life, as life? On the contrary, life begins for him where this activity ceases, at table, in the public house, in bed.[33]

Marx argued that the struggle to reduce the length of time that workers must participate in the labor market in order to survive is, in effect, a struggle to assert the "political economy of the working class" against the interests of capital.[34]

Giddens, however, rejects the notion that the chance to sell one's labor power entails any kind of unfreedom. When Giddens proposes an end to the fixed retirement age, for instance, he does not argue that this is an unfortunate but politically unavoidable concession to what Marx would call "the political economy of the bourgeoisie." Rather, he insists that inclusion in the labor market is valuable for workers under any conditions. Nowhere in these three books does Giddens engage questions of working time, wages, workplace safety, or rights on the job—all issues that labor movements and social democratic parties have seen as crucial elements of the political economy of the working class. It is one thing to argue that modern economies require a "flexibility" that necessitates compromises in such conditions. However, this is not Giddens's point. What is important in Giddens's argument about labor market inclusion is that, in his analysis, the embrace of market forces appears as a cost-free choice. It is not that exploitation is unavoidable; it simply does not exist.

Likewise, Giddens's proposals for the regulation of corporations are curiously weak, despite his bluster about "confronting corporate interests where it is necessary to do so." Giddens calls on governments to encourage competition and discourage monopoly, to monitor corporate behavior, to reward "responsible" corporate policies, and to recognize that not all areas of public life should be commercialized. In the workplace, Giddens lauds employee stock ownership plans and labor–management cooperation. In the global economy, the primary need for regulation stems from the unpredictable and "erratic" effects of capital mobility.[35] Giddens is not simply a neoliberal. Nevertheless, his regulatory proposals suggest that markets need assistance only in running more smoothly and including more people, with the occasional tug toward niceness and with minimal barriers to keep them from engulfing all of society. This is a vision of business regulation that poses few threats to corporate power and offers many rewards to corporations and those who own them.

This profit-friendly form of business regulation is one of the points at which Giddens's abandonment of the notion of class undermines the usefulness of his analysis. Giddens is right that class plays a smaller role in most individuals' understanding of their relationships to other people and to the economy than it did several decades ago. However, class as a category of analysis remains crucial. The concept of class entails a recognition that those who own something for a living gain more economic and political power than those who must sell their labor power, and that without resolute political efforts toward equality of outcome, these class divisions tend to grow wider over time. Deep class divisions, in turn, undermine the political equality on which democratic institutions depend. With an analysis that ignores class divisions, as does Giddens's, the snowballing inequalities that result from profit accumulation become invisible.

Giddens's Third Way therefore represents a real departure from the social democratic tradition. Social democrats have long accepted that they work within capitalist economies and will do so for the foreseeable future; a social democratic accommodation with market forces and the presence of an owning class is nothing new. However, this accommodation has generally been an uncomfortable one. Social democrats have sought to use democratic politics to constrain markets and advance working-class interests, even though their capacity to do so has been limited. Giddens parts with this history. Rather than seeking to contend with market forces, Giddens embraces them. Rejecting the idea that capitalist markets are necessarily characterized by exploitation, Giddens sees "dynamism" as the primary quality of "market societies."[36] Likewise, by setting aside any analysis of class, Giddens is able to offer an account of profit making that lauds economic growth without recognizing why some people benefit from growth much more than others. Where Marx and social democrats after him have seen exploitation and class divisions as quintessential components of capitalism, Giddens sees only dynamic markets that must be made more inclusive.

NEW IDEAS FOR SOCIAL DEMOCRACY

Since Eduard Bernstein launched his famous revision of Marxism by calling for a reformist theory to match the socialist movement's reformist practice, social democracy has been a critical and self-transforming tradition. There is no reason why the present era should be any different, and there is every reason why today's social democrats need to develop new ideas. Social conditions have changed profoundly in the past few decades, and a political movement that does not seek to understand the conditions it faces is likely to run up against barriers it does not anticipate and cannot understand. "In the years to come," Giddens asserts, "Third Way politics will be the point of view which others will have to engage."[37] He is right, and not only because of the enormous influence that Third Way ideas have achieved among politicians. Even where his theoretical framework is wanting, Giddens points to vital questions. Five of Giddens's themes demand particular attention: globalization, risk, life politics, gender, and the crisis of politics. While taking Giddens's arguments seriously, however, readers must pay as much attention to the questions he does not ask as to those he does.

1. Giddens is correct in pointing to the central importance of globalization. The economic integration of the world's economy has immense effects on daily life and on public affairs in every country. The cultural changes accompanying globalization—both the possibility of cosmopolitanism and the real threat of fundamentalism—are urgent concerns as well. Giddens does not, however, focus on the ways in which globalization may constrain egalitarian policy making or the possible transnational solutions to those constraints.

2. The related concept of risk is a valuable way to conceptualize the new problems that are inherent in modernization, in terms of both large-scale risks, such as global warming, and the smaller-scale risks that accrue in individuals' lives. Perhaps the most useful aspects of the notion of risk, however, are those developed more clearly by Beck than by Giddens. Beck uses the concept of risk to uncover new inequalities and to trace the dangers produced by modern economic and technological development—the very elements of risk that Giddens downplays.

3. Giddens's idea of a politics of life choices aims to illuminate a real and profound change in how people in modern, developed societies understand politics as well as themselves. A sense that individuals can, should, and must define their own identities and chart the course of their own lives, and a corresponding interest in personal freedoms and a pluralism of lifestyles, have gained new prominence in recent decades. These questions are of particular importance for the social democratic tradition, rooted as it is in notions of class solidarity that now seem out of tune with the self-understandings of many people in developed societies—whatever the analytical value of class analysis may still be. There is clearly something new at work here; the question is how to describe it. As useful as his attention to the politics of individual self-definition may be, Giddens's use of his own concepts creates too sharp a distinction between life politics and emancipatory politics. Arguably, an emancipatory politics of life chances must form the foundation for any meaningful politics of life choices. If it is true that life choices are predicated on life chances, then anyone seeking to build a solid political analysis of these new developments needs a different formulation—or at least a deep revision of Giddens's concepts.

4. By placing a high priority on gender equality and by relating changes in family life and personal identity to macro social changes, Giddens helps correct the historical gender-blindness of the socialist tradition. Giddens is right that equality between women and men and the shakeup of old gender roles must be fundamental components of a left agenda and that gender matters are closely tied to other political questions. However, Giddens's failure to discuss the role of activism in challenging old gender norms is both analytically wrong and politically problematic. Changes in relations between husbands and wives, new forms of families such as same-sex partnerships, increased labor market opportunities for women, and a new degree of freedom regarding sexual and gender identity all seem to have happened by themselves, or as automatic by-products of a broad detraditionalizing trend. Giddens's account omits the political struggles of feminists and lesbian and gay activists to achieve greater gender equality and the weakening of traditional male and female roles that Giddens lauds. But without recognizing the role of social movements in bringing change, Giddens can offer no suggestion for how to extend the new "democracy of the emotions," except to call for an embrace of the detraditionalizing effects of globalization. Giddens's dismissal of the importance of social movements makes his argument less useful.

5. At the heart of Giddens's Third Way project is the hope of rehabilitating politics and political activity from the doldrums of public disinterest and mistrust. Giddens is again correct in pointing to these issues; the crisis of the democratic state is one of the underlying difficulties of social democratic parties everywhere—indeed, of all nonextremist parties. Participation in and passion about public life are fading and, where they remain strong, are shifting away from the state. Giddens is right in pointing out that no other institutions can match the state and the political parties that seriously vie for a share of state power in their capacity to govern or to draw together majorities of citizens around common concerns. Ultimately, Giddens's work must be judged by the capacity of the politics he proposes to achieve the ends he sets: that "political idealism [be] revived" and, in the process, social democracy renewed.[38] However, it is not clear that Giddens has shown how these goals can be realized.

BEYOND THE THIRD WAY

Giddens's Third Way is far from the spirit of Harrington and Jacobs's War on Poverty memos. Past the careful equivocations—and these seem to come by the bushel—Giddens's three Third Way manifestos are characterized above all by a refusal to recognize tragedies and trade-offs. For Giddens, the acceptance of market dynamism is neither a compromise that cannot be refused nor a historically unavoidable choice that will sustain or create as many problems as it solves. It is simply a good thing. Giddens's failure to engage seriously with the critics he cites seems in keeping with his blithe dismissal of any negative implications of the policies he advocates.

Any attempt to outline a social democratic alternative to the Third Way must grapple seriously with the questions Giddens raises. What it does not need to do, however, is accept Giddens's proposition that the immediately available political options are anything other than tragic. Globalization, the weakness of the state, the breakdown of class solidarity and nonindividualistic understandings of individual life, and the marginality of social movements all make the achievement of social democratic goals difficult at best. Victories for the Left, in the foreseeable future, are likely to be few and partial. What the Left does achieve is likely to be undermined by factors—such as class divisions and the power of market forces—that remain uncontrolled.

Gloominess is not known to be a winning basis for election campaigns. The hope of making left parties electable runs subtly but consistently through Giddens's work. The Third Way project, after all, has its roots in frustration with the electoral failures of the Labour Party in the United Kingdom and the Democratic Party in the United States. Disasters at the polls led to internal restructuring and debate within Labour, which seemed to pay off enormously in the 1997 landslide victory.[39] Similarly, crushing defeats in the 1984 and 1988 U.S. presidential elections were followed by intense organizing—and fundraising—on the part of the New Democrats, who saw Bill Clinton's 1992 election as a vindication of their policies.[40] Given the commitment of Third Way proponents to left electability, Giddens might argue that the cheery tone and optimistic analysis he offers are just what social democrats need.

This is where Giddens's hopes of revitalizing political idealism collide with the structure of his argument. A political framework that promises roses everywhere might help telegenic politicians win votes. However, in the long run, political trust and involvement are not likely to be relegitimated by an approach that denies the significance of real troubles in people's lives. Giddens's policies, at bottom, are likely to exacerbate the inequalities and frustrations inherent in a market-dominated society. Sooner or later, people notice that problems such as unemployment, overwork, financial strains, or yawning cultural divides are not going away. A political framework that cannot effectively confront or even talk about such issues will not be successful at reviving political participation and trust.

Any Left beyond the Third Way, however, cannot promise to make policy just as it pleases. Rather, it must make compromises with open eyes, always attentive to the limits of the reforms it can offer even as it fights hard for those reforms.

If no change short of abolishing capitalism will do more than create marginal improvements in a particular situation, and if no one has any notion of how capitalism might be abolished, then perhaps the Left needs to say so—while making sure that those marginal improvements are still achieved. Giddens, for all his calls for new thinking, helps very little in the construction of a Left that can be viable under such terms precisely because he offers optimism and cheer where irony and discomfort make more sense.

Oddly, an awareness of the tragic dimension to available political options may be better, not worse, for Left morale. Here, it matters greatly that Giddens is constructing a political theory for politicians and not for movements. Giddens ignores social movements in his analysis in part because he has nothing to offer them. Candidates running on optimism can survive from election to election, at least for a while. Movements, in contrast, need to win hearts for the long haul, and thus need ideals. It may not be a bad thing if those ideals are demanding enough to grate against reality. When Giddens gives up the radical core of socialist analysis, he also surrenders the dreams that give activists a reason to keep fighting in hard times, along with the honesty that can help relegitimate the very political idealism Giddens seeks.

Giddens puts some crucial questions on the table. His answers are flawed in large part by the absence of the questions he does not ask. Moving beyond the Third Way means starting with the questions around which Giddens builds his theory and filling in the gaps—with more questions. Even though honest social democrats cannot promise policy achievements radically different from what the Third Way offers, they can still talk about the persistence of exploitation, the endurance of class divisions, and the encumbrances that capitalism places on democratic politics. These are the traditional concerns of social democracy, and the absence of a systemic alternative to capitalism does not mean that these structural problems have gone away. Whereas Giddens would drop the analytic categories—such as exploitation and class—that point to what may be insoluble problems, social democrats seeking an alternative to the Third Way must retain and use those troubling concepts. Critiques need not be matched with solutions, especially in a politics concerned as much with orienting movements and sparking idealism as with catching the momentary attention of voters.

This is not to say that any political movement can eschew short-term questions of electoral victory. Rather, it is to propose that such questions are not the only ones that matter. Any viable politics to the left of the Third Way will define itself by asking how it can rebel against the structural limits to reform even while acting intelligently within those limits, how it can relate individual life choice concerns to issues of collective emancipation, how it can manage the sometimes conflicting requirements of conventional politics and social movement activism, and how it can confront globalized capitalism in the absence of global democratic institutions.

Asking only questions for which he has answers, Giddens offers a theoretical framework that blinds us to the very concerns that define social democratic aspirations. Today's Left may not be able to talk about the abolition of capitalism—even half jokingly—as did Harrington and Jacobs. Still, the willingness to keep in mind the incompleteness of achievable reforms must be part of any social democracy beyond the Third Way. It is jarring to question the fundamental inhumanities of capitalism when there are no apparent means of replacing capitalism with something wholly different. Yet maintaining the tension of unanswered questions will be part of the work of whatever Left is next.

NOTES

1. Maurice Isserman, *The Other American: The Life of Michael Harrington* (New York: PublicAffairs, 2000), 212.
2. Anthony Giddens, *The Third Way: The Renewal of Social Democracy* (Cambridge: Polity Press, 1998), 2.
3. Ibid., 28–33, 34–37; Anthony Giddens, *Runaway World: How Globalization Is Reshaping Our Lives* (New York: Routledge, 2001), 35–37; Anthony Giddens, *The Third Way and Its Critics* (Cambridge: Polity Press, 2000), 65.
4. Giddens, *Runaway World*, 45–46.
5. Ibid., 44–50; Giddens, *The Third Way and Its Critics*, 132–39.
6. Giddens, *Runaway World*, 50–53; Giddens, *The Third Way*, 62.
7. Giddens, *The Third Way and Its Critics*, 40; Anthony Giddens, *Beyond Left and Right* (Stanford, Calif.: Stanford University Press, 1994), 14–15.
8. Stephen Driver and Luke Martell, "Left, Right and the Third Way," *Policy and Politics* 28, no. 2 (2000): 147–61.
9. Giddens, *Runaway World*, 83.
10. Ibid., 60–68.
11. Giddens, *Beyond Left and Right*, 44, 160.
12. Giddens, *The Third Way*, 100.
13. Ibid., 101–14; Giddens, *The Third Way and Its Critics*, 85–89.
14. Giddens, *The Third Way*, 102–3.
15. Ibid., 103, 121; Giddens, *The Third Way and Its Critics*, 40.
16. Giddens, *The Third Way*, 106–12; Giddens, *The Third Way and Its Critics*, 104.
17. Giddens, *The Third Way*, 109.
18. Giddens, *Beyond Left and Right*, 1; Giddens, *The Third Way*, 44–45.
19. Giddens, *The Third Way*, 45–46.
20. Ibid., 70–78; Giddens, *The Third Way and Its Critics*, 60–62; Giddens, *Runaway World*, 93–100.
21. Giddens, *The Third Way and Its Critics*, 150; Giddens, *The Third Way*, 53.
22. Giddens, *The Third Way*, 51–53.

23. Ulrich Beck, *Risk Society: Towards a New Modernity* (London: Sage Publications, 1992), 7–8.
24. Ibid., 21–23; Giddens, *The Third Way*, 59–60.
25. Beck, *Risk Society*, 20, 123–24, 41, 91.
26. Ibid., 92, 99.
27. Ibid., 23, 46, 98.
28. Ibid., 21, 49, 57.
29. Giddens, *Runaway World*, 65; Beck, *Risk Society*, 76, 100.
30. Beck, *Risk Society*, 183–87.
31. Giddens, *The Third Way*, 53.
32. Giddens, *The Third Way and Its Critics*, 36.
33. Karl Marx and Friedrich Engels, *The Marx-Engels Reader*, ed. Robert C. Tucker (New York: W. W. Norton, 1978), 205.
34. Ibid., 517.
35. Giddens, *The Third Way and Its Critics*, 142–53; Giddens, *The Third Way*, 148.
36. Giddens, *The Third Way*, 15.
37. Giddens, *The Third Way and Its Critics*, vii.
38. Giddens, *The Third Way*, 2.
39. Colin Leys, "The British Labour Party since 1989," in *Looking Left: Socialism in Europe after the Cold War*, ed. Donald Sassoon (New York: New Press, 1997).
40. Richard D. Kahlenberg and Ruy Teixeira, "A Better Third Way," *Nation*, March 5, 2001.

How Dinesh Gets Over
The Unmeritorious Scholarship of Dinesh D'Souza

Christine Kelly

For about a decade now, Dinesh D'Souza has been vexing serious left and liberal intellectuals. D'Souza's meteoric rise—from Bombay Rotary Club exchange student at the University of Arizona in 1978 to media-renowned political "expert" and Rishwain Scholar at Stanford University's conservative Hoover Institution today—might be cast as one of the great immigrant success stories of our times. That along the way D'Souza has, as he puts it, "harpooned" battalions of liberal and left Americans in the process is his peculiar distinction. After all, it isn't every day that liberal and left America draws its most enthusiastic and anointed critic from the ranks of third-world university exchange students. Equally distinctive to D'Souza's profile is that he has remained immune to serious counterattack. This is not to say that he has not been criticized, but the most energetic efforts to curb his increasing influence have been undertaken by student activists unhappy that student fees are underwriting his campus appearances—a questionable tactic that often backfires. This immunity from serious challenge is in part the result of the choice by noteworthy liberal or left intellectuals to ignore him, based on two core assumptions: (1) no one could possibly take him or his work seriously; and (2) serious engagement would only bring him more attention. But ignoring D'Souza has not diminished his influence. D'Souza's books continue to make best-seller lists while his professional credibility only increases.

A second explanation for the fact that retaliation has largely passed D'Souza by might be that liberal and left intellectuals remain attached to a type of civility unrecognized by D'Souza. It is not typical of people holding academic positions—left, right, or center—to commit to print the kind of no-holds-barred polemics for which D'Souza is best known. Without sinking all standards, it may be due time to give Mr. D'Souza a little of his own medicine. After all, one who lives by the harpoon might expect to see one coming now and then. And now in his latest two titles, D'Souza has provided plenty of political and professional reasons for, as they say, taking off the gloves.

* * *

EASY STREET

There is nothing typical about Dinesh D'Souza's ride to the top. His is an exceptional journey, but exceptional only in the sense of odd or irregular. He holds the post of "scholar" but has earned only a BA in English from Dartmouth, where he eventually transferred. At age twenty-six, he served as senior domestic policy analyst under Reagan without a shred of serious policy training. In fact, D'Souza, the political "expert," has no training whatsoever in social science. Moreover, he has been appointed to two research institute positions without a single peer-reviewed essay or publication. And, perhaps not surprisingly, he is treated like a serious intellectual in the media and publishing world, despite the remarkable lack of research that goes into his books.

As an immigrant "success" story, his is more reminiscent of the political patronage and smoke-filled backroom promotions of over a century ago—only this time, ethnicity and tribalism are denounced and denied as the source of D'Souza's power. But in reality, D'Souza has little in the way of credentials or training to merit any of his promotions.[1] In transparent violation of his own meritocratic fanaticism, D'Souza's rewards are, in the end, a result of his willingness to fill the role of brown-skinned provocateur for the Right. The rest of his booty comes in the forms of both party paybacks and the ironic glory bestowed on him by the low-brow media (including a profit-anxious publishing industry) that he bashes. Though race, ethnicity, and identity are all liberal bogeymen for those on the Right, it is they who so skillfully play the race card. If Dinesh D'Souza were not East Indian, he would simply have no role to play for the Right: there would be no White House credentials, no appointments as "scholar," and no press. Nothing can better testify to the truth of this perhaps disquieting charge than the evidence of his own poor scholarship, his philosophical inconsistency, and his signature but shamelessly sophomoric panache. In the two titles he released in 2002—*What's So Great about America?* (Regenery Press) and *Letters to a Young Conservative* (Basic Books)—D'Souza has outdone himself. Indeed, the real story between these two books is the utter laziness and flouting of academic integrity their author displays.

A few things dawned on me while reading these two works in the space of two weeks. One was that it would have been a better investment if the Right had funded a proper graduate education for Dinesh rather than permitting him to hone his "writing" and oratory while on staff at the American Enterprise Institute and, more recently, the Hoover Institute. With proper graduate school training in, for example, political science, D'Souza would have experienced three years of seminar reading, writing, and evaluation; a year of preparation for and completion of rigorous qualifying examinations; and another year of guided doctoral research. Finally, in another year's time, he might have produced a scholarly dissertation reviewed and approved by a committee of senior faculty.

Had any of this happened, D'Souza might have gone on to become a truly formidable foe. Certainly, he would have harnessed the scholarly standards that he and other conservatives such as Bill Bennett and Lynne Cheney hysterically defend. He might also have picked up some social science research skills in the meantime. And perhaps a graduate school education would have softened the arrogance that characterizes so little effort in his pages. Among the many things that a PhD education can bestow on someone is the humility of reason in the face of a political passion.

In the scholarly universe, it is not enough to be deeply committed; one must skillfully search for the most reasonable, most consistent, and most demonstrable argument possible. Scholarly standards in the service of a political cause also keep one honest. Contrary to D'Souza's cartoonish characterizations of left scholarship, it is the Left that has historically cherished reason and the attendant standards of verifiability. Contrarily, the Right's strategy, historically, has rested on appeals to faith and sentiment—most often in the form of nationalism, religious zeal, and patriotism. Assertion, not argument; passion, not reason; and symbolism, not evidence, have long been the building blocks of right-wing ideology. In the absence of reasoned argument, patriotism and nationalism are more than wholesome passions; they are threats to the very Enlightenment ideals that D'Souza tortures to fit his agenda. Perhaps this is because D'Souza doesn't really understand the Enlightenment tradition's cosmopolitan legacy. This explanation is preferable to the alternative, which is that D'Souza knowingly engages in the capricious denial of the egalitarianism inherent in the tradition in order to protect his own unearned privilege and power. Regardless, in the course of these two titles, he plays to fear, chauvinism, and provincialism while advancing a set of dangerously unreasonable claims, which I discuss later. Equally unreasonable is the "scholarship" D'Souza pastes together to defend God and country.

This brings me to the second thing that dawned on me while reading these two texts: how they began to blend. At first, I thought this was just the effect of D'Souza's narrow and shallow range of topics (why multiculturalism and antiracism are evil, why Reagan was great, and why capitalism and the West are as good as it will ever get). But for anyone familiar with D'Souza's methods of operation, the feeling of a rehash—be it a rewrite of a transcript from the lecture circuit or a TV appearance or the repositioning of a previous book's argument—isn't a surprise.[2] D'Souza has gotten the game of publishing down to a near science of efficiency. After the lull between his first smash hit *Illiberal Education* (1991) and *The End of Racism* (1996), he has become a virtual pulp machine, putting out *Ronald Reagan: How an Ordinary Man Became an Extraordinary Leader* (1997), *The Virtues of Prosperity* (2000), and now these two titles in one year.

But what at first seemed like a an eerie repetition in the current two texts turned out to be hundreds and hundreds of words in verbatim passages appearing without notes in both books. Given that these books were put out by different publishers, I began to think that Dinesh imagined that no one would actually read both books all the way through—including his editors.

That D'Souza's editor at Basic Books, Liz McGuire, brought him to Basic from the conservative Free Press, where she had also been his editor, might have contributed to the lack of oversight.[3] Although plagiarism of one's own work is unlikely to produce a lawsuit, it is a violation of academic culture and, under normal circumstances, contractual standards. Though I can only speculate, based on the evidence presented by these two texts, I venture to guess that if some eager researcher were to scan all of D'Souza's books and perform a Google string search across them in chronological order, this type of verbatim repetition without notation might be traced back even further.

Whether this is a high crime or not, it is evidence of the sloppiness and laziness characteristic of D'Souza's work generally. That a "scholar" like D'Souza—whose arguments in both books celebrate standards, merit, and virtue—should provide such a poor example should bother, at the very least, the Hoover Institution. That, as a trade author, he has pulled down $250,000 in advance money for a single book also makes it clear that the standards of the marketplace are less than meritorious. It is a lovely example of how the twin souls of modern conservatism—moral virtue and market principles—simply do not abide in the same house.

WHAT'S SO GREAT ABOUT AMERICA? THE EMPIRE STRIKES FIRST

In this post–September 11 defense of U.S. policy, culture, and might, D'Souza begins with a preface in which he likens the U.S. role in the "war on terrorism" to that of the Athenians facing Sparta. In long excerpts from Pericles' funeral oration, D'Souza dramatizes the conflict today as one of clashing moral orders: one premised on freedom, and the other on militarism. Like Athens, America is "a unique civilization that holds itself up as a universal model for civilized people everywhere" (xii). Despite the obvious incongruity of the analogy in military terms, D'Souza's mission in this book is to convince readers that America today offers the "best life" possible and that America deserves absolute defense by its citizens, including the willingness to give their lives in the fight against its enemies. That the terrorists of 9/11 were willing to make this sacrifice for their "side," D'Souza suggests, is not in itself "contemptible or ridiculous; indeed it raises the question of what we in America would be willing to give our lives for. No serious patriotism is possible that does not attempt to answer that question" (7).

Though the initial question is fair, the suggestion that the answer requires a renewal of patriotism—or love of fatherland above all—is an entirely different proposition. Despite his promise to deliver a "reflective," "thoughtful and affirming patriotism" based on "first principles" (30), we end up instead with attacks on procedural liberalism and freedom of expression and an unconditional privileging of what D'Souza argues is the Constitution's foundation in property rights.[4] Equally defining for D'Souza are the prerogatives of might that unfettered accumulation delivers to whichever party garners the greatest wealth. In this sense, D'Souza's assertions are in keeping with the current assertion of American unilateralism based on naked power.

Despite the urgent need for a new politics of multilateralism in an era of globalization and international terrorism, the world watches the American Right—most notably from within the Bush administration—vigorously assert the prerogatives of might in a demonstration of unilateralism grounded in nationalism and militarism. The administration's obsession with a "preemptive" war on Iraq dramatically illustrates the shift. As Philip Golub of the Institute of European Studies in Paris has observed:

> The "operational response" to 9/11 has been accompanied by systematic unilateralism in U.S. foreign policy, that is the single minded pursuit of narrowly defined American national interests, and a complete disregard for the concerns and interests of other members of the international community, including the U.S.'s historic allies in Europe. . . . In effect, the U.S. has abandoned multilateralism and law, that is institutionalized cooperation, or "soft" forms of global governance, in favor of purely coercive methods of management of the world system.[5]

This shift in foreign policy under the Bush administration has its domestic and ideological counterparts as well.[6] And D'Souza does his best in this work to construct a new definition of American patriotism suited for the era. But just as the new Bush doctrine of American unilateralism ultimately rests on the use of force in the face of international law, D'Souza's claim for American moral and cultural superiority is possible only by way of willful, ad hoc assertion in the face of established standards of reason. Little in these five chapters can possibly fit together in any reasonable philosophical frame. Indeed, D'Souza's "talents" as a polemicist have always dominated anything like a theoretically cogent argument. This is not D'Souza's problem alone but the problem of American conservatism generally, with its two internal and contradictory impulses—one of attachments to religion, the traditional family, and virtue; and one of attachments to the market, individualism, and antistatism.[7]

Accordingly, there is constant praise of capitalism as a system of merit and progress, but there are also episodic and histrionic indictments of the widespread decline in respect for external moral authority (i.e., God). D'Souza's Herculean task in this book is to simultaneously hold the United States up as a model while diagnosing its serious moral decline. More challenging is his task of distracting readers from the spectacle of corporate dominance that marks our era and of finding a convincing "other" to blame the moral decline on; after all, corporate America doesn't have an ethics problem, does it? How he meets this challenge is classic D'Souza.

America's "moral" decline, by the way, is relevant to a discussion of global terrorism because, D'Souza reveals, the real Achilles' heel of the otherwise impeccable "American way of life" is indeed its lack of moral virtue. This is what al Qaeda insightfully identifies, and so should the rest of us, if we know what's good for us. Of course, some groups in America are more responsible for this decline than others—later, I discuss D'Souza's scapegoating of African Americans, liberals, and the Left. But how is D'Souza going to square his beloved capitalism with the loss of morality in American life? What follows is the magic of D'Souza's ipso facto, *ala-kazam* philosophical reasoning. With a wave of the wand, D'Souza can make claims that range from the preposterous to the outrageous. Examples include: Nietzsche is a liberal and Francis Fanon is, literally, the Western intellectual behind Osama bin Laden; the three-fifths compromise was a favor to black Americans; and Jean-Jacques Rousseau—yes, Rousseau—is the real culprit behind the "torment and division" in contemporary American society.[8] Such panache characterizes the broader argument as well—and all of it is equally forced.

How the West Won

What is revealed almost immediately in this book is its hypernational framework. In these chapters, D'Souza attempts to place the United States on such hallowed ground that its actions, domestic and international, are always justifiable—unless, of course, they are the result of liberal policies. The pedestal is provided by D'Souza's inventive and incredible narrative in which all civilizational developments are credited to the United States and, tautologically, the United States is the most civilized nation on earth. It is a cartoonish world in which Europe, once past its colonizing period, simply does not exist and every developing nation is depicted as either hopelessly mired in barbarism or desperate to be like "us." The only redeemable developing nations are those on which European colonialism has left its indelible marks—like D'Souza's own India, of course.

It is actually creepy the way the terms *the West* and *America* are interchanged throughout the book. D'Souza's privileging of America as the ultimate expression of the Western tradition serves as both claim and defense. But what characterizes this thing called the West, which D'Souza demands that America represents and therefore deserves our lives to defend? The Western tradition turns out to be valuable not because of the contribution of Enlightenment ideals per se; nor is it the political embodiment of those ideals in constitutionalism and the rule of law. No, instead, D'Souza casts the Western tradition in less expansive terms that—it should come as no surprise—look a lot like the principles of realpolitik, only with a dollop of God on the side.

D'Souza's defense of the West/America begins with a new version of the history of civilization. It is a story in which he concedes that the West/America isn't the only one to contribute to civilization; it's just that America does civilization better than anyone else. D'Souza's narrative on pages 42–45 pays a kind of lip service to what classicist Martin Bernal, in his two-volume study *Black Athena*, has termed the Afro-Asiatic roots of Western culture (a work I'm betting D'Souza has not bothered to look at). Still, D'Souza's strategy is to claim all credit for the "victors" of history and, it follows, to enshrine that victory as moral. Despite their early developments, Asia, Africa, and Latin America just didn't have what it takes to become really civilized. He explains: "civilizational development does not always go to the group that invents things. It frequently goes to the people who are able to take the inventions and run with them" (51). Indeed, it is Western ingenuity—and America as the highest expression of that can-do spirit—that ultimately packaged the "inventions" in the winning combination: science, democracy, and capitalism. This recipe for civilization triumphs, D'Souza suggests, because science, democracy, and capitalism each reflect a natural and universal human impulse—the desire to inquire, the desire to be heard, and the desire to barter (?). And what scholarly evidence for this set of naturalist claims does D'Souza offer? Of course, none. The only justification is yet another tautological reference, but this time he manages to fit God into the otherwise secular-sounding formula: You see, the Judeo-Christian tradition is the only tradition to grasp the universality of these three natural impulses, which ipso facto explains why wherever there was Christianity, there arose civilization.

In an effort to give some intellectual "credibility" to this silly justification of American hegemony, D'Souza relies on Francis Fukuyama's Hegelian-like end-of-history thesis. Although Hegel's philosophy of history was premised on a dialectical unfolding of "world spirit," which, he argued, came to "rest" in the German state, it is a claim that admits teleological closure based on a metaphysic. In contrast, Fukuyama's end of history is justified only by the "last man standing" post–cold war reality. More important, as with any philosophy of history, the horizon of possibilities—future invention, creative progress, and freedom itself—is eclipsed in the name of the status quo. Hegel's philosophy of history denies freedom's future possibilities in philosophical terms, but the damage it could have inflicted as public or state ideology was constrained by Germany's contestable military power. Whereas the German state of 1830 (and subsequent regimes) was militarily disposed, there were other nation-states that could and did contest any purported universality and future efforts to control the world. But in our context, Fukuyama and D'Souza are rationalizing an empire that really has no match, no genuine military competitor, and one that possesses every ability to impose its will—nuclear or otherwise—on the entire planet. End-of-history premises like theirs in today's context rationalize a whole host of chauvinist claims and iron-fisted forays abroad—and they threaten worse. Given this, D'Souza's simpleminded conclusions are really more dangerous than silly:

> In Fukuyama's view, history had ended, not in the sense that important things would cease to happen, but in the sense that the grand ideological conflicts of the past had been forever settled. Of course, the pace of liberalization would vary, but the outcome was inevitable. The destiny of *Homo sapiens* had been resolved. We are headed for what may be termed Planet America. (13–14)

Planet America? Lest we be demurred by D'Souza's suggestion a few paragraphs later that confidence in the Planet America thesis has been shaken recently by the realization that there are "people, especially in the Muslim world that apparently hate our guts and want to wipe us off the face us the earth" (14), he assures us by page 175 that Planet America remains uncontested: "Moreover, given the things that people want, it is entirely reasonable to assert that some cultures (say, capitalist cultures with a Protestant heritage) are superior to other cultures (say, African socialist regimes or Islamic theocracies) in achieving these shared common objectives."

Just as D'Souza loads our choices here, his entire argument is loaded with the preordained conclusion that the world is unable to achieve higher standards for human organization than those found in the American state. That conclusion ultimately permits the United States to impose and defend its interests however and wherever it sees fit.

One Book for the Price of Two

D'Souza's self-serving and cockeyed attempts at constructing a new patriotism are only part of the problem with this text. After the first chapter, the book lapses into old, stale material. There are the all-too-familiar and vitriolic attacks on "multiculturalism" throughout. It is as if D'Souza, having scored big with the PC assault in 1991, just can't stop running the same play. This continued assault seems particularly gratuitous given the fact that the fictionalized multiculturalists he's been shadowboxing for ten years now don't even have a shadow anymore. Since Reagan, the Right in America has been taking, holding, and conquering new ground almost without pause. And it's not as if the Democrats' move-to-the-right strategy hasn't helped them. Hasn't D'Souza noticed that all the actually existing liberals are now, officially, demolished and in total disarray? Especially after the last two election rounds? As for the Left, access to power has long been severed. Let's be honest here: the Right has the presidency, both chambers of Congress, and the high and most lower courts, and it is dominating in the international arena. In this sense, D'Souza reminds me of Senator Joe McCarthy. And like McCarthyism, the attack on multiculturalism was never an attack on the enemies of democracy, but an attack on democratic dissent. In that sense, even after the dissident elements have been marginalized, the chill—or confusion—requires renewal. I suppose that giving up the fight against the imaginary multiculturalists would mean giving up a whipping boy, and whipping boys are good insurance against the possibility of dissent in the future. The only other reasonable explanation is that D'Souza has no new cash-worthy ideas.

Once again, in *What's So Great* we are subjected to a full round of multicultural bashing. Whereas D'Souza has always had a bad habit of beginning his arguments with false propositions—usually in the form of hyperbolic characterizations of American liberals and the Left (and black Americans in general)—this time the multiculturalist argument is so stretched and extreme that, hopefully, the excess itself will be enough to put this dead horse to rest. First, D'Souza repeats the same definition of multiculturalism that has been loaded from the start; he insists that the multiculturalists contend that "all cultures are equal" and therefore are guilty of cultural relativism. On both counts D'Souza has always been wrong. To the degree that multiculturalism is an actual paradigm, the notion of respect for the genuine contributions of other cultures has never amounted to a claim of cultural relativism. Second, D'Souza yet again claims that this nonexistent movement of "cultural relativists" is the intellectual paradigm of choice among American liberals and the Left—who also happen to dominate college faculties and public education. The idea that cultural relativism is the dominant intellectual paradigm in postsecondary humanities and social science curriculum or that it is dominant in American primary and secondary public education is utter nonsense. It is a charge he has never mustered any actual evidence to support and therefore requires no detailed refutation. It is he who owns the burden of proof. The purported damage being caused by this fictional movement is, therefore, even harder to take seriously.

Still, D'Souza has managed to outdo his own past definitions of multicultural crimes. In this book, what was first identified as a threat to the freedom of expression of conservative college students on American campuses in the 1980s turns out to be a domestic threat to American security likened to the threat of the militant Islamists of September 11. This smearing is accomplished by placing all critics of America in the same category. (The chapter in which most of the smearing occurs is titled "Why They Hate Us: America and Its Enemies.") This attempt to liken American intellectuals to Islamic terrorists is performed explicitly and by inference. For example, after quoting one critic of American military interventions abroad, D'Souza quips: "Could bin Laden have put it better?"[9] More explicitly, D'Souza labels all critics of U.S. policy—whether reasoned or extreme—the "Blame America First" crowd: "The moral superiority of America is vehemently denied in three camps: among leftist intellectuals, especially in Europe and the Third Word; among American multiculturalists; and among Islamic Fundamentalists" (170).

But who are the American multiculturalists that he tars with the bin Laden perspective? Among the many he targets are Howard Zinn, Barbara Ehrenreich, Noam Chomsky, and "literary critic [sic] Cornel West"—all of whom are also charged with the high crime of "cultural relativism." D'Souza's effort here to tar some of America's best-known left intellectuals with the terror of September 11 ranks among his lowest and most provocative slurs to date. To suggest affinities of any sort between these intellectuals and those who embraced the September 11 attacks on innocent U.S. civilians shows a total lack of scruples. And, as a matter of some significance, not one person on this list could ever conceivably be labeled a cultural relativist. D'Souza's claim to the contrary is either simply idiotic or knowingly dishonest. This kind of unprincipled baiting might be tolerated in a college newspaper such as the right-wing *Dartmouth Review* (where D'Souza picked up his political panache), but it is entirely beneath anyone with the title "scholar."

And so goes the tone in the rest of *What's So Great*. Old arguments and insults are dressed up for the post–September 11 climate. There is nothing new here except the opportunism D'Souza displays in hawking his old stuff in the midst of a crisis. To be fair, there is the new twist of taking up the "identity" of immigrant as credentials to speak to the virtues of American life—a profound irony, given his relentless denouncements of the politics of identity. But much of the remaining chapters is just a rehash of D'Souza's past three books: all the passages about the evils of multiculturalism *(Illiberal Education)*, all the references in chapters 3 and 6 to how technocapitalism produces "mass affluence" *(Virtues of Prosperity)*, and the tirades against black families, black intellectuals, black SAT takers, and black activists in combination with the obligatory attacks on left intellectuals and activists *(Illiberal Education* and *The End of Racism)* are all here and just as overwrought as they were the first, second, and third times around.

Indeed, African Americans, for whom D'Souza has always reserved his most puerile and vindictive rhetoric, receive the same shameful treatment here as they did in D'Souza's *The End of Racism*. There, he argued that given the state of black culture in America today, private individuals are rational to discriminate. The law should permit such discrimination—and in order to accomplish that, D'Souza calls for the repeal of the Civil Rights Act of 1964. Other examples of D'Souza's race-baiting commentary include his response to the idea that lower-income African Americans could benefit from federal jobs and recruitment in the private sector: "it seems unrealistic, bordering on the surreal, to imagine underclass blacks with their gold chains, limping walk, obscene language and arsenal of weapons doing nine-to-five jobs at Procter and Gamble or the State Department."[10] D'Souza's commentary on African Americans can be so inflammatory and derogatory that it led black conservative Glenn Loury to resign from the American Enterprise Institute, where D'Souza was on staff at the time.[11] But instead of an admonishment, D'Souza's career took an upward turn when he was promoted to the far more prestigious Hoover Institute. No wonder he repeats himself; it works.

The only remaining section of the book that actually seems "new" is D'Souza's "reading" of Rousseau in chapter 5, titled "When Virtue Loses All Her Loveliness." Though it is new, I must say that I almost felt embarrassed for D'Souza after reading it. D'Souza somehow manages to blame (credit?) the 1960s rebellions on Rousseau. With Marx seemingly out of the picture, it is obviously difficult for the Right to find a major thinker to revile—let alone one who can be linked to the imaginary domestic assaults on Western civilization currently being waged by the multiculturalists. But this is a stretch beyond stretches, and one that D'Souza's painfully amateurish "interpretation" of Rousseau (and total ignorance about the actual movements of the 1960s) makes even more ridiculous. Here Rousseau is turned into a navel-gazing, New Age hippie concerned not with virtue, law, community, and limits but with the opposite—atomistic, self-referential authenticity. Though D'Souza grounds this claim in a discussion of Rousseau's *Confessions,* he does so in total disregard of those works that were in fact influential: *The Discourses* and, most important, *The Social Contract.* But still, the idea that the mass movements for civil rights, peace, and women's rights were actually influenced by Rousseau, and that this influence is evident in the American cultural decline in obedience to external moral authority, is, to say the least, inventive. D'Souza is weakest when he tries to act like an intellectual; his efforts here demonstrate pointedly that he should stick with the street-corner polemics he is so good at, or go to graduate school.

What is even more annoying is that I had to read this stuff twice, since this is one of those many verbatim sections that *What's So Great* and *Letters to a Young Conservative* share. One of the more minor consequences of D'Souza's own pilfering is that such moments make for a rather awkward transition between books.

LETTERS TO A YOUNG CONSERVATIVE: DÉJÀ VU ALL OVER AGAIN

I am far more comfortable with D'Souza in his role as a seasoned polemicist and right-wing prankster giving advice to undergraduates (after all, this is at least a more honest description) than in his grandiose role as scholar. At the same time, *Letters to a Young Conservative* reflects the same choplogic of a politico with little respect for the responsibilities of reasonableness that we find in his other work. The format of the book is a series of "personal" letters from D'Souza to a fictional but beleaguered campus conservative. It is a fairly self-congratulatory setup in which D'Souza gets to talk a lot about himself, his family, his friends, his great pranks, his promotions, and his courageous choice to become a writer and not go to business school (most of which we also get to read about in *What's So Great*). But there is greater honesty and even less couching of his prejudices here than in his other titles. There are no scholarly pretensions—no footnotes, no studies cited, and no grand argument. One might even call it refreshing, given the subterfuge of credibility D'Souza yearns for elsewhere. This is pure, unadulterated polemics often delivered to the imaginary "Chris" in the form of "how-to" advice; D'Souza suggests that Chris develop a guerrilla strategy just as he and his pals at Dartmouth did in the 1980s:

> Where to start? I don't know. Conduct a survey to find out how many professors in the religion department believe in God. Distribute a pamphlet titled "Feminist Thought" that is made up of blank pages. Establish a Society for Creative Homophobia. Prepare a freshman course guide that lists your college's best, and worst professors. Publish Maya Angelou's poems alongside a bunch of meaningless doggerel and see whether anyone can tell the difference. Put a picture of death-row inmate Mumia Abu-Jamal on your website and instruct people who think he deserves capital punishment to click a button and execute him online. (36)

This is the real D'Souza, who reminds us less of the wide-eyed Jesuit-trained schoolboy who arrived in America in 1978 and more of a southern posse leader on his way to an execution. Perhaps D'Souza's parents were right to have worried about what America would do to their boy.

The book contains thirty-one letters whose titles include "Pig Wrestling at Dartmouth," "Fighting Political Correctness," "How Reagan Outsmarted the Liberals," "How Affirmative Action Hurts Blacks," "More Guns, Less Crime," "How to Harpoon a Liberal," "Against Gay Marriage," and "Why Liberals Hate America." As you might guess, though more brash in tone, the fare is not new. It reads like a condensed version of D'Souza's most provocative charges: On why gay men shouldn't marry: because "marriage isn't what civilizes men, women do." On the quality of immigrants coming to America today: "Immigrants from Thailand are, in general, greater assets to America than immigrants from Tijuana." On the self-esteem of black males: "Self-esteem in these students is generated by factors unrelated to studies, such as the ability to beat up other students or a high estimation of one's sexual prowess." On U.S. support for Somoza, Pinochet, Marcos, and the Shah: "This support is fully justified when we consider [that] the operating principle of American foreign policy . . . is the doctrine of the lesser evil." Yes, Dinesh, that worked well with the Taliban, too.

The list goes on, and the great temptation for critics is to try to refute his more outrageous and provocative comments. But in this book there are so many that one could spend many more pages than D'Souza has written in an effort to set the record straight (after all, argument always takes longer than assertion). But I am not interested in debating D'Souza in an effort to show why he is manipulative and racist in his handling of SAT data by race, ethnicity, and class; or how his reading of the three-fifths compromise (and much of what he says about the founding fathers) is not only factually incorrect but also excruciatingly twisted so as to justify the unjustifiable—slavery; or why his refusal to acknowledge corporate responsibility for widespread environmental damage is a cruel gift to his seven-year-old daughter; or why he should be embarrassed to put into print statements such as, "ordinary people from Asia, Africa and Latin America are conspicuously absent from demonstrations against globalization." It is an endless and largely futile thing to argue with unreasonableness. (Instead, see the appendix of this chapter for an example of passages that I found particularly annoying.)

To conclude, D'Souza's latest two titles testify to his salesmanship, not scholarship. His ability to produce at the rate he has is a result of his knack for selling the same couple of manuscripts over and over again, in varying combinations. And the products he hawks have been successful in America not because America is a meritocratic nation. D'Souza has been anointed an intellectual by a commercial culture interested only in what sells. D'Souza's media success is related to his shock value, which now dominates the pop-culture industries. His mean-spiritedness and chauvinism also enjoy a political context backed by a party-of-the-same now controlling all levers of institutional power. If D'Souza's "U.S. as moral and cultural superior" caricature was hard to square before, his own slacking in these two books further discredits the claim. One can only wonder why the Hoover Institution keeps him on.

APPENDIX

Besides their obvious deficiencies as credible arguments, each of the passages excerpted below also serves to demonstrate D'Souza's resale of a previous product. Following each passage is the related passage as it appeared in *What's So Great*. This will give you a taste of D'Souza's standards for scholarship—my intention being only to let D'Souza's work speak for itself.

On the three-fifths compromise, and on the question of whether the Constitution of 1789 was racist:

> But the charge is totally false. The notorious three-fifths clause of the Constitution makes no denial of the equal worth of African-American. Indeed, it has nothing to say about the intrinsic worth of any group. The clause arose in the context of a debate between the northern states and the southern states over the issue of political representation.
>
> The pro-slavery South wanted to count blacks as whole persons to increase its political power. The North wanted blacks to count as nothing, not for purposes of rejecting their humanity but to preserve and strengthen the anti-slavery majority in Congress. It was a northerner, James Wilson of Pennsylvania who proposed the three-fifths compromise.
>
> The effect of the compromise was to limit the South's political representation and thus its ability to protect slavery. Frederick Douglass, the black abolitionist, understood this. He praised the three-fifths clause as a "down right disability laid upon the slave holding states" that deprived them of "two-fifths of their natural basis of representation." So the notion that the three-fifths clause demonstrates the racism of the American Constitution is both wrong and unfair. (*Letters to a Young Conservative*, 146)

> Are the founders guilty as alleged? Let us consider the evidence fairly beginning with the notorious three-fifths clause to which [John Hope] Franklin alludes. To the modern mind, this is one of the most troubling pieces of evidence against the founders. And yet it should not be, because the clause itself has nothing to say about the intrinsic worth of blacks.
>
> The origins of the clause are to be found in the debate between the northern states and the southern states over the issue of political representation. The South wanted to count blacks as a whole person, in order to increase their political power. The North wanted blacks to count for nothing—not for the purpose of rejecting their humanity but in order to preserve and strengthen the anti-slavery majority in Congress. It was not a pro-slavery southerner, but an anti-slavery northerner James Wilson of Pennsylvania who proposed the three-fifths compromise. The effect was to limit the South's political representation and its ability to protect the institution of slavery. Frederick Douglass understood this: he called the three-fifths "a downright disability laid upon the slave-holding states" which deprived them of "two-fifths of their natural basis of representation." So a provision in the Constitution that was antislavery and pro-black in intent as well as

HOW DINESH GETS OVER 113

effect is today cited to prove that the American founders championed the cause of racist oppression. (*What's So Great*, 109–10)

On feminism:

> Then something happened that pushed women into the male sphere and career women aspired to compete effectively with men for the most lucrative rewards of the male sphere. According to feminists, the large-scale movement of women into the workforce was the consequence of the great feminist revolution that stormed the barricades of the patriarchy and won a glorious victory, although the battle is ongoing. This is a lovely fairy tale, but when exactly did the battle occur? . . .
>
> Let us put this buncombe aside and talk a little sense. Technology not feminism paved the way for mass female entry into the workforce. The vacuum cleaner, the forklift and the birth-control pill had far more to do with this than all the writings of Betty Friedan and all the press releases put out by the National Organization for Women. Think about this: until a few decades ago housework was a full time occupation. Cooking alone took several hours. The vacuum, the microwave oven and the dishwasher changed that. Until recently work outside the home was harsh and physically demanding. Forklifts and other machines have reduced the need for human muscle. Finally, before the invention of the pill, women could not effectively control their reproduction and therefore, for most women, the question of not having a full-time career simply did not arise. (*Letters to a Young Conservative*, 104–5)

> Technology has also helped to change women's roles and thus destabilize traditional "family values." Here the great catalyst of social transformation was the mass movement of women into the workplace. Feminists fought for women's right to have careers, but their success was made possible by the pill, the vacuum cleaner, and the forklift. Think about this: only a few decades ago, housework was a full time occupation—cooking and cleaning took up virtually the whole day. The vacuum cleaner and other domestic appliances changed all that. Until recently, work outside the home was harsh and physically demanding. Forklifts and other machines have reduced the need for human muscle. Finally, before the invention of the pill, women could not effectively control their reproduction, and therefore, for most women, the question of having a full-time career simply did not arise. (*What's So Great*, 138–39)

On Rousseau:

> The second liberal revolution in occurred in the 1960's. Its watchword was liberation and its greatest prophet was Jean Jacques Rousseau. Before the

1960's most Americans believed in a universal moral order that is external to us, that makes demands on us. Our obligation was to conform to that moral order. Earlier generations right up to the "greatest generation" of World War II took for granted this moral order and its commandments: work hard and try to better yourself, be faithful to your spouse, go when your country calls and so on.

But beginning in the sixties, several factions—the antiwar movement, the feminist movement, and the gay activist movement, and so on—attacked that moral consensus as narrow and oppressive. They fought for a new ethic that would be based not on external authority but on sovereignty of the inner self. This is the novel idea that received its most powerful expression in Rousseau's writing. To the American list of freedoms, Rousseau added a new one: inner freedom or moral freedom. Rousseau argues that we make major decisions by digging deep within ourselves and listening to the voice of nature. This is the idea of being "true to yourself." It is the new liberal morality. (*Letters to a Young Conservative*, 4)

The 1960's & 1970's witnessed a moral revolution in the United States in which the idea of freedom was extended beyond anything the American founders envisioned. The change can be described in this way. The American founders set up a regime dedicated to three types of freedom—economic freedom, political freedom and freedom of speech and religion—so that peopl\e could pursue happiness, or what we call the American dream.

But this notion of freedom was radicalized in the 1960's. The change was brought about by the "counter-culture," the melange of anti-war activists, feminists, sexual revolutionaries, freedom riders, hippies, druggies, nudists and vegetarians. Rebels they all were and bohemians of one sort or another. The great thinker who stood behind them, the philosopher of bohemia was Rousseau. . . . The counter-culture did not reject morality; it was passionately concerned with morality. But it substituted Rousseau's conception of the inner compass for the old rules of obligation. Getting in touch with one's own feelings and being true to oneself were now more important than conforming to the preexisting moral consensus of society. (*What's So Great*, 140, 145)

NOTES

1. D'Souza's "political" career began under the tutelage of English professor Jeffrey Hart of Dartmouth College, who happened to be a senior editor at the *National Review*. It was Hart's contacts that landed D'Souza a post at the *Review* after his graduation. After a short stint there, D'Souza went into the Reagan White House for two years, then on to the American Enterprise Institute from 1989 until 2001, followed by his most recent post at Hoover.

2. Of course, something like a rehash can be tolerated under academic standards. Frequently a seminar paper turns into a dissertation chapter, which is then reframed as a journal article, which might eventually appear as a chapter in a full-length book. But when published material is republished, standards require a note of any previous publication.
3. Liz McGuire and D'Souza's publicist at Basic, Johanna Pinsker, declined comment when contacted, except to indicate that they were not aware of previously published material in the text.
4. D'Souza makes the broad claim that "the American system is founded on property rights and trade, and *The Federalist* tells us that the protection of the unequal faculties of obtaining property is 'the first object of government'" (90).
5. For Golub's complete analysis, see "From Neo-Wilsonian to Militarism: Shifting Patterns of U.S. Governance," in *Global Dialogue* (Paris: 2003); the quotation cited here is from the unpublished English translation.
6. The now infamous Patriot Act of 2002, with its excessive expansion of government surveillance power into the lives of private citizens who are considered "suspicious," is yet another example of how the new "patriotism" operates.
7. For a concise and clear discussion of the conservative tradition and its challenges in the American context, see Stephen Eric Bronner, "The Conservative Disposition: Custom, Stability, Markets," in *Ideas in Action: Political Tradition in the Twentieth Century* (Lanham, Md.: Rowman and Littlefield, 1999).
8. For a more detailed discussion on this embarrassing reading of Rousseau, see the section of this chapter titled "One Book for the Price of Two."
9. "If what these people say is true, then America should be destroyed" (26).
10. Quoted in Michael Berube, "Extreme Prejudice," *Transition* 69 (1996): 93.
11. In particular, Loury condemned the phrasing D'Souza chose to dramatize white reaction to blacks' IQ scores: "We can almost hear the roar of white supremacists. Forget about racism and discrimination. These people are naturally stupid" (PBS transcript, *Think Tank,* "The End of Racism—Part I").

A Mills Revival?

Stanley Aronowitz

Perhaps you know Foucault's remark that despite the torrent of criticism directed against Hegel's philosophical system, "Hegel prowls through the twentieth century." Consigned to a kind of academic purgatory for the last three decades of the twentieth century, at a time when social theory migrated from the social sciences, obsessed with case studies and social "problems," to literature and philosophy, where he was rarely discussed and almost never cited, C. Wright Mills was an absent presence. All sociologists, and most people in other social scientific disciplines, knew his name and, in their political unconscious, recognized his salience, but they were deterred by fear and careerism from following his path as a public political intellectual. Yet in the wake of scandals involving leading corporations and their chief executive and chief financial officers, which have become daily fare even in the mainstream media, and the hegemony of corporate capital over the American state, which was widely reported in the press and television with unembarrassed approbation, Mills's work is experiencing a small but pronounced revival. Although his name rarely appears on the reading lists of fashionable graduate courses in social and cultural theory, the republication of four of his major books, with new introductions by historian Nelson Lichtenstein *(The New Men of Power)*, social critic Russell Jacoby *(White Collar)*, political theorist Alan Wolfe *(The Power Elite)*, and sociologist Todd Gitlin *(The Sociological Imagination)*, is likely to aid in exposing his work to students and younger faculty.

For some, Mills does not qualify in this era when social and cultural theory is dominated by European influences. Except for his dissertation *Sociology and Pragmatism,* he rarely engaged in philosophical speculation; more to the point, apart from some essays, in only one major instance, *Character and Social Structure,* did he address the "meta" questions such as method or the underlying presuppositions of theorizing. Marxists criticize the lack, even disdain, of "class analysis" in his work; indeed, the commentaries in his collection of annotated readings, *The Marxists,* constitute both an appreciation and an unsystematic critique of Marx and Marxism. And social historians, most of them informed by class and class struggle, object to his focus on the study of elites rather than popular expressions from below, even within social movements.

Yet Mills remains a model for those who wish to become intellectuals: based on the evidence of his massive output in twenty-three years of publication, he was the antithesis of the specialist or the expert. When most in the human sciences followed the path of least resistance by writing the same articles and books over and over, Mills ranged widely over historical, cultural, political, social, and psychological domains. He was interested in the labor and radical movements and wrote extensively on them; as a close student of Max Weber, he made some of the most trenchant critiques of bureaucracy; he was among the leading postwar critics of the emergent mass culture and the mass communications media; and, despite its ostensibly introductory tone, *The Sociological Imagination* may be America's best contribution to the ongoing debate about the relationship of scholarship to social commitment, a debate that has animated literary as well as social science circles for decades.

His literary executor and biographer, Irving Louis Horowitz, turned against him, for the most part, so the biography tells us more about the author than about Mills. Other book-length treatments are sympathetic but limited and, to a large extent, dated. With the partial exception of some excellent dissertations and master's theses, notably Tom Hayden's insightful *Radical Nomad* more than forty years after Mills's death, Mills awaits a major critical study, not to mention a full-length biography.

We may speculate that among putative readers his contemporaneity, the sharp focus on the United States and its traditions, and, most of all, his annoying habit of writing plainly (substituting vernacular expressions for scientific terms) turned away some who can respect only writers who invent neologisms and whose simple thoughts require complex syntax. But at a moment when these fashions have lost some of their luster, those who yearn for substance as well as style may return with pleasure to the dark ruminations of C. Wright Mills.

C. WRIGHT MILLS IS EXEMPLARY OF a vanishing breed in American life: the public political intellectual who, despite his grating message, often received a hearing in the mainstream media. For almost fifteen years, beginning with the publication of *The New Men of Power* in 1948 and ending with his untimely death in 1962, at age forty-six, Mills was among America's best-known social scientists and social critics. During the late 1940s and 1950s he published three books that constitute a theory and description of the post–World War II American social structure. His *Sociological Imagination* remains widely read in college classrooms, both for its attempt to provide a socially committed introduction to the discipline and for its fierce critique of the prevailing tendencies in American sociology, what Mills calls "Grand Theory" and "Abstracted Empiricism." The grand theorist's scope is much too wide to yield practical and theoretical insight. And Mills criticizes the legions of abstracted empiricists who, in the service of incrementally accumulated verifiable scientific knowledge, confine themselves to producing small-scale investigations. Together with his collaborator and mentor, Hans Gerth, he edited one of the earliest and best collections in English translation of Max Weber's essays. *Character and Social Structure* (1954), written with Gerth, is an unjustly neglected work and may be considered Mills's premier work of social theory. This book elaborates what I claim was the "scaffolding" on which he hung his major works of middle-range theory, especially the trilogy. In fact, it is difficult to fully comprehend the harsh critiques of *Sociological Imagination* and Mills's method without the elaborated theoretical framework of *Character*.

Though not exactly a household name, he was widely known among the politically active population and among circles of academic and independent intellectuals. Unlike many public intellectuals, he was neither a servant nor a supplicant of power but, in the sense of the seventeenth-century English radical, was a "ranter"; in American terms, he was a Paul Revere whose job it was to sound the alarm. Indeed, some of his writings recall the pamphlets of the decades of the American Revolution, when numerous and often anonymous writers addressed the "publick" of small farmers and artisans as much as those holding political and economic power. Much of his later writing may be compared with that of turn-of-the-twentieth-century populist and socialist pamphleteers, whose aim was to simultaneously educate and arouse workers and farmers to the evils of corporate power.

Yet in his most fertile period of intellectual work—the decade and a half ending with the publication of *The Sociological Imagination* (1959)— with the possible exception of *The Power Elite,* Mills hardly expected to reach a popular audience, let alone the mass public. Nevertheless, he always attempted to reach out to a wider public than did his fellow academics, even when he was formulating new theories, let alone engaging in public criticism. But Mills's intention was entirely subversive of contemporary mainstream social science, especially the notion that intellectuals should remain neutral observers of economic, political, and social life. Although he performed his fair share of funded research—notably his study of Puerto Rico and the collective portraits of characteristic social types—most of his writing is addressed to potential and actual political publics. Following Marx and Weber, who at the end of his life was a major contributor in shaping the moral and legal framework of the Weimar Republic, Mills held that intellectuals and their ideas were embedded in the social antagonisms and struggles of their own time; they bring to their analysis a definite standpoint, whether or not they are prepared to acknowledge it.

Yet Mills adhered to none of the mainstream parties nor to those on the fringes of mainstream politics. Although he was a figure of his own time (his main work was done in the 1940s and 1950s, when issues of sex, gender, and ecology were barely blips on the screen), his position was congenitally critical—of the Right, conservatives, liberals, the relatively tiny parties of the Left, and especially members of his own shrinking group, the independent leftists. Like one of his heroes, the economist and social theorist Thorstein Veblen, himself a pariah in his chosen discipline, Mills was (to paraphrase a famous aphorism of Marx) "in but not of" the academy, insofar as he refused the distinction between scholarship and partisanship. But unlike Veblen, whose alienation from conventional economics was almost total, Mills was, for most of his professional career, a sociologist in his heart as much as in his mind. The rhetoric and the methods embodied in his books on American social structure—*The New Men of Power, White Collar,* and *The Power Elite*—are firmly rooted in the perspectives of mainstream American sociology at the end of the war. These perspectives owed as much to the methodological precepts of Emile Durkheim as they did to the critical theory of Karl Marx and Max Weber. Using many of the tools of conventional social inquiry—surveys, interviews, data analysis, charts included—Mills takes pains to stay close to the "data" until the concluding chapters.

But what distinguishes Mills from mainstream sociology—and from Weber, with whom he shares a considerable portion of his intellectual outlook—is the standpoint of radical social change, not of fashionable sociological neutrality. At the height of the cold war and in the midst of the so-called McCarthy era, he fearlessly named capitalism as the system of domination from within one of its intellectual bastions, Columbia University, and distanced himself from ex-radicals among his colleagues who were busy "choosing the West," otherwise giving aid and comfort to the witch hunters, or neutering themselves by hiding behind the ideology of value-free scholarship. Anti-Stalinist to the core, toward the end of his life he was, nevertheless, accused of pro-Communist sympathies for his unsparing criticism of the militarization of America and his spirited defense of the Cuban revolution.

In light of his later writings—which, to say the least, held out little hope for radical social change in the United States—*The New Men of Power,* Mills's first major work, occupies a singular place in the Mills corpus. Written on the heels of the veritable general strike of industrial workers in 1946, and the conservative counterattack the following year embedded in the Taft-Hartley amendments to the Labor Relations Act, the study of America's labor leaders argues that, for the first time in history, the labor movement, having shown its capacity to shape the political economy, possessed the practical requisites to become a major actor in American politics as well. But as both "an army general and a contractor of labor," a "machine politician" and the head of a "social movement," the labor leader occupies contradictory space. By 1948, the year of publication of the first edition of *The New Men of Power,* a powerful conservative force, buoyed by American capitalism's unparalleled global dominance, was arrayed against labor's recently acquired power and, according to Mills, had no intention of yielding more ground without an all-out industrial and political war. Yet he found union leaders curiously unprepared for the struggle. Even as their cause was being abandoned by liberal allies and belittled and besmirched by their natural enemies among the corporations and their ideological mouthpieces—the right-wing intellectuals and conservative politicians—union leaders remained faithful to the Democratic Party and to the New Deal, which was rapidly fading into history. Mills and his collaborator, Helen Schneider, found that the concept that working people needed a labor party to truly represent their political interests had declined from the perspective of most labor leaders, whereas a decade earlier, at the apex of industrial unionism, a majority had favored the formation of such a party, despite their expedient support of the Democrats.

You might say that Mills's notion of power owes much to Machiavelli's *The Prince*. Just as Machiavelli reminds the prince that the old rules of the feudal oligarchy no longer suffice to retain power, and that a public has formed that intends to call the ruler to account for his actions, in his book on the labor leaders, Mills is, at first, in dialogue with a leadership increasingly attracted to oligarchical rule and to the liberal center and whose love affair with established power has lasted to this day. His study admonishes the labor leadership to attend to the postwar shift that endangers their and their members' power. Arguing that the "main drift" is away from the collaboration between business and labor made necessary and viable by the war, he suggests that labor leaders of "great stature" must come to the fore before labor is reduced. "Now there is no war," but there is a powerful war machine and conservative reaction against labor's power at the bargaining table. "Today, knit together as they are by trade associations, the corporations steadily translate economic strength into effective and united political power. The power of the federal state has increased enormously. The state is now so big in the economy, and the power of business is so great in the state, that unions can no longer seriously expect even the traditional short-run economic gains without considering the conditions under which their demands are politically realizable." Top-down rule, which implies keeping the membership at bay, was, according to Mills, inadequate to the new situation in which a military-industrial alliance was emerging, among whose aims was to weaken and otherwise destroy the labor movement.

How to combat this drift? Mills forthrightly suggests that the labor leader become the basis for the formation of a "new power bloc." Rather than make deals on the top with powerful interests, "he will have to accumulate power from the bottom.... If the democratic power of members is to be used against the concentrated power of money, it must in some way create its own political force ... the left would create an independent labor party" based on labor's formidable economic strength. At the same time, Mills argues, it must enlarge its own base to include the "underdogs"—few of whom are in the unions. By underdogs, Mills does not mean those at the very bottom. They are, in his view, too habituated to "submission." He means the working poor, the unskilled who were largely left out of the great organizing wave of the 1930s and the war years. And he calls for the organization of elements of the new middle class and the rapidly growing white-collar strata whose potential power, he argues, will remain unrealized unless they are organized.

One may read *The New Men of Power* through a number of lenses. At minimum, it can be read as a stimulating account of the problems and prospects facing post–World War II American labor. It is descriptively comprehensive of the state of organized labor and the obstacles it faced in this period. If Mills was mistaken to believe that unions would have to become an independent political force to meet the elementary economic demands of their memberships, it may be argued that this limitation applies only to the first three decades after the war. Unions did deliver, and in some cases handsomely, to a substantial minority of the American working class. They organized neither the "underdogs" nor the new middle-class and white-collar clerical, technical, and professional workers, who were all but ignored by the postwar labor movement, but they forged a new social compact with large employers for their own members. For a third of the labor force in unions, and a much larger percentage of industrial workers, they succeeded in negotiating what may be called a "private" welfare state, huge advances in their members' standard of living, and a high degree of job security and individual protection against arbitrary discharge and other forms of discipline.

Ironically, Mills's book is far more accurate in its central prognostication of labor's decline in the years since 1973. Labor has paid a steep price for its refusal to heed Mills's admonition to forge its own power bloc. Buffeted by economic globalization, corporate mergers, the deindustrialization of vast areas of the Northeast and Midwest, and the growth of the largely nonunion South as the industrial investment of choice, many unions have despaired of making new gains and are hanging on to their declining memberships for dear life. Labor is, perhaps irreversibly, on the defensive. In this period, union density—the proportion of union members to the total workforce—has been cut in half. Collective bargaining stills occurs regularly in unionized industries and occupations, and employers still sign contracts. But the last two decades have been marked by labor's steady retreat from hard-won gains. In many instances, collective bargaining has yielded to collective begging.

Corporations and their political allies have succeeded in rolling back one of the most important features of the New Deal–era reforms: the provision of a minimum income for the long-term unemployed (pejoratively coded as "welfare" by post–New Deal politicians). Many who still collect checks are forced to work in public and private agencies for minimum wages, in some states replacing union labor. Social Security is on the block, and privatization of public goods, especially schools and health care facilities, seems to be the long-term program of conservatives and many in the liberal center.

Mills recognizes, as few labor leaders do, the importance of reaching out to the various publics that frame the political landscape. During the era of the social compact, union leaders saw little value in taking labor's case to the public during either strikes or important legislative campaigns. As junior partners of the power elite, they were often advised to keep conflicts in the "family" and rely on lobbying, influence with leading politicians through electoral support, and other traditionally elite tactics to achieve their goals. Labor leaders would rarely divulge the issues during union negotiations and the final stages of bargaining because they had agreed to a press blackout. Only as an act of desperation, when an organizing drive or a strike was in its losing stage, did some unions make public statements. Following Mills's advice, one might argue that, especially for public employees' unions and unions in major national corporations, the public is always the third party at the bargaining table, and the struggle to win it over has generally been won by management.

The ambiguity comes in when subsequent writings are considered. Discouraged by the labor movement's inability to reverse or halt the reactionary legislative and political offensive, by the early 1950s, Mills had abandoned hope that the labor movement was capable of stemming the tide of almost complete corporate capitalist domination of economic, political, and cultural life. Discussion of the labor movement's social weight is largely absent from *White Collar*, published in 1951, only three years after *The New Men of Power*. *The Power Elite*, which appeared in 1956, more or less permanently consigns organized labor to a subordinate status within the pantheon of national power. In Mills's view, the moment had come and gone when unions could even conceive of making a qualitative difference in power arrangements. Whereas in 1948 Mills's address was chiefly to the labor leaders themselves—it was both a careful sociological portrait of these new men of power and an attempted dialogue with them—the subsequent works do not have a specific labor public in mind.

It was the theory of mass society, a concept that spans radical and conservative critiques of late capitalism, that informed Mills's later pessimism. Mills was a leading figure in the sociology of mass culture and mass society that developed along several highly visible lines in the 1940s and 1950s. He observed the increasing homogenization of American culture and brilliantly linked some of its more egregious features to the decline of the democratic public. Although his rhetoric was distinctly in the American vein, his views paralleled, and were crucially influenced by, those of Theodor Adorno, Max Horkheimer, and Herbert Marcuse, the leading theorists of the Frankfurt school. There is little evidence that he was similarly impressed by psychoanalysis, but like them, he linked cultural "massification" to mounting political conformity associated with the emergence of fascism and other authoritarian movements in nearly all advanced industrial societies.

This pioneering study of the emergence of the middle class of salaried professional, technical, and clerical employees situates the spread of mass culture after World War I to their growing significance in advanced industrial societies. Consistent with Mills's emerging obsession with questions of political and social power and of the prospects for radical social transformation, *White Collar* may be read not only as a traditional sociological analysis of the occupational situation of the "new" middle class but also as an assessment of its social psychology. The book opens with an obituary of the "old" middle class—farmers, small merchants, and manufacturers—perhaps the leading class of the eighteenth century and the first half of the nineteenth century. The transformation of property from a welter of small, independent producers and merchants to the large concentrations of capital that marked the second half of the nineteenth century reduced the economic and political influence of the old middle class to the middle levels of power, mostly in local communities. The functions of administration, sales, and distribution grew faster than manufacturing, but even in production industries, the traditional blue-collar industrial workforce expanded more slowly than the bureaucracies of the various strata of white-collar employees.

By World War I, the oligopolistic corporations in basic industries such as steel and energy, large light-manufacturing industries such as textiles and durable consumer goods, banking and insurance, and wholesaling and retail enterprises were hiring huge armies of clerical employees and sales personnel and smaller but important coteries of engineers, technicians, and managers, the latter growing numerically with the decline of the family-owned and -operated firm. To be sure, the small firm survived, according to Mills, but small businesses of all types were increasingly unstable: "Nationally, the small businessman is overpowered, politically and economically, by big business; he therefore tries to ride with and benefit from the success of big business on the national political front, even as he fights the economic effects of big business on the local and state front."

Small entrepreneurs go in and out of business, their chance of survival diminishing with the growth and scope of large-scale enterprises: grocery chains, department stores, and large manufacturing corporations, all of which are able to benefit from economies of scale and ample supplies of capital with which to invest in technological innovations to drive prices down and their small business competitors out of the marketplace.

Among the diverse strata of the new middle class, the managers, according to Mills, occupy a unique place. The "managerial demiurge" signifies a new form of power, and not only at the workplace. Their numbers are growing rapidly, and, to the degree they run corporate and government bureaucracies, "the managerial type of man becomes more important in the total social structure." Top managers are given the task of controlling the underlying population at every level of economic, political, and cultural activity—middle managers, supervisors, and line foremen, as well—but the job of coordination and control expands with the complexity of the occupational structure and the manifold problems associated with advanced capitalism. Mills accepts the idea, first advanced by Berle and Means in the classic *Modern Corporation and Private Property*, that advanced capitalist societies are marked by the separation of ownership and control in the everyday functions of the large corporate enterprise; the owner has gradually handed more power to the manager. In turn, government and private corporations are run as rationalized bureaucracies rather than in the image of the individual corporate tycoon of the late nineteenth century, who ran his business like an old-fashioned sovereign.

Although little more than elevated wage workers and, for this reason, deprived by their subordination to management of the work autonomy enjoyed by the "old" middle class, the salaried professional and technical strata remain culturally tied to capital. Mills saw little hope for their unionization as long as mass culture—their indigenous culture—was the "main drift" of mass society. On the one hand, reared in images of American exceptionalism, they were the embodiments of the cultural aspiration for individual social mobility; on the other, their growth was accompanied by the proletarianization of the professional and technical strata—proletarian because they neither owned their own productive property nor controlled their labor. Some might earn higher salaries than industrial workers, but in contrast to unionized workers, who have the protection of a collective bargaining agreement limiting management's rights, they were subordinated to arbitrary managerial authority in the performance of their tasks. Yet their eyes were fixed on the stars. Lacking a secure class identity, which is intrinsic to those engaged in the production and appropriation of things, as producers of "symbols," they were likely to remain an atomized mass, an oxymoron that signified what Erik Olin Wright later described as the "contradictory class location" into which they were thrust. As for the clerical and administrative employees, they were cogs in the vast machinery of the "enormous file"; they were keepers of information and of the proliferating records accumulated by the growing significance of sales.

In the absence of social movements capable of making a genuine difference in power relations, these studies are directed to the general, largely "liberal center" for whom Mills never ceased to have mixed feelings. The liberals were a necessary ingredient of any possible grand coalition for social change, but this center was marked by the "looseness of its ideas," an attribute that led it to "dissipate their political attention and activity." Yet, in the wake of the labor leaders' failure to face the challenge posed by the rightward drift of American politics, the hardening of corporate resistance to labor's economic demands, the freezing of the political environment by the cold war, and the virtual disappearance of the Left, especially the independent Left, until the late 1950s, Mills's public address shifted decisively to the center, even as his political position remained firmly on the independent, noncommunist Left.

The central category that suffuses Mills's social thought and to which he returned again and again was that of power, especially the mechanisms by which it is achieved and retained by elites in the economy and social institutions. This is the signal contribution of the Italian social theorists Gaetano Mosca and Vilfredo Pareto to Mills's conceptual arsenal. In Pareto's conception, elites, not classes, constitute the nexus of social rule. To derive his conception of power, Mills focuses neither on the labor process, the starting point for Marxists, nor on the market, the economic focus for Weberians. In contrast, Mills is a state theorist: elites are, for Mills, always institutionally constituted. He recognized the relative autonomy of corporations, but consistent with the regulation era of advanced capitalism, he argued that the state had become the fundamental location of the exercise of economic, as much as political, power. So, for example, in *The Power Elite*, his most famous and influential work, three "institutional orders" that are closely linked but spatially and historically independent—the corporate, the political, and the military—constitute what others might, in Marxist vocabulary, describe as a ruling class. Except that it isn't a "class," either in the sense of those who share a common relationship to the ownership and control of productive property or, as in Max Weber's conception, in the sense of groups that share a common interest in gaining access to market opportunities for employment and to acquire goods. The power elite is an alliance of the individuals who compose the top layers of each of the crucial institutional orders and whose relative strength varies according to historical circumstances.

In the immediate post–World War II period, Mills detects the autonomous power of the military as, increasingly, the driving force in the alliance, just as the political elite occupied that position during the 1930s slump, when the provision of social welfare attained an urgency, lest by neglecting the needs of the underlying population the system might be endangered. The military, as a relatively autonomous power center, gained sustenance from the rearmament program leading to World War II, but since there was no peace after 1945, it retained its central position in the power structure. Almost immediately, the United States and the Soviet Union, the two remaining superpowers, were engaged in a new "cold" war in which nuclear and conventional weapons played an enormous economic as well as political role in world and domestic politics. And the cold aspects of the war were punctuated by discontinuous but frequent "hot" wars, such as those in Korea, Southeast Asia, China, and Israel. Under these circumstances, the military, allying itself with those large corporations engaged in defense production, accumulated substantial independent power. Needless to say, the corporations, the holders of what Mills calls "big money," are by no means ignored. After all, they remain the backbone of the entire system.

But in his analysis of the commanding heights, Mills is not content to describe the three institutional orders that constitute the power elite. He shows that the scope of its power embraces wide sections on which the legitimacy of American society depends. Chief among them are the celebrities, who, as the premier ornaments of mass society, are routinely recruited to lend prestige to the high officials of the three principal institutions of power. Political parties and their candidates eagerly showcase celebrities who support them; corporate executives regularly mingle with celebrities in Hollywood and New York at exclusive clubs and parties; and "warlords"—high military officers, corporate officials, their scientists and technologists engaged in perfecting more lethal weapons of mass destruction, the politicians responsible for executive and congressional approval of military budgets—congregate in many of the same social and cultural spaces, as well as in the business suites of warfare. In short, following the muckraking tradition, but also the international sociological discourse on power, *The Power Elite* uses the evidentiary method first perfected by independent scholars such as Ferdinand Lundberg of tracing interlocking networks of social and cultural associations as much as business relationships to establish the boundaries and contour of power. Moreover, in this work we can see the movement of individuals among the leading institutional orders that constitute the nexus of power, so that their difference tends to blur.

Naming the power elite as the only "independent variable" in American society, Mills was obliged to revise his earlier estimation of the labor movement. Barely eight years after designating labor leaders the "new men of power" who had to choose whether to lead the entire society in the name of working people and other subordinate groups, he designated them a "dependent variable" in the political economy. Accordingly, he lost all hope that working people and their unions would enter the historical stage as autonomous actors, at least until a powerful new Left of intellectuals and other oppressed groups emerged to push them.

Mills's identification of power with the triumvirate of corporation, military, and national state was offered in the same period that political theorists and sociologists were proclaiming the concept of pluralism as a more accurate description. Robert Dahl's *Who Governs*, a study of the city of New Haven's power structure, construed power in the metaphor of a parallelogram of forces, none of which dominated political decision making. Business, labor, consumer groups such as parent associations, and taxpayers and other organized groups constituted power relationships through the mechanisms of compromise and consensus. Although not denying that big business and the political directorate exhibited oligarchic tendencies, Dahl vehemently refuted the concepts associated with both Marxism and elite theory that held that clearly articulated ruling groups were the only genuine independent force. Dahl's study became a model for the understanding not only of local power but of national power as well. As persuasive as Mills's argument may have been for progressives and other political skeptics, his views were subject to the severe criticism of many of his fellow academics as well as reviewers. For some, he had failed to appreciate the resilience of American democracy, was importing ideas inherited from the nonapplicable European context to American circumstances, and, in any case, had offered yet another exercise in debunking.

MILLS DID HIS GRADUATE WORK at Wisconsin under the mentorship of, among others, Hans Gerth, whose powerful mind was never matched by a body of equally compelling written work. In some respects, Mills gave an English language voice to Gerth's ideas (although the collaboration has lately been subject to critical scrutiny by some scholars who contend that Mills took advantage of Gerth). These ideas—a complex synthesis of Marx, Weber, Mosca, and Pareto—introduced a wide range of concepts into the study of modern institutional life. Crucial to Gerth and Mills's understanding of how modern institutions work was Weber's theory of bureaucracy, read through the pejorative connotation of its system of rules and occupational hierarchies as inimical to democratic decision making. Rather than viewing bureaucracies as necessary institutions to make complex industrial societies work more efficiently, as Weber argued, Gerth provided Mills with the idea that bureaucratic control of institutions entailed domination, which Robert Michels extended to socialist organizations in his classic *Political Parties*. For Michels, the mechanism of domination was the leadership's monopoly over the means of communication. Mills sees the development of the state, no less than the labor movement, as a series of highly institutionalized bureaucracies that, in contrast to his preferred model of unions—voluntary, democratically run, and controlled by the rank and file— were rapidly mutating into oligarchies of power.

Mills's dissertation, *Sociology and Pragmatism*, completed in 1943, was an explicit attempt to draw the implications of European sociological theory for the United States. He himself exemplified that connection. For pragmatism, there is no question of intrinsic "truth" if, by that term, we designate the possibility that truth may be independent of the context within which a proposition about the social world is uttered. The truth of a proposition is closely tied to the practical consequences that might, under specific conditions, issue from it. And practical consequences may be evaluated only from the perspective of social interest. But, unlike John Dewey's concept, there is no "win-win" thinking here. In the end, Mills adhered to the notion that whether a particular power arrangement was desirable depended on whose ox was being gored.

Mills drew heavily on Karl Mannheim's concept of ideology but also adopted his lifelong preoccupation with the intellectuals, whom Mannheim designated as the only social formation capable of independent thought and action. Mannheim's major work, *Ideology and Utopia*, is a critique of the Marxist designation of the proletariat as a universal class and, particularly, of Georg Lukács's argument adopting the standpoint of the proletariat, which, in relation to knowledge, has no interest in reproducing the mystifications that buttress bourgeois rule. According to Lukács, Marxism can penetrate the veil of reified social relations to reveal the laws of motion of capitalism and, therefore, produce a truthful account of how society works. Mills was much too skeptical to buy into this formulation; Mannheim's relativism—the view that "standpoint" thinking inevitably led to partial knowledge—was more attractive and corresponded to his own pragmatic vision. Accordingly, knowledge is always infused with interest, even if it occurs behind the backs of actors. But Mills leans toward ideology as an expression of intentionality, and this characterization is particularly applied to the labor leaders who are the subjects of *The New Men of Power* and the business elite described in an essay republished in the collected essays *Power, Politics and People* and later incorporated in *The Power Elite*. Lacking an explicit ideology does not mean that labor or corporate leaders can dispense with the tools of persuasion. But according to Mills, these are the tools of a "practical politician" rather than those of an ideologue. Thus, Mills employs the word *rhetoric* to describe how leaders persuade and otherwise justify their constituencies of policies and programs that may or may not be in their interest.

Mills was also a close reader of the political and social thought of John Dewey, perhaps America's preeminent philosopher of the first half of the twentieth century and one of the leading figures in the development of pragmatism. The debate between Dewey and Walter Lippmann on whether there was a chance for a genuine democratic society and governance in an America increasingly dominated by experts was among the most important intellectual events of the 1920s. Mills derived the concept of the "public," or, in his usage, "publics," from this controversy. By the time Lippmann's *Public Opinion* (1921) appeared, many intellectuals expressed doubt that the ideal of the public as the foundation of a democratic polity, which made decisions as well as conferring consent, was at all possible in the wake of the emergence of mass society with its mass publics and massified culture.

Lippmann argued, persuasively to many, that a public of independent-minded individuals was, by the end of World War I, decisively foreclosed by the complexity of international relations, advanced technology, the reduction of genuine knowledge from which to adduce opinion to slogans by the mass media, and the growing role of the state. For a society of citizens, in the sense of the Greek city-state, who are capable of making vital decisions affecting the polity, he held out no hope. Given the conditions for its formation, the public was shortsighted, prejudiced, and, most of all, chronically ill informed. While defending the claim that the elite of experts, which came into its own with the consolidation of the modern state and the modern corporation, was as desirable as it was inevitable in complex societies, Lippmann retained a trace of his former socialist skepticism. He wanted a democratic public to force experts and political leaders to obtain consent on a regular basis and, through the ballot, to pass judgement on their quasi-sovereign actions. Thus, democracy was conceived purely negatively, as the barrier against authoritarian, technocratic rule.

Deeply affected by this powerful argument against participatory democracy, John Dewey was moved to respond. *The Public and Its Problems* (1925) is, for all intents and purposes, the most penetrating case for an active polity and for radical democracy that any American has ever written. With Dewey, Mills held that the promiscuous use of the term *democracy* to describe the de facto plebiscite of electoral politics, and other mechanisms by which consent is achieved by representative political institutions, is unwarranted. The institutions of the liberal state still need the consent of the governed. But the legislative and executive branches are increasingly beholden to the holders of institutional power, not their electors, except insofar as the public refuses to consent to policies that it perceives to be contrary to its interests and, as in the case of Social Security "reform," succeeds in staying the hand of legislators beholden to corporate power, at least for a time. Having entered into an alliance with the military and corporate orders, the political directorate becomes a self-contained body, undemocratic in both the process of its selection and its maintenance.

Dewey's concept of democracy recalls the New England town meeting in which the "public" was not a consumer of the work of active and influential people but a participant, a decision maker, in the community's political and social life. In this respect, it is important to recall Mills's "Letter to the New Left" (1960). The letter outlined the principles of participatory democracy on the basis of Dewey's concept of the public and was, perhaps, the single most influential document in the early history of Students for a Democratic Society (SDS), one of the key organizations in the development of the social movements of the 1960s. SDS's program, enunciated in its manifesto *The Port Huron Statement*, was constructed around the concept of and demand for a "participatory" democracy in which "ordinary people" could control the "decisions that affected their lives." It presupposed the same distrust of the state and its branches that Mills evinced years earlier. But unlike the immediate post–World War II years, when, notwithstanding its de facto expiration, the New Deal still inspired broad support for what Herbert Croly termed *The Promise of American Life* (which Mills names as the most important work of liberal statism), two decades of militaristic statism and the appearance of a new generation of political activism made Mills's radical democratic appeal more audible.

MILLS WAS ALSO A GREAT TAXONOMIST. With his mentor, Hans Gerth, he published in 1953 a major social psychology, *Character and Social Structure*, which situates the self firmly in the social and historical context that shapes and is shaped by it. This work is, perhaps, the premier instance of Mills's efforts to combine theoretical social science with the distinctly American psychology of William James and George Herbert Mead, but these days, when the little boxes of the mind seem to pervade social thought, this book languishes in the archives of largely unread masterworks. Gerth and Mills's bold juxtapositions are simply too adventuresome for a social science academy for which conventional wisdom seems to be the farthest horizon of possibility. And his numerous essays covered the broad expanse of issues in American politics and culture, a range that has caused more than one detractor to complain that he is "all over the place." In this respect, Mills is a true scion of the great thinkers who founded the social sciences. Their task was to provide a philosophical scaffolding to the disciplines, a project that, as Mills understood, did not end with the canonical works. As a pragmatist, he was acutely aware that theory requires constant renewal and revisions and that, contrary to much current thinking, the problem is not one of applying received wisdom but one of interrogating the wisdom in the light of contemporary developments. So, even as Mills borrows concepts such as "elite" from eminent forebears, he refuses the hierarchical thinking that informed the writings of theorists such as Mosca and Pareto. For example, he invests new significance in the process of investigating historically situated elites. As a result, the labor union elite and the power (ruling) elite display different characteristics, although in *The New Men of Power* we can see the first pass at the development of a new theory.

His main theoretical project, explicated most fully in *Character and Social Structure*, was to situate the biographies of leading economic and political actors—labor leaders, the main figures in business, military, and political institutions—within the social structure and the spatiotemporal context that set the limits and provided the opportunities for their activity. This methodological imperative is designed to account for individual variation among broad types, but also to demonstrate the degree to which the social structure—explicitly named in terms of key institutional orders—sets, at a specific time and specific place, the limits as well as the opportunities for individual and group action. Thus, our biographies mediate, and are mediated by, the institutional frameworks that condition decision making. Except in *White Collar,* Mills is interested mainly in describing and explaining the structure of power rather than the worlds of the relatively powerless, but this work is always undertaken in the interest of reconstructing a democratic public. "We shall use this term *psychic structure* to refer to man conceived as an integration of perception, emotion, and impulse. Of course there are other psychic functions, memory and imagination for example, but we shall limit our terms at this point. For our purpose, 'psychic structure' will refer to when, how and why man feels, perceives and wills."

At the core of Gerth and Mills's theory are the concepts of "institution" and "self." The notion of institutional order connotes the complex of institutions that, taken together, constitute what we loosely designate as the structure of power in "society," chiefly the political, economic, and military orders. Thus conceived, the character structure of individuals formed by physical and social conditions, particularly those of childhood biography, including family and schooling, prepares them for playing certain "roles" within the institutional orders to which they gravitate or are assigned by virtue of their education and training, situations that themselves are the outcome of certain interactions and relationships. The formation of the self in childhood is crucial for structuring the life chances of individuals, conditioning, if not completely determining, the ways they structure knowledge and their emotional and volitional proclivities. But these processes are only relatively unique in individuals; conditions of social location, class, race and ethnicity, and education play a decisive part in shaping the choices available to whole groups of people. The basic unit of analysis, then, is not the individual but collective selves.

Thus his writings are suffused with "ideal types"—Weber's methodological prescription to fashion composite profiles against which to measure any particular instance of the type—arranged horizontally as well as vertically. The models assembled in *The New Men of Power,* of labor leaders; in *The Power Elite,* where he provides a collective portrait of business leaders; and in his essays published in the collection *Power, Politics and People,* which contains several composites of the various publics he addresses and to which he is obliged to respond, give a glimpse of Mills's lifelong approach to social knowledge: First, produce a composite profile of the subject. Then, provide detailed, historically informed descriptions of the context within which the subject operates, and evaluate the relative salience of each element of this context to how the subject is shaped. Then, return to the subject by unpacking the composite to break down the different social and character types. Finally, replace them in the larger political, economic, and cultural situations. To what end? To find out the alternatives to the main drift of politics and ideologies. Needless to say, although he is a student of elites, Mills asks whether the democratic movement from below, of the rank-and-file union members, of the fractured publics of consumers and intellectuals, may succeed in overcoming the pervasive tendency toward oligarchic domination of government and civil life.

For most of his academic career, Mills taught sociology at Columbia University. He produced social knowledge but was also an intellectual agitator. He was deeply interested in advancing the science of sociology as a means of giving us a wider understanding of how society worked. But from the late 1940s, when, at age thirty-two, Mills and Helen Schneider produced their landmark study of the American labor union leaders, he remained a close student of social movements; his writings span analyses of the labor movement, the student Left, the peace movement, and others. He swam, intellectually, against the current, yet unlike many independent leftists who saw only defeat in the postwar drift toward a militaristic-corporate political economy and despaired of relevant political practice, he was, above all, a practical thinker whose interest was always to describe the "main" chance as a dead end and to counterpose the chances for leftward social change. Consequently, even when he is the most descriptive of, say, labor leaders and portrays the new middle class in terms of subordination and as allies of the leading elites, his eyes never stray far from the question, What is to be done? What are the levers for changing the prevailing relations of power? How can those at or near the bottom emerge as historical subjects?

Mills is aware that to reach beyond the audience of professional social scientists he is obliged to employ a rhetoric that, as much as possible, stays within natural, even colloquial language. Addressing the general reader as well as his diminishing audience of academic colleagues, Mills conveyed difficult and theoretically sophisticated concepts in plain but often visual prose, described by one critic as "muscular." And, perhaps most famously, he was a phrasemaker. For example, his concept of the "main drift" to connote conventional wisdom, as well as centrist politics, encapsulates in a single phrase what others require paragraphs to explain. And instead of using the Marxian-loaded term *crisis* or the technical dodge *recession* to describe conditions of economic woe, he employs the colloquial *slump*. He characterizes the rise of industrial unions after 1935 as the "big story" for American labor, a term that encompasses history and common perception. But the imperatives of the cold war—especially the emergence of the military as a dominant institutional order—constitute the big story of the immediate postwar era.

Mills wrote scholarly works, but in keeping with the style of a public intellectual, he was also a pamphleteer, a proclivity that often disturbed his colleagues and, in one of the more odious forms of academic hubris, led some to dismiss him as a "mere journalist." In fact, this dismissal may account in part, along with his boldness in attacking the big themes of social theory and analysis, for the sad truth that since the late 1970s, his major works are virtually unread in social science classrooms, have disappeared from many scholarly references, and are largely undiscussed in the academic trade. In the last decade of his life, manifestos and indictments of the prevailing social and political order issued from his pen as frequently as sociological works. In fact, *The Power Elite*, which has inspired a subdiscipline whose academic practitioners include G. William Domhoff and America's leading consumer advocate and anticorporate campaigner, Ralph Nader, as well as a veritable army of "public interest" researchers, has always been controversial on theoretical grounds. But also, despite its often meticulous and comprehensive collection of "data," it has been criticized for a lack of objectivity in its clear democratic bias. These days, most members of the professorate have retreated from public engagement except as consultants for large corporations, media experts, and recipients of the grant largesse of corporate foundations and government agencies that want their research to assist in policy formulation, or they confine their interventions to professional journals and meetings. Mills, however, remains an embarrassing reminder of one possible answer to this veritable privatization of legitimate intellectual knowledge. In 1939 his colleague Robert S. Lynd published a probing challenge to knowledge producers of all sorts called *Knowledge for What?* He asked the fundamental question: to whom is the knowledge producer responsible? To the state? To private corporations? To publics that are concerned with issues of equality and social justice?

Mills rejects as spurious the prevailing doctrine according to which the social investigator is obliged to purge the work of social and political commitment. His values infuse the sociological research and theorizing, and he never hides behind methodological protestations of neutrality. Mills is, instead, a partisan of movements of social freedom and emancipation while, at the same time, preserving his dedication to dry-eyed critical theory and dispassionate, empirical inquiry. An advocate of a democratic, radical labor movement, he was nevertheless moved to indict its leadership not by fulmination but by a careful investigation of how unions actually worked in the immediate postwar period. A self-described "man of the Left," in the late 1940s Mills provoked his left publics to outrage when he concluded that the "old" socialist and communist movements had come to the end of the road. By the late 1950s, as the frost of the cold war melted a bit after the rise of Nikita Khrushchev to power in the Soviet Union and the power elite's recognition that the anti-Communist purges had hurt U.S. domestic as well as foreign policy, he was loudly proclaiming the need for a "new" Left that had the courage to throw off the ideological baggage of the past, especially Marxist orthodoxy and Stalinism.

Like Jean-Paul Sartre, whose *Critique of Dialectical Reason* appeared in 1960, he came to regard tradition, even radical tradition, as a political albatross. He never used Sartre's fancy term "practico-inert" to mark the encrusted habits that induce people to reproduce the past in the present, but he was a persistent critic of the habituation of the Left to old ideas. A withering opponent of the Communists, sensing the impending doom of the Soviet Union after the opening provided by Khrushchev's revelations of Stalin's crimes at the Twentieth Communist Party Congress in 1956, he was among the first to urge the young to disdain their elders' preoccupation with the "Russian" question and instead attend with fresh eyes and hearts to the tasks at hand: to oppose U.S. intervention in the affairs of revolutionary societies and to establish the framework for a radical democratic society.

I have no doubt that he was right to urge the young radicals to distance themselves from the past, at least in the short or intermediate term. But he never made it clear that he himself had been reared, politically, on the Russian question, and he forgot that those who ignored the failure of the revolution were doomed to relive it, an eventuality he was never cursed to witness. That the New Left, which soon captured the imagination of an entire generation, went awry may not be attributable exclusively to its refusal to address existing socialisms of the Stalinist variety. But it was entirely disarmed when, as the war in Southeast Asia heated up, various Marxist ideologies became matters of urgent debate; most young leftists found themselves overwhelmed. They were moved as much by guilt as by ignorance to give uncritical support to the Vietnamese communists and even hailed the efforts of Pol Pot in Cambodia. By 1970, many reared in the New Left were no longer Mills's spiritual children; they all but renounced his democratic faith in favor of a "third-world" dogma of national liberation at all costs. But ironically, Mills himself was not immune from such enthusiasms.

The book-length pamphlets were received as more than controversial, not only because they were, to many minds, notoriously heretical for their tacit violation of academic insularity but also because they broke from the main tenets of the cold war anti-Communist consensus at a time when, under siege, political repression was still alive and well in the United States. *The Causes of World War Three* (1958) is, in many respects, a popularization of *The Power Elite* and its application to the international scale. It depicts world politics in terms of the rivalry between two power blocs, one led by the United States and the other by the Soviet Union, both of which are governed by irresponsible elites whose conduct of the nuclear arms race threatens the very existence of humanity. Written in a period when one could count the number of radicals with full-time appointments in American universities on one hand and when the preponderant ex-radicals had "chosen the West," this equalization of responsibility for the world crisis between East and West endeared Mills neither to the communists and their periphery, for whom the Soviet Union was virtually blameless for the state of things, nor to the cold war liberals, for whom any suggestion that U.S. foreign policy could contribute to the outbreak of World War III was as shocking as it was absurd.

Hidden in the pages of his work is the influence of the one rather obscure strain of radicalism that, after the war, declared both camps to be forms of a new antidemocratic, militaristic capitalism and boldly, but futilely, called for the formation of a "third" camp whose base would be a radicalized labor movement in alliance with other anticapitalist elements of the population. The project failed because, at the time of its formulation, the leading unions in every capitalist country were busy making deals with their own corporations and with the capitalist state, and leftists were divided between those who were safely ensconced in the cold war consensus and those who, despite everything, remained Soviet apologists. Mills's appeal to the "public," translated in this context as the middle-class liberal center, proved more effective, for it corresponded to the emergence of a mass movement against the testing and use of nuclear weapons and for an end to the cold war. Needless to say, most American labor leaders—including Walter Reuther, the liberal president of the largest industrial union, the autoworkers—were aligned with their own government's policies and were convinced that the price of demilitarization was nothing less than a new slump. And even as he discounted the politicos as allies to the top layers of corporate and military power, Mills was equally skeptical that the intellectuals, the social type on which political dissent conventionally relies, were adequate to the occasion.

A self-declared independent leftist (which, in the cold war era, meant an anti-Stalinist but unaligned radical), Mills had been influenced by Trotskyism early in his life. He carefully separated the still-influential Communists from radicalism. The Communists were influential precisely because the party had been an important vehicle for organizing major industrial unions and for bringing militant workers into the New Deal. During the war, they played a major role in enforcing the wartime no-strike pledge and the government's drive for productivity. Mills believed that whatever oppositional politics they evinced after the war was due, almost exclusively, to the chasm between the United States and the Soviet Union.

Listen Yankee (1961), an exemplary instance of Mills's penchant for rowing upstream, was a fierce defense of the Cuban revolution when, even for many anti-Stalinist radicals, it appeared that the regime was dedicated to raising living standards and was still open to a democratic society. At a time when even the liberal icon, Oregon senator Wayne Morse, was a vocal advocate of counterrevolution and supported the Kennedy administration's ill-fated Bay of Pigs invasion, Mills asserted the right of the Cuban people to determine their own destiny and sharply condemned U.S. policy in the Caribbean and Latin America. He excoriated liberals and conservatives alike for their support of antipopular regimes such as that of Batista in Cuba and Somoza's brutal Nicaraguan dictatorship, pointing out that the U.S. government had opposed democratic efforts by financing military counterinsurgency, especially against the Arbenz regime in Guatemala, as well as Cuba's new revolutionary government. Though he had been a lifelong anticommunist, Mills saw the Cuban revolution as a harbinger of the long struggle of peasants and workers for liberation from colonialism and imperialism and predicted serious future confrontations between the spreading insurgencies and the United States, which, under Democratic and Republican national administrations alike, became the main defender of the dictators.

Indeed, in the 1960s and beyond, Mills's provocative intervention seemed prescient. In Colombia, Douglas Bravo led a formidable armed uprising, and Che Guevara led a band of guerrillas into the Bolivian jungle; both revolts failed. But with Cuba's material help, the Sandinistas in Nicaragua and the National Liberation Front in El Salvador were alive with revolutionary activity, and by the mid-1960s, the dormant Puerto Rican independence movement revived under Marxist leadership that closely identified with the Cuban revolution. In the 1970s, Maurice Bishop organized a successful uprising in Grenada that openly aligned itself with the Cuban revolution, and Michael Manley's democratically elected leftist social democratic government in Jamaica forged close ties with Cuba. However much he was smitten, Mills framed much of his own discourse in terms of the significance of these events for America's neocolonial foreign policy and for America's future. Lacking the tools of discriminating evaluation, many young radicals not only gave their unconditional support but also enlisted as volunteers in Grenada's, Cuba's, and Nicaragua's education and health efforts.

MILLS IS BOTH an exhilarating exemplar of the role and reach of the public radical intellectual and, at the same time, a sobering reminder of how far the human sciences have descended since the end of the Vietnam War. Even in death, Mills was an inspiration to a generation of young intellectuals estranged from the suburban nightmare of post–World War II America and eager to shape their own destiny, and to some in his own generation, who, in fear and trembling, had withdrawn from public involvement but yearned to return. The decline of social engagement and political responsibility that accompanied the ebbing of the impulse to reform and revolution in the 1970s and 1980s witnessed the shift of labor, socialist, and social liberal parties and movements to the liberal center. Many erstwhile radical intellectuals who retained their public voice moved steadily to the right, motivated, they said, by the authoritarianism of the New as well as the Old Left and by their conviction that American capitalism and its democratic institutions were the best of all possible worlds.

Mills suffered the sometimes scorching rebuke of his contemporaries and, even as he won the admiration of the young as well as the tattered battalions of leftist intellectuals, had severed ties with much of the liberal center, which sorely needed to hear his argument that, in the face of the awesome and nearly complete hegemony of the power elite, American democratic institutions were in a state of almost complete meltdown. That a small body of scholars has recently revisited his legacy should be welcomed. Whether intellectuals will remain tucked into their academic bunkers depends not only on depressions or wars to pry them out. Indeed, the economic slumps that have punctuated the last two decades have failed to move most to utterance, although there is evidence that, after 9/11, some radical intellectuals have engaged in protest against the U.S.-promulgated war on Iraq or have entered the debate on the side of the government. After 1950, most of Mills's tirades were self-motivated, and a decade later, Mills looked to an aroused coterie of young intellectuals as the source of a new democratic public. But in the final reckoning, it is usually resurgent labor and other social movements to which intellectuals respond. Though it can be argued that prior to 9/11 there were signs of revival in the political opposition, it remains to be seen whether, after suffering the defeats of the early years of the twenty-first century, the radical, nomadic spirit of C. Wright Mills will inculcate the minds and hearts of the intellectuals and activists on whom he bestowed so much hope.

Part III
Political Recollections

The Price of Heavenly Peace
Tiananmen Square Fifteen Years Later

Michael J. Thompson

THE BURDEN OF HISTORY

Anyone who has walked along Chang'an Boulevard in Beijing in the last fifteen years cannot help but be transported back to the spring of 1989. The ground still elicits the images of the tens of thousands of students and workers who gathered there to demand democratic reform of the communist state. Even today, it is as if the square itself still vibrates with political meaning. This often happens when politics, history, and location meet and intertwine. But whereas certain locales such as Berlin's Brandenburg Gate have come to represent the victory of freedom and democracy over fascism and totalitarianism, Tiananmen Square has taken on the opposite meaning: of the crushing and inevitable collapse of the democratic impulse and the gradual erasure of its memory. Students of history know all too well that the pursuit of democracy usually has more powerful enemies than allies; in Beijing on June 4, 1989, this historical lesson was to prove harrowingly true.

In the West, the crackdown was seen as the bloody result of the actions of a totalitarian government. But the realities of the situation are more complex. Even though the 1980s saw dramatic reforms in communist countries, Chinese reforms were more moderate and cautious. Mikhail Gorbachev's reformist agenda was echoed in China by the liberalizing vision of major political figures such as Hu Yaobang and Zhao Ziyang, who saw China's opening to the world as being more than merely economic in nature. The rigidity of the political systems that were formed and hardened during the cold war were beginning to show signs of thawing. The word *reform* became as dangerous in certain circles as the word *revolution* had been eighty years before—it was a threat to all that existed—and the encrusted, conservative elite that held power could smother the newborn impulse in its cradle.

But even the most conservative of the ruling elder statesmen knew that economic reforms were needed. The political and economic disasters of the Great Leap Forward in the 1950s and the Cultural Revolution in the 1960s and 1970s had brought the Chinese economy to the verge of collapse. Reform meant absorbing ideas and institutions from the West, but only in terms of economics, technology, and science; what was explicitly excluded were the political and moral ideas of the Western political tradition and its cultural products. In 1983, a political movement under the title Eliminate Spiritual Pollution was initiated to eradicate what the conservative elite saw as "decadent" and bourgeois elements in Chinese culture and art. But despite this, a "futurologist school" began to emerge. Through an analysis of Western thought and science, the reality of the gap between their "backward society" and the "modern world" was discovered, and the futurologists—led by figures such as Jin Guantao and Li Zehou—opened up a new horizon of consciousness for younger students and intellectuals. The centuries of Chinese isolationism had created not only a thirst and hunger for modernity but also a bitterness and anger at being held back from realizing it.

Meanwhile, the realities of the newly reformed economy that Deng had created by allowing markets to be resurrected in the countryside and allowing international capital investment and joint enterprises between Chinese and international companies were extraordinary. As the new economy flourished and reform deepened, the calls for democracy were once again, after decades of silence, beginning to be heard. The 1980s saw the emergence of a "market fever" *(shichang re)* that gave birth to a "cultural fever" *(wenhua re)*. The rise of living standards and the yearning for a "true" modernity rekindled the old yearnings from the radical movements of the 1920s. The slogan "Democracy and Science" had been the perceived solution to Chinese backwardness back then, and it was only logical that it was seen as the solution to the same problem in the 1980s. In literature, with novelists such as Gu Hua and Can Xue, and in films, with directors such as Chen Kaige, Zhang Yimou, and Tian Zhuangzhuang, Chinese culture was preoccupied with a project of self-critique that fed desires for political reform. It was only a matter of time before social and political crisis would shake China to its foundations.

Throughout the twentieth century, democracy was never a foreign idea to Chinese intellectuals or activists. It is common for conservatives in the West to see the 1989 protests as the outgrowth of the American idea of freedom and democracy penetrating the Chinese walls and infecting its populace. But this is little more than a display of historical ignorance. After the collapse of the Qing dynasty in 1909, movements for democratic reform and modernization were incessant, consistent, and unwavering in their demands for Chinese modernization—democracy and Western science were seen as the paths to modernization, and students and intellectuals took up the banner of modernization under the auspices of both. Lacking a developed, industrialized economy throughout the first half of the twentieth century, students and intellectuals—instead of a mobilized working class or newly emergent bourgeoisie—were the engine behind demonstrations and protests for democratic reform.

It was in 1978–1979, after the deep freeze of Maoism began to give way, that the issue of democracy once again became the focus of mass appeal and government reaction. The "Democracy Wall" *(Minzhuqiang)* in Beijing was located in the Xidan section of the city, where citizens gathered to read political tracts in the form of posters that advocated an open and democratic China. It was there that Wei Jingsheng wrote about China's need for democracy. For Wei and other activists of the Democracy Wall movement, such as Liu Qing, Cai Song, and Lü Pu, democracy was a precondition for all other forms of modernization and progress. They paid the price for their ideas and their forceful arguments. Wei was sentenced to fifteen years in a "reform through labor" camp, and Liu Qing would serve ten years. This was a mere prelude to what would come a decade later.

China had struggled throughout the twentieth century with feudal traditions and power structures that dated back to its Confucian past. A line from Book VII of Confucius' *Analects* says: "I transmit but do not innovate; I am truthful in what I say and devoted to antiquity." It was this burden of history and tradition, as well as the conservative bias of Chinese culture, that was coming into question in the 1980s with increased intensity. And it was this type of culture that was easily manipulated by the Communist Party to ensure devotion and minimize dissent. Democracy and Western science were seen as the means to throw off these historical burdens, as they had been in the West throughout the eighteenth and nineteenth centuries. Translating these needs into the language of politics was only a matter of time. When the Tiananmen protesters came to the square in the spring of 1989, the cultural fever of the 1980s had been smoldering for at least seven years. They were a truly new generation with new ideas; the consequences of the end of their movement and the reforms they sought are only now beginning to be seen, and they require interpretation.

This was not a movement of only students and intellectuals, nor did it spring from a mimicking of the student movements of the West during the 1960s, as many in America believed. The Tiananmen Square demonstrations included workers who formed unions and demanded labor reforms and slowly began to involve the entire citizenry of the city. In other major cities in China, student and intellectual supporters marched and rallied, as they did in Hong Kong, which was still under British rule at the time. It was a mass movement, a national movement in the classic sense of the term. And as such, in the end, the events that unfolded in the spring of 1989 ought not to be seen as being of consequence only to China and Chinese politics. It is difficult not to equate the political and moral impulse of the students and workers who demonstrated and opposed the communist state in China with the impulse of the revolutionaries of the late eighteenth century in Europe and America. What the students and workers sought were not simple reforms. They sought the modernization that the Chinese revolution of 1949 had promised: to be free from despotic rule and centuries of social and political dependency, as well as cultural paternalism and the canons of oppressive tradition. In the face of a liberalizing economy, one that had become more private and generated more wealth, they sought not only to spread reforms to other spheres of society but also to protect their interests as workers and as young intellectuals from the growing capitalistic nature of economy and society.

CHINA, CAPITALISM, GLOBALIZATION, AND DEMOCRACY

Although China has continued on its course of economic reform, incorporating more market institutions into its quasi-socialistic economic framework and moving increasingly toward Western economic institutions, "liberalization" has come to mean nothing more than economic liberalization. The hope for political reform, democratization, and liberalization now seems to be little more than a utopian ideal for liberal-minded Chinese intellectuals and their foreign sympathizers. Today, as a world economic power, China may have less to fear from chants for democracy than ever before. The turn to capitalism may effect certain reforms and transformations, but it is increasingly clear that a return to the sentiments of the spring of 1989 will not be one of them.

In his now classic study of the development of democracy and dictatorship in the modern world, Barrington Moore wrote, from the vantage point of the 1970s, "the partial truth emerges that non-democratic and even anti-democratic modernization works." What we see in China is the evolution of a new kind of relationship among economics, politics, and society. It is one that flies in the face of one of the core insights of neoliberal Western social science: that the emergence of capitalism and its development will give rise to democracy. The neoliberal mantra wedding markets, democracy, and human freedom could not be more incorrect when considering the case of China, whose private sector has grown to eclipse the once predominant public sector.

In the social sciences, the classic argument about the development of democracy was that capitalism was a precondition for democratic development. This view—primarily of American bastions of conservatism such as the Hoover Institution at Stanford and prominent sociologists and political scientists such as Seymour Martin Lipset—gave primacy to markets as the engine for the development of democracy. The argument was simple: as free markets developed and people entered commerce, wealth would be created by a talented entrepreneurial class that would seek democratic political reforms as its wealth grew and its interests in autonomy and an emerging civil society became more concrete. Thus the link between capitalism and democracy has always been strong in American understandings of economic and political development, and it was premised on giving primacy to economic liberalization.

China's path toward economic and social modernization was heralded as going against state ownership of economic enterprises, which the Communist Party termed "wild and ultra-leftist socialism." What the new elite in the 1980s sought was the rapid economic development of the country. The Communist Party saw its interests as being at one with those of the nation, and it was right about this for quite a while. People did want their living standards to rise, and they have risen steadily throughout the last two decades. But what Chinese capitalism has also created is a massively unequal society marked by brutal capitalist exploitation, environmental degradation, and little regard for human welfare in individualist terms. China's capitalism is what Western capitalism would have become if it were not for radical workers' movements to curb the excesses of the industrial workplace. Lacking unions or any other kind of political or legal protection, Chinese workers and their families have few prospects for progressive change.

Even when it operates within a democratic framework, capitalism is an abusive, destructive economic system. Without the checks and steering capacity of some kind of democratic accountability—something that has been eroding in the West over the past two decades—it is an economic system that can lead to horrible results. Liberal capitalism is therefore in stark contrast with Chinese capitalism. Liberalization of the market means that its effects—the generation of inequality, environmental degradation, the lack of regulations of all kinds—go largely, if not completely, unaddressed. When there is a liberal polity, however, these effects can be contested by social movements to mitigate the market's effects. The lack of a liberal (i.e., democratic) polity means that this mitigation cannot take place, and the operation of the market goes unchecked, its effects unaccountable to any sector of the public.

This has also affected Chinese culture, but not in the way that neoliberal apologists have argued. Instead of economic development leading ineluctably to further calls for democratic reform, a massive consumerist culture has emerged in China that seems to take after the contemporary United States. What Bin Zhao has called "Confucian capitalism" now mirrors what Daniel Bell referred to as the solution to the "cultural contradictions of capitalism": consumerism on a mass scale is the new face of capitalism, one untied from its traditional Protestant ethical foundations of thrift and asceticism. When capitalism is fed by raw, superficial consumerism, apathy in the political sphere is almost always a consequence. America and China may be more similar now than they have ever been—certainly more so than in the spring of 1989, when broad forms of democracy were on the minds of so many politically conscious citizens.

EXPANDING THE LEGACY OF TIANANMEN: PROSPECTS FOR DEMOCRACY IN A GLOBALIZING WORLD

The age of democratic revolution is over. The era of democratic reform looks bleaker than ever. Tiananmen Square was the last gasp of the impulse for mass democracy on a national scale. One would be hard-pressed to think of another movement even half its size in the last fifteen years whose objective was national democracy. It is not that the ideas no longer have appeal; that would be absurd. Rather, the brutal fact remains that as long as the ideas and traditions of democracy are undermined and successfully countered in the developing world, democracy has little chance of succeeding. Economic imperatives have won out over political principle. What we are witnessing in the context of globalization is the narrowing of the political sphere and the expansion of the economy as the road to modernization. Political instability—so long as it translates into economic instability—will be brutally quashed, and it is difficult to see how any movement can compete with the technological and military power of the state, as well as the effects of depoliticization that are implemented through educational programs and other ideological apparatuses. In China, this combination has been particularly effective, but even in places such as Iran, which has a considerably more robust movement for reform and the political institutions to effect real change, there has been a slow weakening of its reform-minded approaches.

As an event, the Tiananmen Square movement should be seen as more than a student movement. It was, in every sense of the word, a mass social movement that lost its political focus and, as it veered toward radicalism, also begged its own violent demise. The politics of social movements is too often seen in naive terms. For any reformist social movement to be effective (as people such as Frances Fox Piven and Richard Cloward have shown), it requires a regime that is in some sense sympathetic to the demands of the movement. This was not lacking in China before May 19, the day that the reformist Zhao Ziyang—China's near-equivalent of Gorbachev and secretary-general of the Chinese Communist Party—was deposed, along with many of his reformist allies. After this, the conservative forces within the party held sway, and the movement could find no one left to continue dialogue.

The Tiananmen demonstrations were the largest movement for democratic reform and political, economic, and cultural change in the twentieth century. Even more, in an era when globalization continues to bind more markets to one another in different locations, the Tiananmen movement can be seen as the last great movement for democracy outside of those places where some form of democracy already exists. The protests and the crackdown therefore need to be placed in a very different historical and political context: the context of global movements for democracy that have taken place since 1989 and the burst of political and social movements and events that occurred at that time. This context tells a different, much more sober tale. The increased power of the state in developing countries and the weakening, or outright lack, of democratic political traditions are at the root of this reality, and the trajectory of globalization seems intent on keeping it that way.

It may be commonplace to blame the nature of the state for the lack of democratic change, identifying it as the source of all problems. But this quickly fizzles into libertarian fantasy. Franz Oppenheimer's view that "a small minority has stolen the heritage of humanity" is no longer a sufficient explanation for the lack of democratic reform in the political sphere in the context of globalization. What we are witnessing is the dawn of a new form of political economy in China—one that will serve as an ideal type for many other developing nations under the auspices of globalization. This is a kind of political economy that stresses the liberalization of markets even as it restrains democratic reforms within the state and its laws. It is one that puts primacy on economic development and growth and does not seek the same kind of development and openness of the state and society. The idea that capitalism and democracy are not only mutually inclusive but also two sides of the same historical coin is nothing more than apologia for capitalism itself and the hegemonic worldview of American liberal capitalism. But even in America, liberalism and capitalism are not wedded in some form of chemical affinity; rather, American society is the result of a liberal-capitalist consensus—one that has been erected between two historically separate social aspirations: the pursuit of profits, and the pursuit of individual freedom and social justice.

It is no longer enough to say that the crackdown and the efforts to quell dissent in China are the reasons for the subsequent political quiescence. Certainly the state's power has always been instrumental in crushing political change, but the reality is, I think, much deeper, both in China and elsewhere. The rapid spread of capitalism has not led to a similarly rapid spread of democracy because capitalism and democracy—real democracy—do not mix well. Rapid economic development and growth require—as political economist Rudolf Hilferding observed—an increased exploitation of labor and the environment; social dissent is therefore an obstruction to the dream of modernization, so tolerance for unrest is rarely prolonged. But what of the predominant theories of neoliberalism? An emergent middle class has developed in China, and it is robust, to say the least. But calls for democratic reform have been lacking from this class because of political apathy, which has been made palatable by a new consumerism and an increasingly powerful state. Thus, the prospects for democracy in China may be worse than ever.

Democracy is more than a framework for political institutions. It consists of more than elections and a system of checks and balances. Democracy is a mind-set that requires a cultural component as well. Democratic impulses move people to solidarity, make movements that push for reform more rational and, ultimately, more successful. But the new dynamic of globalization should be seen for what it really is, and hyperoptimistic predictions about the future of democracy ought to be tempered by reality. The increasing power of economy over society—and the ability of the economy to play into a consumerist and politically apathetic populace—can only weaken chants for democracy, even by the most disadvantaged. In Europe, the Middle Ages went on for centuries with peasant revolts from below, but real change was not possible without a broader solidarity among different social strata.

We may be witnessing the victory of a capitalist form of globalization at the expense of robust democratic change. Indeed, the authoritarianism of modern Russia and China does not elicit the anxiety and fear in the West that their Soviet and Maoist manifestations once did, but at best, these regimes are only marginally more democratic than their predecessors. If Marx was right that men make history, but never under the conditions of their own choosing, then the conditions of the present need to be clearly demarcated. The context of global capitalism—which comes at the expense of democratic ideas—may be paving the path toward the death of the political itself, with its emphasis on market processes and the interests of capital. In such an inverted world, the prospects for democracy depend not only on the infusion of democratic ideas but also on an opposition to the effects of capitalism and the illusion that capitalist development is somehow equivalent to human development.

But on a Quiet Day ...
A Tribute to Arundhati Roy

Fred Dallmayr

Sometimes one feels like "tuning out." Faced with the incessant noise of warplanes and propaganda machines, one sometimes feels like stopping up one's ears in order to shut out the world. The impulse is particularly strong in the "developed," industrial North, given the fact that development almost invariably means a ratcheting up of the noise level. Although amply motivated, the attempt does not quite succeed, for in muffling the roar of military-industrial noises, our ears become available for and attuned to a different kind of sound: the recessed voices of the persecuted and exploited, the anguished cries of the victims of development and military power. A great philosopher of the last century vividly described the tendency of modern lives to become submerged in societal noises, in the busy clamor of social conformism (what he called "das Man"). But he also indicated a different possibility, a different path involving a kind of turning around or a movement away from "tuning out" to a new kind of "tuning in." In his portrayal, this attunement, or tuning in, meant an opening of the heart and mind to recessed voices drowned out by societal pressures—above all, to the voice of "conscience," which calls us into mindfulness, into a new mode of careful being in the world.

Note that conscience here does not call one into a solipsism far removed from the world, but rather onto a road leading more deeply into the world, into its agonies and hidden aspirations. Not long ago, such a call struck me somewhat unexpectedly. It happened in the midst of a new war, while firebombs were dropping on distant cities and the roar of warplanes rocked that part of the world. At that time, I began reading a book called *The God of Small Things* and was transported beyond surface events into the deeper recesses of human agonies. The book is from the pen of a writer I had not encountered before (I shamefully confess) by the name of Arundhati Roy. She hails from the "South," more specifically from Kerala, India, and now lives in Delhi. Happening in the midst of a war ostensibly launched by the North, the encounter had special significance for me—awakening me again to the enormous rifts tearing our world apart and urging on me a renewed mindfulness. In the meantime, I have read several of Arundhati Roy's other writings, including a series of essays collected in her books *The Cost of Living, Power Politics,* and *War Talk*. The following pages are meant as a tribute and an expression of gratitude to her for serving as a voice of conscience, calling on people everywhere, but especially those in the North, to step back from the pretense of cultural superiority and return to the cultivation of our shared humanity.

A WRITER-ACTIVIST?

Paying tribute to a writer like Arundhati Roy is risky and difficult, especially for a nonwriter (or a nonliterary writer) like me. The difficulty is particularly great in the case of a novel like *The God of Small Things,* an outstanding work that deservedly received the distinguished Booker Prize. Not being a novelist or a literary critic, how could I possibly do justice to the vast richness of this book, the immense subtlety of its nuances, its stories within stories and echoes within echoes? How could I fathom its depth of imagination and the intense agonies of its characters? Famous writers East and West have celebrated her work; John Updike compared it to a Tiger Woods story, and Salman Rushdie praised her combination of passion and intellectual verve. My own approach has to be somewhat different. Having spent most of my adult years mulling over ponderous philosophical texts, I have to link her work with my own background, which has always hovered between philosophy and politics or between theory and praxis.

The aspect I want to address first is the title of her prize-winning novel. The very phrase "the god of small things" is, in a way, counterhegemonic if not seditious. Traditional religion, especially in the West, has always associated "God" with bigness or greatness. Of all the things in the world, and of all the big things, God was held to be the biggest or greatest; among all the many causes and moving engines in the world, God was seen as the first or primary one. Due to the traditional linkage of throne and altar, the bigness of God has tended to rub off on the status of princes, kings, and political rulers. This fascination with bigness has proved to be hard to shake, and it persists in some form even today. Thus, when world leaders or presidents claim to be mouthpieces or "stand-ins" for God, their power appears to be wielded by "divine right." To be sure, this pretense of leaders is contested and debunked by modern democracy, with its emphasis on the importance of ordinary people and ordinary lives. As it happens, these ordinary lives—although seemingly small compared with the power of potentates—are by no means "small" in terms of dignity and moral-spiritual significance. For grown-up people in democracies, God no longer needs pomp and circumstance but is content to remain sheltered in ordinary phenomena and inconspicuous places and events. As Walter Benjamin remarked, ordinary lives at any moment can become the narrow gate through which the Messiah suddenly and without fanfare enters. Thus, it is a small, nearly imperceptible change that changes everything.

In Arundhati Roy's novel, the change is so unobtrusive that it is not specifically elaborated or thematized. However, on some other occasions, she has shed light on the book's title. In her 1999 essay "The Greater Common Good" (reprinted in *The Cost of Living*), we find some tantalizing lines. "Perhaps," she writes, "that's what the twenty-first century has in store for us: the dismantling of the Big. Big bombs, big dams, big ideologies, big contradictions, big countries, big wars, big heroes, big mistakes. Perhaps it will be the Century of the Small." She adds: "Perhaps right now, this very minute, there's a small god up in heaven readying herself for us." As we know, of course, this "small god" (if she comes) will be up against all the old bigness: the big old God associated with the biggest country, the biggest superpower, the biggest wealth, the biggest arsenal of weapons of mass destruction, the biggest bigness. If the small god were to come, she would certainly not arrive in a mammoth conflagration or on top of a nuclear mushroom cloud—as some devotees of Armageddon now predict and propagate. She would come on the feet of a dove, as the consoler of the desolate, the healer of the wounded, the liberator of the oppressed. As Arundhati Roy herself stated in a recent interview, commenting on the title of her novel: "To me the god of small things is the inversion of God. God is a big thing and God's in control. The god of small things . . . whether it is the way children see things or whether it is the insect life in the book, or the fish or the stars—there is no accepting of what we think of as adult boundaries. This small activity that goes on is the under-life of the book. All sorts of boundaries are transgressed upon."

In many quarters, and not without reason, Arundhati Roy is considered a political activist and public intellectual—in addition to, or apart from, being a writer. Yet as the preceding passages make clear, her activism does not subscribe to any "big ideology" or overarching platform seeking to mold and reshape social life; nor does she favor mass organizations wedded to rigid marching orders or agendas. As she remarked coyly about her childhood in Kerala, she grew up in a state where different "religions coincide" and coexist, where "Christianity, Hinduism, Marxism and Islam . . . all live together and rub each other down." The point of her remark was not simply to debunk these "religions," but rather to relativize them slightly and thus prevent them from becoming ideological straitjackets. As it seems to me, a main feature of Roy's work is that it escapes ready-made formulas or pigeonholes.

In a nimble way, she refuses to accept the rubrics offered by contemporary society: the options of ivory-tower retreat (literature for literature's sake) or mindless street activism or the super-option of the writer-intellectual as the architect of grand social platforms. What is intriguing and even dazzling is the manner in which she is both a writer and a political activist—the manner in which writing and doing, thinking and acting, are neither radically separated nor fused in an ideological stew. As she remarked in an interview given at the World Social Forum in early 2003: "When I write, I don't even think consciously of being political—because I am political. I know that even if I wrote fairy stories, they would be political." As she added, literature and politics (contrary to widespread belief) are not "two separate things," which does not mean that there is not a world of "difference between literature and propaganda" (the latter instrumentalizes the former for extrinsic goals). For Roy, writing and acting are not at odds but reflective of a "way of being"—reflective of the writer's distinctive way of being in the world.

In a fashion reminiscent of Edward Said, Roy asks a question that is too often sidestepped by contemporary intellectuals: the question regarding the social responsibility of literature and art (and, one might add, philosophy). "What is the role of writers and artists in society?" she queries in *Power Politics*. "Can it be fixed, described, characterized in any definite way? Should it be?" In a poignant way, this question was raised by Said in his Reith lectures of 1993, subsequently published as *Representations of the Intellectual*. At the time of his lectures, Said was renowned as a writer; but he was also suspect in many quarters as a political activist. As he noted in his introduction, "I was accused of being active in the battle for Palestinian rights, and thus disqualified for any sober or respectable platform at all." His lectures pinpointed the public role of the intellectual as that of a peculiar insider-outsider, in any case of an "amateur and disturber of the status quo." If intellectuals were complete "outsiders," they would enjoy the alibi or refuge of an ivory tower, far removed from Julien Benda's *"trahison des clercs"*—what Said calls "Benda's uncritical Platonism." But if they were complete "insiders," they would become accomplices and sycophants of the ruling power, thus robbing the intellect of its critical edge. "Insiders," he writes, "promote special interests, but intellectuals should be the ones to question patriotic nationalism, corporate thinking, and a sense of class, racial or gender privilege." For Said, the "principal duty" of intellectuals, writers, and artists resides in the search for "relative independence" from societal pressures—an independence that justifies his characterization of the intellectual "as exile and marginal, as amateur, and as the author of a language that tries to speak the truth to power."

Without implying any direct influence, Roy's outlook broadly concurs with Said's. In *Power Politics* she lays down two guideposts for writers—first, "there are no rules," and second, "there are no excuses for bad art"—with the second guidepost severely complicating the first. The absence of formal, externally fixed rules does not mean that everything is left to arbitrary whim. "There is a very thin line," she writes, "that separates the strong, true, bright bird of imagination from the synthetic, noisy bauble." The point is that the writer (or the intellectual) constantly has to search for that line and allow herself to be measured by its standard: "The thing about this 'line' is that once you learn to recognize it, once you see it, it's impossible to ignore. You have no choice but to live with it, to follow it through." (In his introduction, Said likewise observed that there are no fixed "rules" by which intellectuals can know "what to say or do," but it is crucial nonetheless to uphold standards of conduct.)

Regarding the public role of writers or intellectuals, this means that there cannot be fixed rules either dictating specific social obligations or mandating radical exile. The rub is again the peculiar inside-outside position of writers or intellectuals: they have to know the language of their community in order to properly address it, and they have to be sufficiently dislodged to contest that language. Whichever way they choose—inside or outside—there is no real escape: "There's no innocence; either way you are accountable." As Roy concedes, a good or great writer "may refuse to accept any responsibility or morality that society wishes to impose on her." Yet the best and greatest also know that if they abuse their freedom—by joining the ivory tower or becoming "palace entertainers"—they inevitably damage their art. "There is an intricate web of morality, rigor, and responsibility that art, that writing itself, imposes on a writer. It's singular, it's individual, but nevertheless it's there."

Roy's entire work is a testimonial to the stringent demands of the "thin line." In her writings and in her public conduct, she has resisted both radical politicization or political co-optation and retreat into the haven of belles lettres. Like every thoughtful writer or intellectual, Roy does not like to be conscripted into ideological agendas or submerged in mindless activism. As a reflective person, she relishes subtle nuances and the open-endedness of many issues. In her own words: "I am all for discretion, prudence, tentativeness, subtlety, ambiguity, complexity. I love the unanswered question, the unresolved story, the unclimbed mountain, the tender shard of an incomplete dream." But she adds an important caveat: "Most of the time." Problems may be so urgent, public policies so threatening or destructive, that even the most pensive person cannot remain uninvolved—without becoming an accomplice. Are there not occasions, she asks, when prudence turns into "pusillanimity" and caution into cowardice? Can a writer or intellectual afford to be "ambiguous about everything"? Is there not a point where circumspection becomes "a kind of espousal"? No one can accuse Arundhati Roy of being pusillanimous or cowardly. Whatever pressing issues or lurking disasters there may be in this world, she has never hesitated to speak out forcefully and without equivocation. In her words again: "Isn't it true, or at least theoretically possible, that there are times in the life of a people or a nation when the political climate demands that we—even the most sophisticated of us—overtly take sides? I believe that such times are upon us. And I believe that in the coming years intellectuals and artists in India will be called upon to take sides." Not only in India, one might add, but all over the world.

THE MILITARY-INDUSTRIAL COMPLEX

The issues on which Arundhati Roy has most frequently and most forcefully spoken are two: big corporate business and the war machine—whose interconnection or collusion President Dwight Eisenhower termed the "military-industrial complex." This interconnection has been steadily tightening since Eisenhower's time. Basically, the war machine is designed to keep markets stable and safe for business investments; in turn, corporate business finances the maintenance of the war machine. For Roy, the most glaring and preposterous manifestations of this collusion in India are the development of the nuclear bomb and the construction of "mega-dams." Some of her sharpest attacks have been leveled at these targets. Although it is not intuitively evident, she has neatly pinpointed the linkage between the two phenomena, while inserting both in the broader framework of globalization. From a global angle, dam construction is part of the global market dominated by Western corporate business; nuclear bombs are compensatory devices meant to provide domestic security and pacify volatile masses.

As she noted in an interview with David Barsamian in 2001, it is crucial to perceive the links among "privatization, globalization, and [religious] fundamentalism." When, by constructing dams, a country like India is "selling its entire power sector" to foreign business firms (such as Enron), pressure is placed on the government to compensate people by building a bomb or else by erecting a "Hindu temple on the site of the Babri mosque." So, this is the trade-off one has to understand: "With one hand, you are selling the country out to Western multinationals; and with the other, you want to defend your borders with nuclear bombs."

Dam construction has been a major preoccupation of modern India. Just as, for Lenin, electrification held the key to Russia's future, dams—in particular mega-dams—were touted as springboards for India's rapid economic development. In a famous speech in 1948, Prime Minister Jawaharlal Nehru proclaimed that "dams are the temples of modern India" (a phrasing he later came to regret). In the period following independence, the country embarked on a craze of dam construction, one more ambitious and extensive than the other. As Roy notes in *The Cost of Living*, India is "the third largest dam-builder in the world," having constructed since 1948 a total of roughly 3,300 big dams. The latest and most ambitious undertaking along these lines is the Sardar Sarovar

Dam, a monumental mega-dam that is being built on the Narmada River in central India—the same river that, according to government plans, is going to provide sites in the future for an additional 3,000 dams. Although big dams are heralded as developmental marvels, their human and social costs have vastly outstripped any economic benefits. In Roy's words, the reservoirs of these dams have "uprooted millions of people" (perhaps as many as 30 million). What is worse, "There are no government records of how many people have actually been displaced," and there is a total lack of anything resembling a "national rehabilitation policy." Against the backdrop of this grim scenario, the Sardar Sarovar Dam is now taking its toll. As the waters at the dam's reservoir are rising every hour, she writes, "more than ten thousand people face submergence. They have nowhere to go."

Dam construction in India is complicated and aggravated by the impact of globalization, which today is closely linked with the panaceas of neoliberalism, structural adjustment, and (above all) privatization. The last policy is particularly grievous when it involves the privatization of water resources in third-world countries. In this case, the policy does not mean an innocuous "structural adjustment" but the transfer of effective control over the daily lives of millions of people. This transfer, one should note, does not signify the end of "power" but rather the replacement of public power—the role of democratically elected leaders—by the unaccountable power of executives of private (chiefly foreign or multinational) businesses. Keeping one's focus on water-generated or electrical power, the deeper meaning of "power politics," in Roy's usage, becomes clear. As she states, "Dam builders want to control public water policies," just as "power utility companies want to draft power policies, and financial institutions want to supervise government investment." In this context, Roy offers one of the most trenchant definitions of "privatization" that one can find in the literature anywhere. "What does privatization really mean?" she asks, and answers:

> Essentially, it is the transfer of productive public assets from the state to private companies. Productive assets include natural resources: earth, forest, water, air. These are assets that the state holds in trust for the people it represents. In a country like India, seventy percent of the population lives in rural areas. That's seven hundred million people. Their lives depend directly on access to natural resources. To snatch these away and sell them as stock to private companies is a process of barbaric dispossession on a scale that has no parallel in history.

Today, the consequences of the privatization of natural resources are no longer left to guesswork. In 1999, Roy recalls, the government of Bolivia privatized the public water supply system in the city of Cochabamba and signed a forty-year lease with a consortium headed by Bechtel, the giant U.S. engineering firm: "The first thing Bechtel did was to raise the price of water; hundreds of thousands of people simply couldn't afford it any more." Something similar may be in store for people in India. With regard to water resources there, the prime advocates and beneficiaries of privatization have been General Electric and Enron. Typically, concerned state governments in India have been induced to sign so-called power purchase agreements with big companies, preferably foreign or multinational companies—agreements that transfer basic control over water and electric power to the purchasers. When such agreements break down or run into trouble with local agencies, they tend to be renegotiated, often at rates of return still more beneficial to the purchasing companies.

In Roy's words, "The fish bowl of the drive to privatize power, its truly star turn, is the story of Enron, the Houston-based natural gas company." The first power purchase agreement between Enron and the state of Maharashtra was signed in 1993. Due to changes in political leadership at the state level, the contract had to be repeatedly rewritten and renegotiated, leading to steadily higher costs to the state. Whereas the initial contract pegged the annual amount owed to Enron at around $400 million, the latest "renegotiated" agreement compels Maharashtra to pay to Enron a sum of $30 billion. As Roy comments, "It constitutes the largest contract ever signed in the history of India.... Experts who have studied the project have called it the most massive fraud in the country's history."

To be sure, the costs of dam construction and the sale of water resources are not borne only by local governments but also (and even principally) by the masses of poor people victimized by "power politics." Despite the huge fanfare boosting big dams and big companies, the results for these masses have been disheartening. After the construction of thousands of dams, Roy notes, some 250 million people have no access to safe drinking water, and more than 80 percent of rural households still do not have electricity. The deprivation is experienced most acutely by the Adivasis (indigenous tribal people) and the Dalits (formerly called "untouchables"), who are also most seriously affected by the big dams. In the case of the Sardar Sarovar Dam on the Narmada River, more than half of all the people displaced are Adivasis; another large segment is made up of Dalits. Here, power politics joins the grim story of ethnic conflict and caste discrimination. "The ethnic 'otherness' of these victims," Roy comments, "takes some of the pressure off the 'nation builders.' It's like having an expense account" whereby India's poorest people are "subsidizing the lifestyles of her richest."

Thus, despite appeals to the "greater common good" (supposedly advanced by big dams), a good part of the "cost of living" of the upper crust of society is charged to the meager fortunes of the poor. When Roy is faced with inequities or injustices of such proportions, her language tends to become stirring and nearly biblical, reminiscent of Lincoln's fulmination against a "house divided." "The millions of displaced people in India," we read in *The Cost of Living*, "are nothing but refugees of an unacknowledged war. And we, like the citizens of White America and French Canada and Hitler's Germany, are condoning it by looking away. Why? Because we are told that it's being done for the sake of the Greater Common Good. That it's being done in the name of Progress, in the name of the National Interest (which, of course, is paramount).... We believe what it benefits us to believe."

As previously mentioned, the construction of mega-dams is closely linked with militarism or the advancement of military power, which, in our age, means the development of nuclear bombs and weapons of mass destruction. In India, the big event happened in May 1998 with the detonation of the first nuclear bomb—an explosion that, according to government reports, made "the desert shake" and a "whole mountain turn white." For Arundhati Roy—voicing the sentiments of millions of people in India and elsewhere—the event was an ominous turning point, steering the country and the rest of the world in a perilous and potentially disastrous direction. As she noted, the case against nuclear weapons has been made by thoughtful people many times in the past, often in passionate and eloquent language, but this fact offered no excuse for remaining silent. Despite a certain fatigue induced by the need to repeat the obvious, the case had to be restated clearly and forcefully: "We have to reach within ourselves and find the strength to think, to fight."

As she did with regard to mega-dams and their social consequences, Roy lent her pen to the vigorous denunciation of militarism and nuclear megapolitics. In language designed to infuriate Indian chauvinists and especially devotees of "Hindutva" (India for Hindus), an essay published in the aftermath of the explosion asserted bluntly: "India's nuclear tests, the manner in which they were conducted, the euphoria with which they have been greeted (by us) is indefensible. To me, it signifies dreadful things: the end of imagination; the end of freedom actually." In still bolder language, the same essay exposed the linkage between mega-bombs and the ruling military-industrial complex, which, in India and elsewhere, constitutes the major threat to the survival of democratic institutions: "India's nuclear bomb is the final act of betrayal by a ruling class that has failed its people [that is, failed to nourish and educate the people]. The nuclear bomb is the most anti-democratic, anti-national, anti-human, outright evil thing that man has ever made."

One of the most valuable features of Roy's antinuclear essay is its realist candor: its unblinking willingness to look at the horrors of nuclear devastation. This candor is particularly important in view of recent attempts—again by ruling elites—to downplay these horrors by throwing over them the mantle of relative normalcy or strategic inevitability (given the global dangers of "terrorism"). Most prominent among these ruses is the rhetoric of "smart nuclear bombs" and (even more hideous) "preemptive nuclear strikes." Piercing this fog of deception, Roy's essay offers a stark description of "ground zero": "If there is a nuclear war, our foes will not be China or America or even each other. Our foe will be the earth herself; the very elements—the sky, the air, the land, the wind and water—will all turn against us." Readers who remember Hiroshima and Nagasaki will find their memories joltingly refreshed by Roy's stark portrayal: "Our cities and forests, our fields and villages will burn for days. Rivers will turn to poison; the air will become fire; the wind will spread the flames. . . . Temperatures will drop to far below freezing and nuclear winter will set in. Water will turn into toxic ice. Radioactive fallout will seep through the earth and contaminate groundwater. Most living things, animal and vegetable, fish and fowl, will die."

Faced with catastrophes of this magnitude, the head of an atomic research center in Bombay (Mumbai) recommended that, in case of nuclear attack, people retire to the basements of their homes and take iodine pills. As Roy scathingly remarks, governmental (so-called) preparedness is a sham; it is "nothing but a perilous joke in a world where iodine pills are prescribed as a prophylactic for nuclear irradiation."

The reasons given by Indian officials for the development of a nuclear capability have been primarily three: the looming danger of China, the ongoing conflict with Pakistan, and the Western example of nuclear power politics. None of these reasons stands up to scrutiny. Regarding China, Roy comments, the last military confrontation happened more than three decades ago; since that time, conditions have by no means deteriorated but have actually "improved slightly between us." Relations between India and Pakistan are more tense and perilous, especially when the focus is placed on Kashmir. However, here the geographical proximity itself undermines nuclear programs on both sides. In Roy's words: "Though we are separate countries, we share skies, we share winds, we share water. Where radioactive fallout will land on any given day depends on the direction of the wind and the rain." Hence, any nuclear attack launched by India against Pakistan will be "a war against ourselves." Somewhat more tricky—but ultimately equally fallacious—is the reference to Western power politics and the obvious hypocrisy involved in Western nuclear policies ("bombs are good for us, not for you"). Although containing more than a kernel of truth, the charge of hypocrisy and duplicity does not vindicate India's nuclear arsenal. "Exposing Western hypocrisy," Roy asks mockingly, "how much more exposed can they be? Which decent human being on earth harbors any illusions about it?" While protesting self-righteously against nuclear proliferation, Western regimes have in fact amassed the largest arsenal of nuclear devices and other weapons of mass destruction, and they have never hesitated to use this arsenal for their own political advantage: "They stand on the world's stage naked and entirely unembarrassed, because they know that they have more money, more food, and bigger bombs than anybody else. They know they can wipe us out in the course of an ordinary working day."

As one should note, Roy's point here is to criticize India's nuclear program, not to shield Western hypocrisy and warmongering. Her book *Power Politics* contains stirring passages condemning the spread of warmongering all over the world, but especially the kind of belligerence unleashed by the so-called war on terrorism (what Richard Falk has called "the great terror war"). Roy is adamantly opposed to the high-handed and unilateral definition of "terrorism" by state governments—especially governments whose own policies may have the effect of "terrorizing" large populations at home and abroad. Here is a memorable statement on behalf of the victims of governmental warmongering: "People rarely win wars; governments rarely lose them. People get killed; governments molt and regroup, hydra-headed. They [governments] first use flags to shrink-wrap people's minds and smother real thought, and then as ceremonial shrouds to bury the willing dead." In our time of unprecedented media manipulation, Roy's denunciation of chauvinistic flag-waving and brainwashing surely deserves close attention. One of her main concerns is the unpredictable outcome of nationalist belligerence: the fact that, in pursuing national glory, governments or ruling elites may unleash or exacerbate "huge, raging human feelings" present in the world today. What warmongering typically ignores are the underlying sources of conflict, especially the misery of common people whose suffering cannot be alleviated by warfare. At the time of the war in Afghanistan (2001), Roy penned a passage whose salience has increased in light of subsequent military adventures: "Put your ear to the ground in this part of the world, and you can hear the thrumming, the deadly drumbeat of burgeoning anger. Please. Please, stop the war now. Enough people have died. The smart missiles are just not smart enough. They are blowing up whole warehouses of suppressed fury."

INDIA AND THE FUTURE

Roy's forthrightness—her role as writer-activist pleading on behalf of common people—has not earned her universal applause. Although celebrated by some literary figures and academic intellectuals, her readiness to "speak truth to power" has irked and infuriated chauvinists, warmongers, and acolytes of "bigness," both at home and abroad. As she remarked once to an Indian reporter,

"Each time I step out, I hear the snicker-snack of knives being sharpened. But that is good; it keeps me sharp." There can be no doubt that, despite the teeth of great power politics, Arundhati Roy has maintained her "sharpness" and intellectual integrity—not out of spite or meddlesomeness, but out of a deep commitment to humanity at large, to a world inhabited and sustained by the "god of small things." In this respect, her work has served as a beacon of hope to the persecuted and oppressed, to the victims of military-industrial complexes everywhere. The presence of such a beacon—or a series of beacons—is crucial today in a world dominated or contaminated by globalizing neoliberalism, structural downsizing, and privatization. In this context, one may usefully recall a phrase Roy used in her conversation with David Barsamian: "The only thing worth globalizing today is dissent." To be sure, globalizing dissent does not mean the construction of grand ideological panaceas or the formulation of general marching orders. Rather, dissenters are called on to resist in very concrete contexts and for a very specific purpose: the alleviation of injustice and misery. "Each person," she commented to Ben Ehrenreich at the World Social Forum in Brazil (2003), "has to find a way of staying their ground. It's not that all of us have to become professional activists. All of us have to find our particular way."

As Roy fully realizes (perhaps better than many "progressive" thinkers), the obstacles to resistance are formidable and nearly overwhelming. Her portrayal of conditions in India and the rest of the world is exceedingly grim—a grimness that has placed her on the "index" of domestic and global ruling elites. Take the example of India first. Her book *Power Politics* opens with passages that are deeply shocking and disheartening. "As Indian citizens," she writes, "we subsist on a regular diet of caste massacres and nuclear tests, mosque breakings and fashion shows, church burnings and expanding cell phone networks, bonded labor and the digital revolution, female infanticide and the Nasdaq crash." As these lines indicate, the country is torn apart by the conflicting pulls of traditional fundamentalism and high-tech modernity; at the same time, society exhibits a widening gulf between a small, globalizing elite and the large masses of people victimized by mega-dams and big bombs. "It is," she adds, "as though the people of India have been rounded up and loaded onto two convoys of trucks, a huge big one and a tiny little one"—with the tiny convoy heading toward a "glittering destination somewhere near the top of the world" as the large one "melts into darkness."

The picture becomes even more disturbing when Roy turns to her immediate environment: the metropolis of Delhi. "Close to forty percent of Delhi's population of twelve million (about five million people)," she comments, "live in slums and unauthorized colonies. Most of them are not serviced by municipal services—no electricity, no water, no sewage systems. About fifty thousand people are homeless and sleep on the streets." Joined by a large army of "informal" laborers, the latter people are the "noncitizens" of Delhi, surviving "in the folds and wrinkles, the cracks and fissures, of the 'official' city."

To be sure, conditions in India are not autonomous or unique; they are merely an outgrowth or reflection of conditions in the world today—a world dominated by the West and its only remaining mega-power, America. Roy's denunciation of Western colonial, neocolonial, and imperial machinations has never been reticent or subdued. As she wrote on the West's domineering impulses: "These are people whose histories are spongy with the blood of others. Colonialism, apartheid, slavery, ethnic cleansing, germ warfare, chemical weapons—they virtually invented it all. They have plundered nations, snuffed out civilizations, exterminated entire populations." What aggravates the situation further is that the plundering of nations has usually been carried out with a "good conscience": for the sake of progress, modernization, or (simply) freedom. In this respect, Americans have an unequaled record of missionary zeal. *Power Politics* offers a long list of countries that America has attacked or been at war with since World War II—a list that includes China, Korea, and Vietnam, El Salvador and Nicaragua, and finally Afghanistan and Iraq. In nearly all instances, military action was justified by the rhetoric of freedom or the defense of Western (superior) values. Referring to America's self-description as "the most free nation in the world," Roy raises the question: "What freedoms does it uphold?" And answers: "Within its borders the freedoms of speech, religion, thought; of artistic expression; food habits, sexual preferences (well, to some extent), and many other exemplary, wonderful things. Outside its borders the freedom to dominate, humiliate, and subjugate—usually in the service of America's real religion, the 'free market.'" Turning specifically to the labels attached to the war against Iraq—Operation Infinite Justice, Operation Enduring Freedom—she comments: "We know that Infinite Justice for some means Infinite Injustice for others. And Enduring Freedom for some means Enduring Subjugation for others."

As it happens, and as Roy fully realizes, the situation is still more complex and hazardous; the neat separation between "freedom at home" and "unfreedom abroad" cannot be maintained for long. Sooner or later, militarism and the insatiable demands of the military-industrial complex are bound to undermine domestic liberties as well. This tendency is well illustrated by the ongoing "war on terrorism" and the prioritization of domestic or "homeland" security. In Roy's words, "Operation Enduring Freedom is ostensibly being fought to uphold the American Way of Life. It will probably end up undermining it completely." The erosion of domestic liberties may proceed slowly and with all kinds of rhetorical subterfuges. However, security demands will ultimately prevail—with far-reaching consequences. The American government and governments all over the world, Roy continues, will use the climate of war as an excuse "to curtail civil liberties, deny free speech, lay off workers, harass ethnic and religious minorities, cut back on public spending, and divert huge amounts of money to the defense industry." Considering the last consequence, there almost seems to be a subterranean complicity between the terrorists and the military-industrial complex, both pulling in the direction of increased defense spending and global militarization. The net result of this collusion is the emergence of a kind of global "empire" wedded to mega–power politics, with potentially totalitarian implications. The sheer scale of surveillance necessary in such an empire is likely to produce "a logistical, ethical, and civil rights nightmare," with public freedom being the first casualty. For Roy, an imperial or ruthlessly hegemonic world is "like having a government without a healthy opposition. It becomes a kind of dictatorship. It is like putting a plastic bag over the world, and preventing it from breathing."

The enormity of the danger—a danger that literally takes one's breath away—may be conducive to discouragement and despair. In occasional passages, Roy herself seems ready to concede defeat and throw in the towel. Reflecting on her native India and its recent infatuation with big dams and big bombs, she sometimes appears willing to beat a retreat or escape into purely imaginary realms. "If protesting against having a nuclear bomb implanted in my brain," she writes in *The Cost of Living*, "is anti-Hindu and antinational, then I secede. I declare myself an independent, mobile republic." This republic, she adds a bit playfully, so far has "no flag," and its policies are simple: "I am willing to sign any nuclear nonproliferation treaty or nuclear test ban treaty," and "immigrants are welcome." Playfulness, however, is only a thin disguise for deep sadness: "My world has died; and I write to mourn its passing." As it happens (fortunately), loss and mourning are not Roy's final words. Even when tempted by despair, she quickly remembers the need to distinguish between oppressive governmental policies and the genuine concerns of common people living ordinary lives, both at home and abroad. Counterbalancing her sharp critique of American mega-politics, she assures ordinary American people "that it is not them, but their government's policies that are so hated." The same trust in ordinary lives also applies to India. Here too, the sparks of common decency have not yet been entirely extinguished, despite massive assaults by ruling elites. Friends of India and friends of democracy are likely to relish the following lines Roy penned in *Power Politics*:

> India's redemption lies in the inherent anarchy and factiousness of its people, and in the legendary inefficiency of the Indian state.... Corporatizing India is like trying to impose an iron grid on a heaving ocean and forcing it to behave. My guess is that India will not behave. It cannot. It's too old

and too clever to be made to jump through hoops all over again. It's too diverse, too grand, too feral, and—eventually, I hope—too democratic to be lobotomized into believing in one single idea, which is ultimately what globalization really is: Life is Perfect.

In the end, Roy's writings exude not despair but hope and commitment to a better—more just, more humane—future. Hope, in her case, is born not from wishful thinking but from a sober readiness to "stay one's ground" in the face of seemingly overwhelming odds. Although severely tested, this readiness is not entirely whimsical or unfounded because, ultimately, hope is sustained by a love that will not quit. "There is beauty yet," we read, "in this brutal, damaged world of ours—hidden, fierce, immense. Beauty that is uniquely ours and beauty that we have received with grace from others. . . . We have to seek it out, nurture it, love it."

Commitment to a better future surely requires active engagement, but—and here is the rub—it requires an engagement that exceeds willful activism. The reason is that the "good life" (so called) cannot be engineered or fabricated in the way devotees of "empire" construct or fabricate their imperial edifice. Although it involves praxis, commitment to a better future also requires a certain reticence, a refusal to dominate, coerce, or construct—hence a willingness to allow the good life to happen when it comes. In this respect, Roy's outlook bears a certain resemblance to Jacques Derrida's notion of a "democracy to come"; he writes that such a democracy must have "the structure of a promise—and thus the memory of that which carries the future, the to-come, here, and now." No one has been better able than Roy to capture the sense of this promise and to articulate it in moving language. Here are the closing lines of "Come September," an address she presented in Santa Fe on September 18, 2002: "Perhaps there is a small god up in heaven readying herself for us. Another world is not only possible, she is on her way. Maybe many of us won't be here to greet her; but on a quiet day, if I listen very carefully, I can hear her breathing."

Flight from Van
Memories of an Armenian Genocide Survivor

Patricia Cholakian

This story was told to me in the 1970s by my mother-in-law, Varsig Pazian Cholakian. I now regret that I did not record it in her own words, but at the time, she insisted that her English was not good enough and that I should write it down for her. Allowances should be made for the fact that these are the memories of a very young child and that many years elapsed between the events and the telling. My original purpose was to preserve her story for the family history, but I believe that it is of interest to a wider audience, not only because it is so compelling but also because it contains a description of life in eastern Anatolia before the 1915 genocide, an eyewitness account of the historic Armenian resistance to the Turkish army during the siege of Van (the siege that Atom Egoyan depicts in his film *Ararat*), the Russian rescue of the city, and the chaotic exodus that followed. It is also possible that the apron Varsig remembers her grandmother wearing was similar to the one worn by Arshile Gorky's mother in his famous painting.

In September 2000 my husband Rouben and I visited eastern Turkey, which had been populated by Armenians prior to the genocide. It is now inhabited mainly by Kurds, who have also been in bitter conflict with the Turks. In Van, nothing remains of the Armenian presence, for the city was completely rebuilt after the First World War. When I asked the hotel desk clerk where the neighborhood of Arakh was located, he had no idea and had never heard of it. In fact, we encountered only one Armenian during the entire trip—the ancient custodian of an Armenian church in Diyarbakir.

SHE WAS BORN ON JUNE 22, 1908, IN TIFLIS, GEORGIA, the first child of Tavit Haroutunian and Lucia Nersesian. It was a premature birth in the seventh month of pregnancy, and Varsig's mother told her later that she was such a frail and ugly baby that she turned her head away at the sight of her, and the doctor offered his condolences. Nonetheless, Varsig had a rugged constitution and survived.

Tavit was a nomadic mechanical engineer who could repair anything from a broken tramway to a ship's engine, but he never stayed long in one place. Seven years earlier he had returned from Russia to his native Van in eastern

Anatolia and settled briefly in a small house belonging to his family, which was on the same street as the large home of the prosperous Nersesian family. To them, this tall, handsome stranger who wore European clothes and had a gold watch seemed an ideal match for their daughter; a son-in-law with contacts abroad could be a real asset to the family if the Turks should attack the Armenians again, as they had in 1895.

At the time she was married, Lucia was still in school. As the pampered daughter of a well-to-do family, she had been exempted from the household tasks usually assigned to Armenian girls her age. Indeed, she was so immature for her age that she barely understood what was taking place and later recalled gazing curiously around her during the wedding ceremony. Once the marriage had taken place, Tavit left Van for Odessa, promising to send for his bride once he had established himself there and found a house for them to live in. He was gone six years.

Lucia's life went on as before. She continued to attend the Armenian school nearby and almost forgot that she was a married woman. During this period, Mooshegh Pazian, a young cousin by marriage, was a frequent visitor to the family. Mooshegh's family were Protestants, and he attended the missionary school. Although not as well-off as the Nersesians, they were more European in their outlook and better educated. They spoke English as well as Armenian, and Mooshegh's older brother was a teacher at the mission. He too had a plan to save his family from the dangerous situation Armenians faced in Turkish Armenia. In 1904, this older brother immigrated to the United States and began saving money to send for his younger brothers and sisters.

Mooshegh was attracted to Lucia, for there were many Armenian girls who were pretty but few who were educated. In the strict Nersesian household, the two were never alone together, but in the presence of family members, they often spoke of their studies and shared their love of Armenian poetry. Lucia too was drawn to Mooshegh, who was so much more intelligent and well read than the other boys she knew. However, Mooshegh was gently reminded that Lucia was already married, and his visits stopped. Soon after, he followed his brother to America. Eventually, Tavit Haroutunian sent for his bride, who was now a young woman, and she joined him in Odessa. From there they went on to Tiflis, where Varsig was born.

The adjustment was difficult for Lucia. Her family had spoiled her by allowing her to stay in school. As a result, she had learned nothing about cooking or housekeeping. The first time her husband brought her a chicken and told her to cook it, she stared at him in dismay. She had no notion what happened between the butcher's block and the table. In addition, she soon discovered that she and her husband had little in common, so with a touch of bitterness, she resigned herself to life as his wife.

The first sight of her baby daughter may not have been a joyful experience, but she soon found herself peeping at the wrinkled little face under the blankets and came to love her. Varsig grew into a toddler, clinging to her mother's skirts. A brother, born a year later, died of scarlet fever in Tiflis, and Tavit decided to move his family to Alexandria. After the death of their son, the couple grew closer, and they welcomed the birth of another daughter, naming her Ishkhanuhi, which means "princess."

The family lived on the verge of poverty, due to Tavit's irregular work habits. They could afford only a tiny third-floor apartment, and Lucia had to take in sewing to make ends meet. She also began to write short stories and poems for the Armenian newspapers. She made friends in the Armenian community, and they encouraged her to work with them as a volunteer for the Red Cross. For the first time since she had left Van, she began to enjoy life. Tavit, however, suddenly decided that they should move on to Istanbul, and then back to Odessa. There they lived in one room with a tiny kitchen and a window that looked out on a courtyard with a fountain in the middle of it.

One day, while Tavit was repairing a boat, he slipped and fell into the water. That evening he went to bed with chills and fever, and it soon became apparent that he was seriously ill. In time he grew better, but he never fully regained his health. Always one to believe that change was the best possible medicine, he decided to return to Van, where the beneficial climate was legendary. Or perhaps he sensed that he would not get well and wanted to see his birthplace before he died.

The journey from Odessa to Van was arduous. There were no railroads once they reached Turkey. They had to buy space in covered wagons that were journeying east. They were on the road for several months, and Tavit's strength was overtaxed by the task of arranging for transportation and obtaining necessities for the family. They arrived in Van in the summer of 1914, and Varsig got her first look at the legendary city of which Armenians said, "Van in this world, paradise in the next." The town was near a lake about twice the size of Lake Geneva, and its water was so alkaline that those who bathed in it emerged wholly clean, as if they had been washed with soap. The walls of the old citadel date back to biblical times, when the Urartians covered them with cuneiform inscriptions that tell of the ancient Vannic empire. In 1914, this part of the city was inhabited mainly by Turks. Its medieval streets teemed with all the hustle and bustle of an oriental bazaar.

On the hills lay the suburb of Ikestan, the garden city where Lucia's parents and most of the other prosperous merchants had their homes. Here, intensive cultivation and artificial irrigation had created plants and trees so perfect that they looked as if they had been grown under glass. Varsig now entered the world of fruit and flowers in which her mother had grown up. The Nersesian property lay in the precinct of Arakh, one of the outermost sections of the city. The house was hidden from the road by high walls, which made it seem like a little world unto itself. To its right were planted, in an order that tradition had made invariable, first walnut trees, then hazelnuts, then pistachios, and finally fruit trees—apples, pears, peaches, and apricots. Even the poorest house in Van had such an orchard, but this was a rich man's house, and it had many trees of each kind. Behind the trees lay the *saku*, a round enclosure in which the family took tea in the afternoon. And beyond it were the grape arbors and flowering trees. To the left, between the garden and the house, lay an area in which many of the menial tasks of the household were performed. It included a sort of covered porch, where fruits and vegetables were hung to dry, and a storeroom containing jars of honey and huge crocks in which meat was salted down in mutton fat for the winter and pickles were set to age in vinegar. In a second storeroom were rows of wooden bins in which the staples of the household were kept—rice for pilaf, bulgur, dried fruits, raisins, beans, peas, and much more. With its colors and smells, this was a fascinating place for a little girl, and there was always the hope of receiving a few dried apricots or raisins, the local equivalent of candy. Beyond the storerooms were the earthenware ovens where the family's bread was baked and the *geraghoors*, or stews, simmered. And finally, there was the bathhouse, in which tubs of water were heated on wood fires.

In a climate where the sun shines most of the year and it almost never rains, it was possible to do a great deal of working and living outdoors. The interior of the house consisted of a parlor, or *mangal*, where the family ate and received guests in wintertime. A pit in the center of the room contained a charcoal heater with benches surrounding it. At mealtimes the family sat there, and the food was brought to them on trays. Benches and walls as well as the floor were covered with rugs. The only other room on the ground floor was a small pantry used to store supplies kept on hand for guests and some small kerosene stoves for brewing the sweet, black coffee demanded by the rules of hospitality. Hospitality played a cherished role in the Armenian household, and no caller could escape without tasting the strong brew. It was served in tiny cups with straight sides to which the grounds clung, enabling the adept to take a quick glance at the future.

The main part of the cooking was done outdoors, however, with the aid of servants, or *mahaghs*. They lived in tiny cells distributed around the kitchen, but in hot weather, they would go up on the roof to play and sing by the light of the stars. One of them always had an oud or a mandolin, and Varsig loved to listen to their music as it floated out over the garden. The servants received only a little spending money, but all their physical needs were taken care of, and their masters were kind. To Varsig, already wearied by years of rootlessness and one-room apartments, this well-ordered household seemed a harmonious haven, overflowing with bounty. She loved to spend her days at her grandmother's heels, following her from kitchen to storeroom. She was always ready to receive one of the dried sweets that her grandmother kept tucked in the pocket-pouch Armenian women wore beneath their aprons.

In the upper story of the house there were several small bedroom–sitting rooms, which were occupied by her grandparents, her uncles, and their wives. It was surrounded on all sides by a glass gallery that led out onto a flat roof, which was used for drying fruit at harvest time. The daughters-in-law, known as *hars*, were expected to be subservient in all things to their mother-in-law. They assisted her in the household duties and spent the rest of their time upstairs sewing or crocheting, since they were not allowed to be seen by any male guests who might arrive on the scene.

The peace and prosperity of Arakh was only surface deep, however, for there were persistent rumors of a war that promised to involve Turkey and thus bring up once more the question of Armenian allegiance to the Turkish government. In addition, within the family itself, a tragedy was approaching. Tavit's health had not improved since his return to Van. He was now bedridden, his ankles swollen to twice their normal size. In addition, Lucia had given birth to twins, who ultimately would not survive, but their constant wailing irritated the sick man.

Despite these troubles, the family did not neglect the annual pilgrimage of thanksgiving to the famous monastery of Varakh, situated in the mountains above Van. The entire population participated in this ancient festival, arising at six in the morning and trudging on foot up to the shrine, where they would make an offering of thanks for the plentiful harvest. Varsig never forgot the sounds, sights, and smells of that wonderful morning as she followed her grandparents up the mountain. The autumn flowers were still in bloom, and she could hear the waterfalls cascading down to the streams below.

The monastery, located about seven miles above the site where Van then stood, was in a mountain pass. It was of great antiquity, built in the Armenian style with a conical dome. It had come to be especially venerated as the seat of the great Abbot Khrimean, who had left it to become the Katholokos of all the Armenians. Khrimean, a man of great personal holiness, had been among the first to inspire the persecuted Armenians to a love of learning and a sense of pride in their heritage. He had founded a school for boys at the monastery and encouraged the opening of Armenian schools in Van. He had even procured a printing press and installed it in the monastery to aid in the dissemination of knowledge.

Unfortunately, the saintly Khrimean had long since departed, and the monastery had fallen on hard times. The school and brotherhood had dwindled in numbers, and the Turks had appropriated the printing press. But to the people of Van, Varakh was still a place hallowed not only by centuries of Christian worship but also by the recent presence of a great spiritual leader. Now, as they made their way along the mountain paths, snatches of song could be heard from various groups, and neighbors exchanged shouts of recognition. Progress was not swift. It was a social occasion, and the Armenians are a gregarious people. In addition, they were burdened with the animals and provisions they had brought with them, for they were about to perform a rite so venerable that it went back to biblical times.

Once at Varakh, each family slaughtered an animal in the cloister enclosure, and the priest cut off a symbolic ear as a token of the sacrifice. Then the animals were roasted in pits specially constructed for the purpose, and the feast was offered to the poor. Only when they had eaten their fill did the offerer and his family partake of what remained. The solemnity of the sacrifice soon gave way to joyous merrymaking, however. There was roast lamb and pilaf for all, with plenty to spare, as well as great quantities of the plump fruits of Van. And when no one could eat or drink anymore, there was singing and dancing in long chains, the dancers linking their little fingers and the leaders waving kerchiefs in the air. Finally, when the sun had sunk low, the long procession made its way back down the mountain, the people now subdued, the children bumping sleepily against their parents' knees and finally drifting off to sleep over their shoulders. They did not know that never again would the people of Van make the pilgrimage to the cloister of Varakh, or that there would soon be other processions in which those too tired to walk would drop by the roadside and not rise again.

As winter approached, it became apparent that Tavit would not recover. The handsome, wandering stranger bequeathed to his wife only the small property in Van. On the night he died, Varsig dreamed that she saw tiny angels singing and going up and down a ladder to heaven. After years spent wandering from one foreign port to another, Tavit had brought his family back to the heart of Armenia on the very eve of a holocaust.

The month after his death, in the spring of 1915, the Turkish government moved to settle "the Armenian question" and began systematically massacring the Armenian people by means of enforced death marches. Although many of the villages and communes submitted helplessly, pockets of resistance flared up, and one of these was in Van. The city was divided into military districts, or *taghs,* by the patriots. The Nersesian home, the largest in the neighborhood, became a fortress, the headquarters for Arakh. The entire population mobilized to resist the invading Turkish armies, certain that failure would mean death for all. It was a heroic attempt with little chance of success, but the alternative only hardened their determination to fight to the last man. "Kill them or die!" was the battle cry.

In the early days of the war, the Turks confiscated all the Armenians' weapons and munitions, claiming that their loyalty was suspect. Armenian nationalists had managed to secrete a few stockpiles of arms, however, and in desperation, they begged the Russians, their potential allies and rescuers, to sell them more. The Turks were literally at the gates of the city, and the sound of gunfire was heard day and night. Everyone was put to work, the elders making gunpowder, the women cooking and caring for the wounded, the young boys and girls carrying messages and supplies, and even the little children making sandwiches for the fighters.

For Varsig, this terrible time was in many ways a holiday, for there were no school lessons. To free their parents for other tasks, all the children were brought together under the supervision of a few capable women. Since the embattled city had to turn night into day, there were no schedules or regulations, and bedtimes were nonexistent. Everyone, including the children, ate and slept where and when they could. Determined to protect the youngest from the horrors taking place around them, the leaders gave strict instructions that no one was to discuss the war in front of the children, and that those who had lost relatives in the fighting should not grieve in their presence. Despite these orders, it was impossible to insulate the children from what was going on, and Varsig often overheard the old women whispering among themselves that if the Turks came, they preferred to die.

She was also aware that children only a little older than she were dying in the effort to save the city. Her grandfather's house was located in the middle of the town on a hill that commanded a view of the surrounding countryside. It had been fortified and connected to the rest of the city by means of a network of trenches that were used to carry messages and supplies. The messengers were often children of about ten, whose short stature made it possible for them to run through the trenches without being seen by the enemy. They were sent out in small groups and instructed to go on no matter what, even if one of them was killed. Beyond the walls of the improvised nursery, Varsig and the other children often heard the screams of the dying. Then the women in the room would quickly whisper, "It's nothing." But as their situation grew more desperate, they frequently heard the harsh command, "Sit still and be quiet!"

After forty days of what had seemed a hopeless struggle, the besieged city was miraculously rescued by the Russian army. The month that followed was a time of almost hysterical jubilation. People greeted one another in the streets with the cry, "Big Bear is here!" After the nightmare of the siege, when everyone had been sure they were doomed, the arrival of the Russians seemed heaven-sent. Meanwhile, the Turkish inhabitants of Van, most of whom lived near the center of town in the old city, had fled, leaving behind their houses and possessions. For years, the Armenians had been forced to buy their safety and well-being from the local Turkish officials with heavy duties and bribes. Motivated by greed and revenge, they now joined the Russian soldiers in an orgy of looting. Varsig's grandmother went to the home of a wealthy Turkish family she had known and took their jewels and diamonds from the safe.

Despite the holiday atmosphere in Van, the war continued, and the Russians began to suffer reverses. They announced that they would be forced to withdraw from Van, but realizing what the fate of the Armenian citizenry would be, they gallantly offered to conduct them into Russian Armenia, where facilities were being set up to receive the thousands of refugees fleeing from the Turks. The people of Van were given eight hours to ready themselves for the departure. Many became hysterical and rushed out of the city, taking nothing with them. Others, sure that they would return one day, spent the time burying their gold and jewels, much of which was later appropriated by the Turks, and much of which may still be hidden underground to this day. The more sensible gathered up food, clothing, and personal possessions. The fortunate piled their belongings into carts or wagons or strapped them onto donkeys and mules; the rest were forced to rely on their own backs.

Lucia found herself abandoned and alone with her two little daughters and only one donkey. For reasons Varsig didn't understand, Lucia's father had packed his belongings into a wagon and set off with his sons without waiting for her. Perhaps he was impatient to be off and thought that she would catch up with them on the road. Probably no one realized how confused and chaotic the enforced exodus of thousands of fear-crazed people would be. Lucia strapped a blanket on the donkey, collected enough food to last a couple of days, and set out. As they walked down the street, Varsig suddenly remembered the baby chicks that had just hatched in the dooryard. She broke away and ran back to fetch them, but her mother commanded her firmly to come back. Protesting vehemently, Varsig rejoined the ever-growing throng, laden with bundles. At the edge of town, they found themselves in the middle of a stampede. People were knocked down and trampled in their hurry to escape the Turks, whom they believed to be just behind them. The air was filled with the sounds of animals bellowing and women screaming. Riders beat savagely at their horses, exhorting them to make haste. Within a few hours, the city of Van was deserted, except for the old and infirm who had been left behind or chosen to stay and die.

Varsig was numb with shock and fatigue. She walked in a daze broken only by her mother's arm pushing her to walk faster, comforted by the monotonous sound of the cart wheels ahead of her on the road. Hypnotized, she imagined that she was once more on the road to Varakh, going to celebrate the festival. "Why don't we have a wagon?" she asked her mother, but Lucia, preoccupied by the struggle to propel herself and the two girls forward, did not answer. More than once, she had to snatch them up to keep them from being stepped on, and as the Russian soldiers rushed up and down the line shouting that the Turks were nearer and that they must make haste, the danger of being crushed to death by the panic-stricken crowd increased. Ishkhanuhi, who was not quite three, was allowed to ride on the donkey, but Varsig had to keep up as best she could. When she saw a Russian cannon rolling by, she demanded, "Let me sit on that!" At times it seemed that she would surely drop to the ground, but each time her body sagged, her mother jerked her up again and dragged her forward.

Finally night fell and they were allowed to stop. The air was stifling, and there was no water. Desperate, the adults gave the wailing children their own urine to drink. The road had been carved out by the Russians through a desolate region, and at night the ground was alive with snakes and scorpions, which terrified the little girls and made it impossible to lie down. They were forced to sleep standing, leaning against something. The halt was only a brief one. Soon they were awakened and urged to move on, for the dreaded Turkish army was still at their backs. Armenian soldiers brought up the rear, and according to rumor, the half-savage Kurds were only an hour behind them. Many of the youngest children were soon dead of starvation. Varsig felt that she had become nothing but a tired lump. She could think only of her desire to lie down and sleep for five minutes, but she did not dare to stop, for she had seen others who had fallen and been trampled to death. Eventually the group passed by a rushing river, and the half-crazed refugees began to loosen their heavy bundles and hurl them into the current. The urge to lighten their loads spread through the crowd, and some of the women, in their eagerness to follow suit, threw in their own babies, which they had been carrying on their backs. Then, realizing what they had done, they hurled themselves into the river and drowned. In the confusion resulting from thousands of people moving forward with no organization, family groups had become separated, and all around one heard the frantic cries of mothers searching for their children. All night, they would go from group to group, peering into the faces of the sleeping children and calling the names of their lost ones, "Haro!" "Maro!" "Sako!" There was never a moment when the air was not filled with their cries.

The little Ishkhanuhi was a winning child, plump and affectionate, with huge dark eyes and fair skin. She soon caught the attention of the Russian soldiers, who found a horse and put both sisters on its broad back, allowing Lucia to follow on the donkey. This turned out to be less than a blessing, however. The horse was nervous and high-spirited. Lucia already had her hands full and could not keep it in check. Suddenly it started violently at a noise in the rear and galloped off with the two terrified children on its back, leaving their helpless mother behind. They were soon out of her sight and could do nothing but hang on for dear life. At last, a man managed to catch the horse and lift them down, but he turned out to be nothing but an opportunist, for he led the horse away and left a shabby little donkey in its place. Varsig now became obsessed with one idea: never to let go of her sister's hand. She was frightened of the braying, stubborn donkey and refused to mount him. With one hand she held tightly to his rope, and with the other she clung to her sister. It did not occur to her to look for her mother. Her only thought was to keep her sister beside her. At last, when they could stumble on no farther, they sat down on the ground and fell asleep. Varsig made sure she kept a tight hold on the donkey's lead, but when she awoke, the donkey had disappeared.

They were now reduced to the state of beggars, living off the handouts of those who took pity on them. Varsig discovered that she had a few raisins in her pocket, and these she rationed out, determined to make them last as long as possible. The days became a blur of hunger, thirst, and fatigue. No one paid much attention to the two children. There were many like them whose parents had been lost or died along the way. The Russians did what they could, but they had no facilities to care for the huge throng, which was totally unorganized and undisciplined. Eventually, despite all her efforts to keep hold of her sister's hand, they were separated, and she was totally alone. Already in a state of shock, her mind became completely benumbed, and she no longer reacted to anything around her.

At last she reached Igdir, a small town to the northeast of Mount Ararat. They had come about a hundred miles from Van. Varsig squatted in the street with the other refugees, dirty, ragged, emaciated, seeing nothing. Those who had lost their loved ones sat there day after day, questioning new arrivals in the hope of learning what had happened to them. The pavement burned her bare feet and legs, for the summer sun beat down mercilessly. High above her head, branches of fruit hung temptingly, but they were jealously guarded by their owners, who hated and feared the hordes of refugees who had turned their village into a nightmarish place filled with sickness and death.

Suddenly, Varsig found herself being picked up and covered with kisses. She heard the sound of a voice calling her pet Armenian names—"Darling, sweet one, little one!" She recognized the face of Ardashes Mirzoian, the husband of her mother's cousin, who had been brought up with Lucia in the Nersesian household. A few months before, he had brought his wife and their child to visit her relatives in Van, so he recognized Varsig. He covered the filthy, half-starved little girl with kisses, laughing and crying as she clung to his neck. A month after their departure from Van, his two-year-old child and his wife had been burned to death by the Turks. He was now a second lieutenant in the newly formed Armenian army under commanding general Antranik Pasha. Ardashes had discovered Lucia at the school-turned-hospital, where she was helping to care for the sick. Some kind people had already brought Ishkhanuhi to her, but she had been sure that she would never see Varsig again. Ardashes had promised to search for her nonetheless, and finding her was like finding one of his own.

When he set her down, he realized that she was disgustingly dirty and covered with lice, so he took her to be washed, shaved her head, and found her some decent clothes before taking her to her mother. Still not recovered from the horrors of the past days, Varsig paid no attention to Lucia, however, but ran to her sister, threw her arms around her, and refused to let go of her. Ardashes, who had connections, had been able to find Lucia a good place to stay in a doctor's house, and Varsig remembered that the three of them slept together on the roof under the stars to escape the heat.

Lucia was now destitute. She had thrown away what few possessions she had managed to save when she lost the children. Since she spoke Russian and had some experience, however, she had found a job nursing the sick. The privations and lack of sanitary precautions during the exodus had led to outbreaks of disease, and the refugees were threatened with a full-scale cholera epidemic. But this job left her no time to look after the children, so she followed Ardashes' advice and placed them in one of the orphanages that had been formed for Armenian refugee children. She had received word that her parents had managed to save a few belongings and some money and were determined to push on to Baku.

Meanwhile, in Igdir, a tall, handsome officer wearing the uniform of the Russian cavalry walked down the street one day and came upon a group of Armenians he recognized as his fellow townsmen. He stopped to talk to them and have his boots blacked, for many of the exiled Armenians were reduced to such tasks to earn their bread. He struck up a conversation with an elderly member of the group.

"Did you by any chance know the family of Nerses who lived in Arakh?" he asked.

"Yes," came the reply, "they've gone on to Baku."

"And did their daughter Lucia go with them?"

"No, she was married to Tavit, you know, and had two little girls by him."

"Then she must be with her husband?"

"No. Her husband died before the siege of Van. She's here in Igdir, working at the hospital."

The cavalry officer stared at the old man as if he had caught him in a lie, until the old man asked grumpily, "And what makes you ask so many questions about Lucia?"

"I am the nephew of her brother's wife," was his answer. "I am Mooshegh."

Then the old man held out his arms. "Mooshegh!" he exclaimed. "Of course you are. I am Lucia's uncle. Come, I'll take you to her."

Mooshegh Pazian had heeded the call for all the Armenian diaspora to serve their country and had returned from America to become a captain with the Russian cavalry under General Yegarian. When the two reached the hospital, someone was sent to tell Lucia that she had a visitor. She came into the room and saw her uncle with a stranger.

"Do you know me?" he asked.

Many years had passed since Lucia and Mooshegh had read together under the fruit trees in her father's garden. She had journeyed back and forth across the eastern Mediterranean world, borne five children, buried a husband, and been driven out of her homeland into exile. Nonetheless, his name rose without hesitation to her lips.

"Mooshegh! You are Mooshegh!" she cried. In her heart, she had never stopped thinking about him, and he had never stopped thinking about her. Both believed to the end of their lives that theirs was a true love made in heaven. On November 20, 1917, Mooshegh married Lucia with General Yegarian's permission. The groom, who had been educated by American Protestants in Van, converted to the Armenian Apostolic faith the same day, and Yegarian served as his best man.

FOR LUCIA, THIS WAS THE HAPPIEST TIME OF HER LIFE. The Turks had once again abandoned Van, and a group of former residents decided to return to the city and rebuild. When she and Mooshegh arrived, they had a bitter shock, however. They found nothing but ruins. The fruit trees were broken and burned, the wells polluted, the fertile gardens flooded by the sophisticated irrigation system that had nurtured them. The house of Nerses, once the proudest of Arakh, was only a shell. Even the stairs had disappeared. Determined to salvage something, Lucia borrowed a ladder and climbed to the second story. There she found a few pictures of her children, including one of Varsig dressed in a Cossack costume, sitting on her father's knee. Sick at heart, she gathered these mementos and turned away. Nothing else was left.

Lucia and Mooshegh remained in Van for about two months, but it became increasingly evident that the destruction of the city had been so complete that it could no longer sustain life; the optimistic citizens who had wanted to rebuild were soon on the verge of starvation. What is more, the dream of Armenian sovereignty was quickly fading as the big powers once again forgot their lofty promises and betrayed the helpless people of Armenia. Mooshegh became convinced that they should go to America. Within a few months, his visa would expire and he would no longer be free to leave. Lucia agreed. If they had to take up residence on foreign soil, she preferred the freedom and opportunities of America to those offered by the Bolsheviks, who now controlled Russian Armenia. Accordingly, she wrote to the authorities and asked that her children be released from the orphanage and returned to her at once. To her horror, the reply came that the officials in Nakhitchevan, where the girls had been sent some months before, had no information on their whereabouts. In the chaos following the Bolshevik Revolution, the Russian bureaucracy had lost track of Varsig and Ishkhanuhi. Lucia was frantic. If she and Mooshegh did not leave immediately, they would be interned in Russian Armenia. There was no time to search the hundreds of orphanages housing Armenian children. Reluctantly, she agreed to leave for America while there was still time and put the case into the hands of the Red Cross. Once Mooshegh, who was an American citizen, had legally adopted her daughters, the Soviet government would be obliged to let them join her. Accordingly, she immigrated with him to the United States.

Once she arrived, she did not give up her determination to find the children, but the situation seemed hopeless. Varsig and Ishkhanuhi, along with thousands of others, had been shipped from town to town, often without enough to eat, sometimes separated from each other, always struggling to stay together. At last, when they had all but forgotten their mother and their homeland, they were located by the Red Cross. Lucia wrote to her daughters, telling them about the new country where they would all live together. There was little money, however. She and Mooshegh were both forced to work hard just to support themselves, but they managed to scrape together enough to purchase two boat tickets. Thus began the last and longest journey for Varsig and Ishkhanuhi, first to Constantinople, and then to the New World.

There, like so many victims of the genocide, Varsig and Ishkhanuhi lived to see their children, grandchildren, and great-grandchildren thrive, living proof of the survival of the Armenian people.

Dharma and the Bomb
Postmodern Critiques of Science and the Rise of Reactionary Modernism in India

Meera Nanda

OF FIREFLIES AND WAR

Amidst the headlines about nuclear war worries in South Asia, a little-noticed news item appeared on the BBC World News.[1] The BBC reported on May 14, 2002, that in the middle of the dangerous military buildup along the border with Pakistan, with careless talk of nuclear war in the air, the Indian government had funded scientists in the nation's premier defense research institutes to develop techniques of biological and chemical warfare based on *Arthashastra*, a 2,300-year-old Sanskrit treatise on statecraft and warfare. The venerable Sanskrit book is supposed to include recipes for "a single meal that will keep a soldier fighting for a month, methods for inducing madness in the enemy as well as advice on chemical and biological warfare," according to Shaikh Azizur Rahman, the BBC reporter from Mumbai. Space scientists and biologists are trying to replicate the ancient formulas consisting of special herbs, milk, and ghee (clarified butter) that will keep soldiers going for a month without food. Other projects include "shoes made of camel skin smeared with a serum from owls and vultures than can help soldiers walk hundreds of miles without feeling tired. . . . A powder made from fireflies and the eyes of wild boars that can endow night vision. . . . A lethal smoke [made] by burning snakes, insects and plant seeds." Rahman reported that scientists next plan to turn their attention to other ancient manuscripts that "claim to provide secrets of manufacturing planes which can not be destroyed by any external force and remain invisible to the enemy planes." The scientists were said to be "excited about the possibilities and do not for a moment think that the idea is crazy."

What is one to make of it? Comic relief? A nostalgia trip for those aghast at the prospect of nuclear annihilation (if only all our weapons came out of fireflies and boars and insects and plants)? Looked at in isolation, this is just a funny little story, a sideshow. After all, what does this minor project matter when India continues to spend millions of rupees (close to 18 percent of the national budget each year) for developing or acquiring modern methods of mass destruction?

But this is no sideshow. This project is not about defense. It is about Hindu supremacy. This project is aimed not at an external enemy but at extending the reach of Hindu nationalism in India's schools and other institutions in the public sphere. This project is about the rising tide of reactionary modernism in India. To place this incidence in a larger context, let us go back to May 1998, when India test-fired nuclear devices in the desert of Pokharan.

THE BOMB: INDIA GOES NUCLEAR

The media around the world carried a picture that should have sent a chill down our collective spine. It showed crowds of ordinary, everyday men and women dancing in the streets of New Delhi to celebrate India's successful nuclear tests. (Think about it: celebrating the making of a nuclear bomb.) For these mobs, the technological hardware of the bomb was a symbol of their national greatness, their strength, and even their virility; it was a Hindu bomb against the Islamic bomb of Pakistan. It is not a coincidence that many among the jubilant mobs also served as foot soldiers in the Hindu nationalist crusade against all those who refuse to accept the equation of India with Hindu dharma. Such persecuted minorities include not just Muslims and Christians but also secular artists, writers, filmmakers, and political activists accused of disrespecting Hinduism. An India that celebrates its bombs is an increasingly intolerant and illiberal India.

Antinuclear activists and progressive intellectuals in and from India, struggling valiantly to retain some degree of hope for a return to sanity, have argued that these pictures pander to orientalist expectations of India—ignorant, nationalist, third-world know-nothings. The Western media's emphasis on mobs celebrating the nuclear tests, the critics claim, misrepresents the actual sentiments of the majority of Indian people who, by and large, are opposed to nuclear weapons or are at least indifferent to them. The overwhelming public approval for the prospect of India building the bomb captured by public opinion polls, the argument goes, was a statistical aberration stemming from the bias of the poll takers for urban folks with telephone connections.

For the sake of peace in the subcontinent, one can only hope that this optimistic reading of Indian public opinion turns out to be true. Yet the fact remains that while the Hindu nationalist supporters came out in the streets, with the full backing and blessing of the ruling Hindu nationalist party, the silent majority remained, well, silent. The scattered, albeit impassioned, protests by communists, feminists, and other leftist peace and disarmament movements failed to bring out the presumably disapproving majority—if it really is disapproving—into the streets.

Although it may be difficult to accurately gauge the width and depth of nationalist sentiment among the Indian public, the jubilant mobs cannot be easily dismissed as a statistical aberration or as an orientalist stereotype created by the Western media. These mobs are only the visible signs of a large ideological counterrevolution that has been going on behind the scenes in schools, universities, research institutions, temples, and, yes, even in supposedly "progressive" new social movements organized to protect the environment or defend the cultural rights of traditional communities against the presumed onslaught of Western cultural imperialism.

DHARMA: HINDU PACKAGING OF THE BOMB

I have a lot more to say later about the antimodernist tendencies of the Gandhian, postmodernist, and old economic nationalist, anti-imperialist left alliance. But for now, I want to focus on how the bomb and the science behind it are being packaged in a Hindu idiom and propagated in schools, temples, and the entertainment media as an unfolding of a holistic, unified, ultramodern science already contained in the ancient texts of the Hindus.

The ideologues of Hindu nationalism and, indeed, many Indian scientists and ordinary people on the streets claimed that the bomb had been foretold in their sacred book, the Bhagavad Gita, in which God declares himself to be "the radiance of a thousand suns, the splendor of the Mighty One. . . . I have become Death, the destroyer of the worlds." Robert Oppenheimer might have used the Hindu imagery after the first nuclear test in 1945 to express fear and awe at what science had wrought, but the Hindu partisans see in this imagery a cultural and religious justification for their nuclear weapons. Indeed, some observers have gone so far as to claim that the detonation of the nuclear bomb was a religious phenomenon in which Indians saw "the triumph of divine power . . . the workings of providence, grace, revelation and a history guided by an inexorable faith."[2]

There is plenty of evidence for a distinctively Hindu packaging of the bomb. Even though the Hindu nationalist Bharatiya Janata Party (BJP) government responsible for the blasts eschewed religious rhetoric in its official pronouncements, it gave its parent organization, the RSS (Rashtirya Svyamsevak Sangh) and its cultural arm, the VHP (Vishva Hindu Parishad), free rein to claim the bomb for the glory of Hindu civilization and Vedic sciences. Shortly after the explosion, VHP ideologues inside and outside the government vowed to build a temple dedicated to Shakti (the goddess of energy) and Vigyan (science) at the site of the explosion. The temple would celebrate the Vigyan of the Vedas, which supposedly contain all the science of nuclear fission and all the know-how for making bombs and much, much more. (It is this ancient science that the defense ministry wants to tap into, as the BBC story reveals.) Plans were made to take "consecrated soil" from the explosion site around the country for mass prayers and celebrations.

Mercifully, the fear of spreading radioactivity scuttled these plans. But the Hinduization of the bomb has continued in many ways. There are reports that in festivals around the country, the idols of Ganesh were made with atomic orbits in place of a halo around his elephant head. These "atomic Ganeshas" apparently brought in good business. Other gods were cast as gun-toting soldiers. At an official level, the weapons and the missiles under construction are given distinctly mythological names, from Agni (the fire god) to Trishul (trident, the symbol of the god Shiva). The religious imagery was sufficiently pronounced to alarm a group of religious studies scholars in America. They issued a letter of concern to "protest the use of religious imagery to glorify and to legitimate nuclear exercises."[3] Indeed, invocation of gods in the context of nuclear weapons has become a constant feature of public discourse. During the recent standoff between India and Pakistan, India's most popular newsmagazine, *India Today*, prefaced its tasteless warmongering with references to Mahabharata and the "thousand suns." The net result of these references is to turn these ugly developments into something like the *Mahabharata,* in which god sided with the virtuous.

The invocation of Shakti and Vigyan is not fortuitous at all. Hindu nationalists have claimed that the bombs and the missiles are symbols of India's advanced science and technology, the roots of which lie in its ancient religious traditions. The idea of constructing a temple to the goddess of learning at the site of the explosion was meant to propagate the age-old myth that Vedas presage all important discoveries of science, especially quantum and nuclear physics. A popular version of this myth was reported by Jonathan Parry in 1985:

> In Benaras, I have often been told—and I have heard variants of the same story elsewhere—that Max Muller stole chunks of the Sama-Veda from India, and it was by studying these that German scientists were able to develop the atom bomb. The ancient rishis (sages) not only knew about nuclear fission, but they also had supersonic airplanes and guided missiles.[4]

The sacralization of war has meant a simultaneous scientizing of sacred Hindu texts. Technological modernization, even in its ugliest form, is being encompassed in the traditional, religiously sanctioned understanding of the natural world.

OF SATELLITES AND HOROSCOPES

Exactly the same pattern unfolded in another episode, this time involving satellites and horoscopes. In April 2001, the Indian Space Research Organization made history by successfully putting a satellite into geostationary orbit, 36,000 kilometers above the earth. In July 2001, the University Grants Commission, the central body overseeing the funding of higher education, announced its plans to offer science courses in Vedic astrology in India's universities and colleges. Astrology has been declared to be on a par with other natural sciences and will be offered as part of the natural science curriculum. This is in addition to other new courses, including training in *karmakanda* (priest craft), Vedic mathematics, and other "spiritual sciences." Other courses in "mind sciences," including meditation, telepathy, rebirth, and mind control, are being planned. The same space power that takes justified pride in its ability to touch the stars will soon start educating its youth in how to read our fortunes and misfortunes in the stars and how to propitiate the heavens through appropriate *karmakanda*. For all we know, the satellites launched by India might someday carry Internet signals that will make horoscopes easier to match!

To outsiders, the ruling Hindu nationalist government likes to present a face of enlightened, forward-looking democracy. Since the September 11 attacks, India has presented itself to the West as an ally in its fight against Islamic fundamentalism. This image hides another reality. Under the cover of democracy, the terms of political discourse in India are changing. Nominally secular institutions in the public sphere—from education and research to the media and government agencies—are increasingly adopting an aggressively Hindu identity.

The Hindu justifications for nuclear weapons, the attempt to read modern science into Vedic texts, and the teaching of Vedic astrology as a science—all these have to be understood in the larger context of Hindu nationalism. When you put these symbolic gestures in the larger context of the BJP-sponsored research into Vedic sciences, the Hindu nationalist project of rewriting the history of Indus Valley as the cradle of the "Aryan" civilization, and the alteration of school textbooks to Hinduize the curriculum and to actively seek religious legitimation for economic and social policies, the dharma and the bomb connection do not seem as "orientalist" as some may think.

A SYMPTOM OF REACTIONARY MODERNISM

I submit that this Hinduization of the bomb is a sign of a phenomenon that is best described as reactionary modernism, in which a society embraces modern science and technology while rejecting the ethos and the ethics of the Enlightenment—or, to put it another way, where technological modernization occurs without the benefit of secularization and liberalism. This phenomenon was first named and described by Jeffrey Herf (1984) in his well-known book *Reactionary Modernism: Technology, Culture and Politics in Weimar and the Third Reich*.

What makes Herf's study of German fascism relevant for contemporary India is his thesis that the Nazi support for cutting-edge technology and science was not merely a strategic bow to modernity to further an essentially irrational and antimodern agenda. Rather, Herf argues—as I will in the case of India—that reactionary modernism in Germany was underpinned by a distinctive, philosophically sophisticated worldview that "incorporated modern science and technology into the cultural system of German nationalism, without diminishing the latter's romantic and anti-rational aspects." Rather than allow modern science and technology to challenge the romanticism and holism of the *volkish* ideology, German reactionary intellectuals, including Ernest Junger, Carl Schmitt, Oswald Spengler, and Martin Heidegger, succeeded in selectively assimilating science into the language of community, nation, Kultur, and finally blood and race. Modern science was disarmed of its critical potential by turning it into an expression of the "Aryan soul" and rejecting whatever could not be so distorted to fit.

THREE THESES

I am now in a position to state three theses on which I will expand. One, under the jargon of cultural authenticity, Hindu nationalists are in the process of absorbing science into myth, making science simply a belated, Westernized, distorted affirmation of the truths already known to Vedic metaphysics of nondualism and holism.

Two, the political legitimacy of and the philosophical arguments for this reconciliation of science and myth have been prepared not by the Hindu Right but by self-described "progressive" intellectuals and activists who broadly share the postmodern suspicion of modern science as a meta-narrative of binary dualism, reductionism, and, consequently, domination of nature, women, and third-world people. In India, for at least two decades now, it has been the populist, anticapitalist Left that has identified the Enlightenment and science as the biggest obstacles to creating a good society. The demand for an indigenous, "patriotic" science has been the loudest among the intellectuals and activists who identify themselves as progressive in politics but indigenist in their cultural beliefs. The left-postmodernists hoped that once non-Western peoples, especially women and other oppressed groups, were allowed to bring their own cultural values and life experiences into knowledge production, they would heal modern science's divide between facts and values, reason and emotions, nature and culture. The Hindu reactionary modernists have claimed these same holistic, nonlogocentric ways of knowing not as a standpoint of the oppressed but for the glory of the Hindu nation itself. The Hindu Right, in other words, enthusiastically accepts the Left's diagnosis that the objectivity and value-freedom of modern science are the source of alienation and domination, but then it offers the high-Brahmanical view of the world—the same worldview that has, incidentally, legitimized the caste system and a stifling form of patriarchy—as the ultimate source of a nonalienating, nondualist science. What's more, the Hindu Right is able to certify elite Brahmanical ways of knowing as scientific by denying, in a postmodern style, that modern science is any more objective, any closer to the truth, than any other way of knowing. Whereas the postmodernists were concerned with exposing the presence of myth and metaphysics in the objective science of nature, the Religious Right has turned the argument around and declared myths to be science.

This brings me to my last and most positive thesis: traditional cultures contain rudiments of materialist, pragmatic thinking that, far from being incommensurable and different, is perfectly compatible with the worldview and methodological demands of modern science. In India, these proto-sciences have existed not in the mystical idealism of the Vedas and the Upanishads but in the heterodox non-Brahmanical traditions of Lokayata and Carvaka. These aspects of traditional cultures, when updated through rigorous scientific education, can serve as seedbeds of a secular and liberal culture in non-Western societies. Thus, contrary to the prevailing wisdom among feminists and multiculturalists, who look to idealized "local knowledge" as an alternative to modern science, I insist that modern science is the standpoint of the oppressed in the third world.

I intend to expand on these three points, but as you well know, this whole issue of the nature of science and other ways of knowing has been at the heart of the so-called science wars. I know I am entering a minefield here. So I want to take a minute to clarify the terms of the debate.

THE TERMS OF THE DEBATE

First, I want to make it clear that I do not see all the good and honorable people who seek solutions to the dilemmas of modern life in traditional societies, religions, or some other kind of noninstrumental community life as reactionary revivalists or backward-looking romantics. I most emphatically do not condemn all attempts to retrieve a usable past from non-Western heritage as reactionary. (I myself look back into India's intellectual history to retrieve cultural roots of the Indian enlightenment from the heterodox anti-Vedic philosophies.) What concerns me about the particular retrieval that has gone on under the postmodernist-Gandhian-ecofeminist alliance is that the Brahmanical past they are retrieving is usable only for a new authoritarian Hindu nationalism.

I grant that the indigenist-left critics of modernity have the best of intentions. If they have quarreled with the Enlightenment, it is because they seek to extend its promise of tolerance and autonomy to other cultures so that they are not forced to conform to one universal story. If they quarrel with science, it is because they think it has become a new source of mystification and domination. I also do not deny that, apart from some notable crossovers, the anti-Enlightenment Left in India has taken a firm stand against Hindu nationalism. Indeed, far from being knowing allies of the Right, the indigenist-left intellectuals and activists are facing persecution from the current regime. While I acknowledge their courage and good intentions, I question the soundness of their diagnosis of the ills of the modern age and the efficacy of their prescriptions for "non-Western modernities." What worries me is that after all the years of denigrating any rational critique of indigenous cosmology and traditions as elitist or Western or both, the Left's present stand for secularism may be too little too late and too rife with self-contradictions.

Second, my critique does not apply to all of postmodernist tradition but only to the so-called science question. Postmodernism at its best aspires to be an equal-opportunity naysayer: if it denies the possibility of truth beyond the local contingencies of language and power, it denies it as much for the holy truths of Hinduism or Christianity or Islam as it does for the grand narrative of modern science. Although some third-world adapters of postmodernism valiantly try to remain evenhanded and take a skeptical, deconstructive look at the grand narratives of their own traditions, in most cases, they end up as essentialists when it comes to their own heritage and deconstructivists when it comes to the West. But all non-Western postmodernists, religious or lay, Left or Right, without exception, resolutely decry one particular grand narrative—namely, modern science. The very rationality and aspiration of modern science and the Enlightenment project more broadly—the ability to put the inherited givens of a culture, paradigm, or mode of life to a systematic, collective test of reason and experience in order to arrive at knowledge that transcends the confines of the givens—are considered theoretically impossible and politically flawed. They are seen as peculiarly Western propensities and a source of the West's colonialism and other pathologies. When I criticize postmodernist influences in postcolonial thought, it is this view of science that I am concerned with.

Third, following the lead of neo-Gandhian antimodernists such as Ashis Nandy, Vandana Shiva, and others, many have become convinced that the very logic of science must be questioned because modern, science-based development has led to an absolute and growing immiseration and cultural displacement of women, native peoples, and traditional family farmers. They also claim that development has given the state carte blanche to coerce people, to tinker with traditional community practices and such. Science, as the phrase goes, has become the reason of the state.

I will cite only two counters to this thesis. First, contrary to the critics' claims, nearly all indices of human development have more than doubled in the last two and a half decades in India. And I am talking here of the Amartya Sen–inspired human development indices of such things as life expectancy, literacy, and gender equality compiled by the United Nations Development Program, not some econometric data from the World Bank or the International Monetary Fund. Yes, the rate of improvement is uneven, with women and lower castes lagging behind. Yes, India could have done much better if it had paid attention to the basic needs of those on the bottom, without sacrificing economic growth. But this is a far cry from saying that things have gotten worse or that people are getting poorer in absolute terms. Second, in one of the rare qualitative studies of its kind, the well-respected agronomist N. S. Jodha found some interesting results that challenge the conventional wisdom of modernization as a source of hardship and anomie. Jodha found that over a period of two decades, even those villagers in western India who had not seen an increase in real income reported a significant increase in well-being. The villagers felt that their lives were getting better because they did not have to depend on the patronage of their caste superiors, they no longer felt compelled to follow inherited occupations, and they had more choices and greater access to modern amenities. Freedom from patronage, opportunities for individual choices, a belief in progress—all these are modern liberal aspirations that these villagers discovered for themselves. Many of these improvements, incidentally, were made possible thanks to state intervention, the same state that is treated by postmodernist critics as authoritarian and colonial in its mind-set.

What I am trying to get to is this: the despair over the violence of modernity is totally disproportionate to the actual facts on the ground. Although much remains to be done, the situation does not call for a total condemnation of modernization.

HINDUIZATION OF SCIENCE

Qualifications and clarifications out of the way, let me now return to my theses, starting with the Hinduization of science. I mentioned how the bomb is being packaged in the idiom of dharma, complete with atomic gods. The Hinduization goes much deeper and wider. All of modern science is in the process of being knitted into a new, Indocentric, Aryan science. If I may borrow a term from Louis Dumont, what we are witnessing is a process through which high Brahmanic Hinduism is encompassing modern science into itself. That is, Hinduism is presenting itself as already containing the worldview, the methods, and even the findings of modern science, especially of quantum physics, ecology, and medicine. Science simply becomes a somewhat inferior, materialistic aspect of Vedic wisdom. (Encompassment is the traditional Hindu way of dealing with heterodox ideas. It leaves room for different views to be accepted on their own terms, but it always tends to include them in a hierarchical relation, subordinated to the ultimate truth of dharma. The other is not recognized as an otherness against which one's own beliefs can be tested but is claimed as an aspect of, approach to, or aberration from the truth contained in its own doctrine.)

I mentioned the work of Jonathan Parry earlier. In his ethnography of Benaras, Parry describes meeting orthodox Brahmans in this ancient city who sincerely believe that Max Muller, a nineteenth-century German orientalist, stole chunks of Sama Veda from India and that German scientists were able to develop their atomic bomb program by studying these texts. This is not just a quaint story. It is part of a widespread, deep-seated belief, at least among the upper-caste Hindus, that the Vedas and the Upanishads are highly developed sciences, on a par with Western science.

This notion of Hinduism-as-science is part of the nationalist myth that recurs repeatedly in the writings of nineteenth- and twentieth-century reformers, including Ram Mohan Roy, Vivekananda, Dayanand, Gandhi, and, to some extent, even Nehru. These reformers hoped to revitalize and modernize Indian culture not by a reformation and an Enlightenment-style critique of traditional ways of thinking but by a restoration of the supposedly scientific spirit of the ancients.

With the Hindu nationalists in ascendance, this idea of Hindu dharma as science has moved, once again, to center stage. The government is funding research projects to modernize astrology, Vastu Shastra, Vedic mathematics, Vedic physics, and traditional medicine. New books have appeared, some of them coauthored by U.S.-based scientists in important universities and sold aggressively around the world through Amazon.com. These books claim to have found such modern discoveries as electricity and the microscope, the solar spectrum and cosmic radiation, photosynthesis and plastic surgery, and binary numbers and advanced computing techniques in the Vedas. Specifically, these scientists claim that the number of syllables in Vedic verses, which supposedly corresponds to the number of bricks in fire altars and the number of beads on the rosary, actually encodes the exact distance between the moon and the sun, the speed of light, the big bang, and so forth. With the Hindu nationalists at the helm, these discoveries are quickly finding their way into school textbooks.

This is not all. Claims for Hinduism-as-science are part of the larger argument that equates ancient Hindus with the original Aryan-speaking people. In the emerging Indocentrism, the landmass of India is claimed to be the original home of the Aryans, who presumably took the Vedic myths and concepts to ancient Egypt and Greece. Thus, the Indocentrists claim, Egyptian and Greek sciences and, by lineage, modern science are Hinduism's "daughter sciences," or at least "sister sciences." Hindu India becomes the cradle of all civilization.

This self-aggrandizing Indocentrism would be laughable if it were not so dangerous. It is laughable because it makes preposterous claims based on shoddy logic and even shoddier evidence. It is dangerous because these claims are made with an earnest nationalistic fervor and backed by the state, which is committed to making India Hindu. I am concerned with Hinduism-as-science not so much because of the harm it can do to the growth of modern science and technology but because of the harm it can do to the development of a secular and egalitarian public culture in India. Hindu ideologues are not going to close down the labs; they are hitching their prospects for entry into the club of elite nations on nuclear, computer, and genetic technologies. Hinduism-as-science is part of the cultural project of modernizing, without the rationalism and secularism of the Enlightenment to challenge the traditional cultural values. Declaring that Hinduism is—by definition—the mother of all science gives the gloss and prestige of modernity to rituals and institutions that are based on a magical understanding of the natural world and a hierarchical understanding of the social world.

Such a glossing is not without serious political consequences. It is true that ideas do not drive history. But the choice between invoking the authority of ancient texts and transcendent myths and seeking publicly testable evidence makes a huge difference in the quality of debate and the terms of sociability in the public sphere. This need to create new democratic norms of sociability is nowhere greater than in India, which has one of the most liberal constitutions, superimposed on a society that lives by the idea of natural inequality. The danger of Hindu science is that it will further entrench the holistic, organismic worldview as our national ethos and a source of public morality. Moreover, absorbing science into myth and rituals—the hallmark of reactionary modernism—makes the defense of religion appear like a defense of reason and modernity, and it brings out the mobs in the streets who want to become modern without losing their traditional identities.

POSTMODERNISM AS AN IDEOLOGY OF REACTIONARY MODERNISM

So far, so good. But recall that I am making a bigger and, to some, more controversial claim—that is, that the postmodern and postcolonial denigration of modern science has provided the philosophical grounds for Hindu science. On the face of it, my thesis sounds highly implausible. Whereas the Hindu Right is busy claiming the products of modern science and technology as part of its own heritage, the postmodernist and postcolonial intellectuals have sought to insulate non-Western cultures from modern science, which they see as alien and oppressive. When the postmodern critics turn to local cultures and "ethnosciences," they are not seeking to establish these as the mother of modern science. On the contrary, the whole point of ethnoscience has been to establish that non-Western cultures can produce wholly different sciences informed by pacific, cooperative, womanly values of nurturance and sustainability that would never lead to such things as nuclear bombs. How can I ignore all these differences and accuse the postmodernists of aiding and abetting the project of Hindu science?

As I said at the outset, it is not the intentions but the logic of postmodernist critics of science that has opened the door to the Religious Right. A logic that denies distinctions between myth and science, ideology and knowledge, might and right runs the risk that myth, ideology, and might will be clothed as scientific truth. And that is indeed what has come to pass in India today. But more specifically, there are at least three postmodernist arguments against science that one finds repeated, almost verbatim, in the arguments for Hinduism-as-science: (1) arguments against dualism as a source of domination of the other; (2) arguments for critical traditionalism and standpoint epistemology; and (3) arguments for epistemic charity. To understand why these arguments would have a resonance for Hindu nationalists, it is important to understand how they argue their case.

The case for Hinduism-as-science hinges on Hinduism's purported holism or nondualism, which does not differentiate between the domains of the material world and the spiritual and social world: all aspects of the entire cosmos are supposed to be products of pure consciousness and eventually merge back into it. Conveniently forgetting that this is a purely metaphysical and mystical unity, not accessible to the ordinary human sensory experience or reason, the Hindu nationalists elevate it to the level of a science—the Hindu equivalent of the unified field theory—that grasps the interconnections of the world. They correspondingly elevate yoga and other traditional methods of divining associations between the heavens and earth as legitimate Hindu methods of science that are supposed to be as rational within the unified cosmopolis of Hinduism as the experimental method is within the Judeo-Christian dualism between a transcendent, law-giving God and his creation.

This holism would have remained a fantastical romance, but for the tremendous philosophical support it has found from the postcolonial feminist and ecofeminist critics of science. Critiques of dualism and binary thinking lie at the heart of these critiques of science as a source of domination. Let me explain.

Gayatri Spivak, a self-described "deconstructivist, feminist Marxist," defined her role as a postcolonial critic as someone who can say an "impossible no" to Western conceptual categories, which she, as an intellectual, inhabits most intimately. Why did she and many other bright, erudite diasporic scholars from India feel compelled to renounce Western concepts, which, as Spivak admits, are an intimate part of their intellectual heritage? They, like the rest of the "new humanities" in North American universities, have taken a linguistic turn: they have come to see Western knowledge itself as a source of colonial power, for it was by objectifying, quantifying, and classifying the colonized that the Western powers were able to control them. Colonialism ceased to be political-economic domination and came to be seen as epistemological domination, a colonization of the mind by alien conceptions of what is real, what is right, and what is desirable. Whereas it was possible for earlier critics of imperialism to oppose the economic and political domination of the West but still accept the universality and legitimacy of Western science, postcolonial and other influential anti-Enlightenment intellectuals demanded that a critique of imperialism must mean decolonization of the mind and culture. The only true progressives were those segments of the Indian population—the peasants, the traditional masses—who lived their lives in community and harmony, as fish in the water, unself-conscious of the basis of these traditions and unsullied by the rationalism and materialism of modern science and Enlightenment. This position was first developed by neo-Gandhian intellectuals led by Ashis Nandy and others at the Center for Study of Developing Societies and the scholar-activists associated with the Patriotic and People's Science and Technology Group, who drew on Thomas Kuhn, Paul Feyerabend, and the 1960s critics of instrumental reason. They were later joined by feminist and postcolonial critics who were influenced by feminist standpoint epistemologies and the Foucaultian equation of knowledge and power.

I submit that this demand for decolonization of the mind is nothing but a demand for a holistic or re-enchanted science that leads straight to Hinduism-as-science. The heart of postmodern, feminist, and postcolonial critique has been that modern science is dualist, that it differentiates and separates the domains of culture from nature, knower from the known, matter from spirit, reason from myths and emotions, public from private, and so on. But, the postmodernists claim, reason is preferred over emotions, objectivity over an open embrace of cultural values, not because they bring us closer to the truth but because they further patriarchal and imperialist goals. This dualism is the source of "epistemic violence" because it forces the "other" to conform to the categories that serve the ends of power. It has became axiomatic in feminist and science studies that women and non-Western people appreciate interconnections; they don't think in binaries but in wholes. This was the whole point of the critical traditionalism of neo-Gandhians such as Ashis Nandy and ecofeminists such as Vandana Shiva.

This position had strong sympathies with feminist standpoint epistemologies, which also saw women as less prone to dualist thinking. Any doubts regarding the validity of feminist or non-Western knowledge are put aside by using sociology of science arguments—which I call epistemic charity—which purport to have shown that all claims to truth are equally socially constructed, and none can claim to bring us closer to truth.

India was a fertile ground for these ideas, not because it is suffering from a bad case of mental and economic colonialism—as the critics of modernity claim—but because of the populist, antimodernist orientation of Indian intellectuals, a legacy of Gandhi's conservative revolution. Indeed, neo-Gandhians, including such influential figures as Ashis Nandy, Vandana Shiva, Clause Alvares, and Ziauddin Sardar, were the major conduits among science studies, postcolonial studies in the West, and popular movements at home. These are important public intellectuals, with a substantial following in new social movements. In my forthcoming book *Prophets Facing Backward: Postmodern Critiques of Science and the Making of Hindu Nationalism in India* (Rutgers University Press and Permanent Black), I document how these ideas spread through the ecofeminist and people's science movements in India. In practical terms, these ideas have meant a defense of the moral economy of the peasant, including the gender and caste relations of traditional family farmers and their caste-based local courts; an opposition to urban industrial intervention in rural affairs; an organized opposition to development projects, sometimes overriding what the local people themselves wanted; a staunch anti-Americanism, which translates into ridiculing liberalism and human rights; and above all, an overwhelming desire to learn from, respect, and cherish "the people." Any critique of the people's self-destructive customs and objectively false knowledge is frowned on as elitist and rationalist. Indeed, "rationalist" has become one of the worst insults that can be hurled at an intellectual. Interestingly, these exercises in postmodernism-inspired populism fed back into science studies and feminism as evidence of the standpoint epistemologies and alternative sciences.

If these good populists ever take the time to read the right-wing critiques of modernity, they will have to, if they are honest, admit a shock of recognition. The populist defense of the moral economy of traditional India is nothing other than the philosophy of "integral humanism," the official doctrine of the ruling Hindu nationalist party. As I mentioned earlier, the epistemological harmony and nondualism between nature and culture, between individual and collective, between facts and values that ecofeminists and feminist standpoint epistemologists celebrate are precisely what Hindu science celebrates as Vedic epistemology. The cooperation, nurturance, and harmony that the Gandhian and postmodernist proponents of marginal knowledge celebrate are precisely what the integral humanists celebrate as the Hindu idea of a good society in which different castes are bound to one another as limbs to a body. The critical traditionalism of Ashis Nandy and the postcolonial insistence on recovering the indigenous conceptual framework are precisely what the nationalists demand when they insist that Hindu dharma should guide what we take from the West.

These resonances are not lost on reactionary modernists, and they have actively sought to co-opt the Left's initiatives in order to win respectability. Indeed, a leading ecofeminist—Vandana Shiva—has become a leading light of Hindu ecology and makes regular appearances in neo-Hindu ashrams in North America. Her work is most respectfully cited in *The Organiser*, the official journal of RSS, the cultural arm of Hindu nationalist parties. India's leading feminist, who long ago took the culturalist turn and formally joined Ashis Nandy's group, is routinely interviewed and cited in neo-Hindu publications. The work of ethnoscience scholars Dharampal and Claude Alvares is cited with great admiration in Hindu science texts. What's more, the populist left opposition to the Green Revolution, genetically modified crops, and other science-intensive initiatives is routinely co-opted by the ultranationalist, autarkic elements of the Hindu Right, as are their more constructive programs for reviving traditional technologies.

The tragedy is that in the rush to denounce the dualism of modern science, the critics have completely overlooked one essential fact: the lack of separation between nature and culture, matter and spirit. The much ballyhooed holism of Indian ways of knowing has traditionally provided the cosmological justification for India's peculiar institution, namely, caste. The natural inequalities of human beings and their separation into hierarchical though intimately interconnected castes is not an aberration of Hinduism but justified by the central dogmas of dharma and karma. These dogmas depend on a unified understanding of nature and culture: the distinctions between human beings are justified by distinctions in the very order of nature. Indeed, the real victims of oppression—namely, the untouchables and other lower castes—understood the hoax of dualism very well. It was for this reason that they have been the staunchest supporters of the Enlightenment in India. The interests of the oppressed are served by breaking the cosmopolis and demanding, unlike the Hindu science, that our knowledge be equally accessible to all through sensory experience and reason.

In conclusion, what I have described is a wedding in progress: a wedding of science and myth, superstition and nationalism. Such a wedding was not ordained by circumstances but was arranged by well-meaning but ultimately dangerous philosophers. This is one marriage that I am afraid is going to last until a whole lot of violence and hatred and misery finally tear the two apart. For the sake of all that is decent, I hope against hope that this union ends in a speedy divorce.

NOTES

This is the text of a paper delivered at the annual convention of the American Sociological Association, July 2000, held in Washington, D.C. A version of this paper also appears in my book *Breaking the Spell of Dharma: A Case for Indian Enlightenment* (New Delhi: Three Essays Press, 2003).

1. Shaikh Azizur Rahman, "Indian Defense Looks to Ancient Text," BBC News, May 14, 2002, at http://www.bbc.co.uk/.
2. William Harman, "Speaking about Hinduism and Speaking against It," *Journal of the American Academy of Religion* 68, no. 4 (2000): 733–40.
3. The text of the letter can be found on the Web site http://www.acusd.edu/theo/risa-1/archive/msg00782.html.
4. Jonathan Parry, "The Brahmanical Tradition and the Technology of the Intellect," in *Reason and Morality*, ed. Joanna Overing (London: Tavistock Publications, 1985), 206.

The Political Legacy of Edward Said

Irene Gendzier

In the fall of 2002, before the United States led the invasion of Iraq, the Israeli newspaper *Ha'aretz* ran an article by Akiva Eldar on a meeting held in Washington for some members of the Pentagon. The host was Richard Perle, then chair of the U.S. Defense Policy Board. The sponsor was an unnamed think tank. The subject was the future shape of the Middle East. The slide show depicted "Iraq: a tactical goal, Saudi Arabia: a strategic goal," as well as stating, "Palestine is Israel, Jordan is Palestine, and Iraq is the Hashemite Kingdom."[1]

Several months later, a leading Palestinian doctor and grassroots activist, Mustapha Barghouti, director of the Health Development and Information Policy Institute in Ramallah, appeared to confirm the ominous "visions" described earlier in Washington. Denouncing "Israeli measures taken against the Palestinians" as "perhaps more dangerous than those taken in 1948," Barghouti observed that, "under Sharon's plan for the Palestinians, they may now be clustered in ghettoes over no more than 9% of historic Palestine."[2]

In the interval, a handful of Israeli journalists and activists regularly denounced the same Israeli policies, demonstrating their solidarity across the landscape of checkpoints and ghettos, pointing, as did Gideon Levy, to the role of the Israeli military in promoting the progressive dehumanization of the Palestinians.[3]

It is safe to say that among consumers of the news in the United States, none of the above sources were familiar fare. Outside of a minority of specialists and concerned activists and intellectuals, reports exposing Israeli policies against Palestinians were viewed with suspicion, if not open disdain, particularly as both the Israeli and American administrations vied to identify Israel with the United States and Palestinians with Arab terrorists. The struggle to maintain this status quo in public opinion was not new, and unfortunately, it was not news. It remained a battle fought at public and private levels, one directed at universities, the media, and offices of congressional representatives and political candidates. The objective was to prevent Americans from confronting Israeli policies, including those exposed by Israeli dissidents.

Challenging such developments, including the persistent myths of "road maps" and elusive peace processes, have been the voices of those raised in support of a binational state encompassing Israel and Palestine. Among those who endorsed such an option was Edward Said, whose endorsement was matched with support for the National Political Initiative in Palestine, involving major social and political reform. The combination constitutes an ineradicable check to Israeli denial of Palestinian rights. It offers, as well, an alternative to nationalist solutions that, Said argued, were no longer tenable, although they required recognition within a new framework.

Said's recent writings on these questions are considered here. They speak to political realities in the Palestinian landscape that remain little known and inadequately appreciated. And they do so by giving voice to "emerging alternatives," as Said described them, revealing the dogged determination of hope and human solidarity as the bases of a Palestinian and Israeli future, unlike the past.

A LEADING LITERARY CRITIC, ACADEMIC, AND MUSICIAN, Said's interests and publications cannot be easily summarized; nor can the range of his writings that deal with matters of culture, politics, and resistance. Suffice it to say that in the political domain, Said was recognized as among the most articulate and passionate spokesmen for the Palestinian cause, a subject that his work effectively internationalized beyond its origins in the Middle East.

Said's political trajectory dislodged him from the role of unengaged bystander, starting with the Israeli-Arab war of 1967. Between 1977 and 1991, he was an independent member of the Palestine National Council, after which he resumed his activism on behalf of Palestine as an independent critic, fully armed with the only weapon that defined him, his words.

In the interval, Said published his first major work, *Orientalism* (1978), followed by *The Question of Palestine* (1979), *Covering Islam* (1981), and *The Word, the Text and the Critic* (1983), a work whose production coincided with the Israeli invasion of Lebanon in 1982. This was a time of grief and suffering for Lebanese and for Palestinians in the Sabra and Shattila refugee camps, who were massacred by Israeli-backed Falangist forces. The events led to a major inquiry in Israel, including an investigation of the role of Ariel Sharon. Said's writings on the events of 1982 can be found throughout his works, attesting to his eloquent defense of Palestinians under siege and of the Lebanese, defeated in their struggle for a secular, democratic state.

Said's literary and political output reflected his conviction that the worlds of politics and culture were not severed but rather parts of a whole whose integrity could not be ignored. His works such as *Culture and Imperialism* and *The Politics of Dispossession* made this clear. The remarks that follow focus on some of Said's more recent political writings, those in which he argued against separation and the myths of the "peace process" and in favor of binationalism and the Palestinian initiative, the groundbreaking grassroots movement that he and other Palestinian professionals, intellectuals, and independent political figures endorsed in the summer of 2002.

None of these issues can be analyzed outside the context of Said's political writings and, notably, his insistence on challenging the Israeli denial of the role of Zionism and Israeli policy in the Palestinian exile of 1948. Implicit in such a challenge was the demand that the "Palestinian narrative" be integrated into that of Israeli history. It is in this context that Said's writings on "invention, memory, and place," on history and memory, can be situated.

In the 1980s he recognized the parallel efforts of Israeli journalists and historians who broke with the apologetic narratives of the past, a development he followed closely from its inception. "In my opinion," Said wrote, referring to those Israelis who contributed to such efforts, "their genesis lay to some considerable extent in the aggravated, but close colonial encounter between Israelis and Palestinians in the occupied territories."[4] Such encounters, he argued, when not undermined by separation and exclusion, permitted the apprehension of the suffering of each community by the other. These were themes to which Said repeatedly returned, even as he denounced the utter imbalance of political and military power between Israel and Palestine, which had increasingly dire effects on Palestinian life.

In his January 1999 article "Truth and Reconciliation," written for the Egyptian weekly *Al Ahram,* Said wrote, referring to Oslo, that it was time to question again the so-called peace process that had brought no peace. "It is my view that the peace process has in fact put off the real reconciliation that must occur if the 100 year war between Zionism and the Palestinian people is to end. Oslo set the stage for separation, but real peace can come only with a binational Israeli-Palestinian state." This, he continued, was scarcely imaginable, because both Zionist Israeli and Palestinian "narratives" were "irreconcilable." Reviewing Zionist history in the recent work of Israeli historian Zeev Sternhell, Said pointed out that the founders of the Zionist movement had not been blind to the presence of Palestinians or to the "insurmountable contradictions between the basic objectives of the two sides," referring to the Zionist movement and the Palestinian national movement. At present, he explained, "the conflict appears intractable because it is a contest over the same land by two peoples who believed they had valid title to it and who hoped that the other side would in time give up or go away. One side won the war, the other lost, but the contest is as alive as ever."

Deeply familiar with internal Israeli politics and with the courageous struggle of Israeli dissidents, Said argued, "I see no other way than to begin now to speak about sharing the land that has thrust us together, sharing it in a truly democratic way, with equal rights for each citizen. There can be no reconciliation unless both peoples, two communities of suffering, resolve that their existence is a secular fact, and that it has to be dealt with as such."

In that frame of mind, he questioned, "What can separation mean?" in *Al Ahram* in November 1999, making it clear that he believed separation to be unworkable. The dream of a Palestinian state, he wrote, was no longer realizable under current conditions. Neither were Israeli efforts at separation. "Neither Palestinians nor Israelis can be made distant from the other. In the area between Ramallah in the north and Bethlehem in the south, 800,000 Israelis and Palestinians live on top of each other, and cannot be separated." Instead of considering partition as the route to independence, he argued that it was "a legacy of imperialism," as ominous in its effects in Pakistan and India, Ireland, Cyprus, or the Balkans as in historic Palestine.

"We must adopt a strategy with like-minded Israelis, this is a crucial alliance, on matters where we have similar interests: secular rights, anti-settlement activities, education and equality before the law, whether it is Palestinian law, which is anti-democratic, or Israeli law, which is equally anti-democratic when it comes to non-Jews as well as secular Jews." He explained that he wrote "in order to be heard by other Arabs and other Israelis, those whose vision can extend beyond the impoverishing perspectives of what partition and separation can offer."

In the period following the second Palestinian intifada in 2000, which coincided with the emergence of the George W. Bush administration and the return of Ariel Sharon as Likud prime minister, Said was unrelenting in his exposé of the hypocrisy of American claims and the denial of Israeli violence and continued expansion into the West Bank and Gaza. He continued to argue on behalf of a political solution to the crisis, albeit one that represented the interests of Palestinians as well as Israelis, a situation belied by the Oslo negotiations. In works such as *Peace and Its Discontents* (1996) and *The End of the Peace Process* (2000), Said excoriated the role of the Palestinian leadership, notably in its accession to the Oslo Declaration of Principles (1993), which Said viewed as "an instrument of capitulation."[5] It would have been preferable, he wrote, to acknowledge that "we have failed as a people in our struggle to restore our rights. Israel has maintained its settlements and very partially redeployed its army. It controls land, water, security, and foreign policy for the Palestinian 'self-rule' authority."

Instead of declaring victory, Said maintained, the Palestinian leadership should have confronted its defeat. "How much more dignified and admirable it would have been to admit defeat and ask the Palestinian people to rally in order to try to rebuild from the ruins" (xxx). Said's criticism of the Palestinian leadership and its lack of preparedness, its ignorance of the United States, was unambiguous, as was his recognition of the utter disparities in power on which such accords rested. What Palestinians and Arabs must remember, he argued, is "that our desire to coexist in peace with each other and with our neighbors is sustained not by blind loyalty to one or two personalities and their rhetoric, but by an abiding faith in real justice and real-self-determination" (xxv).

Said's appraisal of Oslo was compatible with that offered by Israeli historian Baruch Kimmerling, who underscored the compromise agreement made in Oslo that left the Palestinians in control of Bantustans. As for Sharon, Kimmerling argued that "Israel has become a state oriented towards one major goal: the politicide of the Palestinian people. Politicide is a process whose ultimate aim is to destroy a certain people's prospects, indeed, their very will, for legitimate self-determination and sovereignty over land they consider their homeland."[6]

Said had supported the two-state solution to the Israeli-Palestinian conflict, which the Palestine Liberation Organization had formally adopted as its position at the Palestine National Council meeting in 1988. In a series of interviews with Israeli journalist Ari Shavit, recorded in August 2000, Said explained his current position. As Shavit observed: "It seems you've come full circle—from espousing a one secular-democratic state solution in the 70s, to accepting the two-state solution in the 80s, back to the secular-democratic idea."[7] Said replied that partition and separation were no longer workable. In its place, he turned to binationalism. Replying to Shavit, he said, "I would not necessarily call it secular-democratic. I would call it a binational state. I want to preserve for the Palestinians and the Israeli Jews a mechanism or structure that would allow them to express their national identity. I understand that in the case of Palestine-Israel, a binational solution would have to address the difference between the two collectives."

Those differences were daily magnified by the continued struggle on the ground, whose consequences Said relentlessly exposed: the increasing number of Israeli military checkpoints that defined Palestinian ghettos, the mounting death toll, the number of people rendered homeless, the expansion of Israeli settlements in violation of U.S. and UN agreements. In the midst of increasing violence, wrote Said in *Al Ahram* (December 19–25, 2002), the continued bleeding of "the Palestinian civilian population" remained "obscured, hidden from view, though it continues steadily all the time: 65 percent unemployment, 50 percent poverty (people living on less than $2 a day), schools, hospitals, universities, businesses under constant military pressure, these are only the outward manifestation of Israeli crimes against humanity."

In the midst of such conditions, Said and other Palestinians turned their efforts to the state of "Palestinian and Arab politics," which, Said argued, had never been as corrupt nor as harmful to its own populations as at the present.

He criticized Arab leaders, not for the first time, for having failed to implement a "systematic strategy, much less even a systematic protest against Washington's announced plans to redraw the map of the Middle East after the invasion of Iraq." Said's sharp criticisms of Arab politics were not unique. They matched those of critics throughout the Arab world whose demands for social justice and secular political reform also went unheard in the United States.

Said joined with other Palestinian signatories, including Dr. Mustapha Barghouti, cited earlier, to found a new, secular Palestinian national initiative. The initiative, as Said wrote in *Al Ahram* (December 19–25, 2002), "puts forward the idea of a national unified authority, elected to serve the people and its need for liberation, for democratic freedoms, and for public debate and accountability." It was supported by a host of professionals in the fields of health, education, and labor, along with political independents. "The old divisions between Fatah, the Popular Front, Hamas, and all the others, are meaningless today," Said argued, calling for a Palestinian leadership capable of speaking "to our need for independence of mind and responsible, modern citizenship."

This was not to be Said's final contribution to the future of Palestine. In their last conversation, Ilan Pappe, the Israeli historian and activist whose work Said respected, reported that Said "beseeched me, as he did others I am sure, not to give up the struggle for relocating the Palestinians' refugee issue at the heart of the public and global agenda. He stressed the need to continue the effort of changing the American public opinion on Palestine."[8] It remains to be seen whether such efforts have reached their audience.

NOTES

1. Akiva Eldar, "Perles of Wisdom for the Faithful," *Ha'aretz,* November 2, 2002.
2. Mustapha Barghouti, press conference, October 16, 2003, Jerusalem, Israel.
3. Gideon Levy, "The IDF's Chorus of Incitement," *Ha'aretz,* October 26, 2003 (online).
4. Edward W. Said, "Invention, Memory, and Place," *Critical Inquiry* 26 (Winter 2000): 189.
5. Edward Said, *Peace and Its Discontents* (New York, Vintage Books, 1996), xxix; subsequent citations, unless otherwise identified, are from this source.
6. Baruch Kimmerling, review of Ran Edelist, *Ehud Barak: Fighting the Demons, New Left Review,* September–October 2003.
7. Edward Said, *Power, Politics, and Culture* (New York: Pantheon Books, 2001), 452. The interview is reproduced in chap. 29, "My Right of Return."
8. Ilan Pappe's tribute to Edward Said, "A Lighthouse that Navigated Us," may be found in the online Edward Said archives and in the Arabic Media Internet Network, September 26, 2003.

Second Letter on Algeria
(August 22, 1837)

Alexis de Tocqueville

Suppose, Sir, for a moment that the emperor of China, landing on the shores of France and at the head of a powerful army, made himself master of our greatest cities and of our capital. And after having destroyed all of the public registers before even having given himself the pain of reading them, destroyed or dispersed all administrators without acquainting himself with their various attributes, he finally rids himself of all state officials from the head of the government to the *gardes champêtres*, the peers, the deputies, and in general of the entire ruling class; and that he exiled them all at once to some faraway country. Do you not think that this great prince, in spite of his powerful army, his fortresses, and his fortune, would soon find himself rather bothered in administering the conquered land; that his new subjects, bereft of all those who did or could manage political affairs, would be incapable of governing themselves, while he, coming from the opposite side of the Earth, knows neither the religion, nor the language, nor the laws, nor the customs, nor the administrative procedures of the country and who took care to send away all of those who could have instructed him in these matters, will be in no position to rule them? You will therefore have no difficulty in seeing, Sir, that if the regions of France that are effectively occupied by the conqueror were to obey him, the rest of the country would soon be left to an immense anarchy.[1]

You will see, Sir, that we have done in Algeria precisely what I supposed the emperor of China would do in France.

In spite of the fact that the coast of Africa is separated from Provence by only about 160 leagues of sea, that there are published each year in Europe the accounts of several thousands of voyages to all parts of the world, that here we study assiduously all of the languages of antiquity that are no longer spoken as well as several living languages that we never have the occasion of speaking, we could not meanwhile face the profound ignorance in which we lived, not more than seven years ago, on all that could concern Algeria: we had no clear notion of the different races that lived there, nor of their customs, we did not know a word of the languages that these people speak; the country itself, its resources, its rivers, its cities, its climate were unknown to us; one could have thought that the whole breadth of the world lay in between us. We know so little even of what regarded warfare, though this was the issue of greatest concern to us at this time, that our generals thought they would be attacked by a cavalry similar to that of the mameluks of Egypt, whereas our main enemy, the Turks of Algiers, have never fought on anything but on foot. It is in ignorance of all of these things that we set sail, which did not stop us from conquering, because on the battlefield victory is to the bravest and the strongest and not to the most knowledgeable. But, after the fighting, it did not take us long to see that to rule a nation it does not suffice to have conquered it.

You remember, Sir, that I had told you previously that the whole government, civil and military, of the Regency was in the hands of the Turks. Barely had we become the masters of Algiers that we hurried to gather all of the Turks without forgetting a single one, from the *Dey* to the last soldier of his militia, and we transported this crowd to the coast of Asia. In order to better eliminate the vestiges of the enemy domination, we took care earlier to tear up or burn all written documents, administrative registers, official or unofficial evidence, that could have kept alive a trace of what had been done before us.[2] The conquest was a new era, and from fear of mixing in an irrational way the past with the present, we even destroyed a great number of the streets of Algiers, with the purpose of rebuilding them according to our methods, and gave French names to all of those that we agreed to conserving. I think, in truth, Sir, that the Chinese of whom I spoke earlier could not have done better.

What is the result of all of this? You can guess without difficulty.

The Turkish government owned in Algiers a great many houses and in the plains a multitude of domains; but its property titles disappeared in the universal wreck of the old order of things. It was found that the French administration, knowing neither what it owned nor what had remained in the legitimate possession of the conquered, was wanting of everything or thought itself reduced to appropriating half hazard what it needed, in spite of law and rights.

The Turkish government peacefully collected the fruit of certain taxes that out of ignorance we were not able to levy in its place, and we were forced to take the money that we needed from France or to extort it from our unfortunate subjects with methods much more Turkic than any the Turks had ever employed.

If our ignorance was such that the French government became illegitimate and oppressor in Algiers, it also rendered all government outside of itself impossible.

The French had sent the *Caïds* of the *outans* back to Asia. They ignored completely the name, composition, and usage of that Arab militia which, as composed of auxiliaries, was used as police and levied taxes under the Turks, and that was called, as I have said, the cavalry of the *Marzem*. They had no idea concerning the division of tribes. They did not know of the existence of the military aristocracy of the *Spahis*,[3] and, of the *marabouts*, it took them quite long to figure out, that when talking of them, one could mean a tomb[4] or a man.[5]

The French did not know any of these things, and to tell the truth, they hardly preoccupied themselves with learning them.

In the place of an administration that they had destroyed down to its roots, they imagined they would substitute, in the districts we had occupied militarily, the French administration.

Try, Sir, I implore you, to picture these agile and untamable children of the desert ensnared in the thousand formalities of our bureaucracy and forced to submit themselves to the inertia, the formality, to the writings and the trifling details of our centralization. We conserved from the old government of the country only the usage of the yataghan and of the stick as ways to police. All of the rest became French.

This applies to the cities and to the tribes that are tied to them. As far as the rest of the inhabitants of the Regency, we did not even try to administer them. After having destroyed their government, we gave them no other.

I would be leaving the framework that I had laid out if I took it upon myself to write the history of what has happened for the last seven years in Africa. I only wish to prepare the reader to understand it.

For the three hundred years that the Arabs living in Algeria were submitted to the Turks, they had entirely lost the impulse to rule themselves. The leaders among them had been distanced from political affairs by the jealousy of the dominators; the marabout dismounted his horse to climb onto a donkey. The Turkish government was a detestable government, but after all it maintained a certain order and, though it tacitly authorized wars between the tribes, it reduced theft and made roads safe. It was furthermore the only link that existed between the diverse peoples, the center at which ended so many divergent rays.

The Turkish government destroyed, with nothing replacing it, the country that could not yet govern itself fell into a terrible anarchy. All of the tribes fell upon one another in an immense confusion, robbery organized everywhere. The very shadow of justice disappeared and each resorted to force.

This applies to the Arabs.

As far as the Kabyles, since they were almost independent from the Turks, the fall of the Turks produced only few effects on them. They stayed vis-à-vis the new masters in an arrangement nearly analogous to the one that they had taken with the former. Only that they became even more inclusive, the inborn hate that they had for foreigners coming to combine with the religious horror that they had for Christians whose language, laws, and customs were unknown to them.

Men submit themselves sometimes to humiliation, to tyranny, to conquest, but never for long do they suffer anarchy. There is no people so barbarous as to escape this general law of humanity.

When the Arabs, whom we often looked to vanquish and submit to our will, but never to govern, were subjected for a while to savage intoxication given birth by individual independence, they began to search instinctively to remake what the French had destroyed. We quickly saw appear among them entrepreneurial and ambitious men. Great talents revealed themselves in some of their chieftains, and the multitudes began to herald certain names as symbols of order.

The Turks had pushed the religious aristocracy of the Arabs away from the use of arms and the direction of public affairs. The Turks destroyed, we saw it almost immediately once again become warlike and governing. The most rapid effect, and also the most certain, of our conquest was to give back to the marabouts the political existence that they had lost. They again took up Mohamed's scimitar to fight the infidels and soon used it to govern their fellow citizens: this is a great fact and one which must draw the attention of all those who concern themselves with Algeria.

We have let the national aristocracy of the Arabs be reborn, it is only left to us to use it.

To the west of the province of Algiers, near the frontiers of the empire of Morocco, was living since long ago a family of very famous marabouts. Its lineage led straight back to Mohamed himself, and its name was venerated throughout the Regency. At the time when the French took possession of the country, the head of this family was an old man named Mahidin. In addition to his illustrious birth, Mahidin joined the advantage of having been to Mecca and a long history of being energetically opposed to the Turks. His saintliness was greatly venerated and his abilities well known. Once the tribes of the surrounding area began to feel the intolerable malaise which the absence of power causes in men, they went to find Mahidin and proposed to him that he take charge of their affairs. The old man had them gather in a large plain; there, he told them that at his age one had to concern himself with the sky and not the Earth, that he refused their offer, but he urged them to bring their suffrage to one of his youngest sons, which he brought before them. At length he enumerated the qualifications of this one to govern his compatriots; his precocious piety, his pilgrimage to the Holy Lands, his descendance from the Prophet; he made known several striking signs of which the sky had made use to designate him among his brothers and he proved that all the ancient prophecies that announced a liberator to the Arabs manifestly applied to him. The tribes proclaimed by unanimous agreement the son of Mahidin *emir-el-mouminin*, that is to say, leader of the believers.

This young man, who then was only twenty-five years old and of a frail appearance, was named Abd-el-Kader.[6]

Such is the origin of this unique leader; anarchy gave birth to his power, anarchy developed it without respite and, with the grace of God and our own,[7] after having given him the province of Oran and that of Tittery, it put Constantine in his hands and made him much more powerful than the Turkish government that he replaced had ever been.

While these events took place in the west of the Regency, the east offered another spectacle.

In the time when the French took Algiers, Constantine Province was being governed by a bey named Achmet. This bey, contrary to all custom, was *coulougli,* meaning the son of a Turkish father and an Arab mother. It was a particular stroke of luck that allowed him, after the taking of Algiers, to stay in power in Constantine with the support of his father's compatriots and later to found his power on the surrounding tribes with the help of his mother's parents and friends.

While all the rest of the Regency abandoned by the Turks and not occupied by the French fell into the greatest disorder, a certain quality of government therefore was maintained in the provinces of Constantine and Achmet by his courage, his cruelty and his energy; there was founded the empire, solid enough, that we look to restrain or destroy today.[8]

Therefore, at this very moment, three powers are present on the soil of Algeria: in Algiers and on various points on the coast are the French; in the west and to the south, an Arab population that after three hundred years awakens and follows a national leader; in the east, the rump Turkish government, represented by Achmet, a stream that continues to run after the source has dried and will soon itself dry up or lose itself in the great flood of Arab nationality. Between these three forces and as though enveloped from all sides by them meet an array of minor Kabyles peoples, who escape from any and all influences and play off of all governments.

It would be pointless to extensively research what the French should have done in the time of conquest.

We can only say in a few words that we should have at first simply settled there, and as much as our civilization would permit it, in the place of the conquered; that, far from wanting from the beginning to substitute our administrative procedures for their own, we should have for a while adapted our own, maintained political limitations, taken control of the agents of the defunct government, included its traditions and continued to use its procedures. Instead of exiling the Turks to the coast of Asia, it is obvious that we should have taken care to keep the greatest number of them among us; bereft of their leaders, incapable of governing on their own, and fearing the resentment of their former subjects, they would not have waited to become our most useful intermediaries and our most zealous friends, as were the *coulouglis,* though they were much closer to the Arabs than were the Turks but nevertheless have almost always favored throwing themselves into our arms rather than theirs. Once we had known the language, prejudices, and the customs of the Arabs, after having inherited the respect that men always hold for an established government, it would have become possible for us to return little by little to our customs, and to gallicize the country around us.

But today that the mistakes are irrevocably committed, what is there left to do? And what reasonable hopes should we conceive?

We first distinguish with care between the two great races of which we have spoken further above, the Kabyles and the Arabs.

When speaking of the Kabyles, it is visible[9] that there can be no question of conquering their country or colonizing it: their mountains are, as of now, impenetrable to our armies, and the inhospitable disposition of the inhabitants leaves no security to the isolated European who would there peacefully go to make himself a home.

The country of the Kabyles is closed to us, but the soul of the Kabyles is open to us and it is not impossible for us to penetrate it.

I saw previously that the Kabyle was more positive, less religious, infinitely less enthusiastic than the Arab. In the life of the Kabyles the individual is nearly everything, the society nearly nothing, and they are just as far from bending themselves uniformly to the laws of a single government taken from their heart than to adopt our own.

The great passion of the Kabyle is the love of material joys, and it is through this that we can and must capture him.

Though given that the Kabyles let us penetrate their society much less than do the Arabs, they show themselves much less inclined to make war on us. And even when a few of them raise arms against us, the others do not stop frequenting our markets and still come rent us their services. The cause of this is that they have already discovered the material profit that they can get out of our being neighbors. They find it greatly advantageous to come sell us their goods and to buy those of ours that can be useful to the kind of civilization that they possess. And, while they are not yet in a state to achieve our well-being, it is already easy to see that they admire it and that they would find it very sweet to enjoy it.

It is obvious that it is by our arts and not by our arms that we will tame such men.

If frequent and peaceful relations continue to be established between us and the Kabyles; that the first do not have to fear our ambition and encounter among us a legislation that is simple, clear, and which they are sure will grant for their protection, it is certain that soon they will fear war more even than we do and that this almost invincible attraction that draws natives toward civilized man from the moment that they no longer fear for their liberty will be felt. We will see then that the habits and ideas of the Kabyles change without their realizing it, and the barriers closing their country off to us will fall on their own.

The role that we have to play vis-à-vis the Arabs is more complicated and more difficult:

The Arabs are not solidly fixed in one place and their soul is even more nomadic than are their dwellings. Though they are passionately attached to their liberty, they adopted a strong government, and they are keen to form a great nation. And, though[10] they show themselves to be very sensual, immaterial joys are of great value in their eyes, and at every moment the imagination whisks them away toward some ideal good that she discovers for them.

With the Kabyles, it is most important to be concerned with questions of civil and commercial equity, with the Arabs of political and religious questions.

There is a certain number of Arab tribes that we can and must govern directly from this moment on and a greater number upon which we must, for the time being, want to obtain only an indirect influence.

After three hundred years the power of the Turks established itself only incompletely over tribes remote from the cities. The Turks nevertheless were Islamic like the Arabs, had habits similar to theirs and had managed to remove the religious aristocracy from public affairs. It is easy to see that what with us not having any of these advantages and being faced with much greater difficulties, we cannot hope to obtain the level of influence on these tribes that the Turks had nor even approach it. On this point our immense military superiority is almost useless. It makes it possible for us to win, but not to keep under our laws nomadic populations that when the need arises will go deep into the desert where we cannot follow them, leaving us in the middle of the desert where we could not survive.

The object of all our present efforts must be to live in peace with those of the Arabs that we have no present hope of being able to govern, and to organize them in the manner least dangerous to our future gains.

The anarchy of the Arabs, which is so deleterious to these peoples, is vastly damaging to us, because having neither the will nor the power to submit them all at once by our arms, we can hope only to act on them indirectly through contact with our ideas and our arts; which can take place only to the extent that peace and a certain order reign among them. The anarchy pushes these tribes one on the other, throws them without end on us and robs our frontiers of all security.

We have then a great interest in re-creating a government among these people and it is perhaps not impossible to succeed in making it so that this government depends partly on us.

Today that the scepter has just left the hands that held it since three centuries ago, no one has an incontestable right to govern nor a good chance now at founding an uncontested power that will last. All of the powers that will establish themselves in Africa will therefore be unstable, and if our support is given with resolution, with justice, and with consistency, the new sovereigns will constantly be driven to resort to it. They will therefore depend in part on us.

We have to aim before anything else at accustoming these independent Arabs to seeing us meddle in their interior affairs and at making ourselves familiar to them. Because we must realize that a powerful and civilized people such as our own exercises solely by virtue of the superiority of its luminaries an almost invincible force on small, more or less barbarous peoples; and that, to force these to incorporate themselves with it, it only needs to be able to establish sustainable relations with them.

But if we have an interest in creating a government with the Arabs of the Regency, we have a much more visible interest in not letting only one government establish itself there. For then the peril would be far greater than the advantage. It is without a doubt very important for us not to leave the Arabs subject to anarchy, but it is even more important for us to not expose ourselves to seeing them aligned all at once against us.

It is with this point of view that the last treaty with Abd-el-Kader and the expedition planned for Constantine are of a nature to arouse certain fears.

Nothing is more desirable than to establish and legitimize the power of the new emir in the province of Oran where his power was already strong. But the treaty concedes to him in addition the government of the *beylik* of Tittery and I cannot stop myself from believing that the expedition that is in preparation will have for a final result of delivering to him the greater part of the province of Constantine.

We can be sure that with the extent of power that Abd-el-Kader has achieved, all of the Arab populations that find themselves without a leader will go to him of their own volition. It is therefore imprudent to destroy or even undermine the Arab powers independent of Abd-el-Kader; it would be better to think of bringing some about if there are not some already. In opposition to all of this, if our campaign in Constantine succeeds, as we have every reason to believe it will, it can only result in destroying Achmet without putting anything in his place. We will overthrow the *coulougli* and we will not be able to succeed him nor give him an Arab successor. Our victory will therefore deliver the tribes that are under Achmet to an independence that they will not wait long to sacrifice in the hands of the emir who neighbors them. We will make anarchy and anarchy will make the power of Abd-el-Kader.

This is what we can foresee from a distance and with our ignorance of the details.

What it is possible to affirm from now with certitude is that we cannot suffer that all of the Arab tribes of the Regency ever recognize the same leader. It is already far too little with two. Our present security, and the care for our future, demands that we have at least three or four.

Independently of the tribes over which it is in our interest to look only to exercise, for now, an indirect influence, there is also a considerable part of the country that our security as well as our honor oblige us to keep under our immediate forces and to govern without an intermediary.

This is the case where we find a French population and an Arab population that must be made to live peacefully in the same region. The difficulty is great. I am far from believing it, however, to be insurmountable.

I do not pretend to engage here, Sir, with you in a discussion on the specific means that we could use to reach this goal. It is enough for me to indicate in broad terms what appears to me to be the principal conditions of success.

It is obvious for me that we will never succeed if we take it upon ourselves to submit our new Algerian subjects to the rules of the French administration.

We do not impose without consequences new concepts in the realm of political customs. We are more enlightened and more powerful than the Arabs; it is for us to bend at first to a certain point to their ways of life and prejudices. In Algeria as elsewhere, the main duty of a new government is not to create what does not exist, but to use what does. The Arabs lived in tribes two thousand years ago in Yemen; they traversed all of Africa and invaded Spain in tribes; they still live this way in our day. Tribal organization, which is the most tenacious of all human institutions, could not therefore be taken from them now nor long from now without sending a shock through all of their sentiments and ideas. The Arabs appoint their own chiefs; it is necessary to let them keep this privilege. They have a military and religious aristocracy; we should not look to destroy it, but to use it as had done the Turks. Not only is it useful to draw from among the political customs of the Arabs, but it is necessary to modify the rules regarding their civil rights only little by little. For you will know, Sir, that the majority of these rules are outlined in the Koran in such a way that with the Muslims civil and religious law are confused without end.

We must be careful most importantly of all in giving ourselves over to this taste for uniformity that torments us and acknowledge that to dissimilar beings it would be just as dangerous as it is absurd to apply the same legislation. In the time of the fall of the Roman Empire, we saw reign at the same time barbaric laws to which the Barbar was submitted and Roman laws to which the Roman was submitted. This model is a good one to follow; it is only this way that we can hope to pass without perishing through the period of transition that takes place before two peoples of different civilizations can come to meld into a single whole.

Once Frenchmen and Arabs live in the same district, we must resolve to apply to each the legislation that he can understand and has learned to respect. That the political leader be the same for both races, but that for long all of the rest differ, the fusion will come later on its own.

It would be quite necessary as well that the legislation that governs the French in Africa not be exactly the same as the one operating in France. An emerging people can hardly tolerate the same administrative hassles as an old people, and the same slow and multiplied formalities that guarantee at times the security of the latter prevent the former from developing and nearly from being born.

We need in Africa as much as in France, and more than in France, fundamental guarantees for the man who lives in society; there is not a country where it is more necessary to establish individual liberty, respect for property, and the guarantee of all rights than in a colony. But on the other hand a colony needs a simpler administration, more expeditious and more independent from the central power than the one that governs the continental provinces of the empire.

It is therefore necessary to retain with care in Algeria the substance of our political state, but to not hold on too superstitiously to its form; and to show more respect for the spirit than for the letter. Those who have visited Algeria claim the opposite is happening: they say that the smallest details of the administrative methods of the mother country are there scrupulously observed and that often are forgotten the great principles that serve as a foundation for our laws. In acting like this we can hope to increase the number of public officials, but not of colonists.

I imagine, Sir, that now that I reach the end of this too-long letter, you are tempted to ask me, after all, my hopes for the future of our new colony.

This future appears to me to be in our hands, and I will tell you sincerely that with time, perseverance, ability, and justice, I do not doubt that we could erect on the coast of Africa a great monument to the glory of our country.

I have told you, Sir, that in the beginning the Arabs were both pastoralists and agriculturists, and that, though they possess all of the land, they cultivate only a negligible part of it. The Arab population is then widely dispersed, it occupies much more land than it can sow every year. The result of this is that the Arabs part with their land willingly and at a low price and that a foreign population can without difficulty settle at their side without their suffering from it.

You then understand from this, Sir, how easy it is for the French, who are richer and more industrious than the Arabs, to occupy without violence a large part of the land and to introduce themselves peacefully and in great numbers all the way to the heart of the tribes that neighbor them. It is easy to see ahead to a time in the near future when the two races will be intermingled in this way in many parts of the Regency.

But it is hardly enough for the French to place themselves at the side of the Arabs if they do not manage to establish a lasting bond with them and in the end form from these two races a single people.

Everything that I have learned of Algeria leads me to believe that this outcome is nowhere as chimerical as many people suppose.

The majority of Arabs still have a spirited faith in the religion of Mohamed; meanwhile it is easy to see in this Muslim part of the territory, as in all others, that religious beliefs constantly lose their vigor and become more and more powerless to fight against the interests of this world. Though religion has played a large role in the wars that we have made up to now in Africa, and that they have served as a pretext to the marabouts for taking up their arms once again, we can say that can only be attributed as a secondary cause for these wars. We have been attacked much more as foreigners and conquerors than as Christians, and the ambition of leaders more than the faith of the people has put arms into hands against us.[11] Every time that patriotism or ambition does not carry the Arabs against us, experience has shown that religion did not stop them from becoming our most zealous auxiliaries, and, under our flag, they make as brutal of a war against others of their own religion as these make against us.

It is therefore possible to believe that if we prove more and more that under our domination or in our vicinity Islam is not in danger, religious passions will extinguish themselves, and we will only have political enemies in Africa. We would also be wrong to think that the Arab way of life would make them incapable of adapting to life in a community shared with us.

In Spain, the Arabs were sedentary and agricultural; in the areas surrounding the cities of Algeria, there is a great number among them who build houses and seriously devote themselves to agriculture. The Arabs are not naturally nor necessarily pastoralists. It is true that as one approaches the desert, one gradually sees houses disappear and the tents erected. But it is because as one moves away from the coasts security of property and person diminishes and that, for a people who fear for their existence and for their liberty, there is nothing more convenient than a nomadic way of life. I understand that Arabs like better to wander in the outside air than to stay exposed to the tyranny of a master, but everything tells me that if they could be free, respected, and sedentary, they would not wait to settle themselves. I do not doubt that they would soon take up our way of life if we gave them a lasting interest in doing so.

Nothing finally in the known facts indicates to me that there is incompatibility of sentiment between the Arabs and ourselves. I see on the contrary, that in times of peace, the two races mingle without difficulty, and that as they get to know one another, the distance between them lessens.

Every day the French develop clearer and more just notions on the inhabitants of Algeria. They learn their languages, familiarize themselves with their customs, and we even see some who show a certain spontaneous enthusiasm for them. In addition, the whole of the younger generation of Arabs in Algiers speaks our language and has already in part adopted our customs.

When it was a question in the area surrounding Algiers of defense against robbery by a few enemy tribes, we saw form a national guard composed of Arabs and Frenchmen who joined the same units and who together shared the same exhaustions and dangers.[12]

There is therefore no reason to believe that time cannot succeed in amalgamating the two races. God does not prevent it; only the faults of men could put an obstacle in its way.

Let us not therefore lose hope for the future, Sir; let us not allow ourselves to be stopped by temporary sacrifices while an immense objective comes to light that with perseverant efforts can be reached.

NOTES

Translated by Valery DeLame, Rutgers University. This translation is taken from volume 2 of the *Écrits Politiques* of the *Ouvres Complètes*, Gallimard.

1. Tocqueville here seems to be paraphrasing the famous parable of St. Simon.
2. Cf. Esquer, *Les commencement d'un Empire, La prise d'Alger* (Alger, 1823), 428–21. The author notes that the occupation of Algiers by French troops was achieved with great disorder, that they neglected to perform administrative duties, and that many soldiers lit their pipes with government papers. To establish the ownership of properties and of public revenue, it was necessary to take the word of claimants.
3. Originally, the term *spahi* (from the Persian *sipahi*, from which the Indian word *cipaye* is also derived) simply designated a soldier. But in the Ottoman Empire, the name was reserved for a corps of irregular cavalrymen, then for the elite cavalry. The Turks organized formations of these cavaliers in northern Africa.
4. Note from Tocqueville: The marabouts give hospitality near the tomb of their direct ancestor, and this place bears the name of he who is buried there. From this came the error.
5. The notion of marabout is much more imprecise than Tocqueville thinks; not only a tomb but also a pile of rocks and storks can be a marabout. Cf. Doutté, *Les Marabouts* (Paris, 1900).
6. Mahidin, father of Abd-el-Kader, belonged to the Hachem tribe and was a marabout venerated by the powerful brotherhood of the Kadria. Once the tribes in the west of Algeria decided to fight against the French settled in Oran, they thought of putting him in command. But at the Essebieh Reunion near Mascara (November 22, 1832), he, enlightened by a dream, had his son Abd-el-Kader, who had just reached twenty-four years of age, nominated in his place.
7. The Treaty of Desmichels, February 26, 1834, named after the general commanding the forces in Oran, affirmed from the beginning the power of Abd-el-Kader by recognizing his title of emir, and by not determining precisely the territorial

limits of his power nor the precise obligations of a vassal state; the treaty of Tafna, signed by Bugeaut on May 20, 1837, ratified it by ceding him the province of Oran and the Tittery.
8. On El Hadj-Ahmed, bey of Constantine from 1826 to 1837, his tyranny, and his cupidity, but also his qualities as a leader, see E. Mercier, *Histoire de Constantine* (Constantine, 1903), 371–436. For his rapport with France in 1837, see ibid., 129 n. 2.
9. Variant: *évident*.
10. Variant: *bien qu'ils*.
11. In a study on the moral and intellectual state of Algeria in 1830 (*L'Etat intellectuel et moral de l'Algérie en 1830, Revue d'histoire moderne et contemporaine,* 1954, pp. 199–212), M. Marcel Emerit writes: "Many French and Arab witnesses tell us that the war did not have, at the beginning of French occupation, the character of a holy war. It was more a movement of resistance on the part of Arabs in the presence of soldiers from a foreign power to whom they had no reason of submitting."
12. On December 24, 1830, Marshall (Maréchal) Clauzel created in Algiers an urban guard whose members were Frenchmen and those natives from twenty to sixty years old who owned property or industrial establishments. But on August 17, 1832, the duke of Rovigo decided to admit only Frenchmen. On October 26, 1836, Clauzel, once again *directeur général,* reversed this decision by creating an African militia to which natives could be admitted with special permission.

Part IV
Israel and Palestine

Who Are the Palestinians?

Henry Pachter

Who are they, the Palestinians, and who has the right to speak for them? Oppressed nationalities find it difficult to get a hearing because those who pretend to represent them are often political adventurers who merely exploit them—whether for other powers' imperialistic purposes or to vent on imaginary enemies their own hatred of the world. This is true of the Somalis, the Irish, the Bengalis, the Ibos; it is twice as true of the Palestinians because their country happens to lie at the crossroads of a world power struggle. Nowhere else do local enmities serve so many outside masters; nowhere else do foreign interests spread so much confusion about the very identity of the people they are pretending to save.

So first of all, let us agree: like most Irish, most Palestinians are not terrorists; but like many Ulstermen or Basques, many Palestinians condone or even applaud acts of terrorism as long as they lack other means to express what they consider their just grievances, and as long as those grievances continue to be seen as just by others. Let us also agree that their plight is not of their own making; they have been objects of other people's policies for 3,000 years.

Palestine, the land of the Philistines, a Semitic people who were once subjugated by Joshua and by David, has retained that name through the centuries as it was conquered by Hittites, Egyptians, Babylonians, Assyrians, Persians, Greeks, Romans, Arabs,[1] Christians from the West, Osmanli Turks, and the British. Until recently, in modern times it was sparsely settled, mostly by Arab Bedouins, and was considered part of Syria. A movement to liberate and unite the Arabs, then under Turkish domination, existed long before the First World War.

Then the British used Arab tribesmen to wrest Palestine, Mesopotamia (Iraq), and Syria from the Turks, promising them "sovereignty" and self-determination. After prolonged uprisings, those parts of Syria that lay east of the Jordan River were given to Hashemite sheiks, who thereafter were called kings; the part west of the Jordan River was styled the British Mandate of Palestine and was supposed to evolve toward self-government; northern Syria became a French mandate. The terms of the mandates were illegal even by the standards of the Covenant of the League of Nations, which was their covering law. Previously, a unilateral declaration by Foreign Minister Arthur Balfour had designated

"Palestine" a "Jewish homeland"; at the same time, however, Chaim Weizmann and Lord Harlech assured the Arabs that this should not interfere with Arab aspirations to sovereignty.

What these terms meant or how to reconcile them was never spelled out, except in Balfour's memoirs, where he wondered how anybody could have been misled into thinking that they meant anything.[2] But based on the evidence of contemporary customs and conditions, the Balfour Declaration was consistent with a Jewish immigration rate of 50,000 a year and a ratio of two to one between Muslims and Jews. In 1930, after serious Arab riots, immigration was severely restricted—just when Jews were desperate not for a homeland but for a place of asylum. At the outbreak of World War II, the population consisted of 456,000 Jews and 1.1 million Muslims; at its end, the census counted 1.143 million Muslims, 583,000 Jews, and 145,000 Christians.

The Holocaust and the war left the Allies with a "disposal problem" in western Europe: nearly 100,000 eastern European Jews who had been made homeless by persecution and political changes were languishing in displaced-persons camps, fed by charitable contributions and government aid mostly from the United States, which, however, did not lift its own restrictions on immigrants from eastern Europe. Responding to strong pressures from Zionist organizations—and minding the electoral situation at home—President Truman resolved the problem by agreeing to the foundation of a Jewish state in Palestine. Soviet diplomacy gladly gave its assent, viewing any diminution of the British Empire as a gain for itself, and hoping to ingratiate itself with both Jews and Arabs.

At first, the British wanted to build a base in Haifa because, ironically, they were about to fulfill another Arab demand: to evacuate the base in Alexandria. But a 1939 white paper also promised independence to Palestine. Weary of Arab terrorism and immediately prompted by Jewish terrorism, the Labour Party government decided to abandon the thankless task of policing the peace between Jews and Arabs.[3] The deal was consummated by a United Nations Security Council resolution,[4] the only instrument of international law on which the state of Israel can base its existence.

It is therefore necessary to remember that the United Nations at that time created not one state but two on the west side of the Jordan: one Jewish and one Arab. The Jewish state was totally nonviable; it consisted of three noncontiguous parts encompassing most Jewish settlements and a like number of Arab settlements. Even David Ben-Gurion, however, accepted this rump territory because, at the time, he still assumed that Palestine would remain an economic unit where two peoples would be able to develop in symbiosis—a binational state in all but name.

A word about this assumed symbiosis is in order. Not only Jews but also

Arabs had come into Palestine, attracted by the higher wages and better working conditions under Jewish employers, or simply by the promise of prosperity that the Jewish immigration and its foreign backers brought to the country. The Jewish labor organization Histadruth had noted with alarm that fellow Jews were hiring Arab labor at low wages while Jewish immigrants were jobless. From the early 1920s on, therefore, the Histadruth had been waging a campaign "to fight for places to work."[5] Its strongly nationalistic appeal brought quick success to this campaign; by the 1930s, Arabs worked for Jews mostly in menial positions that Jewish workers would not accept. Even so, a remarkable number of Arabs in Palestine prospered, learned mechanical skills, and went to college, so that former Palestinians now occupy enviable positions in all Arab countries as executives, opinion leaders, professional people, foremen, and skilled workers.

There is no doubt that the socioeconomic upset emanating from Jewish Palestine was one of the reasons for Arab sheiks, kings, and capitalists to fear the establishment of a Jewish state. Another was the threat of Jewish mass immigration and the growth of a new power center that was bound to subvert the status quo in the Middle East. At that time, only twenty years after the Balfour Declaration, Zionism was still considered a tool of British imperialism, and the muftis of Jerusalem broadcast for Hitler from Berlin during the Second World War. To him, as to many Arabs today, Zionism was the imperialists' base in the Middle East.

A lot of silly arguments have been heard about this catchword, *imperialism.* Does it apply to Zionism? It is true that Orde Wingate trained the Haganah (Jewish underground defense organization), but another British officer, Glubb Pasha, led the army of Transjordan. And eighty years before these events, Lord Palmerston sponsored the unification of Italy, but does anyone charge that Garibaldi was a tool of British imperialism? The Jewish state was the goal of a national conquest; its conflict with Arab states or Arab interests is on the order of national rivalries, and this remains true even if Jews or Arabs or both are allied with imperial powers. At one time, the British favored the Jews, but after 1930 they found Zionist presumptions increasingly embarrassing. Zionism exploited British power and then turned against it. The British, in turn, contrary to Lenin's theory of imperialism, did not mean to "exploit" Palestine economically but, as the mandate power, to prohibit the development of Jewish industries.

The United States has invested heavily in Arab oil developments. The charge that it uses Israel to keep the sheiks docile, however, is totally unfounded and, on the face of it, ridiculous. The policy of the oil companies and of the State Department has been consistently pro-Arab, unless one defines as pro-Israel any policy not aiming at the destruction of the Jewish state. The responsibility for Israel's preservation, as for some other elements of the status quo that the United States is committed to defend, has been a heavy burden. But it is in the nature of empires to be drawn into national border conflicts where their clients have interests, and often they would rather not have to support them. Far from being used by the Russians or the Americans for their purposes, both Arabs and Jews have deliberately involved their big brothers in their own defense concerns.

Much has been made of the Histadruth's job policy. Obviously, in terms of Lenin's theory of imperialism, Jewish business has not been guilty of exploiting cheap Arab labor; rather, Jewish colonists have been guilty of making Arabs jobless and driving them from their lands. I have to explain here a subtlety of feudal law: fellahin can be sold along with the land on which they have been sitting, but the land cannot be sold without them; it cannot be pulled out from under their feet. When the Jewish agency, aware only of capitalist law, bought land from the callous effendis, it honestly may have thought that it had acquired the right to expel the fellahin, which repeats the story of the "enclosures," well known to readers of Marx's *Capital*. As the Phoenicians had done at Carthage and the Athenians in Sicily, the Jews acquired land, and Jewish colons "settled" it. This is the original meaning of "colonization."[6]

Notwithstanding Lenin, it may be called an imperialist policy on the part of the nation that hopes to prevail in such a fight for the land. Jewish settlers, who had naively begun to cultivate this ground—including kibbutzniks, who did so in the name of socialism—wondered why the former owners or tenants of those grounds were firing at them or staging surprise attacks on their innocent children; from the vantage point of the expelled Palestinians, the settlers were usurpers, colonizers, imperialists in flesh and blood, not just the tools of mysterious powers across the sea.[7]

This is the background of the war of 1948, which resulted in Israel's conquest of a contiguous territory (within the boundaries of 1948–1967) and in the Hashemite annexation of territory west of the Jordan River, including part of Jerusalem and such biblical cities as Bethlehem and Nablus. Perhaps even more important for our present purposes, it resulted in the flight of 600,000 Arabs from their native home.[8] In the light of the communal strife that had preceded the British pullout, that flight is totally understandable. A sensible person avoids being in anybody's line of fire, especially in this kind of civil war. The Jewish defense organizations had taken care to project an image of fierceness. Some, like Menachem Begin's Irgun Zwai Leumi and the Stern gang, were outright terrorists; their tactics appalled even Ben-Gurion.[9] In June 1945 the Irgun blew up the King David Hotel, causing ninety-one deaths. British soldiers were shot by snipers; cars loaded with dynamite were driven into British army camps. Do these people have a right to complain about terrorism? Even the Palmach, the combat organization of the Haganah, blew up bridges and derailed trains. The crimes that had been committed in a few—fortunately very few—places frightened the Arabs; when war came to their area, they followed the advice to stay clear of it. In so doing, they indicated that they were taking no part in the war operations. Clearly, in all wars of the past, displaced populations expected to eventually go back to their places of home, of work, of personal contacts. To keep them from returning, to forbid them a choice between staying abroad and accepting conquest, violates custom and international law—in fact, it is a crime. Yet, for reasons of national policy, the Israeli government seized this opportunity to create a demographically homogeneous Jewish state.[10]

IT WAS AT THIS MOMENT, and through this deed, that the issue of "the Palestinians" was created. So far, we have encountered Palestinians as the inhabitants of an area that might include all of the present state of Jordan or only the population of the mandate territory. Now the name has come to define almost exclusively the million Arabs who claimed that they had been expelled from their homeland and forced to live in primitive camps spread outside Israel in the Gaza Strip, on the West Bank, in Lebanon, and in Syria. These camps were maintained by the United Nations Relief and Rehabilitation Administration and financed mostly by American contributions.

Aside from the moral and humanitarian outrage they constitute, maintaining these camps was a political mistake of the first order. They became hotbeds of unrest, recruiting grounds for terrorist organizations, breeding places for corruption, blackmail, and crime. A few cents a day per head, amounting to many millions of dollars per year, meant an invitation to count many heads twice. The fraudulent claim that there were 2 million people in those camps is clearly exposed by the census figures of 1946. Even if every single Arab in all of Palestine had fled, there could not have been more than 1.2 million. Of course, in the thirty years that have elapsed, the original 600,000 have been blessed with children and grandchildren; even some "dead souls" may have been procreative.

No one denies that many Arabs on the West Bank considered the miserable allowance in the camps preferable to their normal subsistence under Arab governments. Some genuine refugees from Palestine left the camps and found lucrative employment in other Arab states; many others died. All remain statistics in the camp population, and so do their children, although the children may live in other countries. By the most conservative statistics, therefore, more than half of the present camp inmates never lived in Israel. The Israelis who justify their claim to the land by the tribal memory of 2,000 years obviously have no argument against people whose claim is based on tribal memories reaching back only thirty years. More than the expellees' actual misery, the bitterness of the sacrifice that was imposed on them intensifies the hatred that defines the Palestinians as a nation distinct from other Arabs.

Should the displaced Palestinians have been admitted by other Arab states? The Germans expelled from eastern Europe after the Second World War were among the Federal Republic's greatest assets. England admitted West Indians and mestizos whose country had become someone's state. Why do not Syria, Egypt, Lebanon, or rich Kuwait, Algeria, and Saudi Arabia help their Palestinian brothers—for whom they shed such abundant tears—integrate into their countries? Although the oil sheiks have the means, they feel no obligation to do so.[11] Actually, they would rather use these unfortunate victims of national wars as pawns in their own game of power politics. They are not interested in healing this wound; they want it to fester, but in the body of Israel, and in the body of world peace.

How could this have been prevented? At some point between 1948 and 1968, the United States should have stopped subsidizing the refugee camps, and Israel should have made an offer that might have, in one bold stroke, drastically reduced the number of "Palestinians" and disarmed their militancy. The offer should have been based on recognition of legitimate claims by those who could prove that they had lost their property, homes, or jobs in the present territory of Israel. They should have been given the option of either a monetary settlement or return under Israeli law. Since the conditions of life as a second-class citizen are never enviable, even when the nationalities are not emotionally hostile to each other, I believe that few Palestinians would have opted for return. Most would have taken the money, especially if, at the same time, U.S. subsidies had been ended.[12]

The Jewish authorities and public opinion have rejected such proposals on the twofold grounds that Israel could not accommodate so many Arabs without disrupting its economy and without endangering the safety of its state.[13] The first part of this rejoinder sounds odd in view of the steady clamor for more immigrants from countries holding more Jews than there are Arab statistics in the camps. The second part is refuted by the results of the Six-Day War, which added another million Arabs to the population of Israel, and the fact that many Israelis now speak of a "Greater Israel."

Most Israelis would probably want to keep the occupied areas if they could move the Arabs out, whereas Arab nationalism, strangely, demands the return of uninhabited desert first and liberation of the bemoaned brothers later.

In fact, Palestinians are not just the refugees in the camps of 1948. There are a million Arabs who live under military authorities in conquered territory. Despite the greater prosperity that annexation has brought to them, they are a source of unrest and an acute danger to peace. There can be no settlement, no truce, and no confidence between Arabs and Jews as long as their status is not determined equitably and as long as there is no international machinery to ascertain the will of the Palestinians themselves. Unless a political dialogue is initiated between Israel and responsible Arab leaders—a dialogue about concrete proposals that will satisfy legitimate claims—Yasir Arafat will step into the vacuum and pretend that he knows what the Palestinians want, and he will go on blackmailing his Arab friends and the international community. He also has rivals: should he not occupy the vacuum, some terrorist group or perhaps even the Communist Party will. The ball, therefore, is in Israel's court.[14]

At the time of the Six-Day War, the Israeli government declared that it would hold the occupied territories only as pawns and evacuate them in return for a peace treaty. It has offered to pay compensation to those who have lost property in old Palestine—or, rather, to allow the United States to make such payments—but it has not given refugees a choice of taking payment or returning. Meanwhile, the cancer of the Palestinians not only continues to fester but is being transplanted to the world arena, where it eats away the possibilities of peaceful coexistence. A decision is urgently needed to attack the primary point of the evil. Neither recriminations about the past nor legal constructions of right and wrong are required. What is required is finding political answers to political problems.

The offer to receive or to compensate legitimate claimants might be made with greater confidence by the Israeli government if the Palestinians were also offered a state of their own. It has been suggested that the West Bank and the Gaza Strip—two noncontiguous territories—would constitute such a state. Unfortunately, that state would not be economically viable; hence, it would be a pawn in the political game of the oil sheiks. Nor would such a proposal be politically acceptable without including the Arab part of Jerusalem. The Israelis are loath to give up any part of Jerusalem, and there is at this time no device of condominium or international control that would make the administration of the city possible without friction. It is clear that the real point of the quarrel is not viability but sovereignty. All the principals are too primitive in their tribal instincts or too immature as nations to be reasonable on questions where self-respect is at stake. Therefore, the solution for Jerusalem will have to be imposed by the great powers; it cannot be negotiated between the parties concerned. As long as they pretend to negotiate about it, they merely indicate that they do not mean to make peace.

By contrast, the return of the occupied territories must be negotiated by Israel itself with its neighbors, and the return of the refugees can be negotiated only privately between the Israeli government and those private parties who claim to have been residents of the area now under the government's jurisdiction. By its very nature, this cannot be a problem between Israel and Egypt or Syria, for neither of these countries claims sovereignty in Palestine. It could be negotiated between Israel and a state that can speak in the name of the Palestinians. These are a distinct people, different in background and culture from the Bedouins of Jordan, from the mercantile Lebanese, from the temperamental Syrians, from the millennia-old Egyptians. They must determine their own fate, both in Israel and in the West Bank area. They would probably prefer to sever their political ties with Jordan and might be interested in economic arrangements, to mutual advantage, with Israel. It stands to reason that they would rather not fight Boumédienne's wars and that the skimpy subsidies some of their guerrillas are getting from oil sheiks cannot substitute for a development plan and a technology to go with it. In the long run, a Palestinian state on the West Bank might easily fall into Israel's orbit, or become a client of Moscow, Beijing, Washington, or Tehran—who knows?

It is not necessary to believe that appeasement will bring an early cessation of terrorist attacks or a lowering of the level of invective in Arab rhetoric. But it may lay the foundation of a more constructive relationship between the Arabs and Jews on the local level and perhaps bring to old Palestine some kind of unity on the basis of economic interests and businesslike relations. In other words, it is necessary to strip this political problem of ideology. Although in this age everybody is "raising consciousness" or seeking to establish an identity, there is altogether too much of that in the Middle East. The Palestinians speak Arabic and worship in mosques, but they have come from many countries and have intermarried with many conquering nations. Their identity is of rather recent origin, through the misfortunes of war and yet another foreign conquest. Their appeasement ought to be less difficult than their arousal. They are looking for opportunities. I am even tempted to say that they can be bought, but they are being terrorized, and this may be the greatest obstacle to peace at this moment.

Can Israel wager its security on the vague prospect that one day the Palestinians might not only awaken but also mature? There are no alternatives, and one must look for solutions that have some promise of lasting. One may hope to prevent an explosion, even though one may not be able to remove the dynamite. Above all, one must divide, not unite, one's enemies. Third-world strategists have made the Palestinian issue into a cutting edge of their attack on Western positions in world politics. To blunt that edge, it is not necessary for the United States to take drastic measures, though it needs to radically rethink the issue. The friends of Israel—and, surprisingly, that includes many who have valiantly criticized "cold war attitudes" in U.S. policies—are tied to the confrontational patterns of the past decades; they think in terms of security rather than in political terms. They have missed valuable opportunities for peace in the past ten years. They gamble on the survival chances of a particular structure of the Israeli state, which is a dangerous gamble at best and is becoming more dangerous every day. The thought of having Arab citizens in their midst horrifies the Israelis, but while staring at that danger, they do not see the gathering of Arab armies outside the gate. They have too much confidence that the gate can be held shut for all time; this is an illusion for which others have paid dearly. In the long run, security lies only in the confidence of one's neighbors.

Aware that I have made some controversial statements, I want to make clear that the issue is neither moral nor judicial but political. Those who wish to debate my proposal should refrain from reminding me who "started it" or who is "more to blame" or whose "rights" are better. Wherever I have touched on such questions, my intention has merely been to show how Palestinians see them, and that is a political fact, not a moral judgment.

NOTES

Editors' note: This essay was originally published in *Dissent* in the fall of 1975 and reprinted in the collection *Socialism in History: Political Essays of Henry Pachter*, ed. Stephen Eric Bronner (New York: Columbia University Press, 1984). Its foresight and contemporary salience led us to republish the article in *Logos*.

1. Arabs today identify themselves only by speech. Originally the term meant conquerors coming from the Peninsula.
2. In 1922, Colonial Secretary Winston Churchill rejected the interpretation that Arab laws and customs had to be subordinated to Jewish interests, and Arab representatives rejected every constitution the British or the League of Nations tried to impose on the country. The Arab Congress in 1928 demanded a "fully democratic" government—whatever that meant in terms of Arab constitutions.
3. Foreign Secretary Ernest Bevin was no "anti-Semite"; he simply dropped a hot potato that cost England 50 million pounds a year. He was not the only Englishman, however, to wonder why the Jews were turning against England—of all nations—which had fought Hitler. Gratitude is not a political word, but bitterness is.
4. The United Nations then had fifty-seven members; obviously, the resolution would not pass today. Except for states recognized in the Westphalian Peace Treaty (1648) and at the Vienna Congress (1815), no other state has received such sanction. States are usually a product of violence.
5. This was the phrase used abroad; in Hebrew, it sounds less offensive.
6. A reader points out that the number affected was comparatively small and that terrorism developed mostly in the cities. Unfortunately, the symbolic and political value of the object does not depend on its size or price.
7. "The revolt is largely manned by the peasantry, that is to say by the people whose life and livelihood are on the soil but who have no say whatever in its disposal; and their anger and violence are as much directed against the Arab landowners and brokers who have facilitated the sales as against the policy of the mandatory Power under whose aegis the transactions have taken place. The fact that some of those landowners have served on national Arab bodies makes them only more

odious to the insurgent peasantry and has rendered it less amenable to the influence of the political leaders as a whole." George Antonius, *The Arab Awakening: The Story of the Arab National Movement* (New York: Lippincott, 1939), 406–7. The Jewish leaders—except for the communists, Martin Buber, and some *chalutzim*—never thought of allying themselves with these victims of colonization. See Bernard Avishai in *Dissent* (Spring 1975).

8. Some say the number was 800,000—more than had been living in the Jewish half of Palestine.
9. Obviously, what applies to Arabs must apply to Jews. Most Jews may not have approved of terrorism (though my father, usually one of the most law-abiding citizens, did), but Arabs are even less able than Jews to distinguish among factions in the other camp. The crime must be condemned; an entire people must not be condemned for it. But I am not arguing here about the morality of terror; my aim is to establish the fact that the Arab population felt threatened.
10. Unfortunately, socialists such as *Dissent* contributors Avishai and N. Gordon Levin have defended this theft on the ground that "socialist values" can be realized better in a securely Jewish environment. Would they agree with the Soviet government that "Soviet values" can be realized better in an environment that does not include Solzhenitsyn, Pasternak, or Trotsky?
11. Israel claims that it accepted a million oriental Jews, mostly expelled from the Arab countries. The rationale of the Jewish "homeland," however, conflicts with the suggestion that these should be balanced against the Arab expellees. They would be entitled to Israeli citizenship even without being harassed in Baghdad. Besides, a forcible population exchange is repugnant from any internationalist perspective.
12. Gordon Levin rejects the notion that readmission could "serve [any] real human interests besides a satisfaction of Arab honor." But that is a question of deep concern, and it is in Israel's power to restore that sense of honor.
13. It seems that Zionism has abandoned its earliest propaganda, which claimed that a Jewish state would make its Arab citizens happy and contented.
14. Arab notables in the occupied areas are subject to intimidation; some Israelis therefore think that Arafat is the only available partner. It is certain that no parley is now conceivable without him, a calamity that conforms to the pattern of the Israelis' poor grasp of diplomatic realities: they have always been forced to choose between two evils after they had rejected an alternative that would have been, after all, second best.

The Power of Myths in Israeli Society
Historical Realities and Political Dogmatism

Ernest Goldberger

Practically all peoples, nations, and societies have recourse to a treasury of legends, tales, or poetic fictions stemming from their more or less remote antiquity. These are mostly enacted by supernatural beings or by human heroes expressing, in terms of fable or story, interpretations of the world and idealized conceptions of life, and they sometimes serve, as well, as models and examples. Such myth formations often have their roots in animism, survive through the various prerational stages of cultures, and become, in modern societies, metaphors and other metarational forms for expressing ideas that are conceptually hard to formulate. Sometimes, actual historical events as well, because of their traumatic effect, solidify into formative concepts with mythical characteristics.

THE OVERSTATED MYTH OF JERUSALEM

In Switzerland, the figure of William Tell stands as the unyielding personification of the will for freedom and independence. His crossbow stands as a mark of virtue; Gessler's hat as an emblem of unendurable oppression; the Tell Chapel as a site of strength and courage; the Rütli meadow as a tableau of ideally like-minded and resolute men—symbols of a specifically Swiss identity. And it simply does not matter if the historian denies the authenticity of these legends. We are dealing with ideal-concepts of a predominantly rational-acting society. In Israel, the dominating influence of myth on politics, on the sense of identity, on historical consciousness, on culture as expressed in behavior, and on other aspects of society is particularly strong and obvious. At the same time, the timelessly valid messages of tradition occupy a less prominent spot in the foreground than do the verbal formulas in which they are bound up, and which are taken literally. Thus their meanings are so alienated that myths often serve to justify and to support unproductive attitudes and measures. The historical, psychosocial, religiohistorical, and cultural origins of this phenomenon cannot be properly dealt with here. We must content ourselves with two examples.

The myth of Jerusalem has established itself deeply in the consciousness of a broad section of Israeli society as the "holy" city of the glorious days of King

David and King Solomon, as the fountainhead of a continuous Jewish existence in that land, as God's locus, as the focal point of religious practice, where the First and Second Temples stood and where ultraorthodox and nationalist groups hope that a Third will soon be established. In the cultic poetry of the Psalms and in the writings of the prophets, Jerusalem is sung over and over again. The city appears innumerable times in prayers, finding entrance as the "golden" or the "eternal" in songs and sayings, and it is the object of theurgic yearnings and oaths.

IMPEDIMENTS TO A COMPROMISE

Official circles unrelentingly pump up this myth to justify their demand that Jerusalem remain the "eternal" and "undivided" capital of Israel and of the Jewish people. Right-wing nationalists successfully fought against Shimon Peres's candidacy for prime minister in 1996 with the assertion that he wished to divide Jerusalem. In the summer of 2000, when former prime minister Ehud Barak flew to Camp David for negotiations with Palestinian leader Yasir Arafat, the cry went up that he wanted to divide and bargain away Jerusalem. Through this compound of religious, ideological, and nationalistic charges, Jerusalem has grown into what it remains: a chief impediment to compromise with the Palestinians. It stands in the way of pacification of the Middle East, which the whole civilized world longs for. Thus has a myth intervened fatefully in contemporary history; it does not serve, rationally, a productive ideal but has degenerated into the dogma of an irrational policy.

Already in 1898, Theodore Herzl was shaken by the discrepancy between the fiction and the reality of Jerusalem. Thus, he confided to his diary: "The dull precipitation of two millennia full of barbarity, intolerance and uncleanliness lie in the evil-smelling alleys." But when a myth—in this case, Jerusalem—hardens into the official dictum and doctrine of the country's leadership, historical truth, frequently misrepresented by leading Israeli politicians, must face the challenge. Thus in 1998, a "Three Thousand Year Celebration" made it seem that the city had been founded as the religious center of the Israelites in 998 BC. In a speech, then-mayor Olmert erroneously invoked King David as star witness to the continuous Jewish history of the city. Prime Minister Sharon, as well, in an interview with the French newspaper *Le Figaro*, advanced the counterfactual proposition that Jerusalem has been "the capital of the Jewish people for precisely 3004 years." In reality, the spot that David conquered from the Jebusites (see, e.g., Judg. 19:10) was south of present-day Jerusalem, and it had already been inhabited for at least 2,000 years. On this, archaeologists, historians, and other scientists are agreed (e.g., see the compilation of research findings in the *Biblical Archeology Review*, August 1998). The original, agrarian inhabitants called it "Urusalim"; the cuneiform writing on a Babylonian clay tablet of the early Bronze Age, unearthed in 1975 in Ebla (in northern Syria), unambiguously shows this. The Hebrew *ir* ("city") derives from *uru,* and the Hebrew word *shalem* ("whole," "perfect") derives from *salim,* which has the same root as *shalom* ("peace").

Jerushalayim, the spiritualized Hebrew designation of Jerusalem as "Holy City" or "City of Peace," is as little the creation of the Jews as the place itself, which, after its conquest by the Hebrews, was inhabited by Jebusites, Phoenicians, Philistines, Cretans, Canaanites, and others.

As the Bible shows, only when David's son Solomon built the Temple on Mount Moriah was this extremely tiny portion of present-day Jerusalem incorporated within the city. After his death, however, the political and religious independence of the Jews disintegrated; in the Temple, the old gods were worshipped again, and those of the oriental powers, Assyria, Egypt, and Babylon, were allowed to be honored there. In 587 BC, the Babylonian king Nebuchadnezzar II destroyed Jerusalem and the Temple and abducted the elite of the Jews to his Mesopotamian country. After the rebuilding of the Temple some fifty years later, the Persians, Greeks, Seleucids, Romans (who destroyed the Second Temple), Byzantines, Arabs, Turkish Seldshuks, Crusaders, Kurds, Mamelukes, Osmanian Turks, and English displaced one another as rulers.

Jerusalem was under Jewish sovereignty only during the relatively obscure era of the Maccabees, as the ruling dynasty of the Hasmoneans is called. The latter liberated the country in 142 BC from the Seleucid Antiochus Epiphanes IV and established a fundamentalist regime, which the Romans brought to an end by 63 BC.

WHAT "HOLINESS"?

With the exception, perhaps, of the 300 years beginning with the rule of Omayeden-Calif Abd al-Malik, who built the Dome of the Rock (i.e., from roughly AD 700 to 1000), Jerusalem was a place of intolerance, inhumanity, and bloodiness. Untold times, it was conquered, reconquered, destroyed, depopulated. Instead of celebrating a city with such a tragic history, it would be better to ask what sort of "holiness" permits such barbarities, or provokes them. And yet "Jerusalem" has become a verbal incitement that immediately conjures up the holy sites in the Old City. Together with the Palestinian-inhabited East Jerusalem, these sections constitute an area of only six square kilometers. The Jewish western section, before the Six-Day War of June 1967, encompassed thirty-eight square kilometers. Since that passage of arms, however, Israel has annexed an additional seventy square kilometers of land in the West Bank, declared it to be urban area, and applied to this augmented Greater Jerusalem the dogma of mystical and religious indivisibility and holiness. By far, the greater part of the city today has simply no relation to the history and culture of the Jews.

Jerusalem is, in actuality—and in the consciousness of the Israelis and the Palestinians—a divided city in which the two populations live separated, each holding on to its own national and religious identity. Nearly a third of the roughly 680,000 inhabitants are Palestinians. They have the status of permanent residents with no Israeli citizenship and live crowded into the officially neglected eastern section of the city, which Israeli Jews have no difficulty avoiding.

The prayers and mystical longings scarcely have reference to the brutalities in Jerusalem's history or to the unedifying current conditions, but rather to a thus far unfulfilled image of a "holy" place and a messianic condition of peace and human dignity. Many Israeli politicians and representatives of the religious elites, however, have affixed this image onto a specific place and have bound it up in the asserted claim to the "eternal" possession of a Greater Jerusalem. Thus do they alienate a productive model that they claim to live by, for the "idea" of the Jerusalem of their devotions is not bounded to any city limits and unites not parcels of property but human beings.

THE TEMPLE MOUNT: MORE IMPORTANT THAN PEACE?

The Temple myth has also grown into a dominant element of policy. Israel wants sovereignty over the hill where the First and Second Temples stood, even at the cost of peace with the entire Islamic world, although the golden Dome of the Rock and the Al-Aksa mosque have been there for many hundreds of years. Natan Scharansky, minister for Jerusalem and Diaspora Affairs in the Israeli government, recently wrote an article in the newspaper *Ha'aretz* with the title "The Temple Mount Is More Important Than Peace."

This kind of dogmatizing and exploitation of myth raises up a further obstacle in the way of reconciliation with the Palestinians, which is so vital for the country. Thus, after the January 28, 2003, elections, we see on placards, in advertisements, and over the radio the declaration that the Temple Mount is "the heart of the nation" and the "identity of the Jewish people." The office of the chief rabbi has announced that a relinquishment of sovereignty would be, "according to Jewish law," forbidden. Groups of fanatics already want to lay the cornerstone for the Third Temple to replace the Muslim sanctuaries.

The Temple myth finds no support in historical truth. In the much-sung "glory days of King David," there actually was no Temple. When strange gods were not being worshipped in the First and Second Temples—by the Jews, as well—their worship consisted mainly of a sacrificial cult, described in the Old Testament but scarcely to be desired today. It was a hotbed of corruption, intrigue, commercialism, and religious power politics. Various passages in the New Testament (e.g., Matt. 21:12, 13 and John 2:14, 17), contemporary witnesses, and even certain passages in the Talmud describe these conditions in explicit terms.

Only after the destruction of the Second Temple and the expulsion of the Jews nearly two millennia ago could the Jewish religion develop those universal values grounded in the ancient scriptures, which themselves, significantly, came into being during the Babylonian exile, unencumbered by a Temple cult and not tied to a specific place or center of power. This Judaism had no connection to the Temple Mount. Affixing "holiness" to a specific location through the building of the Temple was of a piece with the Zeitgeist of idolatry and served as an inducement for the Crusades of the Middle Ages, which were a Christian variant of the same syndrome. More modern religious thinking holds that "holy" places are merely symbols or models for a transcendence that can be lived and practiced anyplace. In this sense, the role assigned to the Temple myth in Israel not only is politically dubious; it also represents, from the standpoint of philosophy of religion, a grave relapse. Thus, tragically, a mythological, site-bound "holiness" stands in the way of the universal holiness of peace.

NOTE

This article originally appeared in the Swiss daily *Neue Zürcher Zeitung* and was translated from the German by Jeffrey Craig Miller.

The Logic behind the Geneva Accord

Menachem Klein

There are three ways in which the Geneva Accord differs from previous documents dealing with an Israeli–Palestinian settlement. First, this is a model for a permanent status agreement that puts an end to the conflict and to all mutual claims. Prior to the signing of the Geneva Accord in Jordan on October 13, 2003, no such model existed, given that the talks held by Israel and the Palestine Liberation Organization (PLO) in 1999–2001 on a permanent status settlement had come to naught. Second, this is a detailed model. Prior to the publication of the Geneva Accord, several joint Israeli–Palestinian declarations on the principles of a permanent agreement were prepared. Some of these documents were prepared in the official negotiations track, and others were prepared by academic experts and civil society activists through unofficial (track 2) talks. Before the Geneva Accord, however, there was no detailed model that included a precise map of the proposed permanent arrangement. Third, as opposed to earlier documents, the Geneva Accord is a signed agreement. The very fact of the signatures creates a personal commitment that differs from a document published by a host institution. Furthermore, the accord was not signed by a few individuals but by more than twenty persons on each side.

The composition of the signatories is also extraordinary. Among the signatories on the Palestinian side are ministers and deputy ministers, Fatah representatives to the Palestinian Legislative Council, senior officials, and academics. Those Palestinians who held official office declared that they were signing the accord as private individuals. The public, however, understands that without the approval of the Palestinian leadership, these individuals would not have been able to take such a dramatic step or even to engage in the Geneva negotiations. On the Israeli side, the signatories include Knesset members from the opposition parties, peace activists, writers, security personnel serving in the reserves, economists, and academics. Appended to the Geneva Accord is a cover letter that emphasizes that the reference is to a model for an arrangement, not a binding document; to a document that complements the road map, not one meant to replace it; to a private initiative, not one that is representative—even in the case of those individuals who hold public office; to an appeal to public opinion on both sides in order to show that a permanent arrangement is attainable, not a pretense meant to create the impression of an accord between governments.

The Geneva Accord is formulated like a legal agreement between two states. In this way, it gives tangible expression to the idea of a permanent arrangement. The text is complex, lengthy, and, as a legal text, is not friendly to the average reader. In the following pages, I outline the principles behind the formulation of the main articles in the agreement.

ACCEPTANCE OF THE "OTHER" AS LEGITIMATE

For many years, Israel and the PLO denied each other's right to statehood. Israel denied the very existence of a Palestinian people and its right to a state, while the PLO saw Judaism as a religion and not a national identity. The two sides have moved closer together since the late 1980s and now recognize the existence of the other as a fact. In the Geneva Accord, the sides take an additional step forward by granting legitimacy to the other based on how the other defines itself. The accord includes the right of the Jewish people to a state and the right of the Palestinian people to a state. In addition, the sides recognize that these states constitute a national homeland for their peoples. They also emphasize that the fact that the states are founded on an ethnic-historical basis should not infringe on the rights of the citizens. In other words, recognition of Israel as a Jewish state (i.e., a state with a Jewish majority) does not legitimize discrimination against Palestinian Israelis.

SECURITY ARRANGEMENTS

The guiding principle in this section is security for Israel without occupation of the Palestinian state. The negotiations on the security arrangements were the relatively easy part of the Geneva talks. This is because the parameters of the security arrangements have not changed significantly since the official talks at Camp David and in Taba. What has changed is the context in which the security arrangements are to be applied. The deeper Israel is willing to withdraw and the broader its acceptance of Palestinian sovereignty, the greater the Palestinian readiness to accommodate Israel on security matters.

The Palestinians have come to terms with Israel's pursuit of almost 100 percent security, although in the course of the talks, they could not understand how it is that this regional superpower perceives such a deep threat to its security. After all, the Palestinians are the weak side in the conflict and have suffered at the strong arm of Israel over the years. As the side that has incurred the heaviest losses, they were amazed by Israel's deep-rooted sense of an existential threat to its security. They did not try to convince Israel that it is making a mountain out of a molehill but rather met Israel halfway on this issue.

Palestine will be a nonmilitarized state, and no armed force that is not mentioned in the accord will be deployed on its territory. The two sides are committed to an ongoing struggle against terrorism (including acts of terrorism against property, land, and institutions). Neither side may desist from this struggle on the pretext of a disagreement with the other side. Given the strong opposition expected from the enemies of a permanent arrangement, and based on the experience garnered during the Oslo years, when extremists on both sides succeeded in torpedoing the interim agreements, it was determined that the very existence of illegal, armed organizations contravenes the accord and that such organizations must be disarmed. The Palestinians agreed to far-reaching security arrangements that include high-altitude Israeli air force training flights in the airspace of the West Bank, the maintenance of two early-warning stations, and an Israeli military presence in the Jordan Rift Valley. This Israeli military presence, however, will be subject to the authority of a multinational force. This force will defend Palestine against invasion by external forces and oversee the security arrangements. The external supervision of the security articles ensures the end of the occupation and of the Palestinians' humiliation at the hands of Israel. The security arrangements will be open to reassessment after a number of years. In the end, the Palestinians understood that they must show consideration for Israel's psychological needs in the security sphere. By responding to this need, the Palestinians both won full territorial sovereignty and put an end to Israel's use of the security issue as a pretext for continuing the occupation.

TERRITORY

The starting point for the territorial discussions was the 1967 borders as the lines that enjoy international legitimacy and beyond which lie land and people under Israeli occupation. The 1967 lines represent a historic compromise in which mandatory Palestine will be divided between the two national movements.

From the territorial aspect, it was clear to both sides that neither the state of Israel nor Palestine—each for its own reasons—can live with the settlements. The 160 settlements and approximately 100 additional outposts that are spread out over the West Bank prevent the Palestinians from establishing a viable state on the 1967 lands. As far as Israel is concerned, the national settlement enterprise is no longer tenable. There is a huge demographic disparity between the two populations: 200,000 settlers, as opposed to more than 3 million Palestinians in the West Bank and Gaza Strip. This tough demographic reality caused Israel to tighten its control of the settlements and over the Palestinian population through domination of the roads, land, water, and main arteries and by means of Israel's military strength and technological superiority. This, of course, led the Arab majority to launch an uprising.

By mid-January 2004, 2,648 Palestinians had been killed and 24,407 wounded in the intifada, and Israel had set up 608 roadblocks and 56 manned barriers on Palestinian land, totally disrupting the daily lives of the Palestinians. All these measures failed to suppress the Palestinian uprising; rather, they drove the Palestinians to seek revenge and liberation from the Israeli stranglehold by means of low-tech but highly motivated combat and vile acts of terrorism. In 2003, the ratio of settlers to soldiers defending them was 4:1, not counting the Israeli General Security Service personnel and soldiers within the Green Line held hostage to the defense of the settlements. In economic terms, maintenance of the settlements came at the expense of the citizens of Israel. In 2001, each settler received approximately NIS 8,600 (about $2,000) more than each Israeli living within the Green Line. It is worth noting that most settlers cannot be classified as low income and that the preceding calculation does not include benefits received from the Education and Defense ministries or government support for settler associations.

Although the settlers (excluding those in East Jerusalem) constitute only 3 percent of the Israeli population, more than half of the country's citizens support them. After close to forty years of occupation, it is impossible to evacuate all the settlements, despite the fact that they are all illegal under international law. In the Geneva Accord, the sides agreed that no settler will remain within the boundaries of Palestine and that Israel will not annex even one Palestinian. The Geneva map proposed a border that annexes only some 2 percent of the West Bank on which 110,000 Israelis live in 21 settlements (excluding Jerusalem). In other words, approximately 50 percent of the settlers living in some 140 settlements will be evacuated. Their homes and the existing infrastructure will be handed over to Palestine. Israel will compensate Palestine for the territory it will annex in the West Bank with lands from its sovereign territory that are quantitatively equal and qualitatively similar. The Gaza Strip will expand eastward by 25 percent, and cultivated Israeli lands will be annexed to it. This will allow the population of the Strip to export agricultural produce and increase its income. The remaining territorial compensation will be made from lands to the southwest of the West Bank. Palestine will receive lands containing the remnants of about ten Palestinian villages destroyed in the 1948 war, and it will be able to turn these areas into sites of commemoration and return.

REFUGEES

The Israeli–Palestinian conflict does not revolve around the 1967 lands alone, but also the 1948 lands. Israel's War of Independence in 1948 was a catastrophe for the Palestinians. Approximately half the Palestinian population became refugees, and the state of Israel took over their homes, land, and property. The attempt of the Palestinian nationalist movement to create a state under the control of the Arab majority ended in disaster. The war turned the demographic ratio of Jews and Arabs on its head and left a solid Jewish majority in Israel.

The two national entities viewed 1948 as a defining event whose overturn would lead to the collapse of the Zionist structure. In order to preclude any subversion of 1948, Israel denied its role in the creation of the refugee problem and denied the existence of a Palestinian national identity; in order to negate 1948, the Palestinians rejected Israel's existence and denied the Jewish people's right to self-determination. They turned their traumatic defeat into the sweet dream of return. This ideal Palestinian dream became the Israeli nightmare of the end of a state with a Jewish majority.

The two sides learned a lesson when the official negotiations failed to reach agreement on a joint narrative regarding the events of the 1948 war. The Geneva understandings leave this task to the two civil societies, with the two governments showing them the way. After all, a diplomatic accord cannot heal national traumas, suddenly change deep-rooted memories, and destroy national and historical myths. A diplomatic accord can outline and map them, defuse them, and ensure that they will not destroy the operational mechanisms. Reconciliation and openness toward the narrative of one's fellow man are the result of long-term processes that take place within civil society. Diplomatic mechanisms can promote reconciliation processes but not dictate them. Therefore, the Israeli partners to the Geneva Accord did not present their Palestinian counterparts with an unequivocal demand that they renounce the right of return to areas within the state of Israel. In effect, the accord leaves this to the consciousness of each individual.

The classic understanding of the Palestinian right of return is that each individual refugee and the Palestinian national collective have the right to return to their homeland and to a specific place of residence. This right is unassailable. Israel must accept it and comply with it. The Geneva Accord is not based on this approach but rather on UN General Assembly Resolution 194 (December 1948), UN Security Council Resolution 242 (November 1967), and the Arab League peace initiative (April 2002).

UN General Assembly Resolution 194 calls on Israel to allow refugees who are willing to live in peace with it to return to Israel at the earliest practicable date. For years, the PLO claimed that this resolution grants every refugee the right of return. Israel, in contrast, claimed that there is no such term in the language of the resolution; moreover, General Assembly resolutions are not binding. Pursuant to this, the Geneva Accord also refers to Article 2B of the Arab League peace initiative, which speaks of a solution to the refugee problem "to be agreed upon in accordance with UN General Assembly Resolution 194." As opposed to the PLO's classic concept of the right of return and Resolution 194, the Arab states accept the principle of the need for Israel's consent.

The Geneva Accord illustrates how this will be implemented. The choice of the state of Palestine as one's permanent place of residence is a right granted to every Palestinian refugee by virtue of being Palestinian, whereas the possibility of taking up permanent residence in the state of Israel may be granted by Israel. Thus, refugees are free to believe that they are returning to their homeland, but this has no legal or institutional expression or backing in the accord. According to the Geneva Accord, the state of Israel is a country to which Palestinian refugees may immigrate. This will prevent the realization of the Israeli nightmare: the return of a mass of refugees as a means of reversing the outcome of the 1948 war. All the mechanisms for dealing with the refugee problem in existence since 1948 will cease to exist, and the legal status of refugeehood will be terminated. Refugees who seek to deviate from the accord and demand the right of return in the classic sense will find no institution that supports their claim and will have no legal standing.

The determination of an individual refugee's permanent place of residence will not be made by him or her alone but by a technical committee to be established by the international commission appointed to oversee the implementation of the accord. The commission will include an Israeli representative who will submit to the committee the number of refugees Israel is willing to accept. In determining this number, Israel will take into consideration the average number of refugees who will immigrate to countries outside the region. Any Israeli administration that seeks to act in a manner contrary to the spirit of the accord may formally rest its case on this article and fix a low number based on the claim that this article does not commit Israel to a high number. The article was formulated in this way not to deceive the Palestinians but rather to show that, contrary to the classic right of return, the reference is to willingness on Israel's part. The parties to the Geneva Accord hope that whatever administration is in power in Israel when the time comes will wish to resolve the refugee issue and that there will be no need for international pressure to this end.

There is a legitimate argument under way in Israel with regard to the country's identity as a Jewish state, the nature of its citizenship, and its characterization as a liberal democracy. The Geneva Accord does not settle this argument. It recognizes the right of the Jewish people and the right of the Palestinian people to their own state and rejects any infringement on civil rights. Anyone who seeks to tip the scales through the return of huge numbers of Palestinian refugees would, in effect, be destroying any chance of a permanent settlement. Anyone who seeks to punish Israel for establishing a state on the land of another nation by changing Israel's ethnic character would, in effect, be destroying the chance for a different kind of future for the sake of the past. The same holds true for anyone who claims that Israel must recognize the right of return as a basic principle and must leave it to each individual refugee to choose whether to exercise this right. In the absence of mechanisms that would limit the implementation to a model similar to that outlined in the Geneva Accord, the Israeli nightmare of the end of the Jewish state would become real. This actualization of the Israeli nightmare is the surest way to prevent an agreement.

The Geneva Accord does not contain an Israeli apology for its role in the creation of the 1948 refugee problem. In the past, Israel denied playing any role whatsoever in the creation of this problem, placing full responsibility squarely on the shoulders of the leaders of the Arab states and the heads of the Palestinian national movement. Today, given the findings of research into the subject, it is difficult to deny that the Israeli establishment played a part in the creation of the Palestinian refugee problem. Historical research into the period in question has been conducted largely by Israeli researchers and is based primarily on Israeli archives. The academic debate is no longer over the question of whether Israel engaged in acts that created refugeehood in 1948 but over the scope of such activities, the motives behind them, and the level of central planning and control over them. Yet in Israel, it is only the academics and the intellectuals who are grappling with the conclusions of this historical research. The findings have not been absorbed by all levels of society and have not been accepted by the main bodies in the Israeli political system. The dominant narrative of the latter has been that Israel was founded in 1948 by the strength and will of the people and that Israel's War of Independence was pure and untainted. In their eyes, any admission that the Israeli forces committed war crimes in 1948 or that central state mechanisms took part in turning many Palestinians into refugees would mean that the state of Israel was founded on the perpetration of a great injustice, and this would divest Israel of the legitimate and moral basis for its establishment and existence. In the dominant Israeli narrative, this lays the groundwork for invalidating Israel's right to exist. In order for the popular Israeli narrative to change and conform with the findings of academic research, Israel needs reassurances with regard to its fear that the outcome of the 1948 war will be overturned. Only when Israel is confident that its darkest nightmare will not come true will it apologize for its role in creating the refugee problem. In this way, Israel will be able to compensate the Palestinian refugees morally and symbolically for what its forces did to them in 1948.

Furthermore, as long as Israel feels a real or imagined threat to its very existence, it will be difficult for Israeli society to shift from the concept that Israel was founded on the basis of its might and victory in 1948 to the concept that its foundation rests on the Jewish people's right to self-determination in its historical homeland. In other words, it is difficult for the majority of Israelis to make the change from the narrative of power and the concept of an existence based on the use of might against outside forces to a concept based on every nation's right to self-determination.

The PLO faces a similar difficulty. The majority of the Palestinian public finds it difficult to admit to the war crimes perpetrated by its forces in the course of their struggle for national liberation and to apologize for the terror its organizations have used and are continuing to use against Israelis and foreigners. Only the educated elites among them are ready to recognize the immorality of Palestinian terror and war crimes. The common people are focused on securing the establishment of a viable Palestinian state through the struggle against Israeli occupation. In addition, they fear that any admission that the national movement engaged in war crimes and terrorism during the struggle for liberation will cancel the recognition of the Palestinian people's right to self-determination. The time for a Palestinian apology will come when Palestinian sovereignty over the 1967 lands is guaranteed and they no longer fear that Israel will exploit this apology to undermine the establishment of a Palestinian state.

JERUSALEM

Israel has controlled Jerusalem longer than the British and twice as long as Jordan did. The Jewish-Israeli city in the west rules over approximately 200,000 Arab Palestinians (approximately 10 percent of the inhabitants of the West Bank) living in the eastern side. The Palestinian city developed because and in spite of the development of an Israeli Jerusalem. From a historical perspective, Israel has scored quite a few accomplishments in Jerusalem, the most prominent being that it is impossible to revert to the reality that existed in the city prior to the Six-Day War.

The fact that some 50 percent of the Jewish residents of Jerusalem live on former Jordanian territory makes it impossible to evacuate the Jewish neighborhoods there. The option of leaving them in place under Palestinian sovereignty is no less problematic. What would be the nature of the Palestinian capital if approximately half of its population were made up of Israelis?

Although it is impossible to return to the reality of June 4, 1967, it is also impossible to turn the annexation lines of June 27, 1967, into the permanent border. Palestinian construction has turned these lines into a virtual border. In many locations, the annexation line crosses neighborhoods, streets, and homes. Palestinian villages that were not included in the annexed territory for demographic reasons have become suburbs of the city. East Jerusalem operates as a metropolitan, religious, and political center and provides services and a source of income to a large population that resides beyond the municipal boundaries. In a nutshell, both of the June 1967 lines have been eroded, and the borders of the city must be redrawn.

Demographic considerations have shaped Israeli policy toward East Jerusalem since 1967. The Israeli establishment invested vast resources in an effort to maintain the demographic balance that it believes will cement the annexation: 75 percent Jews to 25 percent Arabs. Paradoxically, the annexation momentum increased the Palestinian presence in East Jerusalem. The demographic balance stands today at 68 percent Jews to 32 percent Arabs. Israel's attempts to change this by confiscating identity cards, revoking residency rights, and demolishing illegally built structures in the eastern part of the city and the metropolitan area have failed. As of 1999, Israel had confiscated from the Palestinians only some 4,000 identity cards out of a possible 50,000 to 80,000, and demolition orders were actually executed in only some 4 to 8 percent of the building violations identified by Israel.

The Arabs of East Jerusalem are not citizens of Israel but rather residents. In other words, approximately one-third of the population of the capital of Israel does not recognize it and rejects Israeli citizenship. In the absence of a permanent agreement, the East Jerusalemites are perceived as a threat to Israeli sovereignty and, as a result, have been the victims of organized and ongoing deprivation at the hands of Israeli governments in terms of allocation of resources, laying of infrastructure, and provision of services. Only a small amount of the meager Israeli investment in East Jerusalem met the needs of the Palestinian population. Most investment was allocated to tourism and to strengthening Israeli control and annexation.

Today, Jerusalem consists of two cities positioned back to back. Jewish-Israeli Jerusalem faces westward, to the state of Israel's natural home front, while Palestinian Jerusalem faces the West Bank. The divide between the two cities runs deep, and only a small number of Palestinian workers cross the ethnic lines for a few hours a day. It is in the interest of both the Israelis and the Palestinians to partition the city in order to allow both cities to develop in their natural space.

The Geneva Accord proposes the division of Israeli Jerusalem and Palestinian Jerusalem into two separate entities with controlled crossing points to the other side. The division provides for the maximum preservation of the current municipal functions and protects the interests of both sides. Coordination on matters of common interest will be handled by a committee made up of an equal number of representatives from each side. A multinational force will oversee the implementation of the agreement and will intervene in any dispute between citizens or agencies of the two countries. The division of Jerusalem is not virtual. A fence will run between the two cities, but it will be both user and environmentally friendly, as opposed to the chain of brutal fences and walls being erected today as part of an enterprise that will lead to nothing short of the destruction of both the western and the eastern parts of Jerusalem. The Arab neighborhoods will be connected by a series of roads, just as all the Jewish neighborhoods will be connected by roads, and every citizen of Israel or Palestine will be able to move freely within the territory of his or her sovereign country. The Geneva negotiating team is working on appendices that deal with a number of issues, such as the gradual separation of infrastructures, the planning of border crossings, and the administration of the border areas, but it has not yet completed this task. It is clear that the transition from the current reality to that which we are proposing must take place gradually, and the negotiating team has begun to address this issue as well.

The Old City will be a free and open city. Sovereignty will be divided, with the Jewish Quarter under Israeli sovereignty and the Christian, Armenian, and Muslim quarters under Palestinian sovereignty. The border will be clearly marked, but there will be no physical barriers between the two sovereign areas of the Old City except out of security concerns, and for a limited time only. Lion's Gate, Herod's Gate, Damascus Gate, and New Gate, which face the Palestinian city, will be under Palestinian sovereignty. Zion Gate and Dung Gate, which serve the Israelis, will be under Israeli sovereignty. Citizens of each side will enter and exit freely via the gates under their sovereignty. An Israeli who wishes to exit the Old City via a Palestinian gate will have to present an entry permit to Palestine, and the same applies to a Palestinian wishing to exit via an Israeli gate. Jaffa Gate will operate as an Israeli gate and will continue to be used by Israelis as the main gate of entry from the west, although it will be under Palestinian sovereignty. As there are no Israeli residences or commercial facilities around Jaffa Gate or along the road that leads from it to Zion Gate, this area will be under Palestinian sovereignty, but Israel will be responsible for the security of those entering or exiting Israel along this route. The same applies to the Jewish Cemetery on the Mount of Olives, which will be under Palestinian sovereignty but under Israeli administration and security. In return, the Palestinians will be guaranteed the continued use of the Christian cemeteries in Israeli Jerusalem.

David's Tower is no less an Israeli and a Zionist symbol than Rachel's Tomb or the Wailing Wall, despite the historical truth that the actual ruins of David's Citadel are located somewhere else. Furthermore, David's Tower overlooks western Jerusalem and serves Israel as a municipal museum, an archaeological garden, and a reception hall. The Geneva understandings preserve the existing Israeli administration of the compound under Palestinian sovereignty.

The Geneva Accord does not ignore the place of the Temple Mount as a holy site and a national symbol. In this regard, it is important to note that the sanctity of the Temple Mount is not derived from state sovereignty. The Temple Mount was a Jewish holy site even when it was under the control of the Crusaders or the Persians, and it remains a Muslim holy site even under Israeli sovereignty. The state and the political regime need the Temple Mount as a rallying symbol that grants them legitimacy. The Geneva Accord divides the Temple Mount compound in accordance with each side's national and symbolic usage and its religious role as a site of active ritual observance: the Temple Mount under Palestinian sovereignty, and the Wailing Wall under Israeli sovereignty. The Palestinian side to the Geneva Accord recognizes the sanctity and the religious and cultural importance of the Temple Mount for world Jewry. Accordingly, the Palestinians agree not to excavate under or build on the Mount without Israeli authorization. In other words, the agreement replaces symbolic Israeli sovereignty with recognition of the site's symbolism for Judaism. Israel's approval of excavation or construction is solely residual, while Palestinian sovereignty over Al-Aksa and the Dome of the Rock will grant Palestine a status in the Arab and Muslim world that is second only to that of Saudi Arabia. One cannot exaggerate the importance of this symbolic resource for Palestine, which is short of territory, natural resources, and infrastructure but has a vast population and is rife with social and economic distress.

Both sides are committed to respecting the existing division of administrative functions and traditional practices at the holy sites. In order to assist them in this and to promote interfaith dialogue, the sides will establish a body comprising representatives of the three monotheistic faiths.

CONCLUSION

The goal of the Geneva Accord is to show public opinion on each side that there is a partner for peace and a way to reach the end of the historical conflict. The Geneva Accord constitutes an alternative to the policies of the central regime in Israel and the Palestinian Authority, to the ongoing deterioration resulting from the violent conflict, and to Israel's plan for unilateral disengagement from the occupied territories. The Geneva Accord was widely publicized immediately after it was signed and has become a focal point in the public debate on the diplomatic process both in the Middle East and beyond.

The formulation of such a detailed accord necessitates tough decision making. We cannot shirk this responsibility and leave it to the leaders and to the hope of future negotiations that are nowhere in sight. At the same time, we cannot avoid decisions by taking refuge in some theoretical or ideal model that will be impossible to implement. To the same extent, we cannot reach an agreement that will fail to pass the political and public test. Political and marketing considerations are part of the package deal and of the compromises each side must make in order to help the other side. In the past, channels of communication between Israeli and Palestinian experts limited their talks to professional matters and avoided political issues. They opted for expert solutions that were impossible to implement from the political point of view. The political, the public, and the professional aspects must meet, however, when two countries are negotiating a peace accord. In this respect, of all the academic and political "track 2" channels, the Geneva Accord is closest to the "real thing."

To reach an agreement, each side must see the interests, sensitivities, and point of view of the other. This proved to be Israel's Achilles' heel in the official talks between Israel and the PLO. Israel saw only its own interest. Even when considering the Palestinians' desires, Israel did so from the point of view of its perception of what those desires were. Israel repeatedly argued that only its interests and its bottom line would determine what the other side received. Unfortunately, the official talks on the permanent arrangement failed to produce a win-win situation. But from its inception, the Geneva channel was based on the win-win concept, and the text, formulated from the point of view of both sides, is equal and balanced.

By its very nature as a compromise, the Geneva Accord cannot constitute the embodiment of absolute justice, especially in a situation in which each side feels that it is totally in the right and that every concession is a blow to the justness of its cause. Yet neither does the Geneva Accord constitute a dictate on the part of powerful Israel; it incorporates Palestinian achievements as well and rests on the international legitimacy of a state based on the 1967 lines. It is an agreement that will enable the two peoples to live in honorable and fair coexistence.

In the short time since it was signed on October 13, 2003, the Geneva Accord has become the term of reference in every political and expert debate on the parameters of a permanent status agreement. Furthermore, the Geneva Accord has become an alternative to the current policies of the Israeli and Palestinian governments. The incumbent Israeli government is vehemently opposed to it, and in reaction to the support the accord has won in Israel and abroad, the government is planning to take unilateral steps in an attempt to ease its plight. The Palestinian Authority, in contrast, has refrained from formally endorsing the Geneva Accord because of the Israeli government's failure to do so and because such a step means grappling with internal political struggles and making decisions that the Palestinian government feels are premature. Apparently, the road to the adoption of the Geneva Accord must pass through the failure of the alternatives, including Israel's plan for "unilateral disengagement" by means of a wall and fences. Once Israel realizes that there is no way to avoid concessions and that an agreement, with its advantages and disadvantages, is preferable to the ongoing conflict, which does only harm, the Geneva model will cease to be an alternative plan and will become policy.

Beyond the question of what chances the Geneva Accord has of being implemented lies the question of whether the model it proposes is durable. Will the accord stand the test of time? After all, the Geneva model does not create equality between Israel and Palestine. In terms of territory, Palestine will extend over only 23 percent of the lands of mandatory Palestine, which the national movement sees as the homeland of the Palestinian people. Palestine will be a young state, laden with social and economic problems and home to strong currents of Islamic fundamentalism. What, therefore, will prevent it from striving in the future to correct the "historical injustice" and cancel the agreement it was forced to accept out of a position of weakness?

In fact, the Geneva Accord is not an agreement between two sides that are equal militarily. Israel's military might is far superior to that of the Palestinian national movement and, under the terms of the accord, will remain superior to that of the state of Palestine. The Geneva Accord, like the historic compromise the PLO has proposed to the state of Israel since 1988, is based on the recognition that the Palestinians and the Arab states do not have the military capability to wipe Israel off the map and will not have such a capability in the future. Nonetheless, the Arabs in general and the Palestinians in particular have the international legitimacy to demand the end of the Israeli occupation that has existed since 1967. Every Arab peace initiative has rested on these foundations and on the decision to transfer resources from the confrontation with Israel to domestic needs. The Palestinians who signed the Geneva Accord have adopted this approach. They opted for the establishment of a state based on the 1967 borders and the realization of its human and touristic potential instead of dreaming of the destruction of Israel and paying the heavy price this would entail. The situation in the economic sphere is similar to that in the security sphere. The economic articles of the Geneva Accord have not yet been written, but they are not expected to create economic equality between Israel and Palestine. Any Israeli–Palestinian agreement will regulate the economic relations between the two states but will not put them on an equal footing. Equality between Israel and Palestine will be anchored in the legal status of the two states. In brief, the large economic and military gap between Israel and Palestine will remain. Even if the radical Islamic forces come to power in Palestine, they will be unable to realize their dream.

The Geneva Accord does not outline the path to realization of the Israeli or

Palestinian dreams of national expansion and exclusive control over what is the shared homeland of two nations. The Geneva Accord rests on the recognition of the need for a historic compromise. The Palestinian dream about the 1948 lands is unrealistic and has taken a heavy toll on the Palestinians. The perpetuation of the occupation of the 1967 lands is beyond Israel's capability and is destroying it. Instead of a lose-lose situation, the Geneva Accord offers a win-win alternative.

West Bank Settlements Obstruct Peace
Israel's Empire State Building

Marwan Bishara

Why is it so hard to make peace in the Middle East? The greatest barrier is the Israeli settlements—these are both the motivation for and the engine of the Israeli occupation of the Palestinian territories. Three decades of objections from the United States and Europe have achieved nothing. The rapid expansion of Israeli settlements—all illegal—has undermined Palestinian attempts at nation building. If they continue to spread, they will end the Israel that its founders envisioned.

As Israel makes more incursions into Palestinian cities, it has placed new restrictions on the movement of their people and goods, stifling the economy. Oslo has ended. And still Israeli settlements increase and expand, in violation of all international resolutions. The settlement drive and its ideology have become a cornerstone of modern Israeli national identity. The policy of settlements and the current violence they are breeding have transcended the country's ethnic and religious divides to create a new Israelism based on a new Jewish nationalism. The settlers and their allies are re-creating Israel in their own image: as a theocracy in permanent conflict. Under the government of Ariel Sharon and with the explicit support of President George W. Bush, this process is becoming a destructive self-fulfilling prophecy.

These new settlers are nothing like their predecessors of the pre-1948 generation who founded Zionism and formed the state as a secular, socialist, and mainly European enterprise. The post-1967 settlers are predominantly religious, conservative, Reagan-style neoliberals. And unlike their predecessors, their settlement activity is state sponsored by Israel. The new Zionists (or post-Zionists) believe that for their Greater Israel nationalism project to succeed, another campaign of ethnic cleansing will be necessary. Many members of Sharon's cabinet are already speaking about "transfer"—the collective expulsion of the Palestinians.

Worse, former general Efi Eitam, a newly appointed minister and leader of the National Religious Party, is a supporter of settlements. Though Eitam was once a Labor supporter, he now says that transfer is politically "enticing" but not realistic without war. In that case, he says, "Not many Arabs would remain." And Eitam has in fact called for war on Iraq and Iran through Israeli preemptive strikes.[1]

Sharon has admitted that without the settlements, the army would have left long ago. But the settlements have a great advantage: they enable Israeli leaders to convince ordinary people that their military is not a foreign army ruling a foreign population. In 1977, when Sharon chaired the ministerial committee for settlement affairs, he oversaw the establishment of new Jewish settlements in the West Bank and Gaza. He planned to settle 2 million Jews there. A quarter of a century later, Sharon remains adamant that Israel has a "moral right" to transform the demography of these territories. Since his election in January 2001, Sharon has built thirty-five new settlements.[2]

In the second half of the 1970s, during the transition from a Labor to a Likud government, Sharon emerged as a leader capable of realizing the dream of a Greater Israel beyond Israel's internationally recognized borders. Shimon Peres's encouragement to Israelis to settle everywhere in the occupied territories strengthened Sharon's drive to implement the program of the influential bipartisan (Likud-Labor) Greater Land of Israel movement, which foresaw an Israel spreading from the Jordan River to the Mediterranean.

The number of settlers in the occupied territories outside East Jerusalem increased from 7,000 in 1977 to over 200,000 in 2002—plus 200,000 others in East Jerusalem. Their 200 settlements take up 1.7 percent of the West Bank, but they control 41.9 percent of it.[3] Many of these settlers are armed and dangerous fanatics with a shoot-to-kill license from the Israeli army. Over the years, settlers' death squads have attacked unarmed civilians, gunned down elected officials, and tortured and killed many other Palestinians.

During the Oslo peace process, Israel doubled its settlements, tripled its settlers, and connected them with a network of bypass roads and industrial parks, ensuring their domination over the Palestinian territories. As the minister of infrastructure in the Netanyahu government, Sharon concentrated Israel's investment programs in the occupied Palestinian lands. The Rabin and Barak governments were no less active. There was an orgy of settlement building during the Barak government under the supervision of Yitzhak Levy, then leader of the National Religious Party and minister for the settlements.[4]

When the time came to end this at the Camp David summit in July 2000, the negotiations stumbled and eventually failed because of Israel's insistence that it hold on to the settlements and 9 percent of the West Bank. The Palestinians were asked to sign a final agreement based on a promise of a quasi-state divided into four separate regions, surrounded by Israeli settlement blocs. Determination to retain the settlements has undermined attempts to end the occupation and compromised peace efforts.

After the Camp David summit failed and the intifada broke out, the internationally commissioned Mitchell Report insisted that the settlement issue should go hand in hand with a peace accord. The commission recommended a freeze on Israeli settlements as a requirement for a cease-fire and a resumption of peace talks. Instead, Sharon's cabinet approved an extra $400 million for the settlements.

Today, 7,000 settlers remain in control of 30 percent of the 224 square kilometers of the Gaza Strip—home to 1.2 million Palestinians, most of them refugees. They cannot travel without passing fortified settlements with their swimming pools and basketball courts, built in the heart of this sandy, overpopulated area where water is scarce and land precious. Israel demolished 400 Palestinian homes in the Gaza Strip during the first year of the intifada to protect the nearby settlements.

When the army asked Sharon to remove a number of distant settlements and regroup them within closer, better defended settlement blocs, he refused; he vowed not to dismantle a single settlement while in office. He then brought in two new ministers from the National Religious Party, which forms the core of the settlements' leadership, and made them members of his security cabinet, which deals with the occupied territories. The new geography of the settlements is like carving a map of the West Bank out of Swiss cheese. The small black holes, disconnected and empty, are the Palestinian cantons, called autonomous regions, and the surrounding continuous rich yellow parts are the Jewish settlements.

There are two laws in Palestine: one for Jewish settlers and another for Palestinians. The settlers have the freedom to move around, build, and expand; the Palestinians are cooped up in 200 encircled cantons. Israelis have access to the land and expropriate more of it; Palestinians have less and less. In recent years, Israel has increased its closures of the Palestinian areas, hermetically imposed either locally or throughout the territories, to allow easy travel for the settlers. According to the International Monetary Fund and the World Bank, these closures have caused more damage to the Palestinian economy and its nation building than any other factor.[5] They have made Palestinians' lives impossible.

Friends of Israel in the West, such as journalist Thomas Friedman, say that if the logic of the settlers wins, Israel will become an apartheid state. Former Israeli attorney general Michael Ben-Yair thinks the logic of the fundamentalist settlers has already won, since Israel has already "established an apartheid regime in the occupied territories."[6]

The settlers do not see it this way. General Eitam, the rising star of the Religious Right, sees a Greater Israel as "the state of God; the Jews are the soul of the world; the Jewish people have a mission to reveal the image of God on earth." He sees himself as standing "in the same place that Moses and King

David stood," where "a world without Jews is a world of robots, a dead world; and the State of Israel is the Noah's Ark of the future of the world and its task is to uncover God's image."[7]

Low- and middle-income families and new immigrants have been enticed to the settlements by offers of cheap housing and financial rewards, at times using U.S. aid money. But as the promise of better living turned into a colonial nightmare, the pragmatic settlers have tilted toward the Right. More than 94 percent voted for Benjamin Netanyahu, and then Sharon in the last elections. Today, the fundamentalist settlers dominate the council that oversees the settlements, and they exercise a formidable influence over decision making in the Israeli government. Almost one out of ten members of the Israeli Knesset are settlers. Three settlers have served as ministers in Sharon's cabinet, and two are now serving as deputy ministers.

Although they are extraterritorial entities in the judgment of the international community, the settlements are the hotbed of pan-Israel nationalism. Unlike those Israelis who seek an internationally recognized Jewish state within sovereign borders, the new zealots insist that their homeland is the land of Israel and not the state of Israel; they will therefore not allow the emergence of another state between the Jordan and the Mediterranean.

The power of the settlers goes beyond their electoral influence. Over the last quarter of a century, with the exception of the short-lived Rabin and Barak governments, the religious settlers' influence increased rapidly as the hard political core of the Likud-led coalitions. They are a threat not only to Palestine and the normalization of Israel but also to the whole region.

Think tanks in the settlements show a war-driven style of thinking that taps into new U.S. concepts such as the war on terror and the "axis of evil," as well as new missile systems and the worst, most sensationalist literature produced by the Pentagon. As they dream of U.S.-style wars, the settlers do not think about such things as coexistence with their next-door neighbors. This is not surprising, since they believe that Israel is the hope of the world and that Palestinian moral savagery is organized to prevent this.

Paradoxically, the latest wave of Palestinian suicide bombings has played into the settlers' hands. Their erroneous claim that the Palestinians want the removal of not only the settlements but Israel as well has relieved the pressure on the settlements—previously seen as an obstacle to peace—and radicalized ordinary Israelis. Israel's settlement policy, continued regardless of signed agreements, has created a new geography of conflict. Millions of Palestinians and Israelis live in fear on account of illegal settlers who are plunging the area into communal and colonial war. If Israel continues the expansion of its settlement activity at the rate it did during the peace process, the settlers will soon reach a million. If that happens, separating Palestinians from Israel and its settlers will be impossible without ethnic cleansing.

That would compromise the future of a Palestinian state and also the chances for maintaining a Jewish state over the long term, since the Jewish majority will diminish in mandatory Palestine (Israel, the West Bank, and Gaza). In ten years, the Palestinians will become the majority—one that will grow. And the millions of Jews and Arabs will become increasingly inseparable.

Sharon and his settlers will continue to sustain a state of permanent conflict and war in Palestine and the Middle East. Unless the international community intervenes, the settlements' logic will eventually lead to the same standoff as on the eve of the 1948 war: either accept a binational state or attempt another ethnic cleansing. That would be a dramatic strategic error for Israel.

NOTES

This article also appeared in a French translation in *Le Monde Diplomatique*, June 2002.

1. *Ha'aretz*, April 12, 2002.
2. *New York Times*, April 27, 2002.
3. See B'tselem, "Israel's Settlement Policy in the West Bank," Tel Aviv, May 13, 2002, at http://www.btselem.org/English/Publications/Summaries/Land_Grab_2002.asp.
4. The Fourth Geneva Convention, which Israel and the United States signed, stipulates: "The Occupying Power shall not deport or transfer parts of its own civilian population into the territory it occupies." The convention is legally binding on member states.
5. Conversation with Osama Kina'an, coordinator of the West Bank and Gaza desk at the International Monetary Fund.
6. *Ha'aretz*, March 3, 2002.
7. *Ha'aretz*, April 28, 2002.

Orwell and Kafka in Israel–Palestine

Lawrence Davidson

In the last two years, I have made three trips to Israel and occupied Palestine (the West Bank and Gaza Strip). Each trip represents a journey into an approximation of the literary nightmares of George Orwell and Franz Kafka. To a certain extent we are all subject to the Orwellian version of these nightmares.[1] It was Orwell's conviction that "political language is designed to make lies sound truthful and murder respectful." Here in the United States we ought to recognize the truth of this maxim, for we have once again been drawn into deadly foreign adventures based on lies and exaggeration. However, in Israel the influence of "political language" has reached a unique level of intensity. Increasingly, many Israelis live in a "closed information environment" wherein an insidious Orwellian "newspeak" (a language of propaganda aimed at creating ideologically determined boundaries for thought) shapes thinking and perception relative to the Palestinians. This is true not just of your average citizen manipulated by mendacious politicians and a censored press. In Israel, as in Orwell's novel *1984*, society's leaders are as shaped by the prevailing "political language" as those they rule. Thus, descriptions of Palestinians by Israeli leaders range from "there are no such things as Palestinians" (Prime Minister Golda Meir, June 15, 1969) to "beasts walking on two legs" (Prime Minister Menachem Begin, June 25, 1982) to "drugged cockroaches in a bottle" (Chief of Staff Raphael Eitan, April 14, 1983) to "people who do not belong to our continent, to our world, but actually belong to a different galaxy" (Israeli President Moshe Katsav, May 10, 2001). For a man like Prime Minister Ariel Sharon, "peace" for Israel comes through dominating and controlling "the enemies of humanity" (January 5, 2004). Oppression and warmaking become peacemaking in the land of Zion.

With the Palestinians, in contrast, the use of language is much more descriptive of their reality. Just about every Palestinian has been negatively impacted by the Israeli occupation, so no propaganda can hide the truth from them. Any politician, of whatever nationality, who tries to tell the Palestinians that the Israelis have their best interests at heart and are in "Judea and Samaria" to raise Arab standards of living, introduce progress, and otherwise help the Palestinians into the modern world (all claims made by Zionists in the last fifty years) would be laughed at and thoroughly despised. Thus, deceptive language that substitutes for reality is not what defines the world of those in occupied Palestine. Instead, the particular nightmare of the Palestinians is best described in the pages of Franz Kafka. In Kafka's world, the prevailing theme is uncertainty and unpredictability. There are no set rules for behavior, and the orders given by authorities seem arbitrary and even contradictory. One does not know what the laws are. The "authorities" in Kafka's work sit in their fortresses and periodically intrude into the lives of the confused and apparently helpless protagonists.

This Kafkaesque situation describes life in occupied Palestine. Israeli authorities suddenly intrude into the lives of the Palestinian population, and they do so in an unpredictable and arbitrary manner. They also destroy in an arbitrary manner. Israel's message to the Palestinians reflects one of Kafka's more depressing maxims: "why build knowing destruction is inevitable?" A Palestinian might be safe one moment and in danger the next. A Palestinian cannot predict if he or she will make it to work, the grocer, or school or, for that matter, back again. As a result, many Palestinians can identify with Kafka's character Joseph K. in the novel *The Trial*, who, "without having done anything wrong was arrested one fine morning."

ISRAEL

Israel has entered into an Orwellian world of inbred perceptions and unanalyzed assumptions. These appear to make sense from inside Israeli society (as well as among the Zionist community worldwide), but from the outside, they seem to be out of touch with reality. The inside "reality" is dominated by the obsessive concept of fortress Israel—that is, Israel against the world. This mental paradigm, which ascribes all criticism of Israeli behavior to eternal anti-Semitism, is assimilated from childhood, taught by one's family and one's teachers at school. It is a belief commonly shared, and thus reinforced, by neighbors, coworkers, newspapers, television and radio, and the military (some of the army induction ceremonies are held at the site of the 73 BCE mass suicide of Jewish zealots at Masada). It is a constant part of one's consciousness and defines patriotic thought.

Nonetheless, the belief in fortress Israel is fraught with Orwellian contradictions. Here are some of the things this paradigm teaches (versus what reality looks like from outside of Israel and the Zionist perspective): The Palestinian Arabs are eternal enemies and want to push the Jews into the sea (even though it is the Palestinians who are being slowly but surely pushed into Bantustans behind a ghetto-like "separation" wall). Given half a chance, the Palestinians can accomplish this new holocaust with the help of allied Arab hordes (even though Israel is among the strongest military powers on the globe, is allied to the world's only superpower, and has never lost a war). The Palestinians, both inside and outside Israel proper, are ersatz Nazis (even though, for hundreds of years before the rise of Zionism, they lived peacefully with their Jewish neighbors and turned hostile only when the Zionists started appropriating Palestine under the protection of British imperialism). Yasir Arafat is the devil incarnate and, as Prime Minister Sharon likes to put it, "the greatest obstacle to peace" (even though, since 1988, he has tried repeatedly to make peace with the Jewish state, but all these efforts have been replaced in the Israeli collective memory by Arafat's refusal to accept the treaty offered at Camp David II, and Israel's rejection of all previous Palestinian efforts at peace has been forgotten). Israel is just a little place with "fragile" borders (which, since 1947, have repeatedly expanded, just as David Ben-Gurion, speaking at the time of the founding of Israel, predicted they would). Only war can bring peace to Israel (which characterizes the thinking and policies of the present Israeli prime minister, Ariel Sharon, who is generally recognized outside of Israel and the United States to be a war criminal).

These beliefs approach the strength of a religious doctrine in Israel. They also restrict the range of thought and narrow the possibilities for action among many Israelis and other Zionists. Most have also shown an inability to critically examine Israel's behavior and how it has evolved from this siege mentality. They have held fast to a selective use of history to support the fortress Israel paradigm and its corollaries. As a consequence of this closed mindedness, those who, for a variety of reasons, have managed to break free of the nationally sanctified blinders and publicly contradict accepted doctrine are seen as heretics or traitors and risk social isolation and the ruination of their careers—and sometimes worse. One can see this clearly in the case of tenured Israeli professors who publicly oppose the occupation. Academics such as Ilan Pappe of Haifa University are periodically harassed by the university administration, being brought up on disciplinary charges for alleged seditious activity. They are denied promotion. Their graduate students have found it hard to get jobs, so now few will work with such professors. Untenured professors are reluctant to take a public stand against government policies because they are more vulnerable and could lose their positions. And finally, Jews outside of Israel who publicly criticize the Israeli government and the Zionist ideology are accused of being "self-hating Jews." Nonetheless, so horrid is Israeli behavior toward the Palestinians that the number of such Jews, best exemplified by the "refuseniks," is slowly increasing both in Israel and abroad.

Behind the wall of fortress Israel, most Israeli Jews are scared and depressed. Popular feelings are affected by a constant concern for personal and family safety. Israelis tend to look over their shoulders and worry about riding the bus or going to a restaurant. Britain's *Daily Telegraph* (September 30, 2003) reported on a poll conducted by the Israeli Hebrew daily *Yedioth Ahronoth*. The report concludes that "Israelis are in a state of open despair about their country's future." Seventy-three percent of Israelis do not think that their children will have a better future. Under these conditions, one may ask why the Israelis simply do not negotiate a just peace with the Palestinians. Give them their state on the 22 percent of Palestine that is on the other side of the 1967 border (the Green Line). This is an offer the vast majority of Palestinians would readily accept. Also, such a move would likely make an ally of a Palestinian government that, predictably, would go to great lengths to control anyone whose actions would threaten to bring the Israeli Defence Force back across the border. Such a scenario was described to me as the basis for peace proposed by Arafat in June 2003. This is also the arrangement Israel has with the Jordanians, who control their border with Israel quite effectively. And, in a quiet way, the same arrangement prevails with the Syrians and the Egyptians.

Yet the Israelis insist that allowing the Palestinians a state of their own on the West Bank and Gaza Strip is impossible and mortally dangerous as well. How do they know? The Orwellian political language that dominates their "closed information environment" tells them so. Remember, such an environment binds one to internal references only. These references become inbred and self-serving so that one's major sources of information function like sycophants, telling one only those things that support and rationalize one's actions. Information that undermines or contradicts a priori points of view remains unseen, unheard, or is magically reinterpreted to fit the set parameters in one's mind.

This closed information environment has led most Israeli (and Diaspora) Jews to believe that (1) it is the Palestinians who do not want peace and (2) Arafat is responsible for this rejection and the subsequent violence. The Israelis make two claims to support the first assertion. They point out that the Palestinians have a long history of attacks against Israelis, and they note that Arafat rejected Ehud Barak's supposed "generous offer" at Camp David II in 2000.

The Israelis reject the Palestinian claim that the intifadas (the word means to "shake off") are episodes of resistance against Israel's aggression and occupation. They point out that Palestinian attacks predate 1967 and the occupation of the West Bank and Gaza. This was the position taken in December 2002 by Major General Isaac Ben-Israel at a Tel Aviv University discussion in which I participated. Because there was violence prior to the occupation of the West Bank and Gaza Strip, there would be violence if Israel withdrew from the territories. It should be noted, however, that most of the cross-border incidents, particularly in the ten years following 1948, involved Palestinians who were simply seeking to return to their homes. According to Israeli historian Avi Shlaim, hundreds of these unarmed Palestinians were shot down by the Israelis. Statistically, Palestinian armed attacks on Israel before 1967 were few and relatively infrequent, and they reflected the slow Palestinian recovery from the shock of the Nakba (or 1948 catastrophe). The Jewish Virtual Library (a Zionist source) lists only twenty-seven Israeli fatalities as a result of Palestinian attacks between 1958 and 1966. In the same period, Israeli retaliatory raids into Jordanian and Egyptian territory killed many hundreds of people. Nonetheless, from the Israeli point of view, these pre-1967 attacks were not a response to anything the Zionists did; rather, they were the expression of an undying a priori desire to destroy the Jewish state. Unfortunately, this line of thinking requires a negation of the history of Zionist goals and behavior and an assumption that past Palestinian behavior will continue indefinitely into the future.

Israelis and other Zionists simply take it for granted that, from 1917 onward, the history of the occupation of Israel proper (i.e., the 78 percent of Palestine that is Israel behind the Green Line) was benign and any Zionist military action associated with it was purely defensive. In reality, as any number of Israeli historians (e.g., Benny Morris, Ilan Pappe, Avi Shlaim) have shown, widespread Jewish immigration under the protection of British imperialism initiated the displacement of Palestinians. Palestinian resentment of and reaction to this process was natural and led to resistance that began as early as the 1920s. In truth, all Zionist history in Palestine is the history of occupation, which has been and is offensive rather than defensive in nature.

The situation today is not the same as it was in the 1920s or in 1948. In 1988 the Palestine Liberation Organization (PLO) recognized the state of Israel within its 1967 borders. This constituted a supreme compromise in that, by this recognition, the Palestinians voluntarily forfeited 78 percent of their historic homeland and restricted their claims to the remaining 22 percent that makes up the West Bank, including East Jerusalem, and the Gaza Strip. It is the refusal of Israel to seriously respond to this recognition and the sacrifice it represents, and to cease its occupation of Palestine beyond the Green Line, that has led to a new level of violent resistance on the part of the Palestinians.

Of course, the Israelis do not believe that they have failed to respond. They believe that in the year 2000, at Camp David II, Ehud Barak put forth a "generous offer." This belief has taken on mythic proportions not only in Israel but also throughout the world's Jewish communities and in the United States as well. It now stands as an excellent example of political language restricting the range of thought and thus resulting in mass self-deception within a closed information environment. According to the Zionist story, this "generous" offer gave the Palestinians the Gaza Strip and almost the entire West Bank. Instead of accepting this deal, the Palestinians, under the leadership of Yasir Arafat, rejected it and launched the ongoing and deadly second intifada (2000 to the present).

Israelis believe that they are willing to make peace through "historic compromises," but there is, in their view, no "partner" on the Palestinian side to negotiate with. Arafat, a man who was shut up in two buildings in Ramallah amidst acres of rubble, his communications monitored and his travel restricted, was seen as being responsible for ongoing terror and, according to Israeli novelist and political pundit Eyal Megged, "employed tactics that remind us of Hitler."

Essentially, what one has here is an alternative history that is accepted by the majority in Israel and also by the present U.S. government. In the summer of 2002, National Security Adviser Condoleezza Rice stated on national television that "Arafat is somebody who . . . failed to lead when he had a chance. . . . Ehud Barak, the former prime minister of Israel, gave him a terrific opportunity to lead. And what did he get in return? Arafat started the second intifada instead and rejected that offered hand of friendship." Unfortunately, both the Israelis and Rice have their facts wrong. The "generous offer" has been disproved by both American and Israeli experts, including Robert Malley, President Clinton's adviser on Israeli–Arab affairs who was at Camp David II; Ron Pundak, director of the Peres Center for Peace; Professor Jeff Halper of Ben-Gurion University; and Uri Avnery, head of Gush Shalom, Israel's foremost peace organization. Ehud Barak himself has twice (*New York Times,* May 24, 2001, and *Yediot Ahronoth,* August 29, 2003) denied that his offer was anywhere near "generous."

What did Barak really offer? According to the above reports, his offer gave the Palestinians a little over 80 percent of the West Bank carved into nearly discontinuous cantons. The Israeli government would have controlled all the Palestinian borders (none of which would touch on another Arab state), the airspace above the Palestinian territory, and most of the major aquifers. It would have retained sovereignty over East Jerusalem, maintained almost all Israeli settlements and access roads, controlled immigration into the Palestinian "state," and retained the Jordan Valley through an indefinite "long-term lease." This is an offer that no Israeli would ever accept. However, most Israelis and Americans do not know these details and believe instead in the myth of generosity.

Unfortunately, what is true is not as important as what one thinks is true. Believing that the Palestinians rejected a generous peace at Camp David II and opted instead for the violence of the second intifada, the Israelis now look to other ways to achieve security. How this is to be done is dictated by their Orwellian Weltanschauung. First, they insist on the elimination of Palestinian militancy while systematically destroying the Palestinian Authority's police capabilities. The Israeli army attacks uniformed Palestinian police on sight, and most police facilities have been destroyed. Simultaneously, the Israeli government demands that what is left of the Palestinian Authority direct whatever security forces it still has to the job of "fighting terrorism," which is code for defending Israeli borders and settlers. Given the position of the Palestinians as an oppressed people facing illegal colonization, this amounts to a demand for the Palestinian Authority to eliminate Palestinian resistance to Israeli occupation. Within this scenario, Palestinian resistance to land confiscation, home demolition, and settlement activities takes the form of offensive action, and the invasion of towns and villages by Israeli tanks and helicopter gunships becomes defensive action.

Second, the Israelis build a "security wall" to separate themselves from the bulk of the Palestinians. However, they do not do this along the 1967 Green Line, which most of the world recognizes as the de facto border between Israel and Palestine. Rather, they build this barrier deep inside of the Palestinian West Bank. Its construction thus facilitates ongoing land confiscation. The Israelis build it so as to confine the Palestinians into a series of walled-off areas of concentration. This transforms the "security wall" into a "ghetto wall." Those West Bank Palestinians who find themselves on the Israeli side of the wall will eventually be transferred into the Palestinian ghettos. This will produce future peace and security for Israelis in the same way that prisons prevent crime.

Third, the Israelis enforce a harsh collective punishment on the Palestinians, entailing draconian curfews, roadblocks and checkpoints, "security" sweeps leading to mass arrests, house demolitions, denial of access to medical facilities, mass shutdown of education, and the "legal" use of torture until they "come to their senses" and negotiate peace on "acceptable terms." This tactic brutalizes both Palestinians and Israelis. As the Israelis have visited violence and destruction on their Palestinian victims, their own levels of domestic violence—spousal and child abuse, violence in schools, road rage, and violent crime—have gone up.

Maya Rosenfeld, a sociologist at Hebrew University and a member of Checkpoint Watch, attributes this downward spiral of Israeli society and culture to the fact that "a military discourse has taken over in Israel." Within the context of this militarized society, who can best achieve peace and security? It continues to be the case that a majority of Israelis believe that it is Ariel Sharon (a general who made his reputation based on personal brutality) and his right-wing coalition. This seems to be so not because these politicians are ideologically committed to retaining the West Bank and Gaza Strip (and also the Golan Heights) but because they are determined to continue the occupation.

This would seem, from an outside perspective, to be yet another Orwellian proposition—that is, the road to peace is found by demanding the right of permanent occupation. Yet this notion does not appear to be contradictory to most Israelis. Among the reasons for this is that Zionist perceptions of reality deny the true nature and consequences for the Palestinians of thirty-seven years of colonial occupation in Gaza and the West Bank. Indeed, for a long time, the Israelis refused to even entertain the word *occupation* for what they were doing. As Israeli writer David Grossman explained in an interview with Bill Moyers in March 2002, "there was a whole machinery of fabricating names to the situation, there was a whole narrative that in a way used words not to describe reality but rather to camouflage it, to protect us the Israelis from the harshness of what we are doing." This is what Israeli lawyer Leah Tsemel calls the "laundering of language." In Hebrew, *occupation* became *release* or *salvation*, while *colonizing* became *peaceful settlement* and *killing* became *targeting*. Orwell would have recognized this use of "political language" without much trouble.

Another Zionist trick of the mind is to assign the blame for any negative consequences arising from the occupation to the Palestinians themselves. For instance, in an August 2002 editorial in the Israeli newspaper the *Jerusalem Post*, the common assertion was made that "the Palestinians' current malaise is no one's fault but their own, considering that they started and are continuing the war that is exacting from them such a hefty price." That the "war" is actually resistance against colonial occupation is lost on the *Jerusalem Post* editors.

In Israeli eyes, the occupation is a warranted defensive action driven by a pervasive national fear and suspicion of Palestinians as terrorists. It should be noted that to most Israelis—and to Americans, too—the terrorist is the essential Palestinian. Each Palestinian—whether man, woman, or child—is just a body potentially encased in dynamite. The Israelis point to occupied Palestine as the place from which suicide bombers come and thus feel that they must "control" these lands. That the occupation and its accompanying colonizing policy are in fact the sources of suicide bombings and overall Palestinian violence is simply not accepted by most Israelis. Instead, they ascribe these actions to Muslim religious fanaticism. This came out clearly in a January 2002 interview by me and others with Benjamin Ben Eliazar, the former Israeli defense minister. Eliazar described how he would interrogate prisoners suspected of being failed suicide bombers. "If you interrogate them long enough you can see the religious fanaticism surface." These interrogations may well have resulted in deception; push a prisoner long enough and hard enough, and the prisoner is likely to say anything, particularly what he or she deduces the interrogator wants to hear.

There are other ways in which the Israelis manage to promote the occupation, arguably the source of their insecurity, as a source of security. Here is how Likud leader and Knesset member Yuval Steinwitz conceptualized the situation to me in December 2002: the occupation is necessary because it alone can give Israel, "this little land with impossible borders," defensive depth. According to Steinwitz, Israel is a "great regional power" that is at the same time "fragile" enough to be destroyed by the Palestinian terrorists allied to the Egyptians.

This is a variation on the notion that Israel is in perpetual danger of being "kicked into the sea." One can locate the origins of this fear in the Holocaust and understand how deep rooted it is, but it nonetheless defies reality. There is no military intelligence service outside of Israel that believes this myth. No military engagement (including those in 1947–1948) has ever come close to suggesting that this scenario was or is possible. Yet the myth is pervasive in Israel and among the Jewish Diaspora community as well. So, acting on what one believes is real (not, in this case, what is in fact real), one can justify colonial occupation, the brutal destruction of Palestinian society, and the slow but sure ethnic cleansing of occupied Palestine of its non-Jewish population (all of which is overtly offensive and brutally aggressive in nature) in the name of needing "defensive depth."

The Israelis and their supporters have other rationalizations for occupation. There is the biblically based claim that "Judea and Samaria" are "covenant lands," that is, lands given to the Jews by God. This, of course, is a matter of faith; it is not provable fact. Many people take the Bible, where this covenant is found, as the word of God. However, this too is faith and not provable fact. Nonetheless, such faith put forth as fact allows some Israelis to see the indigenous population as "strangers in the land" and Jewish folks from Brooklyn as rightful inhabitants. This leads to more tricks of the mind. For instance, Carolyn Glick, associate editor of the *Jerusalem Post,* told me and others that the removal of the West Bank colonies would constitute the "ethnic cleansing of Judea and Samaria."

Whether it is for imagined military reasons (which entails a denial that occupation is the source of their insecurity) or faith-based religious reasons (which entails exoneration from responsibility for brutal actions because they are doing the work of God), the majority of Israelis have come to the conclusion that there is no alternative to a hard-line, right-wing government that can conceptualize only a peace treaty that ghettoizes, economically emasculates, and subordinates any eventual Palestinian political entity. And even then, most Israelis do not believe that such a treaty will lead to real peace, not because it fails to satisfy Palestinian needs but because the Palestinians are all anti-Semites who will forever want to destroy all of Israel.

PALESTINE

Palestine is a land of deep despair, growing poverty, and pervasive insecurity. In a slow but sure fashion, the Israelis are reducing the Palestinians to an impoverished, cheap labor pool within ghetto-like areas of concentration. Here is how they are doing it.

First, the ancestral lands of the Palestinians are being confiscated: 78 percent of Palestine was taken in 1948. According to Israel's Central Bureau of Statistics, the over 1 million Israeli Palestinians who now live in Israel proper (behind the Green Line) make up 20 percent of the country's population (40 percent of Israel's population growth rate) and are confined to 3 percent of the land. And this 3 percent is subject to continuing periodic and unpredictable confiscation. Israel's Palestinian communities are not allowed to geographically expand. In 1967 the Israelis took over the remaining 22 percent of Palestine (now designated the occupied territories) and immediately began a colonization program that is illegal under international law. To date, they have confiscated some 40 percent of this remaining 22 percent of Palestine and now operate more than 200 colonies that hold nearly 400,000 illegal residents. They are continuing to expand these "settlements" through the continuous confiscation of land in occupied Palestine (i.e., beyond the Green Line). This means that the Palestinians, both within and without Israel proper, are being relentlessly ghettoized into smaller and smaller areas.

Second, besides the loss of their land, the people in occupied Palestine are experiencing the destruction of their property on a daily basis. According to B'Tselem, Israel's own civil rights organization, hundreds of thousands of olive and other fruit trees have been destroyed, and hundreds of water wells have been sealed (90 percent of all the water resources of occupied Palestine are now reserved for the exclusive use of the occupier). According to the Israeli Committee against Home Demolitions, about 11,000 Palestinian homes have been demolished since 1967. The population is also subjected to periodic indiscriminate artillery shelling and automatic weapons fire; American-made jet planes and helicopters discharge high-explosive missiles and bombs in crowded civilian areas. Some of these bombs and missiles are made of depleted uranium-infused metals. All this is illegal under international law as promulgated in the Hague Conventions of 1907 and 1987 and the Fourth Geneva Convention.

Third, Palestinians have seen their rights of free movement, free association, access to education, access to medical care, and ability to transport and market goods (most of which rights are guaranteed by the Declaration of Universal Human Rights adopted by the United Nations after World War II) severely restricted by the creation of some 480 checkpoints and roadblocks. Most of these are placed not between Israeli and Palestinian towns and villages but between Palestinian locales. These checkpoints, the purpose of which seems to be harassment rather than security, attack the most basic personal rights. The most tragic example of this is the collapse of the Palestinian medical system. According to Human Rights Watch, Israeli soldiers purposely harass and sometimes target for injury or death Palestinian doctors and medical personnel. Checkpoints prevent ambulances from getting to hospitals or to the residences of ill people, and they prevent pregnant women about to give birth from going to hospitals. The soldiers at the checkpoints do not prevent these things all the time, but they do so in an unpredictable, random fashion that heightens the sense of uncertainty and vulnerability of the Palestinian population. I asked Eliazar, the former defense minister, about this practice in the January 2002 interview mentioned earlier. He asserted that the Palestinians use ambulances to transport weapons and "wanted criminals." When I pointed out that there was a qualitative difference between stopping an ambulance and searching it for weapons or wanted individuals and stopping an ambulance until the patient inside died, he became sullen and said that he did not need any help from me when it came to security. Since their tactics have left the Israelis continuously insecure, this is a questionable claim. At the very least, the Israelis need help in maintaining a basic level of humanity. As a result of the policies just described, the rate of death from curable diseases is on the rise among West Bank and Gaza Strip Palestinians, and preventive medicine such as vaccination is almost nonexistent.

In addition to the checkpoints, draconian curfews keep entire populations of cities and towns under forced house arrest for weeks on end, contributing to the breakdown of medical care, education, and employment. (According to the United Nations Relief and Works Agency, unemployment in the occupied territories now stands at over 65 percent, and more than half the population lives in poverty.)

It bears repeating that much of this harassment and destruction occurs in a random and arbitrary fashion. Palestinians never know if they will make it through a checkpoint to get to school or work. And if they do get through, they do not know if they will be able to return home through the same checkpoint. Curfews can be imposed without notice, and Palestinians can be arrested at any time for any reason. It is a Kafkaesque world wherein one cannot predict the consequences of one's daily behavior.

Under these circumstances, 90 percent of Palestinians in the occupied territories see no hope in their future without international intervention. Yet intervention is consistently blocked by the United States, which vetoes any UN resolution that seeks the creation of such a policy. It is because the resolutions are not "balanced," says the U.S. State Department, but this is ridiculous in the face of Israel's brutal behavior. The United States uses its veto to protect Israel because Zionist interest groups have such powerful influence with the American government and political parties. In any case, the Israeli government is adamantly against such intervention and would resist it by force. As a consequence, there is no choice for the Palestinians but to continue their resistance to Israeli occupation, for to concede defeat would mean to acquiesce in the death of Palestinian society and culture.

When it comes to resistance, it is historically the case that the violence of the oppressed usually rises to the level of the violence of the oppressor. That is what has happened in Palestine. The Israeli occupation constitutes thirty-seven years of institutionalized terror that has just about destroyed the economic, social, and political lives of all Palestinians under Israeli rule. Civil society and its infrastructure are nearly gone. Civilian deaths due to direct military action and indirect consequences of Israeli colonial policies now (November 2003) stand at just over 2,700 people (compared with about 800 Israelis). Palestinian civilian injuries due to Israeli action stand at over 47,000. Resistance is all that remains.

This brings us to the issue of suicide bombings. The context for understanding this tactic is the occupation itself. The consequences of the occupation do not discriminate between men and women, adults and children. Confiscations impact them all, home demolitions displace them all, curfews confine them all, Israeli violence targets them all. This is the truth. I have seen much of this with my own eyes. Americans and many Israelis may not believe it, but their disbelief does not change the Palestinian reality. That reality produces deep despair, feelings of humiliation, and unavoidable hatred. It is from this context that the bombers come. Their tactic is the reverse coin of Israel's own practices and not the product of some innate religious fanaticism.

This despair and rage, not religious fanaticism, lead to popular support for Hamas and Islamic Jihad. They are supported so widely not because they represent Islamic fundamentalism but because, in an atmosphere of despair, they serve the needs of the rapidly growing numbers of poor, and they resist the Israelis. If the Palestinians are given back their hope for a just settlement by moving concretely toward the satisfaction of their basic demands, support for Hamas and Islamic Jihad will diminish. This is not mere conjecture. Right after the Oslo Accords were signed, and despite their serious flaws, there was much hope for peace among the Palestinians. As a consequence, support for groups like Hamas fell to under 10 percent of the population in the West Bank and Gaza. By the middle of 2003, in an atmosphere of near hopelessness that still prevails, polls taken by the Palestine Center for Policy and Survey Research indicated that support for Hamas and Islamic Jihad stood at 58 percent.

ANY HOPE?

It is important to realize that most ordinary people on both sides say that they want many of the same things: normal lives, security for themselves and their families, acceptance by the other side. And although the majority of Israelis, and a number of Palestinians, cannot get past perceptual barriers dominated by fear, suspicion, and anxiety, there are factors that can, at least in theory, result in movement toward real peace if they are given a chance to come to the fore.

The vast majority of Palestinians know (even if the Israelis do not) that they cannot destroy the Israeli state. Most Palestinians in occupied Palestine are willing to negotiate compromise solutions to all issues (including the controversial issue of the "right of return"), with the exception of their right to a viable state occupying roughly the 22 percent of Palestine beyond Israel's 1967 borders. For the Palestinians, this is the sine qua non of a just peace. This is not a new stance on the part of the Palestinians or their leaders. Here is a list of peace initiatives that the Palestinians have welcomed (and various Israeli governments have rejected): the Rogers Plan (1969), the Scranton Mission on behalf of President Nixon (1970), Sadat's land for peace mutual recognition proposal (1971), Carter's call for a Geneva international conference (1977), Saudi King Fahd's peace offer (1981), the Reagan Plan (1982), the Shultz Plan (1988), the Baker Plan (1989), a continuation of the Taba negotiations (2001), the Saudi peace proposal on behalf of the Arab League (2002), the unofficial Geneva peace initiative of November–December 2003. And, of course, in 1993, Arafat signed the Oslo Accords, which unraveled after Yitzhak Rabin's assassination (November 1995) and the subsequent return to power of the Likud party.

To the extent that the Israelis block the possibility of a viable Palestinian state, Palestinian leaders and intellectuals put forth the idea of a one-state solution—that is, the acceptance of one state from "the sea to the river," with the struggle then directed toward bringing about equal rights for all citizens. This would, of necessity, negate the idea of a "Jewish state." I do not believe that this is the preference of most Palestinians, but it may be made inevitable by the shortsighted policies of the Zionist movement.

The recent Geneva Accord (November–December 2003) is at least a sign that Israelis and Palestinians can work together to reach a settlement. It certainly is not the end game, for it fails to give adequate attention to the fate of millions of Palestinian refugees who have rights under international law. If this initiative is to be seriously pursued, negotiators need, at the very least, to improve the water rights package and add an Israeli acceptance of responsibility for the Palestinian refugee problem, plus a pledge of compensation. It should be noted that the Geneva Accord has been endorsed by Arafat and the Palestinian Authority. It has, however, been attacked by the Sharon government as a traitorous act.

On the Israeli side, there is a growing number of influential military men (such as Amram Mitzna and Ami Aylon) who have credibility with the Israeli public and understand that continuing the occupation will not bring security and normality but rather a continuing brutalization of Israeli society. There is also a very small but growing number of resisters both within and without the army who refuse to cooperate with the Israeli government's occupation policies.

The problem is that whereas those who are ready to take risks for peace appear to be a majority on the Palestinian side, they are still a minority on the Israeli side. In the end, what we have is a horrible process of physical and emotional destruction that can be overcome only by a psychological leap—mostly among Israelis. They must come to a realization that the occupation is the source of Israeli insecurity, and only by giving it up can there be security and normality; only through peace with the Palestinians can Israel be a safe haven for Jews. Whether the Israelis can achieve this level of awareness while in the grips of a historically rooted, paralyzing fear and anxiety (played on by a Likud government and right-wing factions that are determined to stay in "Judea and Samaria" forever) remains to be seen. Nonetheless, it is their occupation. They have brought to life the nightmare worlds of Orwell and Kafka. If things are to change, they must wake up.

NOTE

1. Here are some additional Orwellian notions and behaviors described to me: (1) Oren Yiftachael of Ben-Gurion University explains that Israel has a "Green Patrol," a special police to keep the Bedouins from developing their land. When Bedouin crops turn green, the Israeli Green Patrol sprays them from the air with herbicides. (2) According to Victoria Buch of Hebrew University, refusal by some soldiers to serve in the occupied territories (which results in the destruction of Palestinian civil society) is regularly described by Israeli politicians as "a knife in the heart of democracy." (3) Michael Warschawski, former director of the Alternative Information Center in Jerusalem, told me that the Israeli government acts to empty Jerusalem of Arabs by creating "green lands" (expropriated Arab lands that cannot be built on without a permit). All the lands between Arab neighborhoods have been declared "green lands," which are then converted into Jewish settlements. Thus the concept of something that preserves and grows is used to destroy and displace. (4) Most of the built-up areas around East Jerusalem, as well as most of the "Jewish-only roads," were created after Oslo, which was supposedly a "road to peace." (5) The Tel Aviv artist Ami Nof was arrested and then committed to a mental institution for publicly suggesting that Israel open peace negotiations with prewar Iraq. (6) According to Israeli writer and poet Yitzhak Laor, reports of Israeli casualties in the occupied territories are referred to as "the result of attacks within Israel," while lethal attacks on West Bank and Gaza Palestinians are referred to as defense of the homeland from foreign attack beyond the borders.

Part V
Iraq: Imperialism and Invasion

The *Guiding Principles* and the U.S. "Mandate" for Iraq
Twentieth-Century Colonialism and America's New Empire

Keith D. Watenpaugh

Late in 2001, the Council on Foreign Relations invited twenty-five academics, corporate executives, oil industry consultants, retired military men, and American diplomats to meet at the James A. Baker III Institute for Public Policy on the oak-shaded campus of Rice University. Cochaired by two former career foreign service officers, Edward P. Djerejian and Frank G. Wisner, the group was charged with mapping out a plan for the United States' role in Iraq after the anticipated war. The final report that followed, *Guiding Principles for U.S. Post-Conflict Policy in Iraq*, outlines a three-phase, at least two-year process by which Iraq would be "liberated," cleansed of Baathists and weapons of mass destruction, and transformed into a democratic, free-market republic fully integrated into the community of nations. The authors of the report never challenge the wisdom of war on Iraq; rather, their plan is built within the framework of what is presumably a "best-case scenario": a short and swift war with low casualties and relatively little urban warfare. The authors also concede that full compliance by the Iraqi state with relevant UN resolutions or a coup might eliminate the need for an invasion.

Although the Council on Foreign Relations is adamant in its assertion that it has no affiliation with the U.S. government, the Baker Institute's close association with the current administration suggests that the report will contribute to the shape of any postwar American occupation of Iraq. This is especially the case with the involvement of Djerejian, who served for much of the 1980s as ambassador in Damascus and Tel Aviv and has often been used to open back-channel contacts in the Middle East and the Caucasus. Djerejian is a careful and sanguine thinker who is deeply sensitive to the history and culture of the region; he understands intimately the explosive power of sectarian and ethnic conflict and how corrosive the asymmetries of American policies toward Israel have been. The report bears his unmistakable imprint in the way it envisions "quiet U.S.–Iranian cooperation," notes that the elimination of Saddam Hussein will not cure all the ills of Iraqi society, and concludes that the United States "must avoid imposing Versailles-style conditions on Iraq" (13).

By the same token, the report's emphasis on the stabilization of Iraq's oil industry—partially for the redevelopment of the country—and on the use of

American power to level "the playing field for awarding energy sector contracts by supporting a transparent and competitive process" (10) reflects the contribution of, among others, cochair Frank Wisner. Wisner has had various jobs in the State and Defense departments since the Vietnam era and most recently served as ambassador to New Delhi. He was appointed to the board of directors of the now bankrupt Enron in 1997 and currently works as vice-chairman of external affairs for American International Group, one of the world's largest insurance and financial services companies. His involvement is a tacit acknowledgment that postwar Iraq policy is predicated less on disarmament or democratization and more on the interests of the American energy sector.

The report envisions a "superintending role" for the United States over a UN-supervised Iraqi administration:

> One that maintains low visibility but is clearly committed to protecting law and order and creating a breathing space for a nascent Iraqi government to take shape. The U.S. role will be best played in the background guiding progress and making sure that any peacekeeping force is effective and robust enough to do its job.... While moving the process along as quickly as possible, the United States must not be limited by self-imposed timelines, but should rather adopt an objectives-based approach. (6)

The "behind-the-scenes" strategy of America's efforts—which would be led by an "Iraqi coordinator"—is calculated to preclude any appearance of colonialism. The anxiety over U.S. actions being interpreted as neoimperialist courses through the document. For example: "A heavy American hand will only convince them, and the rest of the world that the operation against Iraq was undertaken for imperialist, rather than disarmament. It is in America's interest to discourage such misperceptions" (10–11). To counteract any "misperceptions" that might arise, the report's authors advocate the use of "vigorous public diplomacy," not just in the Arab and Muslim worlds but also in the United States and Europe to "deflate ... local criticism in the region and help deny terrorists and extremists the ability to use the military action to their own political advantage" (3). "Public diplomacy" is a euphemism for highly coordinated pro-American propaganda that has gained wider use since the aftermath of 9/11 and the appointment of Charlotte Beers, a distinguished advertising executive, as the undersecretary of state for public diplomacy and public affairs.

The stress placed on issues of appearance and the borrowing of the vocabulary and personnel of Madison Avenue amount to a concession that American plans for Iraq at least resemble colonialism and at most constitute the formulation of a neomodern version of it. What is left unsaid in the report's analysis, and a telling lacuna in a document whose authors seem so sensitive to history, is that Iraq itself, and indeed all the states of the eastern Mediterranean—Syria, Lebanon, Jordan, and Israel—are the end products of a similar style of colonialism, the interwar phenomenon of League of Nations mandates. From a comparative perspective, the parallels are striking. What is a constant in the historical experience of the mandate system in the Middle East and the planned American mandate for Iraq is that both are predicated on orientalist and essentialized conceptions of Arab and Muslim society and the unique identification of liberalism with Western hegemony. And just as the mandate system contributed to the destabilization of colonial and postcolonial Middle Eastern society, the lack of democratic structures, and the failure of the interwar international system, the cost of the American mandate for Iraq will be similar, especially in the weakening of the UN and the permanent radicalization of the region.

COLONIALISM IN DRAG: SYKES-PICOT IN THE WILSONIAN MOMENT

During World War I, and long before its outcome was clear, representatives of France and Britain met to divide the Ottoman Empire (1916). The plan, remembered as the Sykes-Picot agreement for the two civil servants who drew it up, assigned to the two states areas of "direct control" and "indirect control." France's area of direct control was along the eastern Mediterranean from southern Lebanon into Anatolia, with inland Syria under its indirect influence. Britain was given exclusive control over southern Mesopotamia—primarily the oil-producing regions adjacent to Kuwait and Iranian oil fields, and indirect control over inland Iraq. Palestine was to be placed under international control.

Growing American influence and pressure at home forced a shift in the way the British and French portrayed themselves in the region. Rather than conquerors, they began to situate themselves as the humanitarian liberators of the Arabs from the authoritarian oppression of the Ottoman Empire. The British instigation of the Arab revolt, which has become a permanent feature of Western popular culture in the form of David Lean's film *Lawrence of Arabia*, was, in part, a consequence of this shift.

With the collapse of the Ottoman Empire, colonial and military officials sought to persuade the local inhabitants that the European liberation-conquest of the region had been done on their behalf. Sykes and Picot themselves toured Syria in late 1918 and early 1919, delivering speeches calculated to lower local expectations of complete independence, no doubt in anticipation of the implementation of the territorial arrangements outlined in the once secret treaty that the pair had engineered. All their presentations included the existence of a separate Arab nation that, Picot maintained, had been oppressed "for four centuries by the government of Istanbul." Both claimed that the goal of liberating the Arabs and other peoples from this oppression had motivated the war on the Turks and that the Arabs were a nation among nations—nations that had joined together to "end Turkish despotism and return freedom to the people."

Stanley Maude, the British general who conquered Mesopotamia, expressed similar sentiments before the incredulous inhabitants of Baghdad:

> O people of Baghdad, remember that for 26 generations you have suffered under strange tyrants who have endeavored to set one Arab house against another in order that they might profit by your dissensions. This policy is abhorrent to Great Britain and her allies, for there can be neither peace nor prosperity where there is enmity and misgovernment. Therefore I am commanded to invite you, through your nobles and elders and representatives, to participate in the management of your civil affairs in collaboration with the political representatives of Great Britain who accompany the British Army, so that you may be united with your kinsmen in North, East, South, and West in realising the aspirations of your race.

By the time of the Paris Peace Conference, and fearing that Wilsonian notions of national self-determination would scuttle their colonial interests, the British and French seized upon a system of temporary "mandates" as a compromise solution that would appear less "colonial." Article 22 of the League's covenant explained the need for mandates:

> To those colonies and territories which as a consequence of the late war have ceased to be under the sovereignty of the States which formerly governed them and which are inhabited by peoples not yet able to stand by themselves under the strenuous conditions of the modern world, there should be applied the principle that the well-being and development of such peoples form a sacred trust of civilisation and that securities for the performance of this trust should be embodied in this Covenant.

In order to bring these peoples into that "strenuous" modern world, "advanced nations who by reason of their resources, their experience, or their geographical position can best undertake this responsibility" would take on the burden of "tutelage." Although the League recognized the "existence [of the Arab states of the eastern Mediterranean] as independent nations," they would be "subject to the rendering of administrative advice and assistance by a Mandatory until such time as they are able to stand alone." Even though the League's guidelines included a clause that the people of the soon-to-be-mandated territories should have some say in their mandatory, Britain and France were given those areas first coveted in the Sykes-Picot agreement. Ultimately, the mandate system envisioned the tutelage and superintending role as temporary, but at the time of its establishment, the voluntary exit of a colonial power was unprecedented, and most considered the French and British presence permanent.

The most immediate consequence of the imposition of the mandates was the drawing of new boundaries and the creation of unprecedented geographical constructs such as Syria and Iraq. The new borders often had disastrous economic impacts and disrupted trade and migration patterns for thousands throughout the region. The territorial divisions cloaked a more concerted effort to create nonviable states (Transjordan) or states in which potentially loyal religious minorities would amount to a plurality (Lebanon). Iraq was the most curious of these creations, binding together three Ottoman provinces of Baghdad, Basra, and Mosul into a new state.

In the fiction of the mandate system, these new states would run themselves with advice and guidance from the mandatory power. Consequently, parliaments were convened, constitutions written, elections held. In the case of Iraq, a new king was imposed. Faysal ibn Hussein (no relation to Saddam), who had briefly ruled in Syria, was elevated to the new throne of Iraq by the British following a questionable plebiscite. The states were systematically prevented from developing independent militaries, and instead, colonial troops from other imperial holdings were often employed to establish control. In the case of Syria and Iraq, men from non-Sunni Muslim minority groups such as the Alawites, Ismailis, Armenians, and Assyrians were often used to bolster military units commanded by European officers. Foreign policy, security apparatuses, antiquities, and tariff and trade policies were the domain of the mandatory power. Education, court systems, and most middle-management positions were left to the locals. In what must have been one of the more humiliating dimensions of the mandate system, mandated states were responsible for paying the salaries of those officials "advising" them. The *Guiding Principles* outlines a similar plan to reimburse nation-building costs with Iraqi oil revenues (11–12).

Nevertheless, in a departure from their previous colonial enterprises, the French and the British sought, for the most part, to remain "behind the scenes." This was done to fulfill the letter of the mandate, but it also made sense from an administrative perspective. Still, the ultimate power in each of the mandated states was the resident "high commissioner," who could and would employ the military to enforce colonial will. Among the many responsibilities of the high commissioner was periodic reporting of the improving conditions in the areas under his tutelage to the League. Rarely did the League challenge the veracity of these reports or criticize the practices of mandatories; consequently, the organization's credibility as an anti-imperialist, liberal entity diminished through the course of the interwar period. A caricature of its former self, the weakened League failed to prevent the brutal Italian colonization of Ethiopia or stand against Japanese militarism in China.

RESISTANCE TO THE MANDATES AND INTERWAR POLITICS

Before the ink was dry on the documents establishing the new states of the Middle East, resistance to French and British neocolonialism began throughout the region. Though many of these movements resembled prototypical national resistance movements and would become more formalized during the interwar period, other types of opposition arose that were less easily understandable in the idiom of nationalism and made more sense when seen through the lens of late Ottoman forms of religious authority and patterns of legitimacy. Regardless of form, the movements against European colonialism pivoted on two major themes: first, the whole notion of who had liberated whom; and second, whether those societies now liberated by the West were in need of "tutelage."

With the exception of a tiny group of Arab nationalists, British and French efforts to liberate the Arabs from Ottoman suzerainty rang hollow. The Arab identity was itself of little relevance to most. Until very recently, the term *Arab* was more commonly associated with desert-dwelling Bedouin; urbane, cosmopolitan inhabitants of cities such as Damascus or Beirut would have bristled at being called Arab. More substantively, notions of identity followed lines of religious affiliation. Indeed, the postwar efforts to enforce an Arab identity stemmed from the need to create Arabs—and Turks, for that matter—in order to obscure the religious bond between the two groups and to disengage the newly imagined ethnicities from a historical dependence on Islam and the very real possibility of an ongoing anti-imperialist solidarity within its structure.

When seen from another perspective, the inhabitants of the Ottoman Empire, despite the authoritarian dimensions of its rule, were loyal to the state inasmuch as it defended and protected Islam. The British and French—as Christians and Westerners—could not accomplish this. Thus, as resistance took shape in the former empire, it acquired an explicitly Islamist character. Exemplary of this moment was a declaration made by one of the groups fighting the French in northern Syria in the early 1920s. The French should leave "because of the existence of the government of the paramount Islamic Caliphate which is giving aid to it [the people], who consider themselves one part of the several parts of the general Islamic community and fight under its flag." Clearly sectarian in tone, the document makes mention of neither Arabs nor Turks but instead embraces a vital Islamic community. As the French abandoned parts of Anatolia to this resistance, campaigns of ethnic cleansing followed in which the residual Armenian population—which had survived the genocide of 1915—was forced to flee again.

The British liberators of Mesopotamia were also greeted by a revolt. Expressing itself equally in terms of local autonomy and Islamic legitimacy, this revolt would bind together urban Muslims with Arab tribal confederations along the Euphrates and last for several months. Following a brutal campaign of suppression that left more than 10,000 Iraqis (and 450 British soldiers) dead, the resistance was broken. Other comparably bloody moments of resistance would occur later, most notably the Great Revolt in Palestine in the 1930s. It is not unreasonable to suspect that American efforts at liberation will be met by similar sentiments—not just in Iraq, but in other predominantly Muslim countries as well.

The assertion that the societies of the eastern Mediterranean were in need of tutelage was likewise met with derision. The territory conquered by the British and the French had been the stage for nearly a 100-year process of modernization and state centralization. Certainly the level of development of the region compared favorably with that of European states that had once been part of the empire of Austria-Hungary—Czechoslovakia or Yugoslavia—slated for complete independence in the postwar settlements. The entire region had been fully integrated—though in a subordinate position—into international patterns of trade. Schools and universities had been established, and chambers of commerce and industry had been formed. With the Young Turk Revolution of 1908, the Ottoman Empire had even begun to embrace liberal notions of political and intellectual freedom and the creation of a national economy that rejected the debilitating economic concessions imposed on the state by the Europeans during the course of the nineteenth century. The various social and economic reforms left the Ottoman Empire as one of the strongest non-Western states on the globe, and the Ottoman military, far from collapsing in the face of the Allied assault, withstood the two major expeditionary forces sent against it in the initial years of the war—Gallipoli and the first invasion of Iraq—both of which left thousands of British, Australian, and Anglo-Indian soldiers dead or captured. The inherent strength of late Ottoman society—and the fact that the Ottoman Empire, if left intact, would have controlled vast amounts of oil—no doubt contributed to the Western efforts to force its division. Thus divided, the residual states still possessed layers of bureaucrats, local notables, and an emerging middle class of liberal professionals and businessmen who formed the backbone of resistance to European colonialism. As the mandates evolved, the British and French turned to older strategies of divide and conquer to moderate the position of those antagonistic to their rule. Such techniques included the encouragement of compradorial cadres within minority groups and the use of bureaucratic strategies to accentuate sectarian and ethnic divisions within the areas under their control. The formation of Lebanon by the French and early British cooperation with the Zionists are the most pertinent examples of this phenomenon. This form of rule was later adopted by most of the postcolonial governments of the region and fully integrated into styles of authoritarian rule.

As both the French and the British grew exhausted by their colonial endeavor, they moved to more open cooperation with the least liberal parts of Middle Eastern society, primarily the semifeudal notability of the Ottoman period who still dominated much of urban life. Ironically, this elite was itself under tremendous threat from an emergent urban middle class that peopled civil society and ideologically and culturally resembled the Europeans. Thus colonialism contributed to the persistence of the Middle East's ancien régime and the political marginalization of a liberal-minded middle class. Planks in the *Guiding Principles* have the potential to do the same. Although the authors of the report seem less committed to the idea of an ethnic division of Iraq, their continued advocacy of a separate de facto Kurdish "enclave" in a federal system is supportive of the Kurdish notability, who, despite taking on the mantle of political leadership, has divided Iraqi Kurdistan into fiefs. The report's intention to employ "consultative councils" made up of "leaders at the national and local level" and "representatives of external opposition" (7) strikes me as an attempt to use a newer version of mandate-era illiberal notable politics to identify a pliant clientele and suppress dissent. This strategy, when deployed in Afghanistan (i.e., the Loya Jirga), did nothing to instill democracy but rather ensured continued warlord hegemony.

EXIT STRATEGIES

The gradual turning over of authority in British- and French-controlled mandated areas to the semifeudal elite anticipated their final "exit strategies." In the case of the French, the election of a socialist premier in 1936 led to a period of direct negotiations between the notable elite of both Syria and Lebanon but not to a complete withdrawal. The Second World War and postwar French efforts to reclaim parts of their empire made their final departure a clumsy affair. The basic colonial ethos of the permanence of sectarianism was left behind in the organic document establishing the Lebanese Republic—making sectarianism a fact of Lebanese political culture and a contributing factor in the 1975 civil war. In Syria, the urban notables who ruled briefly were replaced almost immediately by military strongmen drawn from the minority groups from which the French had built the armed forces. The ascendancy of the Alawites in the person of the recently deceased Baathist dictator of Syria, Hafiz al-Assad, is a residue of this aspect of French colonial policy.

Great Britain's failures in Palestine are legendary, and in 1948 the British merely abandoned it to the United Nations. However, the British exit strategy for Iraq most closely resembles that implicit in the *Guiding Principles.* By the early 1930s, the British had grown confident that their imposed king, Faysal, would be able to rule by employing a mix of divide and conquer and the British Royal Air Force. The treaty negotiated between Baghdad and London is a blueprint for neocolonialism and anticipates the way various European countries and the United States would deal with former colonies or conquered states in the post–World War II era. By the terms of the 1930 treaty, the British retained two air bases in the country and reserved the right to unilateral intervention in Iraq. The Iraqi military would be developed under close British supervision: all military hardware was to be purchased from British companies; foreign trainers were to be British; and if Iraqi military personnel traveled abroad for training, they were required to go to the United Kingdom. The question of oil had been handled previously in a 1925 agreement under which the Iraqi Petroleum Company—a British firm—had exclusive rights to the development of Iraqi oil reserves in return for the payment of modest royalties. Far from completing the developmental and liberal process envisioned at the award of the mandate, the British had merely identified a limited number of strategic interests in Iraq—access to oil and military assets—and abandoned Iraqi society to those who could best dominate it. Exemplary of this British abandonment was their failure to stop the immediate postindependence genocidal massacres of the Assyrian Christian community of Iraq. The Assyrians, most of whom were refugees from Anatolia, had made up a significant portion of the colonial military and served as a convenient stand-in for anti-British anger. Bakr Sidqi, the officer most responsible for the massacres, used his newly acquired prestige to mount a military coup in 1936, thus setting the stage for Iraqi political instability for the next forty-five years. And although the British did intervene in Iraqi affairs in 1941, it was not to reassert civilian constitutional rule but rather to suppress the government of Rashid Ail al-Gaylani, an Iraqi nationalist who expressed pro-German sympathies and moreover sought to abrogate the terms of the 1930 treaty.

The *Guiding Principles* includes a similar strategy to disengage access to oil from the process of democratization. In the short term, the report advocates "isolating the [oil] industry from domestic turmoil" (16). The report envisions this isolation as only temporary, with American withdrawal from the oil fields contingent on the stability of Iraq, defined as an Iraqi commitment to the "depoliticization" of the oil industry and, again, the "leveling of the playing field." In this sense, the American plan copies the underlying sense of the 1930 treaty: the Iraqis will have sovereignty over their oil resources, as long as sovereignty does not interfere with the American strategic access to those resources. The physical format of the report itself seems to mimic this stance. The working group's report fills the first fourteen pages. The sole addendum, "Oil and Iraq: Opportunities and Challenges," takes up the next thirteen.

CONCLUSION

Perhaps hoping to make the best of a terrible situation, the authors of the *Guiding Principles* have failed to imagine a solution for Iraq that transcends the basic formulas of twentieth-century colonialism. The inherent illegitimacy that will adhere to any U.S. occupation of Iraq—no matter how sheltered by "public diplomacy"—will tar any who seek to cooperate in democratization as collaborators. That the plan includes the obvious limitation of Iraqi sovereignty means that any Iraqi leader who cooperates will be viewed as a servant of American interests, no matter how enlightened. Other questions remain: Would the United States allow an Iraqi government to continue to oppose Israeli policies, or perhaps force it to recognize Israel? To facilitate security, would it place permanent bases on Iraqi soil such as those in Turkey, Qatar, or Afghanistan? More to the point, any ruler who rules only with the aid of American—Christian—occupation forces would lack, in a prima facie sense, any effective legitimacy. Consider for a moment Osama bin Laden's criticism of the Saudi royal family's support of American troops in Arabia.

Certainly the use of the UN to "supervise" an American mandate on Iraq will add credibility to those who denounce that body as a tool of Western imperialism. Likewise, the use of trials for "crimes against humanity" to purge the upper echelon of Iraq's domestic oil industry, as the *Guiding Principles* advocates (17), is a conscious perversion of international norms of justice for purely corporate ends. Any such efforts would turn farcical the whole system of human rights jurisprudence.

Ultimately the plan points to some of the reasons why colonialism in any form must be opposed. By the late 1930s, the peoples of the Middle East had experienced the liberal age promised to them by the League of Nations only as an oppressive mixture of brutish colonialism, political instability, social and cultural dislocations, and Great Depression economic hardship; liberalism had lost credibility and grown hollow. It was in that context that young, educated Arab men began to turn to more radical and racist pan-Arab ideologies such as Baathism. Simultaneously, that was the era when more conservative Islamic movements emerged that were opposed to both the secularizing dimensions of nationalism and Western imperialism. Present-day radical Islamist groups such as al Qaeda and Islamic Jihad trace their lineage to groups of the interwar period of European colonialism, such as the Muslim Brotherhood. The people of Iraq and, by extension, those in the remainder of the Arab world stand to suffer promised American liberation in the same way.

NOTE

A full-text version of the *Guiding Principles for U.S. Post-Conflict Policy in Iraq* is available at http://www.cfr.org/pdf/Iraq_TF.pdf.

The Iraqi Conflict and Its Impact on the Israeli–Palestinian Conflict

Eric Rouleau

There is a widespread belief in the Arab world—and in Western pro-Palestinian circles—that there is a strong Israeli connection to the invasion of Iraq and, more generally, to American policies in the Middle East. Such a conviction is based more on prejudice than on facts. It is widely assumed that the political interests of the United States and Israel are the same with regard to the Middle East and that the hard-line pro-U.S. Jewish faction led by Ariel Sharon represents the views of "the Jewish community" both in Israel and in the world at large. In actuality, however, the relationship between the United States and Israel, and the connection between the Iraqi conflict and the Israeli–Palestinian conflict, is extremely complex. In place of the gross distortions that have permeated popular discourse on the subject, I seek to present a more accurate, multifaceted view of the relationship between the Iraqi conflict and that of Israel–Palestine. By clearly defining the roles and interests of the various actors involved, I hope to move beyond generalizations to form a clearer conceptualization of the way the conflicts overlap and the reasons why they do so.

U.S. AMBITION AND THE IRAQI CONFLICT

The United States has been acting as an empire with imperial ambitions for quite some time, certainly long before President George W. Bush came to power. The administrations of George H. W. Bush and Bill Clinton functioned according to the same imperial logic that guides the current Bush administration; the current administration is set apart from its predecessors only by its commitment to use force to achieve its global ambitions. This difference can be explained by the fact that the current President Bush and his Republican Party represent the interests of the neoconservatives, who will do whatever it takes to achieve their goals. The ideology of these neoconservatives is based on an objective fact: since the disappearance of the Soviet Union, the United States is the sole world superpower that has the capacity—economic, financial, political, and military—to exercise global power. The neoconservatives seek to use the reality of American strength to establish American hegemony.

The invasion of Iraq plays a crucial role in the agenda of the neoconservatives. Iraq has the second-largest oil reserves in the world. If necessary, it could replace other producers such as Saudi Arabia, a fragile ally of the United States. The control of oil production and prices gives the United States the potential power to pressure consumer states such as Russia, China, and many in western Europe. As early as 1997, the neoconservatives recommended that no industrial power—besides the United States—be allowed to play any role on the international oil scene. They were aware of the importance of oil, and it was clear that they intended to dominate the world oil market.

In addition to the control of Iraqi oil, the U.S. invasion provides other benefits to the neoconservatives. The establishment of military bases in Iraq consolidates America's hegemony in the Persian Gulf region, central Asia, and beyond. In addition, it is assumed that the "democratization" of the Middle East, which will include regime changes if necessary, will destroy the bases of terrorism and create a better environment for countries allied to the United States. These friendly states would make peace with Israel even if the Palestinian problem had yet to be solved. Israel, America's surrogate state in the Middle East, would then be given a dominant role in the region.

In terms of domestic politics, the invasion of Iraq allows the neoconservatives an opportunity to entice much of the Jewish vote away from the Democratic Party. The invasion has also strengthened the ties between the Republican Party and millions of sympathizers of the Christian Right, thereby achieving two seemingly contradictory goals at once. The invasion of Iraq allows the neoconservatives to consolidate their power both at home and abroad, bringing them closer to their goal of global hegemony. It is within the context of U.S. interests that the Unites States' relationship with Israel is best understood. Most of the neoconservatives are right-wing Zionists—sometimes more to the right than Sharon—who believe that peace should be imposed on the Palestinians, a peace that would be acceptable to the expansionist rulers of Israel. This "peace" would form a small part of the wider U.S. strategy for dominance, which includes the so-called democratization of Iraq, followed by regime change in Syria, the withdrawal of Syrian troops from Lebanon, and destabilization of the Iranian regime, thus leading to the withdrawal of Hezbollah from Israel's borders. The dramatic change in the regional balance of power would then bring about the desired Pax Americana.

Given U.S. priorities, it should be clear that a strong Israel is desirable only insofar as it will aid the United States in its quest for power. Because the United States is not interested in Israel for its own sake, Israel often does not take priority: in its battle against terrorism, the United States chose to invade Iraq rather than to solve the Israeli–Palestinian problem, even though involving itself in the latter conflict would have been the more logical and obvious choice. Let there be no confusion on this point: Israel is the satellite of the United States, not the other way around.

ISRAEL, THE JEWS, AND THE UNITED STATES

It is a common misperception that Israel's relationship with the United States is inherently symbiotic. In reality, Israel often pays a high price for its ties to the United States. Recently, the perceived connection between the Israeli–Palestinian conflict and the Iraqi conflict has inflicted great harm on Israel, the Jews, and the peace process. International public opinion hostile to the invasion of Iraq, especially in the Arab world and in Europe, makes little distinction between Bush's United States and Sharon's Israel. In most if not all demonstrations, slogans are hostile to both Israel and the United States, and both are accused of warmongering. A poll organized by the European Union in November 2003 indicated that 59 percent of the citizens of Europe considered Israel to be the greatest threat to world peace and stability—greater than the United States, North Korea, or Iran. Undoubtedly this negative view can be partly attributed to the behavior of the Israeli army in the occupied territories. Yet this is a relatively new phenomenon in Europe, and one that should be noted: pro-Palestinian sympathies are becoming more widespread than support for Israeli policies.

The war in Iraq is also seen by many as a worldwide Jewish conspiracy. The government of Israel and Jewish organizations supporting it are partly responsible for this anti-Semitic perception. Israel has always presented itself as the representative of the whole Jewish people, including those in the Diaspora. Organizations of the Jewish establishment around the world that have adopted a hard-line attitude toward the conflict also pretend to speak for the Jews in their respective countries. Unfortunately, the hard-liners have convinced most of the world, and especially the Arab world, that they represent the "Jewish community" as a whole. If we are to more clearly understand the connection between the Iraqi conflict and that of Israel–Palestine, we must disentangle the facts from the distortions and recognize the variations of thought and belief that exist within and among the Jewish communities. On the issue of the U.S. invasion of Iraq, it should be noted that the Israeli government did not represent even the Israeli people as a whole. According to one poll taken on the eve of the Iraqi war, public opinion was evenly split: 46 percent in favor of the American-led war, and 43 percent against a war undertaken without international legitimacy. Furthermore, on February 15, 2003, both Palestinians and Israelis demonstrated against Bush and Sharon, along with millions of others in at least 600 cities around the globe.

Similarly, Jewish establishment organizations in various countries do not represent all their Jewish countrymen and countrywomen. These affluent, powerful lobbies are unconditionally supportive of the Israeli state and attempt to stifle dissenting opinion by labeling those who are openly critical of Israeli policies as "self-hating" Jews.

The role of the Jewish lobby in the United States is further complicated by the fact that it must ally itself with the Christian fundamentalists if it is to have the influence it desires. On its own, the Jewish lobby in the United States is not as efficient as it is said to be. The Christian fundamentalists, who are heavily represented within Congress and the Bush administration, are much more influential. Together with the neoconservatives, Jewish or not, they have played and continue to play a major role in the state's decision-making process. The Jewish lobby is not proud of its alliance with the Christian fundamentalists, who are not only expansionist Zionists but also implicitly anti-Semitic.

Indeed, there is no one "Jewish community" to speak of, only fragmented, dissenting communities with different interests and different alliances. Though this should be an obvious point, distortions and misperceptions about Israel and the Jews have become so commonplace that common sense and rational critique have been discarded in favor of simple, sweeping generalizations.

No matter how strong the relationship between the United States and Israel may become, its fundamental basis will not change: U.S. interests and the U.S. vision of global hegemony will dictate the terms of its existence. For this reason, if for no other, Israel cannot rely on the United States to solve its problems. Indeed, neither the Israelis nor the Palestinians should look to foreign powers for the solution to their conflict. Only when they agree on the basics of a settlement will they obtain the outside support they need. This is why the peace movements in both communities have a historic mission to accomplish, and this is why they badly need the solidarity and the support of all peace-loving organizations around the world.

NOTE

This essay was adapted by Margot Morgan from a talk given in Geneva in July 2004.

Iraqnophobia versus Reality

James Jennings

Incredibly, in less than eighteen months, the Bush administration has turned worldwide support for the United States following the September 11 attacks into the biggest foreign policy debacle since the Vietnam era. This administration's policies on Iraq have bitterly divided NATO, the UN Security Council, the U.S. Congress, the European Union, and even the Arab League. It's an old joke in Washington that a politician's most embarrassing moment is when he (or she) inadvertently blurts out the truth. Both President Bush and Secretary of State Colin Powell had such moments recently.

In his 2002 State of the Union speech, President Bush inadvertently mouthed a line written by either Condoleezza Rice or some obscure White House speechwriter: "Iraq has great potential wealth." Exactly. That's the whole point of the aggressive U.S. posture. It would be hard to imagine the United States amassing 180,000 troops for a preemptive strike on Rwanda. It therefore turns out, if one examines the United Nations Monitoring, Verification, and Inspection Commission (UNMOVIC) reports and looks more deeply into the situation, that the present conflict is not really about weapons of mass destruction after all, despite years of hype from the Western media. Nor is it about oil or even wealth per se, but about the vision Iraq has for the future of the Middle East, as opposed to the vision the United States projects.

The conflict is therefore about ideas—specifically, political ideas. Consequently, the deeper conflict with Iraq cannot really be fought and won by bombs and missiles. It will have to be fought on the airwaves, on television and the Internet. It is more about winning hearts and minds than winning territory. If that is so, and regardless of what happens on the battlefield or to the regime in Baghdad, the real front lines of the war are to be found in the field of communications.

The chief correlate of that proposition is that this will be a long-term battle. The widespread belief that the 1991 Gulf War was a real war and that it would settle the issue of Iraq turns out, in retrospect, to have been mistaken. Long-term observers of the Middle East know that the Gulf War was not so much a war as the first battle of a long campaign or series of wars. For the most part, people in the Middle East understood it that way from the beginning.

In that region, events are measured in generations and centuries, not in quarterly phases, as insisted on by American corporations, or in two- or four-year cycles, as U.S. politicians tend to think. Often in the history of the Middle East, it has taken three wars in succession to settle a question, and sometimes not even then. Europe is not much different, where we have the examples of the Thirty Years' War and the Hundred Years' War. And in our lifetime, we have endured a decades-long cold war that ended not in a quick military victory but in a drawn-out economic triumph. As far as the Middle East is concerned, "If you are not prepared to stay, then don't go" would be the rule taught by experience.

THE IDEAS THAT DRIVE THE CONFLICT WITH IRAQ

The Baath ideology is not well known to Westerners, but the essence of its philosophy is expressed in the term *renaissance.* In short, the Baathists stand for an Arab renaissance. On the surface, there should be no objection to this idea from anybody. The Universal Declaration of Human Rights supports the concept that every group of people deserves to enjoy its own culture and celebrate its own history. In principle, a coalition of Arab states is just as legitimate as a European Union. But when it comes to history, there is a rub. To Arabs, the idea of renaissance evokes powerful political and territorial ambitions that cannot help but create fear and rejection from the West. The remembrance of an overarching Islamic threat to the West, present in some degree since the seventh century, may have faded during the latter half of the twentieth century, but it still exists and was revived in large part at the beginning of the twenty-first century by the methodology of terror exhibited by small bands of extremist Muslims.

A succession of Middle Eastern political leaders has created extraordinary fright in the West. These leaders have consequently been vilified as monsters, elevated to archenemy status, and then destroyed. Generally, the reaction has greatly exceeded the reality. It is true that their images, and especially their more prominent misdeeds, have been jarring to Western culture, making it easier for people in the West to hate them. For various reasons, beginning with Mossadegh in Iran in the period following World War II, a constant and bitter campaign of vilification has been waged against Arab and Muslim leaders in the Western press. Yet Mossadegh, a principled nationalist and democratically elected prime minister of Iran, was deliberately destroyed with the backing of the CIA in favor of restoring the antidemocratic shah.

When the revolution against the monarchy took place in Egypt in 1952, it was the Arabs' turn, with Nasser as the ideal bogeyman. Egypt was attacked in the so-called tripartite aggression of the 1956 Suez War jointly by Britain,

France, and Israel, and again by Israel with U.S. backing in 1967. Later figures like Khadafy, Arafat, Khomeini, Saddam, and bin Laden have also inspired great fear, whether justified by reality or not. For Westerners, behind all these figures has lurked the shadow of a greater nemesis: the fear of an incipient Muslim or, more narrowly, Arab renaissance.

THE PERSECUTION OF IRAQ

The U.S.-led policy of persecution against Iraq is related to these concerns. The American public has yet to face the appalling human cost of the catastrophic embargo against Iraq from 1991 to the present. The number of unnecessary and preventable deaths of children alone—credited by reputable and conservative public health specialists as in the hundreds of thousands—cannot tell the whole story. The economic, cultural, intellectual, and psychological damage to an entire society has been devastating as well.

The closest analogy to Iraq in the 1990s is Germany in the 1920s when, as a means of punishment, it was choked with trade sanctions and the German people starved for three years until the peace settlement was reached. Everybody knows what happened next, with the rise of Hitler and the Nazis. Yet Iraq has been similarly persecuted for nearly thirteen years. What kind of radical hatred can we expect to arise from Iraq's youth in the coming decades? We need only look at the lack of jobs, nutritious food, education, health care, psychological counseling, and, most of all, opportunity to get some idea of the desperation of Iraqi youth. Viewed in this way, the future may well become a reflection of the past.

Among the things that people in the West must do is to pay closer attention to the semantics and rhetoric of war: What is the definition of "terrorist"? Who are the "terrorists"? Why does much of the Muslim world call the United States and Britain "crusaders"? What are "weapons of mass destruction" really? Does a 5,000-pound bomb, deliverable from 50,000 feet half a world away, count as a weapon of mass destruction, or does the term apply only to the possibly nonexistent and certainly nondeliverable stockpile of degraded chemicals or biologicals belonging to a third-rate military power like Iraq? There has been a constant barrage of fear-mongering and warmongering against Iraq in the Western press, but at some point, the question needs to be asked whether such extreme "Iraqnophobia" corresponds to reality.

The worldwide revulsion against American leadership evident in the February 15, 2003, protests was not because of any great love for the Iraqi regime, but because millions of people felt that Iraq had been unjustly persecuted for over a decade and was being unfairly targeted for a new and unnecessary war.

Typical of the protesters, said to have totaled 10 million persons in 603 cities around the world, was the reaction of a Canadian veteran of the Allied army of occupation in Germany during World War II. He said, "The U.S. has always been my favorite country—but I've changed my mind. Now it's France. Your government is lying too much. Why do so many Americans not see the truth?"

THE POLITICAL STRUGGLE FOR DOMINATION OF THE MIDDLE EAST

One way to gain insight into the political ideology behind the present conflict with Iraq is to view the iconography of the Baath regime in Baghdad. In Iraq, mosaic art, paintings, monuments, medals, and coins sometimes depict a map of all the Arab nations with Iraq's president as the leader. This is wishful thinking, of course, but it is a wish that seeks transformation into reality. The map extends from the Atlantic shores of Morocco all the way across North Africa to the Zagros Mountains frontier of Iran. This is the Arab empire that used to exist under the Umayyads and Abbasids and that, deep down, every Arab heart still resonates to, even though it may seem far-fetched today. History suggests that this construct is, and always will be, inimical to Western interests. Therefore, it makes a certain amount of sense for the West to resist any such rebirth of Arabism or, to an even greater degree, a resurgence of the transnational phenomenon of Islamism.

Yet, in reality, the present universal political system of nationalism works against such visionary ideas. With Middle Eastern countries having developed, to a greater or lesser degree, their own national identities over the last century, the political unification of all the Arabs, much less all the Muslims, seems impossible. The interposition of modernity, secularism, and materialism, along with the ideals of the American and French revolutions (which percolated very slowly into the Middle East over more than a century), offer strong countervailing trends.

That said, the way the West has chosen to offset any gains in Arab unity, such as those made by Nasser in his heyday, may be criticized as faulty and certainly counterproductive of good interregional relations. The United States and Britain, followed to a lesser extent by France and at times Russia, have generally sought to (1) destroy or marginalize any charismatic leader who might arise in the Arab world; (2) lure both small and large Arab states into various kinds of alliances with Western powers; and (3) most important, follow the Roman Empire's maxim of *divide et impera*, which means not "divide and conquer," as it is so often translated, but more literally "divide and rule."

Consequently, under this logic, it becomes the task of the West, and particularly of its Middle Eastern colony Israel, to follow a policy of breaking large states into smaller states and small states into tribal and clan rivalries. This plan was implemented successfully and with utmost cruelty for more than fifteen years in Lebanon. Under conditions dominated by Israel following 1982, the Lebanese civil war was supported (largely passively) by the Western alliance and became a theater of the cold war due to input from Syria and its Soviet patron. The losers were the Lebanese themselves, the historically fractious ethnic and religious entities of the country. Eventually, following the end of the cold war, Lebanon managed to reconstitute itself into an uneasy nation once more, but the rifts still exist and could easily reemerge.

Iraq is destined, if the U.S.–U.K.–Israeli alliance has its way, to be more or less permanently split into three parts, despite the oft-stated position of the U.S. Department of State that Iraq should remain as a single entity. The lie is given to this policy line by the reality of the present "no-fly" zones under U.S. Central Command. In the event of an American occupation of Iraq, there is little doubt that these lines will become realities on the ground as well. By no stretch of the imagination can it be said that the United States truly wants Iraq to both stay united and be democratic. A democratic election for all of Iraq would likely ignite a civil war, because the Shia are in the majority, and the Sunnis would not accept such a government. The Kurdish zone would also probably rise up in a new revolution and declare statehood. Since a long U.S. occupation is unthinkable, and leaving a vacuum in the Gulf is unwise, the best course would be for the United States to stay out of Iraq's internal affairs. One thing is certain: Iraqis will not accept a government imposed from outside.

Therefore, the conflict with Iraq is not about a single leader or about specific armaments that Iraq may or may not possess. It goes much deeper. It is an existential struggle for both the Arabs and Israelis. The present gigantic, world-encompassing political struggle must be understood as the Arab-Israeli conflict in macrocosm, the conflict having at last reached its climactic phase. Even so, this phase will likely be extended for many years before a final settlement is reached. The struggle for the domination of the Middle East, regardless of a U.S. victory in the second Gulf war, will not be over soon. It may in fact just be beginning.

Unfortunately for the coterie of swaggering hawks now in power in Washington, no one among them seems to have the prescience to see the issue this way. For years it was steadfastly denied in Washington and by leading political pundits that there was any linkage at all between the Arab–Israeli conflict and the sanctions on Iraq. But in fact they are inextricably linked, exactly because of the collision of ideologies and Iraq's "great potential wealth."

A unique and spectacular opportunity for a way out of this morass has been deliberately ignored by the Bush administration. The most recent Arab League summit in Beirut produced the best offer for a comprehensive settlement that

Israel has ever received. Of course, the U.S. administration is not the only one that has acted arrogantly. Israeli Prime Minister Ariel Sharon insultingly refused for a week to even read the peace plan for Palestine proffered by Israel's number-one patron, the United States, and then curtly rejected it.

COMPARING RHETORIC WITH REALITY

The United States' overall vision of democracy, women's rights, and free secular education for everybody in the Middle East, set forth in one of Secretary Powell's major policy speeches, is a noble one, capable of generating great enthusiasm from the Western point of view. But it is sure to run into incredibly high resistance in the region itself; in fact, it could be described as largely a pipe dream. The United States does not have a convincing record of providing a consistent supply of money and a steady commitment to such schemes anywhere in the world, the Marshall Plan excepted. Experienced observers believe that no such thing is likely to happen in the region short of two or three generations of strenuous efforts from progressive, pro-Western elements within Arab society itself. At the moment, those elements either are not in control in the various Arab countries or hold power so tenuously that their survival is in doubt.

When it comes to weapons issues, one can ask why Iraq's nuclear file has been pronounced satisfactory by the International Atomic Energy Agency (and, incidentally, by the CIA, which says that Iraq might have a bomb within eight years if an improbable series of contingent events occur), yet a huge hue and cry continues to be made over chemicals and biologicals that have not been found. When do people take leave of reality and allow mass paranoia to set in? Former secretary of defense Cohen has stated that twenty-five nations have these prohibited weapons. So far, Iraq is the only nation on earth that has been inspected so intensively—and for years, at that. A reality check is badly needed.

Chief UNMOVIC inspector Hans Blix quietly and neatly used a few verbal pins to burst the balloon of Powell's celebrated UN speech, revealing just how much of it was factually untenable. This came on the heels of Tony Blair's own debacle, when a supposedly definitive British intelligence dossier was publicly debunked as being a crib sheet from a California graduate student's outdated paper. After showing that the vaunted U.S. intelligence establishment was indeed putting the worst possible interpretation on its aerial photographs of the Ibn al-Haithem site, which might simply be normal activity, Blix intoned, "We have found no weapons of mass destruction." As quiet as his delivery was, it was nevertheless a dramatic moment—exactly the reverse of Adlai Stevenson's famous "gotcha" confrontation with the Soviets at the time of the Cuban missile crisis.

Frustrated, Powell threw away his prepared remarks and shot from the hip. He said, "Nobody likes war . . . but sometimes war is necessary to maintain world order." He might have said *"the* world order," for that is precisely the implication of his remark. The "new world order" seeks to impose political, economic, and military order wherever there is resistance or perceived disorder, all under U.S. hegemony, of course.

We need to ask, What is that order? And who exactly is threatening the peace and stability of the region? We need to be sure we are asking the right questions. The first of those questions should be the most basic one: Have we in fact addressed the real problem in going after Iraq's presumed stocks of prohibited weapons? Or is it a dodge for a more fundamental objective: U.S. control of Iraq's "great potential wealth" and the preservation and extension of U.S. "order" throughout what is admittedly a tumultuous region? This order now includes the placement of U.S. military forces in Uzbekistan, Pakistan, Afghanistan, Kuwait, Turkey, Saudi Arabia, and Qatar, not to mention Colombia and all the forgotten places where U.S. troops are stationed as leftovers from World War II, the Korean War, and the cold war.

Since the Bush administration's agenda is being driven by the ideological Right, it makes sense to listen to what they are saying. Former Speaker of the House Newt Gingrich, appearing at an American Enterprise Institute forum in November 2002, along with Caspar Weinberger and Jeanne Kirkpatrick, urged the clash of civilizations mantra: in his mind, the "green threat" of Islam has replaced the "red threat" of communism. Of course. How else could these people hope to maintain their power, except by scaring the public with a bogeyman image of Islam that does not exist? It is true that radical Islamism presents a problem, no less to Muslim countries than to the West, but this is a clash of political ideologies and cannot truthfully be described as a "clash of civilizations."

When this approach was first bruited about in the wake of the cold war, it was ridiculed as improbable, if not impossible. Events have proved otherwise, not so much because of a unified Islamic threat from Muslim states, which in fact does not exist, but because of small radical terrorist cells and the shock of their disastrous attacks on September 11, coupled with a swaggering response to the trauma by American policy makers. "Rather like using a sledgehammer to kill a fly," one lady remarked at the onset of the U.S.–Afghan war.

Soon after September 11, Pentagon planners began organizing for an attack on Iraq. Secretary Powell tried unsuccessfully to demonstrate a linkage between Iraq and Islamist terrorism. Most European intelligence agencies remain unconvinced. Iraq is not al Qaeda, nor is al Qaeda Iraq. But the administration's spokespeople keep insisting that the two are somehow connected, despite the evidence. At least half of Americans accept the administration's logic, ill informed and convoluted as it is.

Islam is multifaceted, diverse, disarticulate, richly textured, and internally conflicted; it appears to be increasingly losing its grip on the young and perceives itself, correctly, as weak. Only by concerted and repetitive blows from the outside can it be made to coalesce, and that with incredible difficulty. Yet that is what the policies of the Bush administration have already begun to achieve. It hardly needs to be said that a different approach is needed.

HAVE WE ADDRESSED THE REAL PROBLEM?

The real problem in the Arab Middle East at the moment is twofold. One crucial issue concerns Arab identity, which involves the evolution of a viable and coherent ideology for Arab peoples generally and for the states of the Arab world in particular. The other concerns regional security and, potentially at least, international security as well. The first problem is internal and can be solved only by the Arabs themselves. The twentieth century saw wild fluctuations in political ideology, political systems, and the structure of political institutions throughout the Middle East.

For countries to move from monarchy to fascism to radical dictatorship to abortive attempts at democracy to socialism to communism to theocracy all in one century is a dizzying set of changes. Although not every country went through every stage, all these ideologies were present in the region at one time or another during the 1900s. One of the underlying problems—perhaps the chief problem—of the region's governments is their lack of legitimacy. This partly explains the typical instability of many of the governments in the region, including that of Turkey and Iran. Turkey endured a severe wave of terrorism in the 1980s and an armed Kurdish revolt during the 1990s. The search for legitimacy became especially evident with the regional rise in Islamism following Iran's turn toward religious extremism under the Ayatollah Khomeini in 1979. The fact that student riots, regional rebellions, and protests continue in Iran is a sign that even under the religious regime, true legitimacy is lacking.

What can the United States do about this issue? First, wish those countries well in their efforts to find suitable identities, establish workable political systems, and build sustainable institutions compatible with their own cultures. Second, stay engaged in appropriate ways, such as many of the programs attempted by the U.S. Agency for International Development over the last half century. Third, encourage more nongovernmental organizations to get involved in people-to-people programs (rather than mere "sustainable development," the current buzz phrase in international aid); they sometimes throw obscene amounts of money into schemes imposed from the outside, most of them destined to fail.

To his credit, President Bush said some of these kinds of things in his speech to Congress and the nation shortly after September 11. Perhaps he counterintuitively engaged a humane and knowledgeable speechwriter for that enterprise. Unfortunately, we have heard nothing more of this approach since that time. The administration's preferred shortcut, to "brag loudly and carry a huge arsenal of bombs," is taking precedence. The ongoing military drumbeat obliterates any thought of diplomacy or an approach like the Peace Corps, which could lead the way to a more peaceful tomorrow.

Afghanistan is a case in point. Despite much high-flown rhetoric about wanting to help Afghans rebuild their nation, the United States continues to spend $2 billion per month in Afghanistan for military purposes but managed to come up with only $750 million for aid projects in a seventeen-month period. That comes out to less than 2.5 percent of U.S. military expenditures for each month. Once again, as the Indians used to say about the Great White Father in Washington, "White man speak with forked tongue." At the international conference in Tokyo devoted to Afghan aid, the nations of the world pledged only $5 billion of the $15 billion needed to reconstruct Afghanistan. So far, only about 20 percent of the amount pledged has been coughed up, and who knows whether the rest will ever be paid, or conveniently forgotten about. And, without much attention by the press, hostile attacks have gradually increased in Afghanistan until U.S. troops are presently receiving an average of one missile attack every day. Did someone say "quagmire"?

At the dramatic "Valentine's Day" Security Council meeting of February 14, 2003, Secretary of State Colin Powell was pushed to the wall diplomatically by the smooth eloquence and strong moral posture of the French foreign minister. Dominique de Villepin's statesmanlike speech instantly catapulted France into the position of leader of European and world resistance to U.S. hegemony. Despite the fact that the French are constantly reviled in Washington as having no principles when it comes to Iraq, but only economic interests, de Villepin succeeded admirably in blocking the U.S. rush to war.

Refusing to be realistic or to face facts about Iraq's supposed threat is itself a threat to the American body politic. Continuing to deal with political differences by the use of hackneyed and demeaning slogans cheapens discourse and leads to the easy recourse to violent "solutions." The American public eagerly swallows the line that the French are ungrateful, cowardly, and sleazy moneygrubbers; the Arabs are liars and terrorists; but the Americans are noble and altruistic. Objectifying people in this misleading way led to the horrors of World Wars I and II. Diplomacy, if we will use it, can provide a way out. The United Nations system, flawed as it is, has helped protect the world from the nightmarish barbarities of the 1914–1945 period for more than half a century. It should be strengthened and encouraged, not ignored and overridden.

Whither Independence?
Iraq in Perspective
From Despotism to Occupation

Wadood Hamad

There has been nearly unanimous consensus among Iraqis that a new age of possible progress and prosperity has dawned on their battered and war-fatigued country with the downfall of Saddam Hussein on April 9, 2003. However, much has tainted this rosy image, and much more could still mar the outcome. A principal factor has been the highly incompetent and nonchalant manner in which the U.S.–U.K. occupying forces have conducted themselves; one wonders if this is a result of sheer imperial arrogance, ignorance of the region, or a combination of both. None of the above reasons is excusable in any way, of course. When a disproportionate U.S. force killed Saddam Hussein's two infamous sons, Uday and Qusay, and a few of their companions and then showed their battered images to the world, two messages were sent: First, the United States will absolutely contravene every mode of rational, moral, ethical, and reasonable behavior to make its point and achieve success (in its own assessment). Otherwise, why not arrest these two criminals and have them justly tried in Iraqi courts? Second, U.S. policy planners have an inveterate attachment to change through force. The lessons from the twentieth century are plenty (as the Hiroshima anniversary, among others, adequately reminds us), and the difference now is of volume and rate rather than quality.

Those of us who vehemently opposed the launch of an immoral, unjust, and illegal war have to seriously address the occupation—not in a romantic, knee-jerk oppositional fashion, which has become commonplace among Westerners as well as Arabs who object to U.S. imperialist plans, but in a calculated manner that puts the interests of the Iraqi people uncompromisingly at the forefront. Thus, what are the facts on the ground, and what can be done? In what follows, I am more interested in raising questions than providing simple, speculative answers. What deeply angers and pains me are the cold, condescending views offered by Arabs and Americans alike when it comes to dealing with Iraq. To these two groups, governments and populace, Iraq seems to be a possession, and each has an opinion on what to do with it. Very little attention is given to how to achieve results, which leads me, and a few others, to believe that no one is really interested in the well-being of Iraqis.

THE UNITED STATES HAS WAGED WAR AGAINST IRAQ in spite of unprecedented worldwide public pressure against it. The pretexts for the war, Saddam Hussein's possession of weapons of mass destruction (WMD) and his alleged link to al Qaeda, have been in dispute from the very beginning, with neither a trace of WMD nor a hint of a connection to the al Qaeda terrorists being found. Rather, there has been an unraveling of a series of apocryphal stories penned by elected and unelected officials in the U.S. and U.K. governments with the sole purpose of manipulating public opinion prior to waging war. Now the sad fact is that such despicable tactics—and the list might be long—have placed the fallen despot and his regime in a rather romantic-heroic position among many in the Arab world, the third world, and elsewhere. Rather than containing terrorist groups and cutting their lifelines, U.S. actions have given life to a litany of fragmented but ruthless reactionary groups intent on inflicting damage on all symbols of modernity—and certainly not limited to the United States and its interests.

To this day, many cannot fathom the horrific and criminal nature of the deposed Iraqi regime, and U.S. tactics in Iraq have allowed people to compare and contrast them with a fictitious version of Saddam Hussein's reign.

Every visitor to Iraq speaks of war-torn cities, devastation, dilapidated services, and a populace fatigued by war and economic sanctions, on the one hand, and the existence of monstrous, grand palaces and edifices, on the other: all are the direct outcome of thirty-plus years of authoritarian rule and twelve years of the most suffocating (U.S.–U.K. instigated and propelled) economic sanctions ever imposed. But Iraqis returning for the first time after decades of exile have observed one thing of significance in the midst of the rubble: people feel free and hopeful. Freedom leads to a satisfying inner happiness that can be understood only by those whose freedom has been curtailed; no explanation, lengthy or terse, would do justice. This is precisely what gives one hope for a better tomorrow. Alas, both the happiness and the hope are slowly being nibbled at, and the prospects are unclear.

Four months after the fall of Saddam Hussein's hierarchical structure of governance, basic municipal and civic services are at an appallingly low level. The workforce has no work, and only a portion of it has started receiving salaries, some of which were paid in useless currency that further aggravates an already drained populace.[1] Security is deteriorating mainly in Baghdad and environs, while most other cities function much better. Further, the rumor mill is grinding absolutely everything imaginable, which only contributes to the increasing level of uncertainty in the country. The Coalition Provisional Authority (CPA) has promulgated actions that can only worsen a very unsettled situation—namely, dissolving the army and affiliated organizations, as well as the Ministry of Information, thus rendering more than 250,000 without any livelihood. Furthermore, the so-called process of de-Baathification is purely ideological in nature—fueled principally by the hawks in the U.S. administration and their Iraqi underlings, most notably Ahmed Chalabi, Kanan Makiya, and company.

In a country where membership in the Baath party was often the only means for advancement, this tactic is bound to engulf the country in a process of vilification and countervilification based on personal, rather than objective, accounts. What would be a more appropriate and just recourse is to judiciously investigate the role of senior Baath functionaries—trying before the law all those guilty of crimes against the people, and pardoning those whose hands are untainted. A national healing and reconciliation process is essential if the tragedies and horrors of the past thirty years are to be constructively addressed, while avoiding the institutionalization of recrimination and guilt by association. The latter is likely to take the country down a dangerous spiral that accentuates antiquated tribal rule, which Saddam Hussein tried to resuscitate in the latter part of the 1990s to further buttress his reign. Iraq's political parties must resist this and instead press for just trials and a process of reconciliation. Interestingly, the majority of Iraqis seems to favor this approach, as evinced by personal and televised accounts (albeit not polled scientifically), thus presenting yet another hopeful scenario for Iraq and its people if they are left alone.

Events indicate that the U.S. invading-cum-occupying forces, though possessing formidable firepower, have less impressive planning and analytical powers. Most echelons of the decision-making process within the U.S. government have apparently been surprised by the run of events. More surprisingly, no contingency plans were prepared for the (speedy) fall of Saddam Hussein's government and the ensuing dissolution of ministries, state organizations, the police, and so forth. What would a rational person expect if a highly centralized structure of governance, dependent on a ruthless social policy grounded in chauvinistic and sectarian politics, suddenly collapsed? Why, then, have U.S. planners and their research centers and institutes been unable to anticipate at least a general framework for dealing with events?

The sanctions-fatigued, repressed Iraqis, who hardly have adequate access to basic food requirements, never mind super-duper search engines, computing power, and the like, could have done much better than the functionaries of the CPA. It is also worth noting that this wait-and-see attitude is essentially the same obscurantism that governs doctrinaire religious teachings (of whatever color): a complete and utter absence of critical thought. This behavior fundamentally stems from the United States' self-image as the unparalleled imperial power of our age. Thus, ideology is fundamentally and intrinsically at the core of all that is happening, and the media have performed a compelling job of disinforming the U.S. populace and effectively contributing to a brainwashing campaign at an astounding rate. The U.S. populace did not change this through the ballot box in 2004. It has not been understood that Americans would not be so hated if they actually thought of the rest of the world on an equal footing and divorced themselves from the condescending attitudes that are so prevalent among those of nearly every class, profession, and ethnic and religious background.

IRAQ IS CONSTANTLY PORTRAYED AS a fragile formation of ethnoreligious groups that are essentially violent and vying for power. Is there a country on this planet that is not an amalgamation of ethnoreligious groups? Even Israel as a Jewish state comprises various ethnicities and hence is heterogeneous.

Modern Iraq has been a staunchly secular country where the separation of religion and the state has been a fact of life—respected and adopted by all, and certainly by its Shiite and Sunni religious establishments. Though not a phenomenon at the popular level, ethnosectarian chauvinism has been institutionalized by the state since its inception—the progeny of the British-concocted Cox-al-Naqeeb plan, laying the foundation for the pyramidal power structure in the nascent government of Iraq in 1921. To ensure reliance on foreign forces, state power was entrusted to a minority elite, with a clear segregation of the largesse among the vying groups: officers of the erstwhile Ottoman army, Sunni landowners and religious notables, and a handful of Shiite landowners and religious notables and Jewish and Christian businessmen.[2] The association was entrenched in the notion of belonging to a group—ethnic, religious, or sectarian—rather than to the country of Iraq. It may be moot to question whether this was a reflection of the lack of a national identity; however, history indicates that the inhabitants of Iraq strongly identified themselves with the land of Mesopotamia, and their association has been with it rather than, strictly speaking, the tribe, religion, or sect.

The year 1958, marking the overthrow of the monarchy and the establishment of the first republic, ushered in a new period when Iraqis identified themselves as citizens and not according to tribal, religious, or sectarian divides. The modern political formations, communist or pan-Arab—principally the Baath party—have been clearly secular and encompassed all sectors of society along ideological rather than ethnosectarian divisions. The Baath party slowly degenerated once Saddam Hussein became the "strongman" in the early 1970s, and in the summer of 1979, he consummated his power by annihilating the leftist wing of the party (led by Abdel Khaleq al-Samarai, who was summarily purged with more than fifty of his comrades, most of whom were executed by Saddam and his underlings). During the 1980s, Saddam Hussein embarked on a policy of entrenching a family-based rule, and the remnants of the party became a façade to one of the darkest periods of Iraq's history. In the 1990s, with the help of the sanctions, the government further degenerated, imposing a brutal mafia-style repression against any modicum of opposition. The inhabitants of the south, mostly Shias, paid a particularly heavy price as a result of their uprising following the 1991 Gulf War. Prior to 1991, the government had forcibly transferred Arabs from the south to the Kurdish north, especially oil-rich Kirkuk, with the objective of creating a new demographic reality. Moreover, a diligent student of the British colonizers, Saddam Hussein fervently adopted an approach favoring one or another Sunni clan for wealth and governmental positions, continually pitting one tribe against the other. This ipso facto created a situation whereby those minority tribes associated their comfortable status with the regime's existence.

The inhabitants of the south have long been suppressed not because of their Shia faith per se but because that region had always been a source of resistance against central authority. The south of Iraq, one of the richest cultural hot spots anywhere, has long been characteristically secular and was the birthplace of Iraqi communism as well as the Arab socialist movement—including the Baath party. Hence, the brutal repression and suppression inflicted on the inhabitants of the south by Saddam Hussein's regime began simply as a measure against a people demanding freedom; then it metamorphosed into a sectarian identity after the disappearance of all secular opposition within Iraq. Saddam's well-practiced technique of punishment was collective and decisively long term: cut off the livelihood of any group of people who dared to pose a threat to his rule. Thus, the marsh Arabs, descendants of Mesopotamia's first dwellers, were dealt a severe blow to their very livelihood and existence for demanding "bread and freedom": the marshes were drained, and fertile agricultural land was turned arid because the Tigris was purposefully redirected away from it.

It is worthwhile to point out that although the south was brutally suppressed, a number of the security apparatus torturers actually came from the south themselves—with the top security echelons coming from the family mafia and affiliated subordinates. Such was the nexus of victim and torturer under Saddam Hussein's reign of terror: entwined to the nth degree.

WHY, THEN, DO ARAB SATELLITE TV STATIONS and most Arab journals maliciously propagate the misconception that every event in Iraq takes place along sectarian lines? Al-Jazeera, in spite of clarifications and corrections from Iraqis inside Iraq, insists on calling the pockets of local fighting "national resistance led by the Sunnis." In many programs where audiences from Baghdad, Cairo, and Beirut talk about the situation in Iraq, rhetorical statements from Cairo and Beirut are devoid of genuine sympathy for the plight of the Iraqis and any concrete plan of how the Arabs wish to assist the Iraqis. Thus there is a strong backlash within a significant portion of Iraqis all across the country, educated or otherwise, against the way Arab governments, the press, intellectuals, and even the public have represented the situation in Iraq under Saddam Hussein's rule and afterward. Iraqis feel disgusted by the hypocrisy practiced by many Arabs. Prior to April 9, 2003, Iraq's children were a mere slogan for Arabs as the murderous sanctions tore them asunder and as years of political repression sought, but failed, to create a docile populace. Most Iraqis contend that no progress can emerge in the Arab world if internal repression persists, and no justification should be given to any form of authoritarian rule, as the history of modern Iraq has amply shown: a rich nation of highly educated people reduced to selling their belongings and rummaging for food for their offspring.[3]

Iraq may now present a scenario for the Arabs to follow. No one in Iraq is oblivious to U.S. reasons for waging war on Iraq, but they recognize their inability to stand against the U.S. mammoth—since neither Europe nor any other state dared to oppose the United States. The split between the dormant Left inside Iraq and their comrades outside specifically addresses this point. They both agreed that no positive change could take place in Iraq while Saddam Hussein's regime was in power, but they differed on the mechanisms for change. Those who lived inside Iraq and were experiencing repression on a daily basis felt that only an outside power could remove the despotic regime. Then, and only then, could work begin to rebuild the country. Hardly any Iraqi welcomed the invading forces, and they all agree that the occupying forces must leave. The collapse of the central government and all its offshoots created a significant power vacuum as well as a security black hole. At the current stage, a foreign presence is required to maintain peace and order. The question is how this should be done and who should do it. No army in the world is trained to maintain peace and order among civilians, thus leading to the tragic, chaotic scenarios that have occurred. All visitors to Iraq acknowledge that the young American GIs are scared witless and therefore shoot at everything that moves. This takes us back to questions I posed at the beginning of this essay: Are the U.S. planners incompetent, nonchalant, or both?

What is clear is that a strict timeline for the speedy withdrawal of U.S. and British forces must be put in place, and at the same time, the United Nations must make a staunch commitment to provide international forces to replace them. There can be no lapse between the two, as the political volatility in Iraq is serious. Moreover, the governing council appointed by Paul Bremer III, though not the transitory national government the Iraqis demanded, is required to form a united front and achieve two goals: restoring peace and security within the country, and restoring the functioning of municipal and governmental activities. The council's efficacy will be judged by whether it achieves these two goals and how quickly. Once this is accomplished, the institution of democratic elections to form a new government must be put in place through a realistic but nonpliant timeline. Achieving success will require a unified approach by the council in order to pressure the CPA into accepting Iraqi demands.

The world can support the Iraqis by pressuring their respective governments to demand that the Iraqis receive the reins of power peacefully, systematically, and quickly. The world has a chance to show that it cannot let the U.S. greyhound loose; it must be tamed.

NOTES

1. The 10,000-dinar note is rumored to be counterfeit and is thus being accepted at a much lower rate, if at all. Furthermore, prices continue to soar.
2. The religious establishment, as elsewhere, was split between submission and opposition.
3. The Arab League, in a meeting of its foreign ministers in early August 2003, refused to recognize the governing council recently formed in Iraq and rationalized the decision on the basis that recognition would be tantamount to accepting occupation. According to the charter of the League, UN Security Council resolutions must be accepted and adhered to, as well as international treaties. Under U.S. pressure, the United Nations passed Security Council Resolution 1483, which basically legitimized the occupation of Iraq and placed the country under the administrative control of the occupying forces. U.S. forces occupy parts of almost every Arab state, kingdom, or sheikhdom; hence the Arab foreign ministers' talk of not recognizing occupation by the United States is nothing but hogwash. Moreover, they are in contravention of the very UN resolutions they proclaim to be enforcing. The real motive for their action lies elsewhere. A genuine change toward democracy in Iraq would threaten all these illegitimate governments; thus they have been united in actively opposing any reasonable resolution of the Iraq crisis. They have proposed no alternative to U.S. occupation nor outlined a road map for ending occupation. Moreover, the official Arab media continue to portray any escalation in Iraq as having religious, sectarian, and ethnic bases, and hardly any notice is given to the secular voices that are widely available inside the country. It is worth noting that the clashes and confrontations with U.S. forces in regions surrounding Baghdad, notably Falluja, have been partly fueled by religious fundamentalists, shipped to Iraq before and after the invasion, bent on destabilizing the country. These deadly confrontations are not supported by most Iraqis and do not represent a form of armed struggle. This is futile violence whose goal is disruption of ordinary life and that serves no useful goal; only innocent civilians die as a consequence.

Part VI
Transnational Realities

September 11 and the Terror War
The Bush Legacy and the Risks of Unilateralism

Douglas Kellner

On September 11, 2001, terrorists seized control of an American Airlines flight from Boston to Los Angeles and crashed it into the World Trade Center (WTC) in New York City, followed by a second hijacking and collision into the other WTC tower minutes later. During the same hour, a third commandeered jetliner hit the Pentagon, while a fourth hijacked plane, possibly destined for the White House, went down in Pennsylvania, perhaps crashed out of harm's way by passengers who had learned of the earlier terrorist crimes and were trying to prevent another calamity.

The world stood transfixed by the graphic videos of the WTC buildings exploding and discharging a great cloud of rubble. Subsequent images depicted heroic workers struggling to save people and then themselves becoming victims of the unpredicted collapse of the towers or shifts in the debris. The WTC towers, the largest buildings in New York City and a potent symbol of global capitalism, were down, and the mighty behemoth of American military power, the mythically shaped Pentagon, was penetrated and on fire. Terrorists celebrated their victory over the American colossus, and the world remained focused for days on the media spectacle of "America Under Attack," reeling from the now highly feared effects of terrorism.

THE BUSH ADMINISTRATION AND TERRORISM

For some weeks after the September 11 attacks, there was ferocious debate and intense speculation concerning the U.S. response. On October 7, 2001, George W. Bush announced the beginning of a military campaign in Afghanistan to destroy the al Qaeda terrorist network and the Taliban regime that was hosting them. Within two months, the Taliban was in retreat and Afghanistan had entered a highly uncertain stage. Whereas the media and the public have generally accepted that the Bush administration's policy was a success, I argue, by contrast, that its terrorism policy is highly flawed and potentially disastrous in its short- and long-term effects.

I will show that the policies of the Bush administration and the Pentagon in the Afghanistan war were poorly conceived and badly executed and are likely to sow the seeds of future blowback and reprisal. Although the overthrow of the Taliban regime and the assault on the al Qaeda infrastructure were justifiable and a salutary blow against global terrorism, the campaign in Afghanistan was arguably misconceived and in many ways unsuccessful. In my view, terrorism is a global problem that requires a global solution. The Bush administration's policy, however, is largely unilateral, and its military response is flawed and has hindered more intelligent and potentially successful efforts against terror networks while quite possibly creating more terrorists and enemies of the United States. A global campaign against worldwide terror networks will require multilateral and coordinated efforts across many fronts: financial, legal-judiciary, political, and military. On the financial front, the Bush administration has failed to adequately coordinate large-scale efforts to fight terror networks, and domestically, there is criticism that fights among the Treasury, Commerce, and Justice departments have hampered coordination even in the United States. The Bush administration systematically pursued a deregulatory policy toward financial markets and has not been able to successfully regulate the flow of funds supporting either the terror networks and other global criminals or corporate allies of the Bush administration that prefer to secure and launder their funds in offshore banks.

On the legal and judicial front, the Bush administration has also failed to construct a lasting and active international alliance against terror. Whereas many foreign countries, including Britain, France, Spain, Italy, and Singapore, have arrested terrorists and broken up terror networks within their borders, the U.S. Justice Department has not been successful in breaking up any major U.S. terrorist networks, and the Bush administration has failed to adequately coordinate global antiterrorist activity with other countries. On the whole, the United States has alienated itself from most of its allies in the war against terror by arresting suspects and then holding them in detention camps without legal rights and forcing them to face military tribunals and the death penalty. In particular, the detention center in Guantánamo Bay, Cuba, has generated worldwide controversy and driven many European allies to question their cooperation with the United States because of the conditions of incarceration, the proposed military trials, and the threat of death.

The Bush administration chose not to criminalize Osama bin Laden and his al Qaeda network, preferring a largely military solution; thus it has been unable to develop a worldwide political and judicial campaign to shut down the terrorists. Many countries are reluctant to send terrorist suspects to the United States because of the secret military courts, lack of standard legal procedures, and danger of capital punishment, practices that are banned in much of the world. Moreover, the Bush doctrine, which maintains that "you are with us or against us" and constantly expands its "axis of evil," has positioned the United States as a strictly unilateral force carrying out its war against terror, thus undermining the development of a more global and multilateral campaign against terrorism. In particular, threatening war against Iraq alienated the United States from both its European and its moderate Arab allies, and the Bush administration's escalating threats against other countries are isolating the United States and making multilateral coalitions against terrorism extremely difficult.

There is also a sense that the United States is losing the struggle for the hearts and minds of Arabs and Muslims because of its bellicose nationalism, aggressive militarism, often uncritical support of Israel, and failure to improve relations with Muslim nations and peoples. The excessive bombing of civilians, the lack of a decent humanitarian program or plan to rebuild Afghanistan, and the unsuccessful propaganda efforts may have produced more enemies than friends in the Arab and Muslim world, increasing the likelihood of future terrorist Islamist cadres rising against the United States.[1]

This situation was especially aggravated as hostilities exploded between the Israelis and Palestinians in 2002. In much of the Arab world, the United States is seen as the major supporter of Israel, and the Bush administration's inability to mediate growing conflicts between the Israelis and the Palestinians, combined with its neglect of the problem during its first fifteen months, has helped create an explosive situation in the Middle East with no solution in sight. In addition, the Bush administration's failure to moderate the aggressive Israeli responses to suicide bombings and other terrorist acts against Israel in 2002 created more hatred of the United States in the Arab world and a growing tendency to perceive Israelis and Americans, Jews and Christians, as the main enemies of Islam.

Thus, the goals of bettering the American image in the eyes of the Arab, Islamic, and global worlds and improving relations between the United States and the Arab world have failed miserably. The incapacity to enhance U.S. and Western relations with Islam is largely the result of a botched military campaign, an inept ideological strategy, and a failure to engage in a fruitful dialogue with Arabs and Muslims. Thus, Bush administration policy is inhibiting the creation of coalitions for peace and the rebuilding of devastated parts of the Arab world such as Afghanistan. One of the goals of and justifications for the Afghanistan war was not only to eliminate al Qaeda terrorist forces but also to forge more creative relationships with Arab and Islamic countries, and this goal remains unrealized and unrealizable under the Bush administration's unilateralist policy.

A successful campaign would communicate the message that the United States respects the Islamic world, wants to carry out more productive activities with it, and desires dialogue, peace, and better relations. But this project has not succeeded, in part because of the violent and destructive military campaign, with the Bush administration and the Pentagon putting military priorities ahead of the reconstruction of Afghanistan. In addition, the propaganda efforts undertaken by the Bush administration have been extremely crude and have mostly backfired, losing more hearts and minds than were gained, as I will document here. Later historians of the Afghanistan war and its propaganda campaign will find Bush administration policy embarrassingly inept and unsuccessful, pointing to another serious deficiency in its handling of the war against terrorism.

From a strictly military standpoint, I would argue that major goals of the Afghanistan war were not achieved and that the deeply flawed campaign will be costly and consequential in its later effects. In particular, the Afghanistan campaign was only a partial success at best, because of the failure to capture or destroy key al Qaeda and Taliban leadership and cadres. This was largely due to a refusal to effectively use ground troops. The Afghanistan campaign, like the Gulf War, Kosovo war, and other U.S. military interventions in the past decade, relied largely on bombing at a distance and little use of U.S. ground troops, following the "zero casualty tolerance" policy of past years. The result was that in the decisive battles of Kandahar and Tora Bora, significant numbers of al Qaeda and Taliban forces escaped, including their leadership and perhaps Osama bin Laden himself.

What is needed, then, is an international and multilateral mission in Afghanistan and elsewhere that combines military, police, humanitarian, and reconstruction efforts. The United States has said that it will train an Afghani army but will not use U.S. forces for police or security duties. In fact, given the chaos in Afghanistan, it is unwise to separate military and police forces. A multilateral force of European Union countries, the United States, and Arab and other countries should train an Afghani military as they police and patrol the country, fight remnants of al Qaeda and the Taliban, and rebuild the country. The Bush administration policy, by contrast, has not adequately dealt with the humanitarian, security, or sociopolitical needs of the country, focusing primarily on military action against al Qaeda and Taliban forces.

The primarily military and unilateral strategy of the Bush administration's response to international terrorism is its major Achilles' heel. The unilateral U.S. policy has produced an excessive militarizing and inadequate criminalizing of terrorism, and Bush administration policies are isolating the United States from potential allies in a global campaign against terrorism. Moreover, such unilateral policies are likely to position the United States and its citizens as the targets of future terrorist attacks. Increasingly, Bush administration foreign policy is being resisted in much of the world, and it is encountering mounting hostility from allies and enemies alike. This is especially so since Bush's "axis of evil" speech and the intensification of the Israel–Palestine conflict, generated in part by the Bush administration's failure to mediate it.

By contrast, a multilateral campaign would make it clear that in the worldwide struggle against terror, the combined forces of civilization are allied against international terror networks. Such a campaign would rely on global forces on the political, judicial, economic, and military fronts, rather than privileging the militarist solution of war. Indeed, since December 2001, the Bush administration has expanded the front of its war against terrorism, sending U.S. troops to the Philippines, Pakistan, and a whole ring of central Asian countries, while threatening military action in Somalia, Indonesia, Yemen, and the infamous axis of evil: Iraq, Iran, and North Korea. The list was expanded in May 2002 to include Syria, Libya, and Cuba. George W. Bush has declared that an unrelenting war against terrorism is the major focus of his administration, and the Pentagon has discussed developing smaller nuclear weapons to be used against terrorist forces, as well as other high-tech weapons, ruthless bombing, and covert assassination.

In addition, the Bush administration manipulated the September 11 terror attacks to push through a hard-right domestic agenda that constitutes a clear and present danger to U.S. democracy. As governor of Texas, George W. Bush consistently performed favors for his largest contributors, such as the Enron Corporation and other oil and energy companies, and as president, he has done the same. Since September 11, the Bush administration has exploited the fear of terrorism to push through further bailouts of corporations that contributed to his campaign, and the center of its economic program has been to create tax breaks for the wealthy while cutting back on liberal social programs and environmental legislation and carrying out the most right-wing law-and-order domestic policy in U.S. history.

On the foreign policy front, the Bush administration used the September 11 tragedy to renounce arms treaties it had already opposed and thus jettisoned the idea of arms control on a worldwide scale. It also used the September 11 attacks to legitimate an increased military budget and a series of military interventions, to test and build new nuclear weapons, to threaten countries such as Iraq and Iran with military attacks, and to abandon multilateralism for a unilateralist "America First" approach to foreign affairs. In June 2002, the Bush administration proclaimed a dangerous "first-strike" policy, saying that henceforth it would engage in "preemptive strikes," abandoning the containment policy and diplomatic strategy for dealing with crises and adversaries in the post–World War II era.

Consequently, the Bush administration has claimed repeatedly that "World War III" has started and that the cold war has been succeeded by a dangerous and long-term period of "terror war." I use this term to describe the Bush administration's "war against terrorism" and its use of aggressive military force and terror as the privileged vehicles of constructing a U.S. hegemony in the current world (dis)order. The Bush administration has developed its war against Islamic terrorism into a policy of terror war by declaring its right to strike any enemy state or organization presumed to harbor or support terrorism or to eliminate "weapons of mass destruction" that could be used against the United States. The right-wing members of the Bush administration seek to promote this terror war as the defining struggle of the era, coded as an apocalyptic battle between good and evil. I will disclose the dangers of such policies and worldviews and depict how the Bush administration's terror war played out in the Afghanistan war and subsequent military adventures.

THE BUSH ADMINISTRATION'S FAILURE TO DETECT AND STOP THE SEPTEMBER 11 ATTACKS

The likely result of the Bush administration's terror war is that in a global world, the United States will become more isolated and will continue to be the major source of international anger and terror attacks. Not only is the Bush administration's foreign policy dangerous and reckless; the administration has also demonstrated stunning incompetence on the domestic front in the so-called war against terror and was highly negligent in allowing the United States to become vulnerable to the September 11 terrorist attacks in the first place. On May 15, 2002, a political uproar ensued when CBS News broadcast a report that the CIA had briefed George W. Bush on August 6, while he was vacationing at his ranch in Texas, about bin Laden's plans to hijack airplanes. There was immediately an explosion of controversy, raising questions publicly about what the Bush administration had known about possible terrorist attacks before September 11 and what it had done to prevent them. Also, during May 2002, a year-old FBI memo from the Phoenix, Arizona, office was released that warned of the dangers of Middle Eastern men going to flight school in order to gain the skills necessary to hijack planes, and of the dangers of the al Qaeda network carrying out such hijackings. Moreover, the arrest of Zacarias Moussaoui, the alleged twentieth al Qaeda hijacker, in Minnesota in late August 2001 should have raised warning flags. He too had been taking flying lessons and acting suspiciously.

Over the summer of 2001, there had been reports of a possible airplane terrorist attack on the G8 economic summit in Genoa that George W. Bush attended. There were purportedly so many intelligence reports of imminent terrorist attacks on the United States circulating that summer that Richard Clarke, the National Security Council's counterterrorism coordinator, warned the FBI, the Federal Aviation Administration (FAA), the Immigration and Naturalization Service (INS), and other crucial government agencies to be on highest alert and not to schedule vacations during a six-week period over the summer. John Ashcroft, U.S. attorney general, was ordered to take government jets instead of commercial airlines, and the FAA passed down several alerts to the commercial airlines.

It was also well known in political circles that in 1994 the French had foiled a terrorist airplane attack on the Eiffel Tower, and in 1995 terrorists were arrested who allegedly planned to use an airplane to attack CIA headquarters. Philippine police subsequently warned the United States that Ramzi Yousef, who had helped plan the 1993 WTC bombing, had schemes to hijack and blow up a dozen U.S. airliners and was contemplating taking over a plane and crashing it into CIA headquarters. Thus, in the light of all this information, it is scandalous that the Bush administration did not take stronger antiterrorist actions. Senate Intelligence Committee Vice-Chair Richard Shelby stated: "There was a lot of information . . . I believe, and others believe, that if it had been acted on properly, we may have had a different situation on September 11."

Furthermore, there had been a whole series of U.S. government reports on the dangers of terrorism and the need for a coordinated response. A 1996 report by the White House Commission on Aviation Safety and Security, headed by Al Gore, warned of the danger of airplane hijacking, but it was never acted on. A 1999 National Intelligence Council report on terrorism specifically warned that bin Laden's al Qaeda network might hijack planes and use them against U.S. targets; the report noted that members of the al Qaeda network had threatened to do this before and that the United States should be alert to such strikes. Perhaps most significantly, blue-ribbon commission reports by former U.S. senators Gary Hart and Howard Rudman, and by the Bremer National Commission, highlighted the dangers of a domestic terrorist attack against the United States and the need to develop appropriate protective measures. The Hart-Rudman report recommended consolidating U.S. intelligence on terrorism and organizing federal responses to prevent and fight domestic terrorist attacks.[2]

Hence, the Bush administration failed to act on warnings of imminent terrorist attacks. It failed to respond to the need to provide systematic government responses and to coordinate information in an attempt to prevent and aggressively fight terrorism. Moreover, it halted a series of attempts to stop the bin Laden network that had been undertaken by the Clinton administration. Just after the September 11 attacks, a wave of revelations came out, ignored completely in the U.S. media, concerning these failures of the administration.

An explosive book published in France in mid-November, *Bin Laden, la verite interdite* (2001), by Jean Charles Brisard and Guillaume Dasquie, claimed that under the influence of oil companies, the Bush administration initially blocked ongoing U.S. government investigations of terrorism, while it bargained with the Taliban over oil rights and pipeline deals and the handing over of bin Laden. This evidently led to the resignation of an FBI deputy director, John O'Neill, who was one of the sources of the story. Brisard and Dasquie contend that the Bush administration had been a major supporter of the Taliban until the September 11 events and had blocked investigations of the bin Laden terror network. Pursuing these leads, the British *Independent* reported on October 30: "Secret satellite phone calls between the State Department and Mullah Mohammed Omar and the presentation of an Afghan carpet to President George Bush were just part of the diplomatic contacts between Washington and the Taliban that continued until just days before the attacks of 11 September." Furthermore, Greg Palast published an FBI memo that confirms that the FBI had been given orders to lay off the bin Laden family during the early months of George W. Bush's rule.[3]

The U.S. media completely ignored these and other reports concerning the Bush administration's shutdown or undermining of operations against the bin Laden network initiated by the Clinton administration. An explosive article by Michael Hirsch and Michael Isikoff entitled "What Went Wrong," published in the May 28, 2002, issue of *Newsweek*, however, contained a series of revelations concerning how the Bush administration had missed signs of an impending attack and systematically weakened U.S. defenses against terrorism and the bin Laden network. According to the *Newsweek* story, Clinton's national security adviser, Sandy Berger, had become "'totally preoccupied' with fears of a domestic terror attack and tried to warn Bush's new national security adviser Condoleezza Rice of the dangers of a bin Laden attack." Although Rice ordered a security review, "the effort was marginalized and scarcely mentioned in ensuing months as the administration committed itself to other priorities, like National Missile Defense and Iraq."

Moreover, *Newsweek* reported that Ashcroft was eager to set a new right-wing law-and-order agenda and was not focused on the dangers of terrorism, while other high officials had their own ideological agendas to pursue at the expense of protecting the country against terror attacks. Ashcroft reportedly shut down wiretaps of al Qaeda suspects connected to the 1998 bombing of African embassies and cut $58 million from an FBI request for an increase in its antiterrorism budget. On September 10, Ashcroft sent a request for budget increases to the White House; it covered sixty-eight programs, none of them related to counterterrorism. Nor was counterterrorism in a memorandum he sent to his departments heads stating his seven priorities. According to *Newsweek*, in a meeting with FBI chief Louis Freeh, he rebuffed Freeh's warnings to take terrorism seriously and turned down an FBI request for hundreds of additional agents to be assigned to tracking terrorists.[4] In the *Newsweek* summary:

It wasn't that Ashcroft and others were unconcerned about these problems, or about terrorism. But the Bushies had an ideological agenda of their own. At the Treasury Department, Secretary Paul O'Neill's team wanted to roll back almost all forms of government intervention, including laws against money laundering and tax havens of the kind used by terror groups. At the Pentagon, Donald Rumsfeld wanted to revamp the military and push his pet project, NMD [National Missile Defense]. Rumsfeld vetoed a request to divert $800 million from missile defense into counterterrorism. The Pentagon chief also seemed uninterested in a tactic for observing bin Laden left over from the Clinton administration: the CIA's Predator surveillance plane. Upon leaving office, the Clintonites left open the possibility of sending the Predator back up armed with Hellfire missiles, which were tested in February 2001. But through the spring and summer of 2001, when valuable intelligence could have been gathered, the Bush administration never launched even an unarmed Predator. Hill sources say DOD [Department of Defense] didn't want the CIA treading on its turf.

A *Time* magazine cover story in late summer by Michael Elliot, "The Secret History" (August 4, 2002), provides more details concerning the Clinton administration's plan to attack al Qaeda in November 2000, when the election battle in Florida was raging. The Clinton administration was unable to implement the plan, however, because "with less than a month left in office, they did not think it appropriate to launch a major initiative against Osama bin Laden." Clinton administration officials claim that Condoleezza Rice was fully informed of this plan and that Sandy Berger stressed the need for a major initiative against bin Laden and al Qaeda, but nothing was done. Moreover, Richard Clarke, head of antiterrorist operations in the Clinton administration, stayed on for the Bush administration and urged implementation of the plan, which he had drawn up himself. Unfortunately, fighting terrorism was not a priority in the Bush administration, so the plan for attacks on al Qaeda went through the usual layers of bureaucracy, finally reaching Bush and his inner circle in early September, too late to prevent the September 11 attacks.

As these revelations unfolded in the summer of 2002, Democrats and others called for blue-ribbon commissions to study the intelligence and policy failures that had allowed the September 11 terrorist attacks to happen. Republicans, led by Vice President Dick Cheney, predictably attacked the patriotism of anyone who ascribed blame to the U.S. government concerning the September 11 attacks. Moreover, according to Democratic Senate majority leader Tom Daschle, Cheney repeatedly urged him not to hold hearings on U.S. policies or failures that led to the September 11 attacks. Bush administration spokespeople also attacked California senator Dianne Feinstein, who retorted in a memo:

> I was deeply concerned as to whether our house was in order to prevent a terrorist attack. My work on the Intelligence Committee and as chair of the Technology and Terrorism Subcommittee had given me a sense of foreboding for some time. I had no specific data leading to a possible attack.
>
> In fact, I was so concerned that I contacted Vice President Cheney's office that same month [July 2001] to urge that he restructure our counterterrorism and homeland defense programs to ensure better accountability and prevent important intelligence information from slipping through the cracks.
>
> Despite repeated efforts by myself and staff, the White House did not address my request. I followed this up last September 2001 before the attacks and was told by "Scooter" Libby that it might be another six months before he would be able to review the material. I told him I did not believe we had six months to wait.[5]

This is highly shocking and calls attention to the vice president's failure to produce an adequate response to the dangers of terrorism. A year earlier, in May 2001, the Bush administration announced that "Vice President Dick Cheney is point man for [the Bush] administration . . . on three major issues: energy, global warming, and domestic terrorism." On the May 19, 2002, episode of *Meet the Press*, Cheney acknowledged that he had been appointed head of a Bush administration task force on terrorism before September 11 and claimed that he had held some meetings on the topic. Yet Cheney and others in the Bush administration seemed to disregard several major reports that cited the danger of terrorist attacks, including the Hart-Rudman report, and failed to act on their recommendations. Obviously, Cheney concentrated on energy issues to the exclusion of terrorism and should be held partly responsible for the Bush administration's ignoring of pre–September 11 terrorist threats.[6]

Crucially, plans to use airplanes as vehicles of terrorist attack should have been familiar to the intelligence agencies and to Cheney and the Bush administration. Furthermore, there were many other reports circulating from foreign and domestic intelligence services provided just before the September 11 attacks that the United States had reason to fear terrorist attacks from the bin Laden network.[7] Thus, there should have been attempts to coordinate intelligence among the various agencies, warnings to the airlines regarding potential hijackings, and security alerts to the public to be on the lookout for potential terrorist activities.

Consequently, serious questions should be asked of the Bush administration and of the head of its antiterrorism task force, Dick Cheney, concerning what they knew and did not know, and what they did and did not do in response to reports from domestic and foreign intelligence agencies concerning the likelihood of al Qaeda airplane hijackings and terrorist attacks on the United States. As head of the task force on terrorism, Cheney should be held especially accountable, but so far, the media and Democrats have not raised this issue, and Cheney aggressively attacks anyone who raises such issues as an unpatriotic enemy of the state. Obviously, there was no coordination of information on terrorist threats, and it is disgraceful that Cheney did not establish a group to centralize information, focus on the dangers of terrorism, and do more to prevent the September 11 attacks.

It therefore appears, as I write in summer 2002, that top officials of the Bush administration did little or nothing to protect the United States against domestic terror attacks. When confronted with reports that he had been advised of impending terror attacks and had not acted, Bush became highly indignant, attacking his critics for "second-guessing" and engaging in partisan politics. He shrilly retorted that if he had known exactly what was going to happen, he would have prevented it. This was not the issue, of course; rather, it was the failure of the Bush administration to take seriously the threat of terrorism and to develop an antiterror policy. In fact, Bush was on an unusually long one-month summer vacation at his ranch in Crawford, Texas, when he was briefed on the dangers of looming al Qaeda attacks, and no one could expect the highly unqualified president to "connect the dots" and see the need to organize the country against domestic terrorist attacks.

The media are also to blame for not focusing more intently on terrorism over the previous decade. During the 1980s, terrorism emerged as a major problem, and there were frequently news reports, specials, documentaries, and media discussions of the problem. Yet in the 1990s, the corporate media became increasingly "tabloidized," focusing on the O. J. Simpson trial, the Clinton sex scandal, and other obsessions of the moment. As noted earlier, major reports on the dangers of terrorism were released without media scrutiny. The Hart-Rudman "Road Map for National Security: Imperative for Change," warning of the danger of a terrorist attack on the United States, was released in January 2001 and was ignored by much of the mainstream media, as well as the Bush administration.[8] Instead, there was an obsessive focus on tabloid stories such as the disappearance of intern Chandra Levy and her affair with Congressman Bill Condit.

Not surprisingly, many elaborate conspiracy theories emerged alleging U.S. government complicity in the September 11 attacks. There were many strange and unexplained elements of the attacks on the WTC and the Pentagon, and the Bush administration and military establishment were the main beneficiaries of the terror attacks. Additionally, the Bush family's shocking history of engaging in daring conspiracies may have contributed to the widespread allegations of

U.S. government involvement. There are, in fact, three major possibilities to explain the Bush administration's responsibility or complicity in the September 11 attacks: (1) the Bush administration was completely incompetent and too focused on pushing through its right-wing agenda to detect the obvious signs of an impending al Qaeda terror attack outlined earlier; (2) the Bush administration knew that the attacks were coming but welcomed them as a chance to push through its stalled right-wing, militarist agenda; or (3) the Bush administration, or rogue sectors of the U.S. government, were actively involved in the conspiracy.[9] As of now, it is impossible to confidently affirm the precise responsibility of the Bush administration, but obviously, this is a matter of grave concern and should be thoroughly investigated.

The Bush administration's surprise call on June 6, 2002, for a new cabinet-level homeland defense agency was seen by critics as an attempt to deflect attention from investigations of its intelligence failures. There were widespread fears that such an agency would increase bureaucracy and even provide the apparatus for a Gestapo-type police state. Indeed, the USA Patriot Act, pushed through by the Bush administration following September 11, was already erecting the powerful trappings of a police state. It allowed the government to eavesdrop on all electronic and wireless communication, to arrest individuals without specific charges and hold them indefinitely, to monitor conversations between lawyers and clients, and to carry out secret military trials of suspected terrorists.

Moreover, the Bush administration's assault on civil liberties has weakened constitutional democracy and the rule of law in the United States. On August 15, 2002, Human Rights Watch released a report that claimed, "The U.S. government's investigation of the September 11 attacks has been marred by arbitrary detentions, due process violations, and secret arrests." Human Rights Watch discovered that more than 1,200 noncitizens were secretly arrested and incarcerated and that "the U.S. government has held some detainees for prolonged periods without charges; impeded their access to counsel; subjected them to coercive interrogations; and overridden judicial orders to release them on bond during immigration proceedings. In some cases, the government has incarcerated detainees for months under restrictive conditions, including solitary confinement. Some detainees were physically and verbally abused because of their national origin or religion. The vast majority are from Middle Eastern, South Asian, and North African countries." The report describes cases in which random encounters with law enforcement or neighbors' suspicions based on nothing more than national origin and religion led to interrogation about possible links to terrorism.[10] Besides dangerously undermining the U.S. constitutional order, the Bush administration's economic policies have produced almost unparalleled economic crisis, scandal, and corruption.

THE BUSH REICH

The consequences of the Bush administration's failed terror war policies and domestic policy outrages are frightening. The Bush Reich seems to be erecting an Orwellian totalitarian state apparatus and plunging the world into ongoing war that could generate military and police states domestically and abroad. In his prophetic novel *1984*, George Orwell depicts a grim condition of total warfare in which his fictional state Oceania rules its fearful and intimidated citizens through war, police state terror, surveillance, and the suppression of civil liberties. This constant warfare keeps Oceania's citizens in a perpetual situation of mobilization and submission. Further, the Orwellian state controls language, thought, and behavior through domination of the media and is thereby able to change the very meaning of language ("war is peace") and to constantly rewrite history itself.[11]

Orwell's futuristic novel was, of course, an attack on the Soviet Union and has been a favorite of conservatives over the years, but it uncannily describes the horrors and dangers of the regime of George W. Bush. Orwell's totalitarian state had a two-way television screen that monitored citizens' behavior and a system of spies and informers that would report on politically incorrect thought and activity. Bush's police state has its USA Patriot Act, which enables the state to monitor communications via e-mail, wireless, telephone, and other media and allows the state to arrest citizens without warrants, hold them indefinitely, monitor their conversations, and submit them to military tribunals, all of which is governed by the dictates of the Supreme Leader (in this case, a dangerously demagogic figurehead ruled by right-wing extremists).

The Bush administration also has its Terrorist Information and Prevention System (TIPS), which would turn citizens into spies who report suspicious activities to the government. Truck drivers, mail carriers, meter readers, and others would be recruited to "report what they see in public areas and along transportation routes," thus turning workers into informants. In addition, Ashcroft has proposed concentration camps for citizens that he considers "enemy combatants."[12]

With its Orwellian-sounding Office of Homeland Security, proposed Office of Strategic Information, shadow government, and Patriot Act, the Bush administration has in place the institutions and apparatus of a totalitarian government. Since the election in 2000, the Bush clique has practiced a form of Orwellian "Bushspeak" that endlessly repeats the big lie of the moment. Bush and his propaganda ministry engage in daily propagandistic spin to push its policies and to slime their opponents, while showing no regard whatsoever for the canons of truth and justice that conservatives have traditionally defended.[13]

To keep the public in a state of fear, Bush and his administration have repeatedly evoked the specter of renewed terrorist attacks and promised an all-out war against an "axis of evil." This threatening axis, to be defined periodically by the Bush administration, allegedly possesses "instruments of mass destruction" that could be used against the United States. Almost without exception, the mainstream media have been a propaganda conduit for the Bush administration's terror war and have helped generate fear and even mass hysteria. The mainstream corporate media have thus largely failed to advance an understanding of the serious threats to the U.S. and global economy and polity, and have failed to debate the range of possible responses to terrorism and their respective merits and consequences.

The Bush administration's terror war raises the specter that Orwell's *1984* might provide the template for the new millennium, as the world is plunged into endless war, as democracy is snuffed out in the name of freedom, as language loses meaning, and as history is constantly revised (just as Bush and his scribes constantly rewrote his own personal history). There is thus the danger that Orwell's dark, grim dystopia may replace the (ideological) utopia of the "information society," the "new economy," and a prosperous and democratic globalization that had been the dominant ideology and vision of the past decade. Questions arise: Will the Bush administration's terror war lead the world to ruin through constant warfare and the erection of totalitarian police states over the façade of fragile democracy? Or can we find more multilateral and global solutions to terrorism that will strengthen democracy and increase the chances for peace and security?

There is indeed a danger that the terror war will be a force of historical regression and the motor of destruction of the global economy, liberal polity, and democracy itself, all to be replaced by an aggressive militarism and totalitarian police state. It could be that Orwell is the prophet of a coming "new barbarism" with endless war, state repression, and enforced control of thought and discourse, and that George W. Bush and his minions are the architects of an Orwellian future.

It could also be the case, however, that the Taliban, bin Laden, al Qaeda, and the Bush administration represent obsolete and reactionary forces that will be swept away by the inexorable forces of globalization and liberal democracy. The opposing sides in the current terror war could be perceived as representing complementary poles of an atavistic and premodern version of Islam and nihilistic terrorism confronted by reactionary right-wing conservatism and militarism.[14] In this scenario, both poles can be perceived as disruptive and regressive forces that need to be overcome to create genuine historical progress. If this is the case, the terror war would be a momentary interlude in which two obsolete historical forces battle it out, ultimately to be replaced by more sane and democratic globalizing forces.

This is, of course, an optimistic scenario. For the foreseeable future, progressive forces will probably be locked in intense battles against the opposing forces of Islamic terrorism and right-wing militarism. Yet if democracy and the human species are to survive, global movements against militarism and in favor of social justice, ecology, and peace must emerge to combat and replace the atavistic forces of the present. As the new millennium unfolds, the human race has regressed into a new barbarism that was unforeseeable prior to September 11. If civilization is to survive, individuals must perceive their enemies and organize to fight for a better future.

Consequently, I argue that Bush administration militarism is not the way to fight international terrorism; rather, it is the road to an Orwellian future in which democracy and freedom will be in dire peril and the future of the human species will be in question. These are frightening times, and it is essential that all citizens become informed about the fateful conflicts of the present, gain a clear understanding of what is at stake, and realize that they must oppose both international terrorism and Bushian militarism and an Orwellian police state.

CONCLUSION

September 11, the subsequent terror war, the Enron scandals, and other Bush- or Cheney-related corporate scandals that have emerged during the ongoing misadventures of the Bush administration constitute what I am calling the new barbarism. It was scandalous that civilized countries tolerated the Taliban and allowed bin Laden's al Qaeda network to develop, and the Bush terror war unleashed new forces of barbarism now evident in Afghanistan, the Middle East, and elsewhere. The term *new barbarism* denotes a frightening historical regression in an era of highly uncivilized and violent behavior. One would hope that the new millennium would signal a chance for progress and historical optimism, but instead, the human species is moving into a situation in which the universal values of the Enlightenment, the institutions of democracy, the global economy, and the earth and human species itself are faced with challenges to their survival.

As a response to the September 11 terror attacks, the Bush administration intensified its militarism, which threatens to generate an era of terror war, a new arms race, accelerated military violence, U.S. support of authoritarian regimes, an assault on human rights, constant threats to democracy, and destabilization of the world economy. The new barbarism also describes Bush administration practices of providing political favors to its largest corporate and other supporters, unleashing unrestrained Wild West capitalism (exemplified by the Enron scandals), and a form of capitalist cronyism whereby Bush administration family and friends are provided with government favors while social welfare programs, environmental legislation, and protections of rights and freedoms are curtailed.

The corporate media, especially television, are part and parcel of the new barbarism, spewing almost unopposed propaganda for the Bush administration, fanning war fever and terrorist hysteria, while cutting back on vigorous political debate and varied sources of information as it produces waves of ideologically conservative talk shows and mindless entertainment. I have been closely tracking the media and the crisis of democracy for over a decade now, and the current crisis marks the low point of U.S. media performance. The U.S. corporate media at first fanned the flames of war and hysteria and then became a conduit for Bush administration and Pentagon propaganda rather than a forum for reasoned debate, serious discussion, exposure of Bush administration failures, and the exploration of saner alternatives.

In view of the enormity of the events of September 11 and their frightening aftermath and consequences, it is now appropriate to reflect on what happened, why it happened, and what lessons we have learned as we seek to apply such insights to the crisis we now find ourselves in. It is a time for intelligence, not knee-jerk reaction; a time for thought, not hysteria. It is a time for reflection, for figuring out what went wrong, and for informed and intelligent action that will get at the source of our problems. It is also a time for taking stock, for examining individually and collectively our views of the world and our everyday behavior. A situation of crisis provides an opportunity for positive change and reconstruction, as well as barbaric regression. Thus, now is the time for reflection on such things as democracy, globalization, and the flaws, limitations, and fallacies in our individual thoughts and actions, as well as problems with U.S. institutions and leadership.

Momentous historical events, like the September 11, 2001, terrorist attacks and the subsequent terror war, test social theories and challenge our ability to provide a convincing account of the events and their consequences. They also give cultural studies an opportunity to trace how political and ideological discourse, propaganda, and mythology play out in media discourse and representation. Major historical events and media spectacles also provide an opportunity to examine how the broadcast media and other dominant modes of communication perform or fail to perform their democratic role of providing accurate information and discussion.

Quite possibly we will never know exactly what happened in the Afghanistan war. In 1992, I published one of the first books on the Gulf War, largely based on Internet sources, the newspapers of record, press conference transcripts, and other government material available on the Internet. I perused subsequent memoirs of military participants in the war, journalists providing first-person accounts, and other studies, but a definitive history of the Gulf War has not yet emerged. We still do not know all the shadowy details about the relationship between George H. W. Bush and Saddam Hussein, why Iraq invaded Kuwait, what knowledge the United States had or did not have of Iraqi plans, how the United States orchestrated the Gulf War, or what actually happened. Yet it is always possible to expose the fallacies and holes in official accounts, to uncover lies and disinformation, and to contextualize and interpret major historical events such as the Gulf War, the September 11 attacks, and the Afghanistan war.

I would argue that a combination of critical social theory and cultural studies can help illuminate the September 2001 events, their causes, effects, and importance in shaping the contemporary moment. Certainly, the spectacle of September 11 is one of the major media and political events of our time, and interpreting the affair and its aftermath provides crucial insight into the dynamics and conflicts of the present era. The subsequent terror war appears to be the major ongoing spectacle of the new millennium, and the Bush administration is using it to promote its agenda and to build up the U.S. military as a hegemonic force, creating the "new world order" that the elder Bush had wanted to create at the end of the Gulf War. As envisaged by the second Bush administration, the terror war is projected as the defining feature of the new millennium for the foreseeable future.

NOTES

1. Although the Bush administration propaganda war was immensely successful at home—85 to 90 percent of those polled supported the Afghanistan war—a number of polls done in the Arab and Muslim world revealed a striking lack of support for U.S. policies, and the majority polled did not even believe that Osama bin Laden and his al Qaeda network were responsible for the September 11 attacks. However one explains this, it is clear that the Bush administration failed miserably in its efforts to communicate and improve relations with Arabs and Muslims. For a variety of polls on Arab attitudes toward the United States pre- and post–September 11, see http://www.zogby.com/main.cfm. For the 2002 Gallup poll on the Islamic world, see http://www.gallup.com/poll/summits/islam.asp. For a Pew poll that cites growing European criticism of and distance from Bush administration policies, see the report "Americans and Europeans Differ Widely on Foreign Policy Issues," which concludes: "The survey revealed considerable European support for taking a more independent course in security and diplomatic affairs. Majorities in France, Germany and Italy think Western

Europe's partnership with the United States should not be as close as it has been in the past. People in Great Britain are divided on the question. European support for a more independent approach is not especially linked to negative reactions to recent U.S. policies, such as the steel tariffs. Rather, it is more associated with general criticism of President Bush, the feeling that the United States has ignored allied interests in conducting the war on terrorism, and general disapproval of U.S. policies in the Middle East" (http://peoplepress.org/reports/display.php3?ReportID=153).

2. For the Gore report, see http://www.fas.org/irp/threat/212fin~1.html; for the Hart-Rudman report, see http://www.nssg.gov/News/news.htm; and for the Bremer National Commission on Terrorism report, see http://w3.access.gpo.gov/nct. See also "1999 Report Warned of Suicide Hijack," Associated Press, May 17, 2001.

3. See Greg Palast, "FBI and U.S. Spy Agents Say Bush Spiked bin Laden Probes before September 11," *Guardian*, November 7, 2001. Palast's article is available on his home page, which has a lot of other interesting reports on Bush administration activities; see http://www.gregpalast.com. See also "U.S. Agents Told: Back off bin Ladens," at http://old.smh.com.au/news/0111/07/world/world100.html.

4. In "Ashcroft Knew" (*Salon*, May 23, 2002), Bruce Shapiro names Ashcroft "the official responsible for the most dramatic failures of September 11." Ashcroft indeed emerges as one of the primary villains because of his stunning incompetence and failure to address the dangers of terrorism due to his fanatic obsession with pushing through a right-wing law-and-order agenda. Ashcroft also carried out the most systematic assault on civil liberties in U.S. history and represents a clear and present danger to constitutional democracy. Yet in my reading, it is the collective responsibility of the Bush administration, which failed to heed warnings of imminent terrorist attacks and systematically carried out policies that made such attacks more likely.

5. The Feinstein memo can be found at http://www.senate.gov/~feinstein/Releases02/attacks.htm.

6. See CBS News, "New Terror Task Force: Cheney to Lead at Terrorist Threats to U.S.," May 8, 2001. A June 30, 2001, CNN report was headlined, "Cheney is point man for administration," noting that Cheney would be in charge of task forces on three major issues: energy, global warming, and domestic terrorism. On May 11, 2001, the Web site http://www.disasterrelief.org also posted a report that stated, "Bush asked Vice President Dick Cheney to lead the task force, which will explore how attacks against U.S. citizens or personnel at home and overseas may be detected and stopped." To prevent future terrorist attacks on the United States, it would thus be very important to see exactly what Cheney did or did not do and address the problems revealed.

7. The *Frankfurter Allgemeine Zeitung* reported on September 14, 2001, that German intelligence sources had gathered warnings from the Echelon spy system that Middle Eastern terrorists were "planning to hijack commercial aircraft to use as weapons to attack important symbols of American and Israeli culture" and had passed the warnings on to the U.S. government. On Israeli intelligence warning the United States of terrorist networks sneaking into the country, see "Officials Told of 'Major Assault' Plans," *Los Angeles Times*, September 20, 2001. Carolyn Kay assembled scores of material from Russian, Israeli, German, U.S., and other

intelligence sources warning that a major domestic terrorist attack was about to unfold against the United States, but Cheney, the rest of the Bush administration, and the national security apparatus failed to respond or prepare for the impending attacks; see http://makethemaccountable.com/whatwhen/index.html. See also Russ Kirk, "September 11, 2001: No Surprise," for an analysis of myriad sources signaling the September 11 attacks (http://www.loompanics.com/Articles/September11.html).

8. See Harold Evans, "What We Knew: Warning Given . . . Story Missed: How a Report on Terrorism Flew under the Radar," *Columbia Journalism Review* (November–December 2001). Evans points out that the Bush administration blocked planned congressional hearings on the Hart-Rudman report in May 2001, instead "forming its own committee, headed by Dick Cheney, who was expected to report in October." Even former Republican House majority leader and conservative ideologue Newt Gingrich concedes, "The [Bush] administration actually slowed down response to Hart-Rudman when momentum was building in the spring."

9. For accounts of Bush family conspiracies, see Douglas Kellner, *Television and the Crisis of Democracy* (Boulder, Colo.: Westview Press, 1990), *The Persian Gulf TV War* (Boulder, Colo.: Westview Press, 1992), and *Grand Theft 2000* (Lanham, Md.: Rowman and Littlefield, 2001). Major conspiracy Web sites for September 11 include Michael Rupert's http://www.fromthewilderness.com, the Emperor's Clothes site at http://www.tenc.net, and the compendium of conspiracy theories collected at the Global Research site at http://www.globalresearch.ca. The best-selling French conspiracy book by Thierry Meyssan was reportedly being translated into English as *9/11, the Big Lie*.

10. See Human Rights Watch, "Presumption of Guilt: Human Rights Abuses of Post–September 11 Detainees," at http://www.hrw.org/press/2002/08/usdetainess081502.htm.

11. For a discussion of Orwell's novel, see Kellner, *Television and the Crisis of Democracy*; in the light of the Bush administration's projected terror war, however, it could well be Orwell—rather than Huxley and Marcuse, as I argue in that article—who provides the most prescient templates of the future.

12. See Jonathan Turley, "Camps for Citizens: Ashcroft's Hellish Vision," *Los Angeles Times*, August 14, 2002. John Ashcroft, who would serve Bush as U.S. attorney general, received the 1984 award for "Worst Government Official" by Privacy International. In 2002, the watchdog group said that the top U.S. law enforcement officer "is responsible for a massive increase in wiretapping of phones and other electronics and for the imprisonment without charge of as many as 1,200 people in the United States after the Sept. 11 attacks on America" (see Reuters, April 19, 2002).

13. See Kellner, *Grand Theft 2000*, for documentation and a systematic critique of Bushspeak.

14. Tariq Ali captures this dialectic in his book *The Clash of Fundamentalisms* (2002), whose cover pictures George W. Bush shading into the visage of Osama bin Laden, two fundamentalists whose families have long been linked to shady business practices and who personally represent the competing fundamentalisms of the ongoing terror war.

Europe as a Political Project

Dick Howard

In the 1980s, with several friends, I helped produce a program called "Europe-in-Formation" at the New York left-wing public radio station WBAI. This was a time well before the ultimate internal weakness of the Soviet Union became apparent and when a true or good or purified socialism remained a hope for many leftists. Our idea was that the model of a European Union, enlarging the welfare state and challenging the realpolitik cynicism of a U.S. government that supported repressive regimes in the name of fighting the communist enemy, would encourage political criticism that was still leftist even though it contained a dose of realism. The process by which Europe was coming into being was to serve as an inspiration for the creation of a Left that was at once democratic and social.

Two decades later, the question of Europe remains relevant, but the challenge it poses is different. Whereas the Left had been the stubborn victim of its own ideological dreams or hopes, today, after the end of the cold war and with the victory of liberalism and capitalism, there is no serious left-wing political project. In the earlier moment, the Left was full of ideas, inventing Projects (with a capital P) and knitting together the undeniably important but always partial and often temporary successes into a global vision. Today, the Left has few ideas; its politics consists in opposing the most egregious elements of the economic free-marketeers and the attempts by social reactionaries to roll back the achievements of modernity.

The European idea has gained some attractiveness as, even in the countries that Secretary of Defense Rumsfeld refers to as the "new" Europe, healthy majorities have appeared to oppose the preemptive unilateralism of U.S. foreign policy. In contrast, the "old" Europe has been denounced—not without some grounds—as the weak-kneed "Venus" whose well-being depends on the military strength of the American "Mars." What is more, in at least some countries (such as France), large minorities within the orbit of the Socialist Party seriously considered the idea of rejecting the ratification of an eventual European constitution if it were put to vote in a referendum. To them, Europe seemed to be the vehicle of an expanded capitalism, its advances in the sphere of human rights standing only as a concession to liberalism. Europe, from this perspective, is said to suffer from a "democratic deficit"—although it is often unclear just what is meant by this vague concept.

To get some perspective on the status and implications of the European model today, I propose to return to the old distinction between two kinds of liberalism and the two models of democratic politics with which they are associated. The roots of this distinction are both historical and conceptual, while its manifestations can be seen in the contemporary political cultures of the Europeans and the Americans.

One appealing approach to the Euro/American cultural distinction is suggested by Pierre Hassner, who traces the difference back to the geopolitical fact that Europe is composed of nations defined by their borders, which entails the need to form alliances and maintain a balance of power, whereas America can choose isolation and decide when to use force or opt to employ the peaceful arms of commerce. As a result, Europe has learned to recognize the usefulness of rules that bind sovereignty, while ensuring that war is limited to those who are actually fighting, whereas the United States refuses to accept limits on its sovereign will and, when it does go to war, accepts no constraints (such as worry about "collateral damage"). Old Europe calls the agreed-on rules "civilization," while virile young America treats them as limits and denounces them as a sign of weakness of will.[1] This difference is manifest, for example, in the different attitudes toward the creation of the International Court of Justice.

But Hassner recognizes that the European solution is threatened. Its civilized rules were based on a Westphalian notion of a sovereign national will (and the material reality of states that could protect their citizens as well as their economies); that vision may be simply a dream in a globalized and "postmodern" society that cuts across national boundaries and transforms the citizen into a mere consumer. This could explain some of the complaints about a "democratic deficit" in the EU. But that is too simple. The institutional question depends on cultural premises. To denounce the incompleteness of democracy is a facile ploy, as nationalists and communists know only too well. By its very nature, democracy is never, and can never be, a true or fully realized political form; to think otherwise is to dream of an end to history. That is why it is better to take some distance on the problem of Europe and its democratic deficit, appealing to those vague but (perhaps for that reason) fruitful notions of culture and history.

The contrast between European and American political culture dates from the French and American revolutions. The Americans had to free themselves from the control of the British Empire. Their new institutions sought to preserve an independent society in which material inequality coexisted with the absence of status hierarchies. That latter absence (rather than the material inequalities) explains Americans' antistatist liberalism in which the (prepolitical) rights of the individual elevate pragmatic self-interest over collective goals.[2] It also explains the oft-remarked absence of social solidarity in a brutally competitive society whose liberalism, in principle, protects the rights of the individual.

In France, in contrast, monarchical power had created national unity out of feudal diversities, but at the same time, it had consecrated a hierarchical society of orders. As a result, it was necessary to seize and then to use state power to institute a society based on (at least the principle of) equal rights for all. The liberalism that resulted appealed to rights that, although they were said to be "natural," could be made effective only by state intervention. Individualism (which Tocqueville saw as the new threat arising in American democracy) is a threat to rule-based and self-limiting civilization created by European states; its concern with private interest is an antipolitical threat to the kind of solidarity needed in a competitive (and anomic) society based on rights that protect individual from the power of the collective. We cannot expect that the associative democracy that Tocqueville hoped would provide a corrective in this regard will be reproduced in the new Europe of the twenty-five. But is there, as another Frenchman would ask a generation later, a functional equivalent?

As Emile Durkheim recognized, forms of solidarity are cultural products whose consequences are neither immediate nor simple. One might ask why the European[3] political culture that emerged from its particular path to liberalism and democracy produced the (nonidentical) twins of socialism and nationalism, which were never able to gain more than a temporary foothold in the United States. The answer depends on cultural expectations. The attempt to institute rights by means of state action cannot stop with the achievement of merely formal equality; the notions of equality and of rights drive each other forward in the (utopian) quest to realize what I call a *democratic republic.* This project seeks to add democratic social policies to the formal framework of the political republic. Its goal is to free social relations from the stain of particularity or hierarchy; unity would replace difference as the alienation of political life is overcome and society becomes fully rational. The problem, however, is that this complete realization of equality and of rights can conflict with the basic liberal right to have rights—which is particular, differential, and individual(ist). For this reason, rights-based liberalism may seem to be the enemy of social solidarity.

A different institutional history produced an American political culture oriented toward *republican democracy.* The distinction is not simply rhetorical. When they freed themselves from Britain, the Americans tried to ensure that their democratic self-rule would not be infringed on by the political state (whose existence, said Paine, is a sign of human sinfulness). But they soon learned the necessary limits that sin imposes on pride; more concretely, they recognized that self-governing society needs to adopt political forms in order to conserve its own autonomy. Their national confederation was too weak to attract the ambitious, who instead made a mess of local politics (particularly in Pennsylvania). A new national constitution was produced and ratified by specially elected conventions. An illustration of the way this republican document not only conserved but also encouraged democracy can be found in the justification of the Senate (in *The Federalist* 63). Although a senate is supposed to represent the aristocratic order, no aristocracy existed in egalitarian America. What, then, does the Senate represent? It represents the people, as do (*The Federalist* insists significantly) all the institutions of a republican democracy. And that means, in turn, that no institution can claim to incarnate fully the sovereign people. Yet that is just what the democratic republic seeks to do.[4]

This distinction suggests why Europe could become the showplace of both nationalist and socialist ideologies. (America, of course, is not exempt from these temptations, particularly in moments when the nation itself feels threatened.) The European model of a democratic republic that seeks to overcome the separation between the society and its political representative illustrates what I call a *politics of will*. The will must be one and harmonious; a divided will is incapable of willing. Socialism, on the one hand, and nationalism, on the other, attempt—each in its own way, of course—to overcome division, to create unity and homogeneity while absorbing (or eliminating) particularity and difference. This tendency to think of politics as depending on the will, whose unity must be achieved and conserved, reached its extreme form in the twin totalitarianisms that disgraced the twentieth century.

The reference to totalitarianism brings us toward our own time. After 1945, nationalism was so discredited that even the all-dominant United States recognized the need for a multilateral world. But the outbreak of the cold war, exacerbated by the socialist dream of real democracy as incarnated in a democratic republic that remained alive in western Europe, suggested to many Europeans the need to find a third way. Fearful of renewed nationalism, but needing to keep their domestic working class satisfied, they took steps toward common economic politics that culminated in the 1956 Treaty of Rome. But the political implications of what was first called simply the Common Market became apparent when it was challenged by Britain's creation of a rival, purely economic association called the European Free Trade Association (EFTA). That reduction of the political to market relations (like the critique of the Rome treaty for consecrating the injustices of international capital) could be said to represent another variant of the politics of will, but based this time on the assumption that the invisible hand of the market would transform competitive individual action into a rational and unified society. Just as the democratic republic reduces politics to social relations, this time, politics is reduced to economic relations. The denial of the autonomy of the political sphere was based on the vision of a society (or economy) wholly transparent to itself. The failure of the British alternative meant that the EU would have to learn to articulate the political essence of its own culture. The third way could not just mediate between two kinds of economic society.

While the cold war continued, the European project could advance only slowly. But the turning point came before the end of the Soviet empire. The antitotalitarian politics that emerged in the wake of the Helsinki Accords[5] made it clear that human rights are not granted by the state; nor are they the private rights stereotypically identified with American liberal individualism. The politics of human rights went together with the idea of an autonomous civil society. But this new vision was still open to the temptation of a politics of will that sought to overcome the separation of state and society in the unity of civil society. (This may explain the attraction of movements such as Solidarnosc or Chater 77 to some of the normally "anti-anti-communist" Western Left, who could see here the *mise en oeuvre* of their own goal of self-managed socialism.) The imposition of a state of siege in Poland should have clarified the need for some kind of political state to protect the rights of the individual, without which civil society cannot maintain itself. But what kind of state? It is at this point that "Europe" begins its contemporary career. The notion of a "third way" is no longer conceived in economic terms; it now has to be conceived politically.

With the unification of Germany and the May 2004 integration of states formerly belonging to the Soviet bloc, what could become of the European political project? The first task is negative: to avoid the missteps of the various forms of what I call a politics of will. It is clear that the enlarged EU cannot be expected to realize the socialist (or the nationalist) project; nor can it restrict itself to simply economic homogenization. It is also clear that it has to face up to the denunciation of a "democratic deficit." But this issue is less institutional than it is cultural; the proposed European constitution cannot solve the problem on its own. Europe has to create a paradoxical kind of unity, one that is more solid because it is plural. Solidarity is the key concept; and it is not based on identity or on the exclusion of difference. This is where the European project can come to a better self-understanding by comparison with the American attempt to maintain a liberal political culture by creating a republican democracy.

A return to the historical roots of America's republican democratic culture illustrates the difficulty of overcoming the unitary temptations of a politics of will. Twelve years after the ratification of the new constitution, Thomas Jefferson was elected president in what contemporaries called the "revolution of 1800." The term is surprising, and it has fallen out of use by historians.[6] Since

Jefferson's support for the French Revolution was well known, it led to the belief that he would bring social change, a kind of American version of 1793. What was in fact revolutionary was not the social content of Jefferson's politics but rather the political fact that power passed peacefully from one political party to another. This had never happened before; it was made possible by the unique political culture that was described at the outset of this argument: the people (in their plurality and difference) are represented in all the institutions of the republic, which means, therefore, that they are incarnated in none. But Jefferson's republicans themselves did not understand this republican democracy, as they showed shortly thereafter when they refused to confirm the ("midnight") appointment of a federal magistrate by the outgoing government. They were, after all, the democratically elected majority and, they assumed, represented the actual will of the people; they were not bound by the action of the previous majority. In 1803, in *Marbury v. Madison*, the Supreme Court issued the decision that was the foundation of its own independent power—a power that, like all powers in the United States, is based on the Constitution rather than on the will of any temporary majority.

These two institutional innovations were made possible by the culture of a republican democracy. The foundation of that political culture can be understood by its contrast to the forms of politics of will. It rests on what can be called a *politics of judgment* that begins from the plurality of rights-bearing individuals in order to make possible a kind of solidarity that need not claim to incarnate the unitary will of a homogeneous nation. Leaving aside the philosophical foundations of this concept, its institutional form can be described in general terms by a closer look at the American constitutional practice of republican democracy. At issue is the relation between the particularity and plurality of socioeconomic relations and the juridical-political framework that unifies society. On the one hand, political parties articulate particular problems that emerge within civil society and aggregate them in the form of a proposed law. The temptation for the parties is to reach for the lowest common denominator and to avoid issues that concern only minorities, with the result that the laws may prove inadequate to protect the rights of this or that group or individual. At this point, the court enters the picture, providing a republican check to ensure that the temporary legislative or executive majority cannot claim to incarnate once and for all the vox populi. This interaction of particular and universal can be repeated in the other direction. There will be times when political debate is blocked, when issues appear too hot to handle; at this point, the court intervenes, this time to make certain that the particular is not blocked from debate. Now it becomes the task of the parties to find a way to deal with the issue at the level of the everyday political life of the citizenry (rather than at the constitutional level).[7]

Two conclusions and a caveat follow from this comparative account. The caveat is most important. It insists that the cultural politics of judgment is not attained once and for all; a fallback to the politics of will is always possible. One cannot expect to introduce (or impose) the American institutional structure in foreign contexts, as if their own political culture and history do not matter. What one can learn from the American experience is what kind of political culture would satisfy the structural imperatives of a politics of judgment. This permits a negative conclusion. The hope that Europe will become that third way formerly identified with the economic policies of social democracy will not be realized. As indicated at the outset, the problem for a liberal political culture is not to add social and material predicates to the formal rights of the individual; the problem, rather, is to imagine and understand the new forms of solidarity that—paradoxically, in the eyes of some—are based on the individual right to have rights. Europeans need to look at their achievements since the 1956 Rome treaty with an eye toward finding the functional equivalent of the American politics of judgment. Meanwhile, from their side, the Americans have something to learn from the "civilized" political culture of modern Europe (which Hassner, in search of a ringing paradox, too quickly identifies with postmodernism). A republican democracy, after all, is possible only when it gives itself rules that limit its will while making necessary the exercise of judgment and the assumption of responsibility for it. Contemporary America seems to have forgotten that basic lesson.

NOTES

1. The debate between such "civilization" and the virile energy of nature can be found already among Greek sophists such as Callicles. It reappears as the Roman republic becomes Hellenized, before it rediscovers its supposed virility and becomes the world-encompassing empire. The astonishing parallels between Roman history and that of America are well illustrated by Peter Bender in *Weltmacht Amerika. Das neue Rom* (Stuttgart: Klett-Cotta, 2003).
2. Cf. Gordon S. Wood, *The Radicalism of the American Revolution: How a Revolution Transformed a Monarchical Society Into a Democratic One Unlike Any That Had Ever Existed* (New York: Knopf, 1992). The subtitle of this fascinating book points to the thesis expressed here, since "monarchical" implies the existence of a status hierarchy.
3. I am equating "French" with "European" for the sake of simplicity.
4. It might be noted that this refusal to admit that any power can incarnate the sovereign will of the people explains why, in the long run, America will prove to be incapable of becoming a truly imperial power.
5. It is worth noting that the chief negotiator of the Helsinki Accords, Henry Kissinger, did not intend the so-called third basket that treated human rights to

be taken seriously; he was operating within a realpolitik framework that sought to make permanent détente.
6. I have been able to find only one book specifically devoted to the theme. See Daniel Sisson, *The American Revolution of 1800* (New York: Knopf, 1974). The book is out of print, and the author seems to have written no other since that time.
7. Illustrations of this process in recent history concern questions of racial integration, sexual (or gender) discrimination, and the rights of women and other minorities. Such contemporary illustrations may suggest that nineteenth-century politics, particularly in the period leading up to and then emerging from the Civil War, was at best only an approximation of the kind of republican democracy that came to exist in the twentieth century.

Multilateralism
For a New Political Enlightenment

Drucilla Cornell and Philip Green

Even if the realization of this goal of abolishing war were always to remain just a pious wish, we still would not be deceiving ourselves by adopting the maxim of working for it with unrelenting perseverance.
—Immanuel Kant, *Metaphysical Principles of Justice*

The war in Iraq, having been publicly declared as an example of our new foreign policy and its commitment to preemptive strikes against anyone who gets in the way of the United States, and the threats to Syria and Iran, first put forward by Secretary Rumsfeld after their incursions into Iraq, are already being ratcheted up. At the same time, the landing of our ever more precise cruise missiles in both Iran and Saudi Arabia angered the leaders and the people of both countries, but none of this bothered anybody in charge. Killing had become a sport, with the media cheering on the administration, producing gleeful headlines about "Smoking Baghdad." As for what is to come, the fall of Saddam Hussein may well be a liberation for most Iraqis, but still, the administration seems utterly indifferent about the foreseeable future of Iraq: tens of thousands of casualties that will never be counted, possible civil strife, starvation, the collapse of public health and the economic infrastructure. The United States has made it clear that the world community, in the form of the United Nations, will not be allowed to help with the occupation and restructuring of the desert we have created. As with everything else, the United States intends to do this unilaterally; not even the faithful ally Britain will be allowed to bring its prime minister's moral concerns to the table where corporate greed will be the main principle of distribution. How did such a political, moral, and human disaster come about? For us, the answer is simple: the United States' unilateral desertion of all established principles of international law, together with its administration's contempt for democratic standards of justice and fairness at home. Liberation, though welcome, if it really comes to pass, will not be welcomed for long if it is brought about only by extending the rule of lawlessness and caprice across the globe.

According to Vice President Dick Cheney, he is proud rather than insulted when he is called a gun-slinging cowboy; proud both because he is a Westerner and because gunslinging is what we need right now. The gunslinging cowboys of the administration don't have any other ethic than might makes right; as has been said of various tyrants of the past, they understand only force. However, even though the invasion and conquest of Iraq continue in this vein—with all its attendant destruction, as seen by the rest of the world, if not by us, given the new system of embedded reporting—we now more than ever need to fight against the adoption of this ethic. Although alternative ethical and political ideals have been made to seem impossibly distant, we must not surrender to the administration's political "realism." On the contrary, we must salvage such ideals, for they are crucial to building movements and institutions for abolishing lawless violence—what the United States has unleashed on Iraq in the horrifying name of shock and awe.

But we also need to develop a political analysis that transcends the rhetoric of the good, democratic United States and its few unquestioning allies versus a world of evildoers and their witting or unwitting collaborators, the world of "with us or against us" that characterizes the propaganda of the Bush administration. Crucial to the complexity of this analysis is the recognition of two salient points. First, the legitimacy of U.S. unilateral mobilization of force anywhere abroad at any time is shored up domestically by the systematic undermining of our most basic constitutional liberties and by the growing militarization of our culture and economy, to say nothing of the attendant demolition of civil society, public education, health care, social services, public safety, and the basic needs of anyone other than billionaires. Second, the only foreign policy compatible with the recovery of our precarious democracy is a true multilateralism, rather than American imperial dominance, as the governing principle of international politics.

BY MULTILATERALISM, we mean that each nation-state as a matter of right should be accorded the dignity of its sovereignty by other nation-states and thereby deserves the same respect that the United States demands for itself and for its laws. Of course, in an age of nuclear weapons, international terrorism, genocide, and state torture, the principle of multilateralism must be subject to reasonable objections. A state that engages in "ethnic cleansing," invades its neighbors, sponsors terrorism, or refuses to accept internationally sanctioned limits on weapons of mass destruction becomes an outlaw state. However, except on the most extreme occasions, a state's moral wrongdoing enters the international political arena by masquerading as self-defense, deterrence, and cultural preservation. Over and against such a state, some other political entity must assert the rule of law, pronounce the sentence of outlawry, and, if necessary, legitimize the use of counterforce. But who can legitimately do this?

By itself, no single nation-state has the moral authority to play that role. Therefore, true multilateralism is inseparable from recognizing the centrality of the United Nations, an organization that, since its inception, has had as its major long-term goal collective security, defined not only as the full termination of particular wars but also as the end of war as a means of resolving conflicts between sovereign nations. This ideal presumes a form of federalism that secures the freedom of each state in accordance with international law and affords each state an equal voice in the federation. To be sure, the UN's actual practice over the last few decades has lagged far behind its stated ideals; it is, after all, a bureaucracy, often no better than any other. Yet its record in food aid, refugee relief, the provision of children's health care, and even peacekeeping is impressive compared with that of most nations—especially the United States. And we must remember that, to a large degree, the UN's well-publicized shortcomings in its peacekeeping role are due to the United States' refusal to commit its economic power to peacekeeping efforts in the way that it has unilaterally used its military might toward destructive and violent political ends. Truly supporting the UN would mean helping it to obtain the resources necessary to enforce its charter, not making it beg for its yearly dues.

What does multilateralism look like, then, under the current UN charter? First of all, "humanitarian" invasions must always proceed under the authority of the UN Security Council, and they must be based on cooperative efforts among nations since, by definition, they deal with collective causes—human rights violations, genocide, civil wars, and so on. It must be emphasized, however, that we should not give a blanket endorsement to the practice of invasion for allegedly humanitarian purposes, even under the auspices of the UN. That a regime treats its inhabitants horribly cannot be made the occasion for aggression, or perpetual war would be the principle of human affairs. The world is and always has been full of tyrants and torturers, and the list of nations, past and present, whose inhabitants, all other things being equal, would probably be better off under a different regime is potentially endless, depending only on one's point of view: Syria, Cuba, China, Nigeria (the regime of women-killers), Algeria, Iran, North Korea, Saudi Arabia, South Africa before the end of apartheid, Sudan, Myanmar, Argentina under the generals, Chile under the colonels. There are those who would add Venezuela to the list, or Israel. The point is not that any item on this list is defensible, but that none is. All other things are never equal. On rare occasions, as was almost certainly the case in Rwanda and Burundi and may have been the case in the former Yugoslavia, the utilitarian calculus of lives likely to be saved by armed intervention versus the unknowable future costs of a supposedly beneficent but humanly destructive intervention may be overwhelmingly clear and unarguable. Iraq was no such occasion. Though we in the United States must in some sense rejoice at

Saddam's absence from the lives of the Iraqi people, we should not rejoice at his overthrow, for there is no possible way that the calculus, applied to Iraq, could justify our contemptuous subversion of the fundamental principles of international law—that national sovereignty is to be respected and that aggressive warfare for any reason must always be an option of last resort.

In any event, we know that prior to the fateful night of March 19, George W. Bush did not proclaim that the war in Iraq was primarily a humanitarian intervention seeking a regime change in the name of freedom and democracy, no matter whose auspices were going to justify it. Rather, throughout the fall and winter, after the passage of UN Security Council Resolution 1441, the administration's rhetoric focused chiefly on whether Saddam Hussein and his regime had refused to comply with the UN demand that they completely disarm themselves of weapons of mass destruction. Only after March 14, when Hans Blix argued with full documentation that slowly but surely Saddam Hussein was being disarmed and that his government posed no serious threat to the United States, did the administration return to its earlier, occasional rationale for a unilateral invasion. This should not be a surprise; the historical record is full of interventions undertaken for "humanitarian" reasons (e.g., the U.S. invasion of Grenada or of Panama) that disappeared from sight the day after victory.

In the same way, the political discourse of security and self-defense has been cynically deployed by the Bush administration ever since September 11. Shortly after September 11, Security Council Resolution 1373 recognized that the kind of terrorism perpetrated against the United States by al Qaeda presented a difficult enforcement problem for the UN: how could it defend not just the United States but all countries of the world from what Richard Falk called megaterrorism and at the same time allow the United States to defend itself, given that terrorism of this magnitude could not be addressed by traditional political negotiation? Earlier, Security Council Resolution 1368 had been used by the Bush administration to justify its attacks on Afghanistan in the name of U.S. self-defense, even though self-defense had already been expanded beyond its traditional definition, since the war was declared against the Taliban regime for harboring and funding al Qaeda. This definitional expansion was widened to include George W. Bush's bellicose condemnation of what he called the "axis of evil"—an axis in which any nation that defied U.S. military or economic operations could be condemned as a threat to U.S. security, thereby justifying a retaliatory attack precisely as a matter of self-defense.

This paradoxical expansion of self-defense can only be offered in the language of just-war theory, because nothing in the language of the UN charter can accommodate or justify it. Just-war theory, however, turns on two basic moral principles: proportionality and discrimination between combatants and noncombatants, both of which purportedly limit human suffering by making war an absolute last resort. Resolution 1368, conceived to deal with more traditional threats between nations, thus had to be stretched to extend to the U.S. pursuit of al Qaeda cells in Afghanistan. It was certainly not meant to justify the aggressive U.S. foreign policy, because it has to be read against the basic presumption of the UN that war, as the last resort, is justifiable only when all other efforts at collective or national security have failed. Nothing, then, in the UN's implicit endorsement of the U.S. bombing and invasion of Afghanistan undermined the fundamental fact that only the Security Council should have decided if and when military action against Iraq was necessary. Indeed, the General Assembly held an emergency meeting in the first week after the war began—a meeting that was not televised or reported widely by the U.S. media. Resolutions decrying the war as illegal and shock and awe as a crime against humanity were brought to the floor of the Security Council, though they were not passed. But the very fact that the meeting occurred illustrates that, by its actions, the United States has significantly undermined the UN as an international institution designed to promote the ideal of peace and collective security.

In any case, let's assume that a material breach of the UN's post–Gulf War resolution on disarming Iraq's weapons of mass destruction had been brought to light by the UN's weapons inspectors. Of course, no such breach has been discovered, despite feverish investigation, accompanied by "revelations" that disappeared by the next day's headlines. This fact aside, though, what should have been done in accordance with the ideal of multilateralism amid increasing U.S. warmongering and boorish threats of U.S. unilateralism? Very simply, the governing resolution ought to have been followed, and the ultimate decision about the means of enforcement used against Iraq should have been made by the United Nations, not by the United States. But this did not happen precisely because the United States counted votes and realized that it could not win, despite its unsuccessful (though clearly cynical) attempts to gather votes by arm-twisting, bullying, leveraging, and bugging the phones of Security Council delegates (as reported by the *London Observer* on March 2). Indeed, in retrospect, it seems likely that the Bush administration (or elements within it) never intended to win UN sanction for an invasion; rather, it preferred to both make war and discard the UN's pretensions as a force for collective security. In this respect, it is apparent that the supposed treaty that ended the Gulf War was not a genuine treaty but a mere temporary suspension of hostilities in the name of an imposed "truce." Because of the horribly punitive sanctions to which the people of Iraq were subjected, this "truce" was really a continuation of war by other means. Thus, the ostensibly new war against Iraq actually began years ago, and that treaty should have been impugned because the United States clearly intended to strike again at Saddam Hussein under its very terms as soon as it could find an excuse (weapons of mass destruction) and muster enough international support—or at least establish a pretense of having tried to do so.

Arguments that national sovereignty is a thing of the past are thus beside the point. No one, after all, can pretend that U.S. sovereignty is dead and buried. This is all the more reason why the United States should be accorded full respect, just like any other state—nothing less, but also nothing more. Certainly one need not be a cynic to know that weapons and money ultimately make the decisive decisions in world politics. Nevertheless, it is also true that naked power can abjure coercive rule precisely to gain moral authority for its actions. An enlightened superpower would be a state that seeks to establish, on the level of international relations, respect for the political dignity of all other states, dignity normally provided to individuals by modern democratic constitutions (though, admittedly, constitutions can take as many different forms as democratic regimes themselves). In the first instance, such a state would seek forms of conflict resolution consistent with international law through means other than war, rather than militarily defending its own naked economic and political interests. For the United States, this would mean joining an international criminal court (something it has consistently refused to do) and thereby showing its commitment to the political enlightenment represented by international law. Instead, the United States clearly pursues what Joseph Stalin would have recognized as a doctrine of "sovereignty in one country."

Of course, international laws and institutions are only as good as the nation-states that abide by and support them, since the particular mechanisms of enforcement within individual states are not powerful enough to enforce them worldwide. The nations of the world, then, are responsible for strengthening these laws and giving them political reality by respecting them. After September 11, some Americans on both the Left and the Right argued forcefully that the bombing of Afghanistan was unnecessary, devastating to an already devastated country. We are among those who would have supported, as an alternative, police action and a criminal investigation culminating in an international criminal trial. Both courses of action would have been in full accordance with international law. Moreover, they would have been the most effective means of actually bringing the perpetrators to justice. The bombing of Afghanistan caused severe harm to the people of that country, and yet for all the political bombast, cultural invective, and military zeal that accompanied it, Osama bin Laden remains at large and, today, is seemingly almost forgotten. Even pursuing a goal that most of the world endorsed, the United States managed to subvert the only principles that could legitimize a long-run counterterrorist policy. That is not surprising—by now, it is all too clear that even "counterterrorism" was only a fig leaf to cover the administration's real goal, the pursuit of empire.

Of course, the disarmament of states with nuclear power, whether or not they belong to an arbitrarily constituted "axis of evil," is also central to multilateralism—perhaps the most crucial goal of all. But if it is going to have legitimate status as one enlightened nation among others, the United States must be the first state to throw down the gauntlet and begin the disarmament process. If the United States is to be just one nation-state in a federation committed to peace and collective security, it should have no need for nuclear weapons—weapons of terror designed only to kill mass civilian populations. The United States does not need, under its own totally recalcitrant control, what is many times over the largest and most threatening military force in the world.

THIS IS YET ONE MORE REASON WHY, at home, we must oppose an ever-expanding debt economy capable of financing an infinite war. "There is no cause for suspicion," Immanuel Kant wrote in his famous essay on perpetual peace, "if help for the national economy is sought inside or outside the state. But a credit system, if used by the powers as an instrument of aggression against one another, shows the power of money in its most dangerous form. For while the debts thereby incurred are always secure against present demands (because not all the creditors will demand payment at the same time), these debts go on growing indefinitely." Kant's point was not that all debts are bad but that the running of an ever-growing military debt cannot but undermine the state's capacity to maintain basic institutions that meet the needs of its citizens and promote democracy.

Thus we are returned to the question of democracy at home. More and more it is becoming apparent that the administration's ultimate goal is the destruction of democracy as we have known it and its replacement by a permanent regime of oligarchy. As we have said, our own civil society is steadily weakening, and some of its institutional necessities—equal economic opportunity, care of the poor and the helpless, equal justice in the courts, maintenance of cities and their infrastructural lifeblood—are threatening to disintegrate. Democracy must begin at home. The ultimate American political fantasy is that a regime that trashes equality at home has carte blanche to spread it abroad. So we must pay close attention to the fraying domestic fabric of democracy, while abroad, we must replace the discourse of "democratic" liberation—in truth, a discourse of *novum imperium*—with a more properly political discourse of mutual support and reciprocity. As the strongest among equals, but still a moral and legal equal, the United States must involve itself in transnational agreements and accords that seek to solve problems that are clearly unsolvable by any one nation-state. It is both unrealistic and normatively undesirable for any state as powerful and wealthy as the United States to be isolationist. Historically, isolationism has always been supernationalist and opposed to collective security; today's imperialists, then, are merely the old isolationists in a new context—new emperors, as it were, in the same old clothes.

An archetypal example of a real attempt at mutual support is the recent international backing of the Kyoto global warming treaty, a treaty the United States refused to sign, arguing that it was unfair because it used a point system that required the wealthier countries of the world (the wealthiest, of course, being the United States) to assume a greater responsibility for curtailing their burning of oil than poorer countries in dire need of industrial development. This point system was eminently realistic and unimpeachably fair in terms of the burden that some of the poorest countries in the world could shoulder in the name of a world problem. In the name of respect for the long-term goal of a more egalitarian distribution of the world's resources, reciprocity must take into account different levels of responsibility. Another example of a world problem that can be addressed only by transnational accords and agreements is the AIDS epidemic currently ravishing whole areas of Africa and Asia. Millions of people around the globe are dying from AIDS. We need to seek a world solution to that problem because no nation or individual—even one as wealthy as Bill Gates—is up to the task. But even after verbally committing a relatively paltry sum to that end, the administration still allows economic blackmail and political scare tactics to keep sex education and condom distribution from being implemented in nations that desperately need them. What kind of nation among nations marshals virtually infinite resources to fight a war against one hideously brutal tyrant but turns its back on much less expensive, less interventionist, and less destructive policies that might avoid hundreds of millions of hideously brutal deaths?

Criticizing U.S. policies in this way, it is necessary to keep in mind two things: first, that endless imperial expansion in the name of democracy is not taking place as the democratic will of the American electorate; second, that we are referring to the newest phase of U.S. imperialism, not to the political novelty of American imperialist dominance (for such dominance has been ongoing and, pace Michael Hardt and Antonio Negri, threatens to continue untrammeled). Because an out-of-control executive branch currently fuels the reckless use of unconstrained power, we remain committed to the claim—at once historical and political—that the U.S. Constitution is a document that reflects a deep and profound suspicion of unchecked executive power. The Constitution not only establishes checks and balances among the major branches of the government; it also contains a Bill of Rights that defends the freedom of individuals against abuse by the government. It should thus protect U.S. soldiers from the abuse of fighting an illegal and unjust war. The best way to support our troops and support democracy would have been to demand that House Resolution HJ20, which would have stripped Bush of his right to continue to wage the war, be removed from committee and brought to the House floor. Genuine American patriotism and multilateralism need not be at variance. After all, patriotism must begin with a defense of the Constitution—a political reclamation of the very political rights on which the USA Patriot Act is trampling.

We have all heard the language of freedom and rights replaced by the language of security. No one would deny that a certain amount of security is necessary, but this does not mean just security against terrorist attacks. It also means that we need the security of knowing that we will not be spied on in our own homes. We need the security of not being thrown in prison unless we have committed an actual crime. We need the security of dissent in all forms—the dissent necessary for individual citizens to defend what they understand to be the values of their country. We need economic security in the form of jobs, health care, and decent schools for our children.

As crucial as it is, the question concerning how we can be safe from terrorism can be answered only through a resolute commitment to law, right, and equal justice—in other words, through a commitment to multilateralism as the guiding principle of international politics. That is the only way that the United States can become a nation-state that respects international law, the UN, and the sovereignty of other nation-states—an enlightened nation-state.

Globalism
The New Market Ideology

Manfred B. Steger

GLOBALISM AND THE SELLING OF GLOBALIZATION

In his celebrated address to a joint session of Congress nine days after the terrorist attacks on September 11, President George W. Bush made it abundantly clear that the deep sources of the new conflict between the "civilized world" and terrorism were to be found in neither religion nor culture but in political ideology. Referring to the radical network of terrorists and governments that support them as "heirs of all the murderous ideologies of the twentieth century," Bush described the sinister motives of the terrorists: "By sacrificing human life to serve their radical visions, by abandoning every value except the will to power, they [the terrorists] follow the path of fascism, Nazism and totalitarianism. And they will follow that path all the way to where it ends in history's unmarked grave of discarded lies."

There are two remarkable pieces of information that stand out in this passage of the president's speech. First, by omitting any reference to communist ideology, the president chose to put political expediency over ethical principle, presumably not to alienate China. In other words, his silence on the horrors of communism makes sense within the administration's overall strategic framework of putting together the broadest possible alliance against terrorism. Second and more important, Bush's reference to the birth of a new totalitarian ideology runs counter to the idea of a "de-ideologized world" that dominated the post-Soviet intellectual landscape in the West. Advanced by social theorists such as Francis Fukuyama more than a decade ago, the "end of ideology" thesis postulated that the passing of Marxism-Leninism marked nothing less than the "end point of mankind's ideological evolution," evident in the total exhaustion of viable ideological alternatives to Western liberalism. Fukuyama explicitly downplayed the significance of rising religious fundamentalism and ethnic nationalism in the "new world order" of the 1990s, predicting that the global triumph of the "Western idea" would be irreversible and that the spread of its consumerist culture to all corners of the earth would prove to be unstoppable.

Bush's emphasis on the continuing significance of ideology also runs counter to the popular thesis of the "clash of civilizations" suggested by Harvard political scientist Samuel Huntington in the mid-1990s. Arguing that the fundamental source of conflict in the new world order would be neither ideological nor economic but "cultural," Huntington identified seven or eight self-contained "civilizations," of which the conflict between Islam and the West receives the most attention. Though seemingly pertinent to the current situation, it is precisely this large-scale scenario of clashing cultures and religions that the president rejected when he insisted that America's new enemy was not Islam per se but "those who commit evil in the name of Allah" and thus "blaspheme the name of Allah." Indeed, in a recent newspaper interview, Huntington himself admitted that the current crisis does not fit his model, since the former appears to be based not on a wholesale civilizational paradigm but on extremist political ideas within Islam. In short, ideology is alive and well.

Given the resilience of ideas, values, and beliefs as the source of major conflicts, I submit that we are currently witnessing the beginning of a new ideological struggle over the meaning and the direction of globalization. If global terrorism constitutes one extreme protagonist in this struggle, then neoliberal globalism represents the other. It is my purpose here to explore the main features of the latter position.

At the outset of the new century, it has already become a cliché to observe that we live in an age of globalization. Although it may not be an entirely new phenomenon, globalization in its current phase has been described as an unprecedented compression of time and space reflected in the tremendous intensification of social, political, economic, and cultural interconnections and interdependencies on a global scale. But not everybody experiences globalization in the same way. In fact, people living in various parts of the world are affected very differently by this gigantic transformation of social structures and cultural zones. Globalization seems to generate enormous wealth and opportunity for the few, while relegating the many to conditions of abject poverty and hopelessness.

The public interpretation of the origin, direction, and meaning of the profound social changes that go by the name of globalization has fallen disproportionately to a powerful phalanx of social forces located mainly in the global North. Corporate managers, executives of large transnational corporations, corporate lobbyists, journalists and public-relations specialists, intellectuals writing for a large public audience, state bureaucrats, and politicians serve as the chief advocates of globalism, the dominant ideology of our time. Saturating the public with idealized images of a consumerist, free-market world, globalists simultaneously distort social reality, legitimate and advance their power interests, and shape collective and personal identities. In order to analyze these ideological maneuvers, it is important to distinguish between *globalism*—a neoliberal market ideology of Anglo-American origin that endows globalization with certain norms, values, and meanings—and *globalization*—a set of social processes defined and described by various commentators in different, often contradictory ways.

Globalists have marshaled their considerable resources to sell to the public the alleged benefits of market liberalization: rising global living standards, economic efficiency, individual freedom and democracy, and unprecedented technological progress. Globalists promise to "liberate" the economy from social constraints by privatizing public enterprises, deregulating trade and industry, providing massive tax cuts, reducing public expenditures, and maintaining strict control of organized labor. Inspired by the liberal utopia of the "self-regulating market," neoliberal globalists have linked their quaint nineteenth-century ideals to fashionable "globalization talk." Thus, globalism represents a gigantic repackaging enterprise—the pouring of old philosophical wine into new ideological bottles.

Dozens of magazines, journals, newspapers, and electronic media feed their readers a steady diet of globalist claims. For example, *Business Week* recently featured a cover story on globalization that contained the following statement: "For nearly a decade, political and business leaders have struggled to persuade the American public of the virtues of globalization." Citing the results of a national poll on globalization conducted in April 2000, the author of the article went on to report that about 65 percent of the respondents consider globalization to be a "good thing." At the same time, however, nearly 70 percent of those polled believe that free-trade agreements with low-wage countries are responsible for driving down wages in the United States. Ending on a rather combative note, the author issued a stern warning to American politicians and business leaders that they should be more effective in highlighting the benefits of globalization. He claimed that rising public fears over globalization might result in a violent backlash, jeopardizing the health of the international economy and "the cause of free trade."[1]

Note the author's open admission that political and business leaders are, in fact, peddling their preferred version of globalization to the public. In fact, the discourse of globalization itself has turned into an extremely important commodity destined for public consumption. Neoliberal decision makers have become expert designers of an attractive ideological container for their political agenda. Indeed, the realization of a global market order depends on the construction of arguments and images that portray market globalization in a positive light. Analyzing countless utterances, speeches, and writings of globalism's most influential advocates, I have identified five ideological claims that recur with great regularity throughout the globalist discourse.

CLAIM 1: GLOBALIZATION IS ABOUT THE LIBERALIZATION AND GLOBAL INTEGRATION OF MARKETS

This claim is anchored in the neoliberal ideal of the self-regulating market as the normative basis for a future global order. One can find in major newspapers and magazines countless statements that celebrate the "liberalization" of markets. Consider the following statement in a recent issue of *Business Week*: "Globalization is about the triumph of markets over governments. Both proponents and opponents of globalization agree that the driving force today is markets, which are suborning the role of government. The truth is that the size of government has been shrinking relative to the economy almost everywhere." Joan Spiro, former undersecretary of state in the Clinton administration, echoes this assessment: "One role [of government] is to get out of the way—to remove barriers to the free flow of goods, services, and capital." British journalist Peter Martin concurs: "The liberal market economy is by its very nature global. It is the summit of human endeavor. We should be proud that by our work and by our votes we have—collectively and individually—contributed to building it."[2]

Most importantly, these globalist voices present the liberalization and integration of global markets as "natural" phenomena that further individual liberty and material progress in the world. Presenting as "fact" what is actually a contingent political initiative, globalists seek to persuade the public that their neoliberal account of globalization represents an objective, or at least a neutral, diagnosis. To be sure, neoliberals offer some empirical evidence for the liberalization of markets. But do market principles spread because of some intrinsic connection between globalization and the expansion of markets? Or do they expand because globalist discourse contributes to the emergence of the very conditions it purports to analyze? In most instances, globalists hold the political and discursive power to shape the world largely according to their ideological formula: LIBERALIZATION + INTEGRATION OF MARKETS = GLOBALIZATION.

CLAIM 2: GLOBALIZATION IS INEVITABLE AND IRREVERSIBLE

At first glance, the idea of the historical inevitability of globalization seems to be a poor fit for an ideology based on neoliberal principles. After all, throughout the twentieth century, liberals and conservatives consistently criticized Marxists for their determinist claims that devalue human free agency and downplay the ability of noneconomic factors to shape social reality. Yet globalists rely on a similar monocausal, economistic narrative of historical inevitability. According to the globalist interpretation, globalization reflects the spread of irreversible market forces driven by technological innovations that make the integration of national economies inevitable. The multiple voices of globalism convey to the public their message of inevitability with a practiced consistency.

Former president Bill Clinton, for example, argued on many occasions that "today we must embrace the inexorable logic of globalization—that everything from the strength of our economy to the safety of our cities, to the health of our people, depends on events not only within our borders, but half a world away. . . . Globalization is irreversible. Protectionism will only make things worse." Likewise, Frederick W. Smith, chairman and CEO of FedEx Corporation, insists that "globalization is inevitable and inexorable and it is accelerating. . . . It does not matter whether you like it or not, it's happening, it's going to happen." *New York Times* correspondent Thomas Friedman comes to a similar conclusion: "Globalization is very difficult to reverse because it is driven both by powerful human aspiration for higher standards of living and by enormously powerful technologies which are integrating us more and more every day, whether we like it or not." Neoliberal elites in non-Western countries faithfully echo this globalist language of inevitability. For example, Rahul Bajaj, a leading Indian industrialist, insists that "we need much more liberalization and deregulation of the Indian economy. No sensible Indian businessman disagrees with this. . . . Globalization is inevitable. There is no better alternative." Manuel Villar, the Philippines' speaker of the House of Representatives, agrees: "Of course, we can not simply wish away the process of globalization. It is a reality of a modern world. The process is irreversible."[3]

The portrayal of globalization as some sort of natural force, like the weather or gravity, makes it easier for globalists to convince people that they must adapt to the discipline of the market if they are to survive and prosper. Hence, the claim of its inevitability depoliticizes the public discourse about globalization. Neoliberal policies are above politics because they simply carry out what is ordained by nature. This implies that instead of acting according to a set of choices, people merely fulfill world-market laws that demand the elimination of government controls. There is nothing that can be done about the natural movement of economic and technological forces; political groups ought to acquiesce and make the best of an unalterable situation. Resistance would be unnatural, irrational, and dangerous.

The idea of inevitability also makes it easier to convince the general public to "share the burdens of globalization," thus supporting an excuse often utilized by neoliberal politicians: "It is the market that made us cut social programs." As German president Roman Herzog put it in a nationally televised appeal, the "irresistible pressure of global forces" demands that "everyone will have to make sacrifices."[4] To be sure, President Herzog never spells out what kinds of sacrifices will await large shareholders and corporate executives. Recent examples suggest that it is much more likely that sacrifices will be borne disproportionately by those workers and employees who lose their jobs or social benefits as a result of neoliberal trade policies or profit-maximizing practices of "corporate downsizing."

Finally, the claim that globalization is inevitable and irresistible is inscribed within a larger evolutionary discourse that assigns a privileged position to certain countries at the forefront of "liberating" markets from political control. Fukuyama, for example, insists that globalization is a euphemism that stands for the irreversible Americanization of the world: "I think it has to be Americanization because, in some respects, America is the most advanced capitalist society in the world today, and so its institutions represent the logical development of market forces. Therefore, if market forces are what drives globalization, it is inevitable that Americanization will accompany globalization."[5]

And so it appears that globalist forces have been resurrecting the nineteenth-century paradigm of Anglo-American vanguardism propagated by the likes of Herbert Spencer and William Graham Sumner. The main ingredients of classic market liberalism are all present in globalism. We find inexorable laws of nature favoring Western civilization, the self-regulating economic model of perfect competition, the virtues of free enterprise, the vices of state interference, the principle of laissez-faire, and the irreversible, evolutionary process leading up to the survival of the fittest.

CLAIM 3: NOBODY IS IN CHARGE OF GLOBALIZATION

Globalism's deterministic language offers yet another rhetorical advantage. If the natural laws of the market have indeed preordained a neoliberal course of history, then globalization does not reflect the arbitrary agenda of a particular social class or group. In that case, globalists merely carry out the unalterable imperatives of a transcendental force. People aren't in charge of globalization; markets and technology are. Certain human actions might accelerate or retard globalization, but in the last instance (to quote none other than Friedrich Engels), the invisible hand of the market will always assert its superior wisdom.

As economist Paul Krugman puts it, "Many on the Left dislike the global marketplace because it epitomizes what they dislike about markets in general: the fact that nobody is in charge. The truth is that the invisible hand rules most domestic markets, too, a reality that most Americans seem to accept as a fact of life." Robert Hormats, vice-chairman of Goldman Sachs International, agrees: "The great beauty of globalization is that no one is in control. The great beauty of globalization is that it is not controlled by any individual, any government, any institution."[6]

But Hormats is right only in a formal sense. Although there is no conscious conspiracy orchestrated by a single evil force, it does not mean that nobody is in charge of globalization. The liberalization and integration of global markets do not proceed outside the realm of human choice. The globalist initiative to integrate and deregulate markets around the world both creates and sustains asymmetrical power relations. Backed by the powerful countries of the Northern Hemisphere, international institutions such as the World Trade Organization, the International Monetary Fund (IMF), and the World Bank enjoy the privileged position of making and enforcing the rules of the global economy. In return for supplying much-needed loans to developing countries, the IMF and the World Bank demand from their creditors the implementation of neoliberal policies that further the material interests of the first world.

Moreover, if nobody is in control of globalization, why do globalists such as former national security adviser Samuel Berger try so hard to convince their audiences that the United States ought to become a "more active participant in an effort to shape globalization"?[7] The obvious answer is that the claim of a leaderless globalization process does not reflect reality. Rather, it serves the neoliberal political agenda of defending and expanding the hegemony of the global North. Like the rhetoric of historical inevitability, the idea that nobody is in charge seeks to depoliticize the public debate on the subject and thus demobilize antiglobalist movements. The deterministic language of a technological progress driven by uncontrollable market laws turns political issues into scientific problems of mere administration. Once large segments of the population have accepted the globalist image of a self-directed juggernaut that simply runs its course, it becomes extremely difficult to challenge neoliberal policies. As ordinary people cease to believe in the possibility of choosing alternative social arrangements, globalism gains even more strength in its ability to construct passive consumer identities.

CLAIM 4: GLOBALIZATION BENEFITS EVERYONE

This claim lies at the core of globalism because it provides an affirmative answer to the crucial normative question of whether globalization should be considered a good thing or a bad thing. For example, former treasury secretary Robert Rubin asserts that free trade and open markets provide "the best prospect for creating jobs, spurring economic growth, and raising living standards in the U.S. and around the world." Denise Froning, trade policy analyst at both the Center for International Trade and Economics and the Heritage Foundation, suggests that "societies that promote economic freedom create their own dynamism and foster a wellspring of prosperity that benefits every citizen." Alan Greenspan, chairman of the U.S. Federal Reserve Board, insists that "there can be little doubt that the extraordinary changes in global finance on balance have been beneficial in facilitating significant improvements in economic structures and living standards throughout the world."[8]

But what about the solid evidence suggesting that income disparities between nations are actually widening at a quicker pace than ever before in recent history? The global hunt for profits actually makes it more difficult for poor people to enjoy the benefits of technology and scientific innovations. Consider the following example: A group of scientists in the United States recently warned the public that economic globalization may be the greatest obstacle to preventing the spread of parasitic diseases in sub-Saharan Africa. They pointed out that U.S.-based pharmaceutical companies are stopping production of many antiparasitic drugs because developing countries cannot afford to buy them. The U.S. manufacturer of a drug to treat bilharzia, a parasitic disease that causes severe liver damage, has stopped production because of declining profits—even though the disease is thought to affect over 200 million people worldwide. Another drug used to combat damage caused by liver flukes has not been produced since 1979 because the "customer base" in the third world does not wield enough "buying power."[9]

Although globalists typically acknowledge the existence of unequal global distribution patterns, they nonetheless insist that the market itself will eventually correct these "irregularities." According to John Meehan, chairman of the U.S. Public Securities Association, such "episodic dislocations" are "necessary" in the short run, but they will eventually give way to "quantum leaps in productivity."[10] Globalists who deviate from the official portrayal of globalization as benefiting everyone must bear the consequences of their criticism. For example, Joseph Stiglitz, the Nobel Prize–winning former chief economist of the World Bank, was severely attacked for publicly criticizing the neoliberal economic policies created by his institution. He argued that the structural adjustment programs imposed on developing countries by both the World Bank and the IMF often lead to disastrous results. He also noted that "market ideologues" had used the 1997–1998 Asian economic crisis to discredit state intervention and to promote more market liberalization. At the end of 1999, Stiglitz was pressured into resigning from his position. Five months later, his consulting contract with the World Bank was terminated.[11]

CLAIM 5: GLOBALIZATION FURTHERS THE SPREAD OF DEMOCRACY IN THE WORLD

This globalist claim is rooted in the neoliberal assertion that free markets and democracy are synonymous. Persistently affirmed as "common sense," the actual compatibility of these concepts often goes unchallenged in the public discourse. The most obvious strategy by which neoliberals generate popular support for the equation of democracy and the market is by discrediting "socialism." As late as the 1970s, socialists provided a powerful critique of the elitist, class-based character of liberal democracy, which, in their view, revealed that a substantive form of democracy had not been achieved in capitalist societies. Since the 1989 collapse of communism in eastern Europe, however, the ideological edge has shifted decisively to the defenders of a neoliberal perspective, who emphasize the relationship between economic liberalization and the emergence of democratic political regimes.

Fukuyama, for example, asserts that there is a clear correlation between a country's level of economic development and successful democracy. Although globalization and capital development do not automatically produce democracies, "the level of economic development resulting from globalization is conducive to the creation of complex civil societies with a powerful middle class. It is this class and societal structure that facilitates democracy." Praising the economic transitions toward capitalism in eastern Europe, U.S. Senator Hillary Rodham Clinton argued that the emergence of new businesses and shopping centers in former communist countries should be seen as the "backbone of democracy."[12]

Such arguments hinge on a conception of democracy that emphasizes formal procedures such as voting at the expense of the direct participation of broad majorities in political and economic decision making. This "thin" definition of democracy is part of what William I. Robinson has identified as the U.S.-backed political project of "promoting polyarchy" in the global South. "Polyarchy" refers to an elitist and regimented model of "low-intensity" market democracy that typically limits democratic participation to voting in elections. This ensures that those elected remain insulated from popular pressures and thus can govern "effectively."[13]

In addition, the globalist claim that globalization furthers the spread of democracy in the world must contend with evidence that points in the opposite direction. Even media outlets that faithfully spread the gospel of globalism occasionally concede that large transnational corporations often invest in developing countries that are not considered "free" according to generally accepted political rights and civil liberties standards. The conservative *Chicago Tribune* recently cited a report released by the New Economic Information Service suggesting that democratic countries are losing out in the race for American export markets and American foreign investments. In 1989, democratic countries accounted for more than half of all U.S. imports from the global South. Ten years later, with more democracies to choose from, democratic countries supplied barely one-third of U.S. imports from developing countries: "And the trend is growing. As more of the world's countries adopt democracy, more American businesses appear to prefer dictatorships."[14]

Why are powerful investors in the global North making these business decisions? For one, wages tend to be lower in authoritarian regimes than in democracies, giving businesses in dictatorships a monetary advantage in selling exports abroad. In addition, lower wages, bans on labor unions, and relaxed environmental laws give authoritarian regimes an edge in attracting foreign investment.

CONCLUDING REMARKS

The five central claims of globalism constitute the foundation of a dominant discursive regime that bestows public meaning on the process of globalization. Yet, as both the terrorist attacks of September 11 and the massive antiglobalist protests from Seattle to Genoa have shown, the expansion of this market narrative has encountered considerable resistance. Ideological challengers on both the political Left (internationalist egalitarians) and the political Right (nationalist protectionists) have already begun to flex their conceptual and political muscles. Far from condemning people to intellectual boredom in a world without ideology, the opening decade of the twenty-first century is quickly becoming a teeming battlefield of clashing ideologies. It appears that globalist forces will continue to struggle with their antiglobalist opponents as each side tries to impress its agenda on the public mind.

Yet it is important to remember that globalization is an incipient process, slowly giving rise to a new condition whose eventual qualities and properties are far from being determined. Globalization does not necessarily have to mean what globalists say it means. However, such a skeptical posture toward globalism should not be interpreted as a blanket rejection of globalization. One should take comfort in the fact that the world is becoming a more interdependent place. One should welcome the progressive transformation of social structures, provided that modernity and the development of science and technology go hand in hand with greater forms of freedom and equality for all people, as well as with a more effective protection of our global environment. The task for critical theorists of globalization is not to denounce globalization but to offer a thoughtful analysis and critique of globalism.

Indeed, it is insufficient to analyze globalization as if it were simply the outcome of objective material processes "out there." Globalization also has important normative and ideological dimensions that are always part of social and economic processes. Hence, we must understand the dynamics of our age, in part at least, as the result of intricately interacting ideas, values, and beliefs. As the events of September 11 have shown, academic observers of the phenomenon can hardly remain untouched by the ongoing ideological battle over the meaning and direction of globalization.

In my view, globalism is ethically unsustainable because it routinely privileges self-interested market relations over other-regarding social relations. Indeed, as extreme market policies impose conditions of inequality on billions of people around the globe, globalism will eventually inflict enough damage to global social relations and the environment to cause severe reactions against those countries and regions that are identified with extreme neoliberalism. Such a violent backlash harbors the potential to unleash armies of religious fundamentalism and irrational hatred that could dwarf even the most sinister forces of the recent past: fascism and Stalinism.

Guided by a vision of an egalitarian global order that may involve the creation of a gigantic "Marshall Plan" for the global South, critical theorists of globalization ought to uncover the ways in which unfettered market forces undermine the capacity of human beings to participate in shaping their own destinies. Once globalism and its corresponding neoliberal power base begin to lose their grip on the construction of meaning, alternative interpretations of globalization centered on the political demands for global citizenship and a redistribution of the world's economic resources will circulate more freely in public discourse. As a result, more and more people will realize that positive change is possible. Indeed, there is nothing "inevitable" or "irreversible" about globalism.

NOTES

1. Aaron Bernstein, "Backlash: Behind the Anxiety over Globalization," *Business Week*, April 24, 2000, 44. This *Business Week*–Harris poll on globalization was conducted by Harris Interactive between April 7 and 10, 2000. A total of 1,024 interviews were conducted.
2. *Business Week*, December, 13, 1999, 212; Joan E. Spiro, "The Challenges of Globalization" (speech given at the World Economic Development Congress, Washington, D.C., September 26, 1996), http://www.state.gov/www/issues/economic/960926.html; Peter Martin, "The Moral Case for Globalization," in *The Globalization Reader*, ed. Frank J. Lechner and John Boli (Malden, Mass.: Blackwell, 2000), 12–13.
3. Bill Clinton, "Remarks by the President on Foreign Policy" (San Francisco, February 26, 1999), at http://www.pub.whitehouse.gov/urires/12R?urn:pdi://oma.eop.gove.us/1999/3/1/3.text.html; President Clinton cited in Sonya Ross, "Clinton Talks of Better Living," Associated Press, October 15, 1997; "International Finance Experts Preview Upcoming Global Economic Forum," April 1, 1999, at http://www.econstrat.org/pctranscript.html; Thomas Friedman, *The Lexus and*

the Olive Tree: Understanding Globalization (New York: Anchor Books, 2000), 407; Rahul Bajaj, "Interview with the *Rediff Business Interview*," February 2, 1999, at http://rediff.com/business/1999/feb/02bajaj.html. See also http://www.ascihyd.org/asci701.html and Manuel Villar Jr., "High-Level Dialogue on the Theme of the Social and Economic Impact of Globalization and Interdependence and Their Policy Implications" (New York, September 17, 1998), at http://www.un.int/philippines/villar.html.

4. Roman Herzog cited in Hans-Peter Martin and Harald Schumann, *The Global Trap: Globalization and the Assault on Democracy and Prosperity* (London: Zed Books, 1997), 6.
5. "Economic Globalization and Culture: A Discussion with Dr. Francis Fukuyama," at http://www.ml.com/woml/forum/globa12.html.
6. Paul Krugman, "We Are Not the World," in *The Accidental Theorist* (New York: W. W. Norton, 1998), 78; Robert Hormats, "PBS Interview with Danny Schechter," February 1998, at http://pbs.org/globalization/hormats1.html.
7. Remarks by Samuel R. Berger, Columbia University, New York City, May 2, 2000, at http://www.usis.it/file2000_05/alia/a0050415.html.
8. Robert Rubin, "Reform of the International Financial Architecture," *Vital Speeches* 65, no. 15 (1999): 455; Denise Froning, "Why Spurn Free Trade?" *Washington Times*, September 15, 2000; Alan Greenspan, "The Globalization of Finance," October 14, 1997, at http://cato.org/pubs/journal/cj17n3–1.html.
9. "Tropical Disease Drugs Withdrawn," BBC News, October 31, 2000.
10. John J. Meehan, "Globalization and Technology at Work in the Bond Markets" (speech given in Phoenix, Arizona, March 1, 1997), at http://www/bondmarkets.com/news/Meehanspeechfinal.shtml.
11. Doug Henwood, "Stiglitz and the Limits of 'Reform,'" *Nation*, October 2, 2000, 20.
12. "Economic Globalization and Culture: A Discussion with Dr. Francis Fukuyama," at http://www.ml.com/woml/forum/globa12.html; Hillary Rodham Clinton, "Growth of Democracy in Eastern Europe" (Warsaw, Poland, October 5, 1999), at http://www.whitehouse.gov/WH/EOP/FirstLady/html/generalspeeches/1999/19991005.html.
13. William I. Robinson, *Promoting Polyarchy: Globalization, U.S. Intervention, and Hegemony* (Cambridge: Cambridge University Press, 1996), 56–62.
14. R. C. Longworth, "Democracies Are Paying the Price," *Chicago Tribune*, November 19, 1999.

The Silence of Words and Political Dynamics in the World Risk Society

Ulrich Beck

September 11, 2001, will stand for many things in the history of humanity. Among these is the failure, the silence of language before such an event: *war, crime, enemy, victory,* and *terror*—the terms melt in the mouth like rotten mushrooms (to borrow a phrase from Hugo von Hofmannsthal). NATO summed up the alliance, but it is neither an attack from the outside nor an attack of a sovereign state against another sovereign state. September 11 does not stand for a second Pearl Harbor. The attack was directed not toward the U.S. military machine but rather toward innocent civilians. The act speaks the language of genocidal hate that knows no negotiation, no dialogue, no compromises, and, lastly, no peace.

The notion of "enemy" is misleading. It stems from an imaginary world in which armies conquer or get conquered and then sign cease-fires and peace treaties. The terrorist attacks, however, are neither just a crime nor a simple case for national justice. The notion and institute of "police" proves to be just as inadequate for acts whose results resemble military attacks, just as the police are in no position to dismiss a cadre of perpetrators who appear to fear nothing. Appropriately, the notion of "civil emergency services" seems to lose its meaning. We live, think, and act according to zombie-like notions, according to notions that have died but continue to rule our thinking and our actions. Yet if the military, trapped in its old notions, responds with conventional methods, such as surface bombings, then it is legitimate to fear these as not only ineffective but also counterproductive: new Osama bin Ladens will be bred.

This is what makes suicide bombings, even months or years after they have occurred, incomprehensible. The notions on which our worldviews are predicated and the distinctions between war and peace, military and police, war and crime, internal and external security, and particularly between internal and external in general, have been magnified. Who would have thought that internal security, even Germany's, for instance, would have to be defended in the remotest valleys of Afghanistan? "Defend!" Again, another false notion. Even the distinction between defense and attack does not hold up anymore. Can one still say that the United States is defending its internal security on foreign soil, in Afghanistan and so forth? What if all these concepts are false and language fails in the face of reality? What has really happened? No one knows. But would it be braver to be silent about it? The destruction of the Twin Towers in New York was followed by an explosion of chatty silence and meaningless action. To quote Hugo von Hofmannsthal, "I succeeded no longer at grasping reality with the simplifying gaze of familiarity. Everything broke down into pieces for me, and those pieces again into more pieces, and nothing else would let itself be encompassed under one concept. Single words would swim around me; they ran into eyes that stared at me and that I stared back into."[1]

This silence of words must finally be broken. We can no longer afford to keep quiet about this. If we could at least succeed in naming the silence of single ideas, to name the distance between idea and reality, to presume and to prudently break the bridges of understanding to the novel reality that stems from our civilizing actions, most likely not much, but something, could be gained. Here I clarify the notion of a world risk society and then, within this context, criticize and redefine a series of notions: (1) war and terror, (2) economic globalization and neoliberalism, and (3) state and sovereignty.

WHAT IS A WORLD RISK SOCIETY?

What do events and threats like Chernobyl, environmental catastrophes, discussions regarding human genetics, the Asian economic crisis, and current threats of terrorist attacks have in common? I will explain what I mean with an example. A few years ago, the U.S. Congress contracted a scientific committee to develop a language to elucidate the danger of America's permanent sites for radioactive waste. The problem to be solved was the following: how do concepts and symbols have to be constructed in order to convey a single, unchanging message 10,000 years from now?[2]

The committee was made up of physicians, anthropologists, linguists, brain researchers, psychologists, molecular biologists, archaeologists, artists, and so forth. It was supposed to answer the unavoidable question: will the United States still be around in 10,000 years? For the government committee, the answer was obvious: USA forever! To be sure, the central problem—how it is possible, at a distance of 10,000 years, to have a conversation with the future—gradually proved to be unsolvable. Scholars began searching for models among the oldest symbols of humanity. They studied the construction of Stonehenge (1500 BC) and the pyramids, researching the history of the reception of Homer and the Bible and wanting the life cycles of documents explained to them. But in any case, these were only enough for looking back a couple thousand years, certainly not tens of thousands of years. The anthropologists recommended the symbol of the skull and crossbones. A historian remembered that to alchemists, the skull and crossbones meant resurrection. A psychologist performed an experiment with three-year-olds: when he pasted the skull and crossbones on a bottle, they yelled "poison"; if he pasted the same symbol on the wall, they yelled "pirates."

Other scientists suggested literally plastering the ground around the permanent waste sites with ceramic, metal, and iron planks that contained all sorts of warnings. However, the judgment of the linguists was unambiguous: it would be understood only for a maximum of 2,000 years. Precisely the scientific meticulousness with which the committee proceeded clarified what the concept of world risk society implies, uncovers, and renders understandable: human language fails before the task of informing future generations of the dangers that we inadvertently put into the world through the use of certain technologies. The modern world increases the differences between the language of calculable risks in which we think and act and the world of noncalculable uncertainty that we create with the same speed of technological developments. With past decisions on nuclear energy and contemporary decisions on the use of genetic technology, nanotechnology, computer sciences, and so forth, we set off unpredictable, uncontrollable, and incommunicable consequences that endanger life on earth.

What is new about the risk society? Were not all societies, all people, all epochs always surrounded by dangers that prompted these societies to unite to defend themselves? The concept of risk is a modern concept. It requires decisions and attempts to render the unpredictable consequences of civil decisions predictable and controllable. When one says, for example, that a smoker's risk for cancer is X amount and the risk of a nuclear power plant catastrophe is Y amount, this means that these risks are avoidable negative consequences of decisions that appear to be predictable through the probability of accident and disease and thus unlike natural catastrophes. The novelty of the world risk society lies in the fact that we, with our civilizing decisions, cause global consequences that trigger problems and dangers that radically contradict the institutionalized language and promises of the authorities in catastrophic cases highlighted worldwide (such as Chernobyl and now the terrorist attacks in New York and Washington). The political explosiveness of the world risk society lies precisely in this fact. Its heart rests in the mass media, politics, and bureaucracy—not necessarily at the site of its happening. This political explosiveness does not allow itself to be described or measured in the language of risk, in the number of victims dead and wounded, or in scientific formulas. This causes it to "explode"—if the metaphor is permitted—with responsibility, demands of rationality, legitimizations through reality checks; for the other side of the present danger is the failure of institutions that derive their legitimacy through a declared mastery of danger. For this reason, the "social birth" of a global danger is an equally improbable as well as a dramatic, traumatic, world-shaking event. In the shock highlighted by the mass media, it becomes evident for a second that the silence of words—or, according to one of Goya's etchings—"the slumber of reason generates monsters."

Three layers of danger can be identified in the world risk society. Each one follows a different logic of conflict, circles around or represses other topics, or crushes or empowers certain priorities: first, ecological crises; second, global economic crises; and third, since September 11, the risk of transnational terrorist networks. Despite the differences, all three possibilities of danger present a common pattern of political opportunities and contradictions within the world risk society: in an age when faith in God, class, nation, and the government is disappearing, the recognized and acknowledged global nature of danger becomes a fusion of relations in which the apparent and irrevocable constants of the political world suddenly melt and become malleable. At the same time, however, new conflict and political alternatives present themselves, which once again question the unity of the world risk society: How could these dangers be overcome within the limits of historical nonsimultaneities of single nations and cultures?

This is how the horrific pictures of terrorism, those obscene images of a live mass murder and a live suicide, staged as a global television appearance, shook people worldwide and triggered a political reflexivity that contradicted all expectations. It was questioned and discussed over and over again: What could unite the world? The experimental answer: an attack from Mars. This type of terrorism is like an attack from an "internal Mars." For a single historical blink of an eye, the disputed sites and nations stand united against the common enemy of global terrorism.

Precisely the universalization of terrorist threats against the nations of the world renders the battle against global terrorism a major political challenge in which opposing camps forge new alliances, regional conflicts are dammed, and the cards of world politics get reshuffled. Until recently, national arms reduction plans still dominated Washington's political actions and debates; now there is no more talk of this. Instead, the belief seems to have taken hold that not even a perfect arms reduction system could have prevented these attacks and that the way to ensure U.S. internal security is not by the United States acting on its own but by forming a global alliance. Relations between former cold war enemies, Moscow and Washington, play an outstanding role. U.S. unilateralism falls flat on its face in the world risk society and for national interests. It is not possible for the United States to arrest Osama bin Laden in an isolated action by the CIA and the Pentagon without the rest of the world. The world risk society requires a multilateralism of the sort in which Russia switches from the role of the petitioner to the role of nation to be wooed. Russian president Vladimir

Putin's decision to completely and unmistakably place himself on the side of modernity, civilized and attacked, opened up new power and opportunities to refashion himself as an important partner in the multipronged balance of power in the global alliance. However, this certainly does not create the illusion that the war against terrorism can underhandedly expand into a war against Islam, that is, a war that does not conquer terrorism but feeds and increases it, or a war that might reduce important liberties or renew protectionism and nationalism and demonize cultural others.

In other words, the global nature of the perceived threat has two faces: it creates both new forms for a political risk society and regional inconsistencies and inequalities with regard to those who are affected by those dangers. The fact that the collapse of global financial markets or climate change in a single region, for instance, has diverse effects does not change the fact that, in principle, everyone could be affected and that overcoming these problems in the present state necessitates global political efforts. Environmental problems such as global warming and world overpopulation (of present and future generations) could promote the idea of a "community of common destiny."

However, this does not by any means occur without conflict. For example, the question is raised, to what extent do industrial nations have the right to demand that developing nations protect important global resources, such as rain forests, while using a lion's share of energy resources for themselves? Yet it is precisely these conflicts that form common ground by underlining the fact that global solutions need to be found and that this will occur not through war but through negotiations.

This does not mean that there is only one answer to the demands of the world risk society. For European and non-European nations and cultures, the ways into the world risk society are just as different as the ways out of it can be. In this sense, it becomes clear that in the future there will be many modernities. The debates surrounding an Asian modernity or a Chinese, Russian, South American, or African one are just beginning now. This type of discourse removes all doubt that the European monopoly on modernity is broken in the world risk society. Seen in such a way, the radical critique of modernity in a non-European realm turns out to be one against "excessive individualism," against the loss of "cultural identity and worth," in short, against a "McDonaldization of the world"; it is not a straightforward rejection of modernity but more an attempt to test and try out other modernities that selectively hearken back to the Western model of modernity.

The everyday realm of the world risk society is not a love affair between everyone and everything. It comes about and consists in the perceived necessity for global consequences to civilizing actions—regardless of whether these consequences create globalization through information technology networking, financial channels, natural crises, cultural symbols, the pending atmospheric catastrophe, or terrorist threats. Therefore, it is the reflexivity of the world risk society that breaks the silence of words and allows globalization to become painfully aware of itself in its own context and builds new approaches to conflicts and alliances. What has been shown for the modern nation-states is that they can keep their vulnerability in check only through constant communication—this has proved true even for the world risk society. This brings me to my first question: how do the meanings of *terrorism* and *war* change in the context of the world risk society?

TERRORISM AND WAR

Even the notion of "terrorist" is misleading when talking about the novelty of the threat because it creates the illusion of a familiarity with motifs of national liberation movements that do not apply to the perpetrators of suicide and mass murder. What is simply inexplicable to the Western observer is the way in which fanatical antimodernism, antiglobalism, and modern global thinking and acting are interrelated.

Hannah Arendt coined the phrase *banality of evil* with the fascist mass murderer Adolf Eichmann in mind. In this vein, we can imagine absolutely evil technocrats who are family oriented but not terrorists in the name of God; they marry in the West, earn engineering degrees in Germany, have a fondness for vodka, and quietly plan years in advance for technically perfect group suicides and mass murders and then execute them in cold blood. How is this at all rooted in modernity and to be simultaneously understood as the archaic selflessness of evil?

Up until now, the military focused its attention on itself and other national military organizations and their defenses, but now it is transnational threats from underground perpetrators and networks that challenge world governments. Just as earlier in the cultural realm, it is possible to experience the death of distance in the military realm as well—that is, the end of the state monopoly on violence in a civilized world where anything can be turned into a weapon in the hands of a few decisive fanatics. Even the peaceful symbols of civilized society could be converted into instruments of hell. In principle, this is nothing new; it is a critical experience that is omnipresent.

With the horrific scenes from New York, terrorist groups have established themselves as new global actors in competition with states, economies, and civil societies in one swoop. Terrorist networks act like nongovernmental organizations—"violence NGOs"—in a non–territorially bound, decentered fashion, acting locally on the one hand and transnationally on the other. They use the Internet. Whereas Greenpeace, for example, uses environmental crises and Amnesty International uses human rights causes against national governments, terrorist NGOs increase their monopoly. This means that this type of transnational terrorism is not limited to Islamic terrorism. Rather, it can align itself with any possible goal, ideology, or fundamentalism. A distinction must be made between the terrorism of national freedom movements, which are nationally and territorially bound, and that of the new, transnational terrorist networks, which act without any territorial affiliations and across national boundaries and manage, as a consequence, to cancel the national language of war and the military with one strike. Previous terrorists tried to save their lives after committing terrorist acts. Suicide terrorists create a monstrous destructive force through the intended surrendering of their lives. The suicide bomber is the most radical contrast to *Homo economicus.* He is both economically and morally uninhibited and, for this reason, is a bearer of absolute cruelty. In a strict sense, the act and the suicide bomber are one. A suicide bomber cannot commit a suicide attack more than once, nor can state authorities convict him. This singularity is marked by the simultaneity of act, confession, and self-extinguishment.

To be exact, governments do not even have to search for suicide bombers in order to find them guilty of their crimes. The culprits have confessed to their crimes and turned their weapons on themselves. For this reason, the antiterrorism alliance need not capture the individuals directly responsible for New York and Washington (they have already pulverized themselves); rather, they seek the people behind them: the puppet masters or the state patrons. Whereas the culprits turn the weapons on themselves, the causalities dissipate and get lost. This means that states are indispensable for building transnational terrorist networks. But perhaps it is precisely this lack of government identification, this lack of functional government structure, that offers the humus for terrorist activities. Perhaps the placing of responsibility on governments and on those behind the scenes who give the orders stems from military thinking. Today, however, we are on the threshold of an individualization of war, a type of warfare in which wars are no longer conducted state against state, but rather individuals against states.

The power of terrorist actions rises with a series of conditions: the vulnerability of a civilization; the global, mass media–informed presence of terrorist risk; the U.S. president's assessment that "civilization" is under threat because of these culprits; and their readiness to extinguish themselves. Finally, the risks of terrorism exponentially multiply with technological advancement. With the technologies of the future—genetic engineering, nanotechnology, and robotics—we are opening a new Pandora's box. Genetic manipulation, communication technologies, and artificial intelligence are all interconnected mean of getting around the government monopoly of violence and will wind up opening, if no international bar is placed in front of it, the door to an individualization of war.

Thus a genetically engineered menace with a long period of incubation that targets specific populations—in other words, a genetically engineered miniature bomb—can be built by anyone without a tremendous effort. This is just one of many examples. The difference between atomic and biological weapons is notable. It is grounded on scientifically based technological developments that can be easily expanded and are capable of revolutionizing themselves again and again. Thus, the possibility of government control and monopoly fails, as it did with atomic and biochemical weapons when they were reduced to specific materials and resources (weapons-convertible uranium, costly laboratories). Politically, this empowerment of individuals against governments could be dangerous. The boundaries between the military and civil society may be torn down, as well as the boundaries between innocent and guilty, between suspects and nonsuspects, where up until now, sharp distinctions have been made. If the individualization of war continues to be a threat, citizens will have to prove that they are not dangerous, because under these circumstances, every individual might be a potential terrorist. Everyone has to accept the fact that he or she, in the absence of any concrete reason, has to be checked for "security reasons." This indicates that, in the end, the individualization of war can translate into the death of democracy. Governments would have to ally themselves with other governments against individuals in order to avert the threat presented by their own citizens.

When thought through thoroughly, a premise in the present discussion on terrorism—namely, the distinction between "good" and "bad" terrorists—crumbles. Nationalists are to be respected, and fundamentalists are to be abhorred. There are no justifications for such value judgments and distinctions in the age of nationalistic modernity; they become a moral and political perversion in the terroristic world risk society and in any consideration of the possibility of the individualization of war.

Is a political response to this challenge even possible? I would like to name one principle: the law. In a nationalist context, allowing the victims of crime to assume the roles of persecutor, judge, and executive power infringes on the legal sensibilities of the civilized world. This type of "self-justice" must also be overcome in international relations. Even if relations between the states are not fully ripe for it, the global alliance against terrorism has to be based on the law. Thus it follows that an international convention against terrorism must be discussed and ratified. It must be a convention that not only clarifies certain notions but also provides a legal basis for the intergovernmental prosecution of terrorists—in other words, this convention has to create a unified, universal space for the law to be executed. This, among other things, requires that the statutes of the international courts of all nations, even those of the United States, have to be ratified.[3] The goal would be for terrorism to be punishable as a crime against humanity worldwide. States that refuse to adopt this convention would have to face combined sanctions from all other states. Would this not be an interest that Europe and Russia, based on their historical backgrounds, could espouse as their own in order to sharpen their political profiles in the global alliance—to help in the battle against terrorism by building their own opposing military momentum to success? This brings me to my second question: how do the meanings of *economic globalization* and *neoliberalism* shift in the context of the world risk society?

ECONOMIC GLOBALIZATION AND NEOLIBERALISM

Allow me to start with an anecdote. When I hear the word *globalization*, the following political cartoon appears before my eyes: The Spanish conquerors, the conquistadors, arrive in the New World in their shiny armor with horses and weapons. The thought bubble reads, "We have come to you to talk to you about God, civilization, and the truth." A group of bewildered native onlookers responds, "Of course, what would you like to know?"

This scenario can easily be transported into the present. Economic experts from the World Bank, the International Monetary Fund, corporate managers, lawyers, and diplomats step off their intercontinental flights in post-Soviet Moscow. A thought bubble reads, "We have come to talk to you about democracy, human rights, and the free-market economy." A delegation of readers responds, "But of course, how else do the Germans go around spreading open violence against foreigners on their streets?"

Perhaps this caricature depicts yesterday's situation, which is no longer valid today. The terrorist attacks and the anthrax scare raise questions that can no longer be swept under the rug: Is the triumph of the economy already over? Will the primacy of politics be rediscovered? Has neoliberalism's apparently unstoppable victory suddenly been broken? In fact, the outbreak of global terrorism resembles a Chernobyl of globalization. With Chernobyl, it was about taking the exaltation of nuclear energy to its grave; with September 11, it is about bidding farewell to the beatification of neoliberalism. The suicide terrorists not only uncovered the vulnerability of Western civilization but also gave us a taste of the sorts of conflicts that are generated by economic globalization. In the world of global risks, the mark of neoliberalism rapidly loses its credibility to substitute the state and politics through economics.

The privatization of airline security in the United States is particularly emblematic of the above point. Until now, there has been a reluctance to discuss this because the tragedy of September 11 was homemade, in part. Moreover, the United States' vulnerability certainly has something to do with its political philosophy. America is a neoliberal nation through and through and is thus unwilling to pay the price for public safety. It was long known that the United States was a target for terrorist attacks, but in contrast to Europe, flight security was privatized and taken over by miracle-working, highly flexible part-time workers whose wages are lower than those of fast-food workers, meaning approximately $6 an hour. The individuals who occupy these important security positions have only a few hours of training and no more than six months of on-the-job experience. Before restricting the basic rights of all citizens to ward against terrorism and endangering democracy, the government should take over flight security and make it more professional. This is just one example of the many improvements that could be made.

It is America's neoliberal concept of itself—its government penny-pinching, on the one hand, and the triad of deregulation, liberalization, and privatization, on the other—that contributes to America's vulnerability to terrorism. The extent to which this realization catches on will break the hegemonic power that neoliberalism has gained in shaping U.S. philosophy and actions in the past. In this sense, the horrific pictures of New York contain a message that has yet to be deciphered: a state, a country can become neoliberal to the point of death.

The economic commentators of the big daily newspapers worldwide suspect this and insist that what was true before September 11 cannot be false after September 11. In other words, the neoliberal model will persist even after the terrorist attacks because there are no alternatives to it. But this is precisely what is wrong. This reveals a lack of alternative thinking. Neoliberalism has always been frowned on for being a fair-weather philosophy that works only when blatant conflicts or crises arise. The neoliberal imperative insists that too much government and politics and the regulating hand of bureaucracy are the real causes of world problems such as unemployment, global poverty, and economic breakdowns. The success of neoliberalism relied on the promise that a free economy and a globalization of markets would solve the problems of humanity. It championed the belief that by giving free rein to egoism, inequality could be battled in accordance with global standards and global justice could prevail. Instead, capitalist fundamentalists' belief in the magical power of the market has recently proved itself to be a dangerous illusion.

In times of crisis, neoliberalism is left standing without a single political response. The approach of increasing the dosage of bitter economic medicine when a breakdown is pending or comes full circle in order to rectify the consequences of globalization is an illusionary theory that only now begins to exact its price. On the contrary, terrorist threats make the simple truths that the neoliberal triumph had suppressed known again: The separation of the world economy from politics is illusionary. There is no security without the state and public service. Without taxation, there is no government, no education, no affordable health care, no social security, no democracy. Without the public, democracy and civil society have no legitimacy. And without legitimacy, there is no security. Thus it follows that without the shape and form of a legally regulated (meaning recognized and not violent) national settlement of conflict in the future—and above all, on a global level—there will be no world economy in any form.

Wherein lies the alternative to neoliberalism? Certainly not in national protectionism. We need an expanded concept of politics that is capable of appropriately regulating crises and conflicts. The Tobin tax—being demanded more and more by political parties in Europe and worldwide—on the unbridled flow of capital is only a first program. Neoliberalism insisted on the economy breaking out of its nationalistic dwelling and building transnational rules for itself. At the same time, it assumed that the government would keep on playing its old game and keep its national boundaries. After the terrorist attacks, even the states recognized the power and possibilities of transnational cooperation, even if only for the scope of internal security. All of a sudden, the opposite of neoliberalism, the importance of the state, becomes omnipresent again, and in its oldest Hobbesian variant: that of guaranteeing security. What was unthinkable up until recently—a European warrant of arrest that disregards the sacred national sovereignty of matters of the law and the police—is now within reach. Perhaps soon we will experience a similar joining of forces in light of the possible world economic crisis. The economy has to prepare itself for new rules and new circumstances. The times of "everyone to the best of their abilities and will" are certainly over.

The terrorist resistance to globalization has achieved the exact opposite of what it sought to achieve. It introduced a new era of globalization of politics and of the states—the transnational invention of the political through cooperation and networking. In this way, the not yet publicly noticed strange natural law has proved that resisting globalization—whether one likes it or not—only accelerates its engine. This paradox is enough to grasp that *globalization* is the name for a strange process that is realized on two opposite tracks: one is either for it or against it. All those who oppose globalization not only share global communications media with those in favor of it; they also operate on the foundation of global rights, global markets, global mobility, and global networks. They also think and act in global categories that they create through their acts of global openness and global attention. One need only think of the precision with which the terrorists of September 11 staged their acts in New York as a television-worthy live catastrophe and live mass murder. They could count on the fact that the destruction of the second tower by a passenger aircraft transformed into a missile would be transmitted live throughout the entire world via the omnipresent television cameras.

Does globalization have to be the cause for terrorist attacks? Is it perhaps an understandable reaction to a neoliberal steamroller that, as critics state it, seeks to flatten every corner of this world? No, that is nonsense. No cause, no abstract idea, no god can justify or excuse these attacks. Globalization is an ambivalent process that cannot be reversed. Smaller and weaker states give up their politics of self-sufficiency and rush to join the world market. How did one of the big daily newspapers headline the German chancellor's visit to Ukraine? "We forgive the crusaders and await the investors." In fact, there is just one thing worse than being steamrolled by foreign investors, and that is *not* being steamrolled by foreign investors. It is necessary, however, to link economic globalization with a policy of cosmopolitan understanding. The dignity of people, their cultural identities, the otherness of others must be taken more seriously in the future. Wouldn't it make sense to build a new pillar in the alliance against terrorism? To build a cultural bridge, so to speak, and foster a dialogue between the cultures on the inside and outside, with the countries in the Islamic world and also with the countries of the so-called third and fourth worlds, which view themselves as victims of globalization? And couldn't a culturally extroverted Europe—in particular, a culturally extroverted Germany—play a leading role, since it is less plagued by a colonial past but still cognizant of its obligation because of the Holocaust?

This brings me to the third and final question: how and to what extent do the concepts of *state* and *sovereignty* change in the eyes of the world risk society?

STATE AND SOVEREIGNTY

To get right to it, terrorist attacks reinforce the state but cancel its central historical form, the nation-state. National security is, in the borderless age of risks, no longer national security. This is the biggest lesson from the terrorist attacks. Certainly, there were always alliances. The difference is that, today, global alliances are necessary not only for external but also for internal security. In the past, it was accurate to say that foreign policy was a question of choice, not of necessity. Today, on the contrary, a new principle governs the scene; national security and international cooperation are directly linked. The only way to have national security in the face of the threat of globalized terrorism (but also of financial risks, the downfall of organized crime) is transnational cooperation. The paradoxical principle is valid here: states need to denationalize and transnationalize themselves. This means that they need to sacrifice certain aspects of their autonomy in order to overcome their national problems in a globalized world. The acquisition of a new space for action and leeway—that is, the expansion of political sovereignty and control—has to be paid for with "self-denationalization." The dismantling of national autonomy and the growth of national sovereignty do not by any means cancel each other out. Rather, they can reciprocally reinforce and expedite each other. The logic of the zero-sum game that was valid for empires, superpowers, colonialism, economic and cultural imperialism, independent nation-states, and military blocs loses its power of justification.

In this sense, it is crucial to introduce the difference between sovereignty and autonomy. The nation-state was based on the equation of sovereignty with autonomy. Viewed in this light, economic independence, cultural diversification, and military, legal, and technological cooperation between states automatically lead to the loss of autonomy and sovereignty. However, if one measures sovereignty by political creative power and the extent to which a state succeeds at gaining power and influence on the stage of world politics and increases its citizens' security and prosperity, it follows that greater interconnection and cooperation lead to a loss of autonomy and a gain in sovereignty. For example, Russia's worth in the world is no longer measured by its potential for confrontation, as it was during the cold war, but by its cooperative potential and art—that is, by its ranking in the networked states of the world and the world market, as well as by its presence in supranational organizations. Separated and united sovereignty does not reduce this; on the contrary, it increases the potential for single-state sovereignty. In this sense, not only the global terrorist threats but also the world risk society in its entirety open a new era of transnational and multilateral cooperation.

The disintegration of the Soviet Union, Yugoslavia, and Czechoslovakia notably led to a large number of nationally defined successor states in which ethnic, national, and civic identities resulted in conflictual overlap and exclusion. This newly awakened national consciousness in the countries and states of central and eastern Europe seems at first glance to be in conflict with the discovery and development of cooperative transnational states in the face of the challenges posed by the world risk society. The opposite is true. These challenges can contribute toward taming the borderless national and ethnic tensions in the post-Soviet states. If these countries concur in defining their position, such that they can be confronted with common historical challenges, it will be possible and necessary to find political frames and coordinates to vote on national solutions and demands on sovereignty under transnational conditions. This is now being experienced and spelled out in geopolitical questions of the borderless "internal security" of states that overlap both ethnically and nationally. In any case, this can be transferred into questions regarding regional world economic cooperation, the curbing of global financial crises, the impending atmospheric catastrophes and environmental dangers, poverty, and, last but not least, human rights. In other words, in the recognized and acknowledged threats of the future, there may be a key to lessen the historical experiences of violence cooperatively.

Two ideal types of transnational cooperation among states emerge: "surveillance" states and "open-world" states, in which national autonomy gets reduced in order to renew and expand national sovereignty in the world risk society. Surveillance states, with their cooperative power, threaten to become fortress states in which security and the military will be writ large and freedom and democracy writ small. The word is already out that Western societies accustomed to peace and prosperity lack the necessary measure of friend-or-foe thinking and the readiness, the advantage that the marvel of human rights had up until now, to give up the now necessary measures of resistance. This attempt to build a Western fortress against the cultural others is omnipresent and will surely increase in the coming years. A policy of state authoritarianism that behaves adaptively in foreign relations and authoritarian in domestic affairs could be the result. For the winners of globalization, neoliberalism is appropriate; for the losers of globalization, it stirs up terrorism and xenophobia and administers doses of the poison of racism. This would amount to a victory for the terrorists, because the nations of modernity would rob themselves precisely of that which makes them attractive and superior: freedom and democracy.

In the future, it will mostly come down to the following question: what are we fighting for if it is about fighting transnational terrorism? An open-world state system based on the recognition of the otherness of others holds the answers.

Nation-states, whether their borders are internal or external, can possess ethnic and national identities that overlap and exclude one another or have not grown together peaceably. Open-world states, in contrast, emphasize the necessity of self-determination and a responsibility toward others, uniting foreigners within and beyond national borders. It is not about denying self-determination or damming it in—on the contrary, it is about freeing it from national tunnel vision and connecting it with an openness toward world interests. Open-world states not only fight terrorism but also fight the causes of terrorism in the world. They gain and renew the powers of creation and persuasion of the political by solving pressing global problems that seem insolvable by single national initiatives. Open-world states are founded on the principle of the state's national indifference. Similar to the Westphalian peace that ended the sixteenth-century religious civil war through the separation of church and state—which is the crux of the argument here—the world national (civil) wars of the twentieth and early twenty-first centuries are also addressed with a separation of church and state. Similar to the way the irreligious state renders the practice of different religions possible, open-world states have to provide for border-crossing closeness of ethnic, national, and religious identities through the principle of constitutional tolerance.

I am coming to my conclusion. It is almost superfluous to pronounce it, but I am hopelessly rooted in the tradition of the Enlightenment, even if self-critically applied. With this in mind, I have attempted to trace how a political handbook, which is seemingly composed for perpetuity, gets dissolved and reshaped. Perhaps it astounds you as much as it does me that the fear of danger, which paralyzes us, also succeeds in obstructing our view of the very broad political perspectives that are opening up. I have hinted at three of these only seemingly paradoxical opportunities that the world risk society has to offer.

First, it seems possible and necessary to create an international legal foundation for the alliance against terrorism. It would entail an antiterror regime that regulates issues such as tax investigation as well as the extradition of perpetrators, the authorization of armed forces, the jurisdiction of courts, and so forth; only in this way can the long-term challenge of shifting historical and political contexts really be met.

Second, it would be necessary to base the promise of the alliance not only on military means but also on a credible policy of dialogue—first of all, with regard to the Islamic world, but also toward other cultures that see their worth as being threatened through globalization. Only in this way can the military actions that only succeed in helping terrorists to ally themselves with worldwide Islamic populations be prevented. Perhaps the more culturally experienced and, in foreign policy, more dialogue experienced Europe is better equipped to do this than the culturally introverted America.

Third, the dangers of the world risk society could be transformed into opportunities to create regional structures of cooperation among open-world multinational states. Let me end with a quote from Immanuel Kant: "To think of oneself as a member of a cosmopolitan society in compliance with state laws is the most sublime idea that man can have about his predicament and which cannot be thought of without enthusiasm."

NOTES

This article is based on a talk given to the Russian Duma in November 2001. It was translated from the German by Elena Mancini.

1. Hugo von Hofmannsthal, *Der Brief des Lord Chandos* (Stuttgart: Verlag, 2000), 51f.
2. See Gregory Benford, *Deep Time: How Humanity Communicates across Millennia* (New York: Avon Perennial, 1999); Frank Schirrmacher, "Ten Thousand Years of Isolation," *Frankfurter Allgemeine Zeitung* 209 (September 2000): 49. I thank the latter for this example.
3. Baltasar Garzón, "Die einzige Antwort auf den Terror" (The only answer to terror), *Die Zeit* 44 (October 25, 2001): 11.

CONTRIBUTORS

STANLEY ARONOWITZ is distinguished professor of sociology at the Graduate Center, City University of New York. He is the author or editor of twenty-three books, including *How Class Works, Just Around the Corner, The Paradox of the Jobless Recovery,* and *The Knowledge Factory.* He is currently writing a biography of C. Wright Mills.

ULRICH BECK is professor of sociology at the University of Munich and the *British Journal of Sociology* Visiting Centennial Professor at the London School of Economics and Sciences. He is chief editor of *Soziale Welt,* as well as editor of *Zweite Moderne* at Suhrkamp. He is the director of a research center at the University of Munich (in cooperation with four other universities in the area), Reflexive Modernization.

MARWAN BISHARA is a Palestinian writer and editorialist and a lecturer at American University of Paris, and he is the author of *Palestine/Israel: Peace or Apartheid.*

STEPHEN ERIC BRONNER is distinguished professor of political science at Rutgers University and a member of the graduate faculties of comparative literature and German studies. The senior editor of *Logos: A Journal of Modern Society and Culture,* he is also the author of numerous books and articles on modern politics and society, including *Reclaiming the Enlightenment: Toward a Politics of Radical Engagement* and *A Rumor About the Jews: Antisemitism, Conspiracy, and "The Protocols of Zion."*

PATRICIA CHOLAKIAN (1933–2003) taught at Hamilton College until her retirement in 1996 and was the author of articles and books on women writers of early Europe, notably, *Rape and Writing in the 'Heptameron' of Marguerite de Navarre.* At her death, she and her husband, Rouben C. Cholakian, were completing a literary biography of Marguerite de Navarre (1492–1549), *Marguerite de Navarre: Mother of the Renaissance.*

DRUCILLA CORNELL is professor of political science, women's studies, and comparative literature at Rutgers University. She is currently working on two books: one about the future of freedom, equality, and global development; another about the future of critical theory.

FRED DALLMAYR is Packey J. Dee Professor of Political Theory at the University of Notre Dame. Among his recent publications are *Alternative Visions, Border Crossings, Achieving Our World, Toward a Global and Plural Democracy, Dialogue among Civilizations,* and *Peace Talks—Who Will Listen.*

LAWRENCE DAVIDSON is professor of Middle East history at West Chester University in West Chester, Pennsylvania. He is author of *Islamic Fundamentalism* and *America's Palestine: Popular and Official Perceptions from Balfour to Israeli Statehood.* He also has written nineteen published articles on U.S. perceptions of and policies toward the Middle East.

IRENE GENDZIER is a professor in the department of political science at Boston University. She is the author of a forthcoming updated edition of *Notes from the Minefield: United States Intervention in Lebanon and the Middle East, 1945–1958.*

ERNEST GOLDBERGER grew up in Switzerland, where he was active as an entrepreneur. He has lived in Israel for twelve years. His book, *Die Seele Israels* (The Soul of Israel), was recently published in Switzerland.

JEFFREY GOLDFARB is chair and Michael E. Gellert Professor of Sociology at New School University in New York. He is the author of several books, including *The Persistence of Freedom: The Sociological Implications of Polish Student Theater* and *On Cultural Freedom: An Exploration of Public Life in Poland and America.*

PHILIP GREEN is visiting professor of political science at New School University Graduate Faculty and a member of the editorial board of the *Nation*. He is the author of several books, most recently, *Equality and Democracy.*

JÜRGEN HABERMAS is professor emeritus of philosophy at the University of Frankfurt and the author of numerous books in social philosophy and sociology. His most recent books in English are *The Future of Human Nature, Philosophy in a Time of Terror* (with Jacques Derrida), and *Truth and Justification.*

WADOOD HAMAD is a research physicist, writer, and activist currently living in Vancouver, Canada.

DICK HOWARD is distinguished professor of philosophy at the State University of New York at Stony Brook. His most recent books are *The Specter of Democracy* and *Aux origines de la pensée politique américaine*. In addition, *Chroniques de la démocratie américaine* and *The Necessity of Politics: Reading the History of Political Philosophy* are forthcoming.

CONTRIBUTORS

KURT JACOBSEN is a research associate in the department of political science at the University of Chicago and the author or co-editor of six books.

JAMES JENNINGS is the founder and president of Conscience International, a humanitarian agency based in Atlanta, Georgia. He appears regularly on television and radio. Trained as an archaeologist, his expertise is in the Middle East.

DOUGLAS KELLNER is George Kneller Chair in the Philosophy of Education at UCLA and is author of many books on social theory, politics, history, and culture, including a trilogy with Steven Best on postmodern theory, as well as *Media Culture, Grand Theft 2000: Media Spectacle and a Stolen Election, From 9/11 to Terror War: The Dangers of the Bush Legacy,* and *Media Spectacle and the Crisis of Democracy: Terrorism, War, and Election Battles.*

CHRISTINE KELLY is director of the American Democracy Project in the department of political science at William Paterson University. She is the author of numerous books, including *Tangled Up In Red, White, and Blue: New Social Movements in America.*

MENACHEM KLEIN is a senior lecturer in the department of political science at Bar-Ilan University, Israel, and a senior research fellow at the Jerusalem Institute for Israel Studies. His books are *Jerusalem: The Contested City* and *The Jerusalem Problem: The Struggle for Permanent Status.*

GEOFFREY KURTZ is a graduate student in political science at Rutgers University. He is writing a dissertation on the political thought of Jean Jaurés.

MEERA NANDA obtained a PhD in biotechnology before turning to history and philosophy of science. Her most recent book, *The Wrongs of the Religious Right: Reflections on Science, Secularism and Hindutva,* was published in India in 2005. She is currently on a research fellowship from the Templeton Foundation.

CHARLES NOBLE is professor and chair of political science as well as director of the international studies program at California State University, Long Beach. He has written widely on American politics, public policy, and political economy and is the author of *The Collapse of Liberalism: Why America Needs a New Left, Welfare As We Knew: A Political History of the American Welfare State,* and *Liberalism at Work: The Rise and Fall of OSHA.*

HENRY PACHTER (1907–1980) was one of the twentieth century's most important scholars of socialism and political history. He wrote several books, including *Magic Into Science: The Story of Paracelsus* and *The Fall and Rise of Europe: A Political, Social, and Cultural History of the Twentieth Century.*

ERIC ROULEAU was the French ambassador to Tunisia from 1985–1986 and to Turkey from 1988–1992. An internationally known journalist and an expert on Western relations with the Middle East, he is currently a special correspondent for *Le monde diplomatique*.

R. CLAIRE SNYDER is associate professor of government and politics in political theory at George Mason University. She also serves as a faculty fellow at the Women & Politics Institute at American University. She is the author of *Citizen-Soldiers and Manly Warriors: Military Service and Gender in the Civic Republican Tradition* and *The Case for Gay Marriage* (forthcoming), as well as numerous articles and essays on topics related to democratic theory and citizenship.

MANFRED B. STEGER is professor of global studies and head of the School of International and Community Studies at the Royal Melbourne Institute of Technology in Melbourne, Australia. He is also an affiliated faculty member with the department of political science at the University of Hawai'i-Manoa. Publications include *Globalism: Market Ideology Meets Terrorism, 2nd ed., Judging Nonviolence: The Dispute Between Realists and Idealists, Globalization, Gandhi's Dilemma: Nonviolent Principles and Nationalist Power,* and *The Quest For Evolutionary Socialism: Eduard Bernstein and Social Democracy.* He is currently writing a book on political ideologies in the age of globalization.

MICHAEL J. THOMPSON is assistant professor of political science at William Paterson University and the founder and editor of *Logos: A Journal of Modern Society and Culture*. His books include *Islam and the West: Critical Perspectives on Modernity* and *Confronting Neoconservatism: The Rise of the New Right in America* (forthcoming).

ALEXIS DE TOCQUEVILLE (1805–1859) is the author of *Democracy in America*, a two-volume study of American political culture.

KEITH D. WATENPAUGH is associate director of the Center for Peace and Global Studies and is assistant professor of Eastern Mediterranean and Islamic history. He is the author of *Being Modern in the Middle East: Revolution, Nationalism, Colonialism, and the Middle Class in the Arab Eastern Mediterranean.*

NICHOLAS XENOS is professor of political science at the University of Massachusetts, Amherst. He is the author of *Scarcity and Modernity* and has contributed essays and reviews to the *Nation, Grand Street, London Review of Books,* and other periodicals.

INDEX

Abd-el-Kader, 205, 208
Abu Ghraib, 43
Adams, John, 28
Adorno, Gretel, 75–79
Adorno, Theodor, 23, 75–79, 123
Afghanistan, 15, 43, 159, 161, 291, 304, 317, 335, 353
Africa, 209–211
Aid to Families with Dependent Children, 46
al Aksa, 230, 243
Albright, Madeleine, 14
Alcibiades, 63
Alfarabi, 62, 63
Algeria, 201–212
Alliance for Marriage, 36
Alpert, Rebecca, 32
Alvares, Clause, 192–193
America
   African-Americans, 21–22, 29, 30, 54, 108–109, 112
   Americanization, 24
   Americans, 19–29, 102–110, 117, 145, 147, 161
   and American society, 21–27
   anti-Americanism, 17–20, 23, 25
   capitalism and, 53
   critical judgments of, 17
   culture, 19–21
   as economic model, 19
   foreign policy of, 13
   founders of, 28
   hegemony of, 105
   liberal capitalism and, 147
   and soldiers' lives, 11
   needs of, 15
   power, 21
   practices, 18
   public, 11, 15
   racism and, 21
   role of, 21
   triumphalism, 20
   way of life, 21
American Constitution, 127
American Enterprise Institute, 100, 109
"American model," 18
American Psychological Association, 35
Anatolia, 165–166
anticommunism, 18
anti-Semitism, 19
Arabs, 203–212, 305–319
Arab world, 14, 243, 279, 305
Arafat, Yasir, 223, 228, 257
Arbenz, 137
Arendt, Hannah, 17
Armenian resistance, 165
Ashcroft, John, 309–311

Baath (Iraq), 284, 286
Bajaj, Rahul, 345
Balfour, Arthur, 217
Balfour Declaration, 218
Balkans, 19, 198
Barak, Ehud, 228, 257
Barghouti, Mustapha, 195, 200
Barsamian, David, 154, 160
Batista, 137
Bayh, Evan, 11, 12
Bay of Pigs, 137
Bechtel, 43
Beck, Ulrich, 87–89
Beers, Charlotte, 270
Begin, Menachem, 220
Bell, Daniel, 145
Bellow, Saul, 60
Benda, Julien, 152
Ben-Gurion, David, 218, 255
Ben-Israel, Isaac, 256
Benjamin, Walter, 75, 150
Bennett, Stephen, 32
Bennett, William, 28, 69, 101

Berg, Alban, 75–79
Berger, Samuel, 346
Berger, Sandy, 310
Berlet, Chip, 33
Berman, Paul, 72
Bernstein, Eduard, 91
Bhagavad Gita, 181
Bible, 31, 32
Bill of Rights, 28, 29
Bishop, Maurice, 137
Blair, Tony, 13, 40, 81–82, 84
Blix, Hans, 288, 334
Bloch, Ernst, 75–79
Bloom, Allan, 60, 73
Bolshevik Revolution, 177
Bravo, Douglas, 137
Bremer, Paul III, 298
Brisard, Jean Charles, 309
Brock, David, 39
Brooks, David, 73
Brown, Sherrod, 12
Brown v. Board of Education, 30
Burkean conservatives, 21
Burnyeat, F. M., 68
Bush, George H. W., 69
Bush, George W., 9, 10, 12, 14, 15, 40–46, 48, 198, 247, 279, 283, 291, 303–319, 334, 341
   administration of, 9–12, 14, 39, 59, 103, 287–289, 303

Canada, 47
Caribbean, 137
Catholics, 21
central Asia, 23
Chalabi, Ahmed, 295
Cheney, Dick, 311–313, 331
Cheney, Lynne, 101
China, 141–148, 158, 161, 201, 280
   capitalism in, 145
Chomsky, Noam, 12, 108
Christianity, 33, 48, 105, 180, 186 203
   and evangelical churches, 30
   and fundamentalists, 42
   moral precept of, 28
   right-wing, 32
"Christian nation," 27–29

Christian Right, 28, 29, 31–32, 34–37
Churchill, 71
CIA, 9, 10
civil marriage, 27–29, 31–32
Civil Rights Act, 30, 109
civil rights movement, 51
Civil War, 29, 69
Clarke, Richard P., 40
Clarke, Wesley, 39, 308, 311
Clay, Jenny Straus, 59, 66, 72
Clinton administration, 309–311, 344
Clinton, Bill, 11, 51, 81–82, 279, 345
Clinton, Hillary, 11, 349
Cloward, Richard, 146
coalition of the willing, 15
Communism, 18, 21
Communist Party (China), 143, 145, 146
Conason, Joe, 39
Concerned Women for America, 36
Concord Coalition, 50
conservatives, 46, 120
   American, 27
   Christian, 28
   and religious organizations, 27
constitutional government, 28
constitutional interpretation, 28
Cook, Robin, 13
Cracow, 24
Croly, Herbert, 131
Cuba, 15, 137
Cuban revolution, 136–137
Cultural Revolution, 141
Cyprus, 198

D'Souza, Dinesh, 99–112
Dahl, Robert, 128
Damascus, 10
Daschle, Tom, 311
Dasquie, Guillaume, 309
Dayanand, 188
Dean, Howard, 11
Declaration of Independence, 28
democracy, 15, 20, 25, 105, 143–148
   in America, 25, 28
   and democratization, 19
   enemies of, 18

liberal, 19, 27, 29, 33
  principle of, 20
Democratic Leadership Council, 11
Democratic Party, 10–12, 14, 15, 30, 41, 50–52, 107, 121, 137, 313
  New Democrats, 51–52, 54
Derrida, Jacques, 163
Dewey, John, 129–130
Dharampal, 193
Diamond, Sarah, 33
dictatorship, 19
Djerejian, Edward P., 269
Dobson, James, 35
Dome of the Rock, 229, 243
Domhoff, G. William, 134
Douglass, Frederick, 112
Duelfer, Charles A. 9
Dumont, Louis, 187
Durkheim, Emile, 325

Egypt, 189, 202, 222–223, 284
Ehrenreich, Barbara, 108
Ehrenreich, Ben, 160
Eisenhower, Dwight, 154
Eisler, Kurt, 75–79
Eitam, Efi, 247
Eldar, Akiva, 195
Eliazar, Benjamin Ben, 260, 263
Elliot, Michael, 311
El Salvador, 161
England,
  foreign affairs ministry of, 13
  political landscape in, 13
Episcopal church, 33
equal rights, 28
Equal Rights Amendment, 29–31, 33
Europe, 14, 19-21, 23, 53, 104, 323–329, 361
  central, 17
  integration of, 17
  "new" and "old," 323–329
European Union, 53, 86
Exodus International, 35

Fahrenheit 9/11, 39–44
Falk, Richard, 159
Family Research Council, 31
Fanon, Francis, 104

far left, 11
FDR, 12
Federal Marriage Amendment, 27, 33
Feinstein, Dianne, 311
feminism, 30, 31, 34, 113
  and anti-feminists, 30
Feyerabend, Paul, 191
First Amendment, 27
Focus on the Family, 31
Foucalt, 117
Fourteenth Amendment, 29
France, 53, 201–212, 285
freedom, 20, 27
  individual, 28
Friedan, Betty, 113
Friederburg, Ludwig von, 75
Friedman, Thomas, 249, 345
Fromm, Erich 75
Froning, Denise, 346
Fukuyama, Francis, 105–106, 341, 349
Fulbright, J. William, 14

Gandhi, 188, 192
al-Gaylani, Rashid Ail, 277
Genesis, 31
Geneva Accord, 233–246
Germany, 53
Gerth, Hans, 119, 128, 131–132
Giddens, Anthony, 81–96
Gingrich, Newt, 289
Gitlin, Todd, 117
Goldwater, Barry, 30
Golub, Philip, 103
Gorbachev, Mikhail, 141, 146
Gore, Al, 12, 41, 52, 309
Gorky, Arshile, 165
government, secular, 27
Great Leap Forward, 141
Great Society, 51
Greece, 189
Greenspan, Alan, 346
Grossman, David, 260
Guantao, Jin, 142
Guatemala, 137
Guevara, Che, 137
Gulf of Tonkin, 14
Gulf War, 297, 319

Halliburton, 43
Harlech, Lord, 218
Haroutunian, Tavit, 165–167, 170
Harrington, Michael, 81, 96
Hart, Gary, 309
Hassner, Pierre, 324
Havel, Vaclav, 17
Hayden, Tom, 118
hegemonic power, 19
Heidegger, Martin, 72, 184
Herf, Jeffrey, 183
Hersh, Seymour, 59
Herzl, Theodore, 228
Herzog, Roman, 345
Hilferding, Rudolf, 147
Hinduism, 180–193
   and Hindu bomb, 180
   and nationalism, 181
   nationalist party and, 180
Hitchens, Christopher, 40
Hobbes, Thomas, 61, 62
von Hofmannsthal, Hugo, 354
Hollywood, 23, 34
Holocaust, 24
Homeland Security, 14
homosexuality, 27, 29, 30, 32, 34, 36, 37
   and gay marriage, 31, 33, 36
Hoover Institute, 100, 102
Horkheimer, Max, 75–79, 123
Hormats, Robert, 346
Horowitz, Irving Louis, 118
Hua, Gu, 142
Human Rights Campaign, 34
Huntington, Samuel, 342
ibn Hussein, Faisal, 273
Hussein, Saddam, 9–11, 14, 40, 293–298, 334–335

IG Metall, 53
impartial laws, 28
impeachment, 11
India, 149–163, 180, 182, 192, 198
Indonesia, 14
Institute of European Studies, 103
International Monetary Fund, 54
Iran, 15, 248, 307, 331
   Iran-contra, 14

Iraq, 9, 10, 15, 40, 43–44, 68, 103, 138, 161, 195, 248, 280, 285–297, 307, 334–335
   invasion of, 13, 280
   no-fly zones over, 40
   and weapons of mass destruction, 10
Iraqi War, 9–12, 331
   and Iraqi lives lost during, 11
Ireland, 198
Irgun, 220
Islam, 33, 186, 211
Israel, 40, 196–200, 217–225, 227–231, 233–246, 254–266, 285
   policies of, 195
   West Bank settlements in, 247–251

Jacobs, Paul, 81, 96
Jacoby, Russell, 117
Jamaica, 137
James, William, 131
Jim Crow, 21
Jingsheng, Wei, 143
Jodha, N. S., 187
Junger, Ernest, 184

Kabyles, 203–207
Kafka, Franz, 253–266
Kagan, Robert, 69
Kaige, Chen, 142
Kant, Immanuel, 337
Kashmir, 158
Kazimierz, 24
Kennedy, Bobby, 12
Kennedy administration, 137
Khomeini, Ayatollah, 290
Khrimean, Abbot, 169
Khrushchev, Nikita, 134–135
Kimmerling, Baruch, 199
King, Martin Luther Jr., 40
Kirchheimer, Otto, 75–79
Kirkpatrick, Jeanne, 289
Korea, 161
Kramnick, Isaac, 28
Kristol, Irving, 45
Kristol, William, 68, 69
Krugman, Paul, 12, 346
Kucharczyk, Jacek, 17

Kuhn, Thomas, 191
Ku Klux Clan, 21
Kurds, 165, 173

Labor Relations Act, 120
bin Laden, Osama, 40, 42–44, 104, 108, 304–319, 336, 356
LaHaye, Beverly, 37
Lang, Fritz, 75–79
Latin America, 20-21, 23, 108, 111, 137
Lee, Barbara, 12
Left, 49, 52–54, 107, 120, 126
Lenin, 154
Lenya, Lotte, 75
lesbian marriage, 27, 29–32, 34, 36, 37
Leviticus, 32
liberalism, 28–29, 100, 103, 104, 107, 120, 192
 capitalism and, 145
 Democrats and, 28, 46
 liberals and, 30, 46
 logic of, 29
 philosophical, and illiberal reaction to, 30-31
 political theory and, 28
liberties, 27
 religious, 28
Lichtenstein, Nelson, 117
Lieberman, Joseph, 12
Lilla, Mark, 73
Limbaugh, Rush, 13
Lincoln, 71, 157
Lippmann, Walter, 129–130
Lipset, Seymour Martin, 144
Lord, Carnes, 68
Loury, Glenn, 109
Loving v. Virginia, 30
Lowenthal, Leo, 75–79
Löwith, Karl, 61, 63
Lundberg, Ferdinand, 127
Lynd, Robert S., 134
Lyons, Mathew, 33

Machiavelli, 121
Mahidin, 204
Maimonides, 63
majoritarianism, 29

Makiya, Kanan, 295
al Malik, Abd, 229
Manley, Michael, 137
Mann, Erika, 75–79
Mann, Thomas, 75–79
Mannheim, Karl, 129
Maoism, 143
Marcos, 111
Marcuse, Herbert, 13, 75, 123
Marx, Karl, 90–91, 109, 119–120, 128, 148
Massachusetts Supreme Court, 29
Mattox, William, 36
Maude, Stanley, 272
Maurras, Charles, 62
McCarthy, Joseph 9, 107, 120
McChesney, Robert, 39
McGirr, Lisa, 33
McGuire, Liz, 102
Mead, George Herbert, 131
Mead, Margaret 67
Meehan, John, 348
Megged, Eyal, 258
Metropolitan Community Church, 33
Michnik, Adam, 17
Middle East, 15, 195, 219, 224, 228, 243, 288–290
Miller, Matt, 52
Mills, C. Wright, 117–138
Mohamed, 204
Moore, Barrington, 144
Moore, Michael, 39–44
Moore, R. Laurence, 28
Morse, Wayne, 137
Mosca, Gaetano, 126, 128, 131
Mossadegh, 284
Moussaoui, Zacarias, 308
Muller, Max, 188
multipolar world, 14
Murrow, Edward R., 13
Muslims, 180, 205
Muslim world, 106, 243

Nader, Ralph, 134
Nandy, Ashis, 186, 192–193
Nasser, 284, 286
National Association for Research and Therapy of Homosexuality, 35

National Liberation Front (El Salvador), 137
NATO, 39, 353
Nazis, 24
Nehru, 188
Nehru, Jawaharlal, 154
neoliberal Republicans, 28
Nersesian, Lucia, 165–166, 175
Netanyahu, 248
Neumann, Franz, 75–79
New Deal, 13, 45, 51–52, 121, 122, 131, 136
New Testament, 31
new world order, 21
Nicaragua, 137, 161
Nicolosi, Joseph, 35
Nietzsche, 104
9/11, 102–103, 107–108, 138, 291, 303–319, 341, 351, 353–356, 363
9/11 Commission, 40
North Korea, 15, 307

Office of Strategic Influence, 15
O'Neill, John, 310
O'Reilly, Bill, 13
"original intent," 28
Oppenheimer, Franz, 147
Oppenheimer, Robert, 181
Orwell, George, 253–266
Orwellian "endless war," 44

Pakistan, 14, 158, 182, 198
Palestine, 196–200, 247–251
  and its people, 195–200, 217–225, 228–230, 233–246, 247–251
Palestine Liberation Organization, 199, 233–234, 237, 240, 244–245, 257
Pareto, Vilfredo, 126, 128, 131
Parry, Jonathan, 182, 188
Pasha, Antranik, 175
Pasha, Glubb, 219
Patriot Act, 43
Penn, Sean, 12
Pentagon, 15
Peres, Shimon, 228
Perle, Richard, 10, 195
Persian Gulf war, 39
Pew Poll, 14

Pinochet, 111
Piven, Frances Fox, 12, 146
Pogo comic strip, 23
Poland, 17–19
Pol Pot, 135
postcommunist world, 20
Powell, Colin, 9, 283, 288, 289–291
Powers, Thomas, 10
preemptive strike, 14
President Johnson, 14
privatization, 48–49
Progressive Era, 13
proletariat, 19
Pu, Lü, 143
Puerto Rican independence, 137
Pundak, Ron, 258
Putin, Vladimir, 356

al Qaeda, 10, 11, 40, 104, 289, 294, 303–319, 335
Qing, Liu, 143
Quayle, Dan, 68

Rabin, Yitzhak, 265
radical socialism, 21
Raffarin government, 53
Rahman, Azizur, 179
Rather, Dan, 39
Reagan, Ronald, 17, 20, 30, 46, 69, 81, 101, 106
  administration of, 45, 68
"Reagan Democrats," 33
Reconstruction, 21
Reconstructionist Judaism, 33
Reform Judaism, 33
Republican Party, 11, 12, 30, 41, 52, 68, 137, 279
Reuther, Walter, 136
Revere, Paul, 119
Rice, Condoleezza, 258, 283
Right, 29, 31, 32, 33, 36, 40, 45–46, 48–51, 54, 100–101, 103, 106–107, 120
  New, 29–31, 33, 50
  Old, 30
  Republican, 51
Robertson, Pat, 13
Robinson, William I., 349

Roosevelt, Theodore, 14
Rosenfeld, Maya, 259
Rousseau, Jean-Jacques, 104, 109, 113, 114
Roy, Arundhati, 149–163
Roy, Ram Mohan, 188
Rudman, Howard, 309
Rumsfeld, Donald, 15, 323, 331
Rushdie, Salman, 150
Russia, 19, 148, 154, 165, 280, 356, 361

Said, Edward, 152, 196–200
same-sex marriage, 27–29. *See also* homosexuality
Sandinistas, 137
Sardar, Ziauddin 192
Sartre, Jean-Paul, 135
Saudi Arabia, 10, 14, 40, 243, 280
Scharansky, Natan, 230
Scheer, Robert, 12
Schindler's List, 24–25
Schlusky, Abram, 59
Scholem, Gershon, 75–79
Schonberg, Arnold, 75–79
Schmitt, Carl 61–62, 184
September 11, *see* 9/11
Shah, U.S. support for, 111
Sharon, Ariel, 198–199, 228, 247–251, 253, 259, 288
Shavit, Ari, 199
Shiva, Vandana, 186, 192–193
Shlaim, Avi, 256
Short, Clare, 13
Sidqi, Bakr, 277
Siegfried, Kracauer, 75–79
Six Day War, 222–223, 229, 240
social contract, 28
Social Security Act, 47, 51
social welfare, 12
Somoza, 111, 137
Song, Cai, 143
South Africa, 23
Soviet bloc, 20
Soviet Union, 130–136
Spain, 209–211
Spencer, Herbert, 346
Spengler, Oswald, 184
Spielberg, Steven, 17, 24

Spiro, Joan, 344
Spivak, Gayatri, 190–191
Steinwitz, Yuval, 260
Stiglitz, Joseph, 348
Stockman, David, 45
Strauss, Leo, 59–73
Students for a Democratic Society, 130
Suez War, 284
Sumner, William Graham, 346
Supreme Court, 30, 41
Sykes-Picot agreement, 271, 272
Syria, 15, 331

Taft-Hartley amendments, 120
Taliban, 303–319
Tarcov, Nathan, 68
Tax cuts, 12
Tehran, 10
Temple Mount, 243
Temporary Assistance to Needy Families, 46
Ten Commandments, 32
Tenet, George, 10
Thatcher, Margaret, 81
Third Way, 81–96
Tiananmen Square, 141–143, 146
Toulmin, Stephen, 67
traditionalists, 30
Traditional Values Coalition, 34
Tsemel, Leah, 260
Turkey, 14, 165

Unitarian Universalists, 33
United Nations, 9, 40
United States, 10–13, 17, 23, 27–34, 40, 47, 50, 51, 53, 54, 62, 63, 104, 106, 120, 126, 137, 145, 195, 198, 253, 279, 304, 331–339, 353
  corporate interest, 20
  distrust of, 14
  foreign policy, 59, 224
  geopolitical interest, 20
  imperial power, 20
  policy, 40, 102, 137, 293
  slavery, 21
U.S. Constitution, 28–30, 41, 112
U.S. Defense Policy Board, 195
Unocal, 43

Van, 168–174
Varakh, 170–174
Varsig, 171–175
Veblen, Thorstein, 120
Vietnam, 39, 161
Vietnam War, 14, 23, 137
   U.S. role in, 14
Villar, Manuel, 345
de Villepin, Dominique, 291
Vivekananda, 188

Wallace, George, 33
Warsaw, 20
Watergate, 14
Watergate hearings, 11
Wayne, John, 42
Weber, Max, 118–120, 126, 128, 132
Weinberger, Caspar, 289
Weizmann, Chaim, 218
Welfare Reform Act, 46
welfare state, 45–47
   Keynesian, 45, 52–53
Wellstone, Paul, 12
West, decline and fall of, 21

West, Cornel, 12
Wilson, James, 112
Wingate, Orde, 219
Wisner, Frank G., 269–270
Wolfe, Alan, 117
Wolfowitz, Paul, 10, 68
women's equality, 30
Woods, Tiger, 150
Woolsey, Lynn, 12
Wright, Erik Olin, 125

xenophobic nationalism, 19
Xue, Can, 142

Yaobang, Hu, 141
Yemen, 209
Yimou, Zhang, 142

Zannusi, Krzystof, 17
Zehou, Li, 142
Zhao, Bin, 145
Zhuangzhuang, Tian, 142
Zinn, Howard, 108
Zionism, 197, 219, 247
Ziyang, Zhao, 141, 146